The Fateful Lightning

SERIES EDITORS

Sarah E. Gardner, *Mercer University*

Jonathan Daniel Wells, *University of Michigan*

Print Culture in the South addresses the region's literary and historical past from the colonial era to the near present. Rooted in archival research, series monographs embrace a wide range of analyses that, at their core, address engagement and interaction with print. Topics center on format/genre—novels, pamphlets, periodicals, broadsides, and illustrations; institutions such as libraries, literary societies, small presses, and the book industry; and/or habits and practices of readership and writing.

THE FATEFUL LIGHTNING

Civil War Stories and the Magazine Marketplace, 1861–1876

Kathleen Diffley

THE UNIVERSITY OF GEORGIA PRESS
ATHENS

© 2021 by the University of Georgia Press
Athens, Georgia 30602
www.ugapress.org
All rights reserved
Designed by Kaelin Chappell Broaddus
Set in 10.5/13.5 Garamond Premier Pro Regular
by Kaelin Chappell Broaddus

Most University of Georgia Press titles are
available from popular e-book vendors.

Printed digitally

Library of Congress Cataloging-in-Publication Data

Names: Diffley, Kathleen Elizabeth, 1950– author.
Title: The fateful lightning : Civil War stories and the magazine
marketplace, 1861–1876 / Kathleen Diffley.
Description: Athens : The University of Georgia Press, [2021]
| Series: Print culture in the South | Includes bibliographical
references and index.
Identifiers: LCCN 2021029500 (print) | LCCN 2021029501
(ebook) | ISBN 9780820358550 (hardcover) |
ISBN 9780820360652 (paperback) | ISBN 9780820358567 (epub)
Subjects: LCSH: United States—History—Civil War,
1861–1865—Literature and the war. | War stories, American—
History and criticism. | Periodicals—Publishing—United
States—History—19th century.
Classification: LCC PS217.C58 D54 2021 (print) |
LCC PS217.C58 (ebook) | DDC 813/.4093581—dc23
LC record available at https://lccn.loc.gov/2021029500
LC ebook record available at https://lccn.loc.gov/2021029501

For Sam, Jessie, Bo, and Jobie

CONTENTS

List of Illustrations xi
Acknowledgments xiii

Introduction: Dépôt Culture 1

CHAPTER 1
Potshots: Border Traffic, International Copyright,
and Baltimore's *Southern Magazine* 22
CAROLINE MARSDALE, "Cousin Jack" 44
"Running Like the Mischief" 51

CHAPTER 2
Old Times There: The Lost Cause, Charlotte's
The Land We Love, and Commemorative Stamps 62
INA M. PORTER, "Road-Side Story" 85
"Dreadful Necessities" 93

CHAPTER 3
Railroaded: The Western War, Railroad Sprawl,
and Chicago's *Lakeside Monthly* 102
HELEN E. HARRINGTON, "In the Palmy Days of Slaveholding" 129
"Deliver a Smeazel" 138

CHAPTER 4
Emancipation and Grizzly Reckoning:
The Advent of Photography, San Francisco's *Overland Monthly*,
and the Model of Parallax 146
JOSEPHINE CLIFFORD, "An Episode of 'Fort Desolation'" 171
"Like—a Sister" 180

Coda: Depot, Culture, 1876 187

Notes 205
Bibliography 225
Index 243

LIST OF ILLUSTRATIONS

FIGURE 1.	*Grand Central Dépôt, New York*	3
FIGURE 2.	Edouard Baldus, *Louvre*	7
FIGURE 3.	Wartime title-page image, *Atlantic Monthly*	8
FIGURE 4.	*Grand Central Dépôt, New York—Interior view*	11
FIGURE 5.	Cows grazing in a pasture at 45th Street and Lexington Avenue	12
FIGURE 6.	First issue title page, *Overland Monthly*	13
FIGURE 7.	*The Underground Railway, New York City*	14
FIGURE 8.	*Waiting for the Train*	15
FIGURE 9.	*Going on Board*	20
FIGURE 10.	Theodore R. Davis, *"Reb" and "Billy Button" Carrying the President's Children to School*	37
FIGURE 11.	*Louisiana*	54
FIGURE 12.	Early commemorative stamps	67
FIGURE 13.	First cover on buff paper, *The Land We Love*	72
FIGURE 14.	Second cover on blue paper, *The Land We Love*	72
FIGURE 15.	A. J. Davis, *Residence of Gov. Morehead, North-Carolina*	74
FIGURE 16.	Samuel Sloan, Home of Governor Morehead's son, John Lindsay Morehead	74
FIGURE 17.	The Confederate Monument at the north side of Montgomery's historic capitol	100
FIGURE 18.	Winslow Homer, *News from the War*, detail	103
FIGURE 19.	*The Lightning Postal Train from New York to Chicago*	109
FIGURE 20.	*The City of Chicago, Illinois*	111
FIGURE 21.	*Very Truly Yours W. B. Ogden*	117
FIGURE 22.	*Hon. Anson S. Miller, LLD*	122
FIGURE 23.	*Lieut. Governor of Illinois, William Bross*	125
FIGURE 24.	*Hotel Ponce de Leon*	139
FIGURE 25.	*Taking Stereoscopic Picture of Near Objects*	147
FIGURE 26.	Alexander Gardner, *The "Sunken Road" at Antietam*	150

FIGURE 27.	Edwin Forbes, *Brilliant and Decisive Bayonet Charge of Hawkins's Zouaves*	151
FIGURE 28.	Edwin Forbes, *The Battle of Antietam—Charge of Burnside's 9th Corps*	152
FIGURE 29.	Alexander Gardner, *Antietam, Maryland. Bodies of Dead, Louisiana Regiment*	153
FIGURE 30.	Alfred R. Waud, *The Battle of Antietam—Carrying off the Wounded after the Battle*	154
FIGURE 31.	*Scenes on the Battlefield of Antietam. From Photographs by Mr. M. B. Brady*	155
FIGURE 32.	Alexander Gardner, *Gathered Together for Burial: After the Battle of Antietam*	156
FIGURE 33.	*Scenes on the Battlefield of Antietam. From Photographs by Mr. M. B. Brady*	156
FIGURE 34.	*A Southern Mansion* and *A Home in Ruins*	165
FIGURE 35.	Joseph Hull, *Which we had small game, / And Ah Sin took a hand*	168
FIGURE 36.	Solomon Eytinge, *In the scene that ensued / I did not take a hand*	168
FIGURE 37.	*Fort Cummings, New Mexico, 1867*	183
FIGURE 38.	Francis H. Schell and Thomas Hogan, *The Centennial—Interior of the Main Building*	191
FIGURE 39.	Theodore R. Davis, *Our Centennial—President Grant and Dom Pedro Starting the Corliss Engine*	192
FIGURE 40.	Theodore R. Davis, *The Centennial—Southern Restaurant, the New Jersey Building, the Women's Pavilion*	193
FIGURE 41.	Alfred H. White, bust of Bishop Richard Allen	199
FIGURE 42.	Alfred H. White, monument to Bishop Richard Allen	201
FIGURE 43.	*Panoramic View of Fairmount Park, Taken from the Pennsylvania Railroad*	203

ACKNOWLEDGMENTS

On the sunny side of this book's long gestation, it is a pleasure to thank those whose financial support has enabled time to reflect and write. I am deeply grateful to the National Endowment for the Humanities and the George A. and Eliza Gardner Howard Foundation for fellowships as this project began. In addition, I want to thank the University of Iowa for a Faculty Scholarship, a three-year award so generous that it no longer exists.

During research leaves and plenty of semesters in classrooms large and small, several writing groups have taken up talks, chapters, and the articles they produced as our drafts have multiplied, often over the course of years. For the kindness of their time and the pleasure of their company, my warm appreciation goes to Joni Kinsey, Teresa Mangum, Kim Marra, Laura Rigal, and Leslie Schwalm, as well as Jennifer Ambrose, Rebecca Entel, Jen McGovern, Lori Muntz, Anne Peterson, and Eve Rosenbaum. Years ago, Richard Adams, Luke Mancuso, Cynthia Stretch, and Mary Sylwester helped a first book become a second in an ongoing project, which Nicholas Borchert and Stephanie Grossnickle-Batterton, Jaclyn Carver, Naomi Greyser, and Miriam Thaggert have more recently nudged into clarity. I am also grateful to Walter Biggins at the University of Georgia Press and two anonymous readers, whose care and encouragement have enabled a better book. May they and all those with a hand in a draft forgive any errors and infelicities that remain.

Every book reconsidering the past that periodicals helped make is indebted to institutions, their holdings, and their people, whose knowledgeable assistance opens unexpected possibilities. At the University of Texas and the Harry Ransom Center, ready thanks go to Coleman Hutchison and Danielle Brune Sigler for the revelations of the Fleur Cowles Flair Symposium they organized in 2014. At the New-York Historical Society, I am grateful to library staff for an unusual photograph of Grand Central Dépôt and permission to reprint it twice. In North Carolina, Sharon Kennedy-Nolle first pointed me toward Blandwood and the executive director of Preservation Greensboro Incorporated, Benjamin Briggs, who has graciously reproduced prints of the Italianate villas once belonging to Governor John Motley Morehead and his son. At the Smithsonian's National Postal Museum, Lynn Heidelbaugh and Bill Lommel have been instrumental, midpandemic, in securing usable scans of early commemorative stamps. Curator Michael Panhorst has been generous with an enviable photograph he took himself, and so has art historian Susanna Gold, who also introduced me to Reverend Mark Tyler, Marian Bennett, and the discovery of an AME Church treasure, now part of the Mother Bethel Archives in Philadelphia. I am grateful for so much openhanded resourcefulness, just as I am beholden to Janalyn Moss, Patricia Baird, and Bethany Davis at the University of Iowa Libraries for their continuing assistance.

I would also like to thank several university presses for their generosity. A portion of the introduction that first appeared as "'Dépôt Culture': The Civil War in Periodical Fiction," in *A History of American Civil War Literature*, edited by Coleman Hutchison (2016), 79–95, has been reproduced with the permission of Cambridge University Press through PLSclear. An earlier version of chapter 1 was published as "Home from the Theatre of War: The *Southern Magazine* and Recollections of the Civil War," in *Periodical Literature in Nineteenth-Century America*, edited by Kenneth M. Price and Susan Belasco Smith (1995), 183–201; portions have been revised and reprinted by permission of the University of Virginia Press. The concluding section of the same chapter appeared as "'Running Like the Mischief': Civil War Louisiana in the *Southern Magazine*," an article published by Taylor & Francis in *Women's Studies* 50, no. 1 (January/February 2021): 10–22 and initially available on February 3, 2021, at https://www.tandfonline.com/doi/full/10.1080/00497878.2021.1874801. A substantial portion of chapter 4 was published as "Emancipation and Grizzly Reckoning: The Advent of Photography, California's *Overland Monthly*, and the Model of Parallax," in *Literary Cultures of the Civil War*, edited by Timothy Sweet (2016), 245–64, and has been reprinted with permission from the University of Georgia Press.

Closer to my heart have been three timely invitations from John and June Lowe, whose friendship I have long held dear. To Peter Antelyes, Barbara Higham, and Geraldine Murphy, thanks for being there—always, always. I am indebted as well to the University of Iowa's Obermann Center for Advanced Studies, which offered the time and windowed space that revived this project amid welcome quiet and even more welcome conversations. It has been a further pleasure to step into any meeting room where the Civil War Caucus gathers. This book has come to life on panels stirred by remarkable caucus scholars and their enterprising attention to work aborning.

During the years since this project began, so many close to home have passed away. But a new generation has also arrived, a generation that will reconstruct my own tantalizing future. To Sam, Jessie, Bo, and his very little sister—sensitive, gutsy, exuberant, newborn—sank ee.

The Fateful Lightning

Introduction
Dépôt Culture

Like many New England regiments in 1861, Julia Ward Howe arrived in Washington by train. Accompanying her husband as he traveled to a meeting of the U.S. Sanitary Commission during the first November of the war, she noticed the federal pickets stationed to protect rail access from enemy threats nearby. Days later, she saw Confederate soldiers in a sudden skirmish that sent parading Federal regiments back to their barracks in the city. Among the troops on a crowded road that autumn afternoon, Mrs. Howe and her Boston party sang familiar songs, including "John Brown's Body." She would later report that, early the next morning, she awoke to scribble new words to the tune, lines the *Atlantic Monthly* would publish anonymously in February 1862. One poem among many during the war's first year, Howe's stanzas were nonetheless reprinted by newspapers and songbooks, then sung with growing enthusiasm by Union soldiers, even in Libby Prison.[1] For the rest of her life, Julia Ward Howe would hear the biblical vineyards of Revelation trampled in cities across the country, often with the same ardor that had once inspired Union troops drawn to divine glory.

Taking its title from the "Battle Hymn of the Republic" and the stanzas first loosed in Boston's premier literary magazine, *The Fateful Lightning* examines the narrative innovations and colloquial vitality that early Civil War stories also provoked in American letters.[2] The flash of local events and the sound of unfamiliar voices in periodical stories do much to suggest why Mark Twain's fiction is so different from Herman Melville's: the Civil War marked the first time that many Americans left the neighborhoods they knew well, the first time that many Northern boys saw slavery at all. The magazines that veterans helped make popular bespoke a hankering for the idiosyncratic, the innovative, and the diverse in literature during a new era when the national "homestead" was opening up.

Anticipating the direction in which American literature would move after its prewar surge, this book couples rising expectations with commemorative priorities to consider newly founded periodicals, specifically in the light of marketplace shifts that would transform the production of postwar magazines and thus the wartime memories that could get into print. Key developments that came to bear on editors and their pages were the renewed agitation over international copyright, the reorganization of a national postal system, the spread of railroads, and the advent of photography. The result in *The Fateful Lightning* is a portrait of strikingly different publishing centers across the country as Reconstruction began, akin to what Perry Miller's *The Raven and the Whale* once revealed about literary "giants" and the antebellum ferment that only began with Poe and Melville.[3] Examining a host of midcentury periodicals, with a steady focus on four that were founded after the rebellion and outside of New England, this book reveals unexpected commemorative practices and narrative upshots complicating the literary Civil War that many believe they know.

To date, Northern publishing centers have been more widely noticed, of course, much like the competing clam chowders in Miller's New England and New York. But just as noteworthy for the spread of alternative magazines and their stories were the national rail networks that were rapidly developing. Of particular moment in understanding postwar literary gatekeeping, of particular use in comprehending the imagined dimensions of the war's distant reach and local clutch, is the New York rail terminus undertaken by Cornelius Vanderbilt, an outsized station designed to serve a diversifying railroad network. Commenced in November 1869 and completed in October 1871, Grand Central Dépôt simultaneously assembled far-flung lines and reoriented local traffic, specifically in Manhattan from 42nd Street to 48th Street (figure 1).

Built of red pressed brick with cast-iron trim painted white to look like marble, the headhouse for passengers was constructed in French Second Empire style and was, with its spectacular train shed, "immense," according to *Harper's Weekly*.[4] Leland Roth has pointed out that Second Empire as an architectural style was eclectic in its historical borrowings but was generally embellished and symmetrical, horizontal in its layering, given to pavilions center and flank, and topped in Paris by the ubiquitous mansard roof, which allowed for dormers and an extra floor while eluding city taxes.[5] The style was "without much pretension to architectural elegance," sniffed *Harper's Weekly*. But there was no gainsaying Vanderbilt's grand scale when construction required twenty thousand barrels of cement, eighty thousand feet of glass in the roof alone, eight million pounds of iron, and ten million bricks, according to the newsmagazine. As a "union" of Vanderbilt's three rail lines, the terminus managed daily hordes

FIGURE 1. *Grand Central Dépôt, New York*. Constructed on 42nd Street to unite the New York Central, the New York and Harlem, and the New York and New Haven Railroads and their tracks. Wood engraving. *Harper's Weekly*, February 3, 1872, 104. Courtesy of the University of Iowa Libraries.

of passengers arriving and departing as surely as steam heat circulated through some seventy-five thousand feet of pipe.[6]

In its witness to proliferating lines and amalgamating terminals, Grand Central Dépôt ably suggests the proliferating magazines and magazine stories of the 1860s and 1870s, as well as an amalgamating master narrative of hard-won liberty and justice that was circulated by the triumphant North. But it is also significant that Vanderbilt's rail lines were no more fully integrated behind their Second Empire facade than the North, the South, and the West were fully integrated in the new nation that emerged from the rebellion. Just as Vanderbilt's terminal housed several railroads that were operated separately, so newly founded periodicals in urban centers like Baltimore, Charlotte, Chicago, and San Francisco were all pavilions of a sort, venues that would become distinct and enterprising forums for the war's first recollections. Inspected more closely, the sprawling network of rails that constituted Commodore Vanderbilt's second empire, after a fleet of ships had made his first fortune, was paradigmatic in being nationally attuned and yet locally complex, as the carts, carriages, omnibuses, and even pedestrians in *Harper's Weekly* suggest. Much like New York's monumental depot, the Civil War stories examined in this book helped engineer a master narrative that was nonetheless open to regional challenges, particularly as "the South" reentered a national lexicon and emancipation helped engender a new nation that the country's founders had scarcely anticipated.

All the more reason to reconsider nineteenth-century periodicals and the variegated fare that once gave recollections of the war an emerging shape, what Alice Fahs in *The Imagined Civil War* has called the war's "commercial print memory."[7] Ever since 1973 and Daniel Aaron's declaration that the Civil War's "seamy and unheroic" epic was "unwritten," skeptical literary scholars have been digging.[8] The fortunate result has been that less predictable fiction and poetry, drama and autobiography, illustrations and memorials have rendered the war's parlored women less polite, its soldier scribes less disengaged, its photographic operators less silent, and its emancipated voices less fugitive than Aaron once believed them. Reckoning archivally with the war's expense and promise has meant considering less familiar texts in ever greater numbers as the earth of the past has been turned to reveal a richer subsoil than Aaron suspected. In place of few reported appeals to dazed readers, it is now instructive to consider multiplying versions of civil trauma and, with them, what David Blight has called "the politics of memory," a phrase that suggests both the varieties of recollection and the dividends of strategic forgetting.[9]

In the defeated South and, more particularly, the emerging West, new literary magazines posited a postbellum nation that was genuinely struck by the loosed bolts of Howe's battle hymn, as well as the "unfinished work" Lincoln proposed at Gettysburg.[10] Countering established venues like the *Atlantic Monthly*, regional magazines and their insurgent narratives regularly fractured antebellum social hierarchies, sometimes simply by enlarging story casts. But even in Chicago and San Francisco, a respect for home as property and the republic as founded would persist, and so would the continuing pull of a plantation past that magazines in Baltimore and Charlotte recognized more readily. Strange bedfellows in many ways, magazines with noticeably different stakes in recollecting the war would demonstrate how quickly Lincoln's "new birth of freedom" could be imagined, and yet how potent for the war's first storytellers the social relations of earlier years remained.[11]

The deliberate work of recovering short magazine fiction grounds midcentury literary developments in the rites of citizenship at that moment when the nation and its Constitution were being redefined. My first book, entitled *Where My Heart Is Turning Ever* after Stephen Foster's "Old Folks at Home," charted the endeavor "to sing the body politic in parlors nationwide" by examining the role of short and widely circulating narratives in domesticating a newly national citizenship, North and South, that was forged by the war and three Reconstruction amendments to the Constitution.[12] In the "Old Homestead" stories, Romances, and Adventures that appeared in sixteen periodicals of the 1860s and 1870s, the same array of sources that continues to orient this second book, a conservative domestic rhetoric proved fundamental in negotiating civil crisis for the varying publics that so many magazines assembled. *The Fateful Lightning* acknowledges the continuing social appeal of the Union as it was. More than a hundred brisk war stories in *Harper's Weekly* alone demonstrate that constitutional amendments abolishing slavery, promoting federal authority over state jurisdiction, and guaranteeing suffrage for black men did not banish conservative priorities or reconceive antebellum social norms by fiat. But an increasing number of stories appearing in or outside Boston and New York demonstrate that familiar social relations could be undone, often with an innovative verbal panache.

Take, for example, the narrative grip of a story by Rebecca Harding Davis. Published in the *Atlantic Monthly* at the end of the war's first year, "John Lamar" (April 1862) casts the conflict between soon-warring sections as a competition between rivals in love. Cousins by marriage, the two have met again in western Virginia, where their continuing friendship and toast to "Liberty!" epitomize antebellum ideals that were already diverging.[13] Despite their sectional differences, Davis's protagonists share a thoughtless disregard for two unusual characters: an evangelical Union volunteer from Illinois and the "gladiator" slave he inflames to murder.[14] These two arresting portraits—sharp-edged, colloquial, malignant—make mincemeat of ongoing sectional debate and John Lamar's Southern solution to slavery's injustice, a gradual education in work and ambition that miscalculates his field hand's fierce revenge. The result of incorporating the brutality of bondage and this man's hidden knife is as fateful as the grapes of wrath, as quick as retributive lightning. Biographer Jean Pfaelzer in *Parlor Radical* calls "John Lamar" and its abrupt climax "a black-white apocalypse brought on by the sins of the white father."[15] The ruptures that war was already bringing to countless households by way of invasion, dislocation, and mounting casualties, in other words, Davis effectively brought to narrative conventions and the hidebound expectations about whose interests American liberty was meant to serve.

Yet turning to neglected periodical forums and their equally neglected priorities, this book discovers in hundreds of Civil War stories the contemporary alternatives to "John Lamar" and good reason to look more closely at four postwar iconoclasts: Baltimore's *Southern Magazine* (1866–75), Charlotte's *The Land We Love* (1866–69), Chicago's *Lakeside Monthly* (1869–74), and San Francisco's *Overland Monthly* (1868–75). Arranged in the order of their postbellum runs and their distance from Grand Central Dépôt, these four Reconstructive monthlies give a startling literary dimension to the midcentury crisis that first erupted in Kansas during the 1850s. Their commemorative agendas, I argue, can best be understood in the midst of their distinctive urban cultures, an approach that can reveal both unrepresented local norms and unnoticed narrative details, both tantalizing deletions and significant substitutions. Guided by their editorial preoccupations and the metropolitan realities they filtered for subscribers, such newly created venues gave a particular slant to narrative space that was at once the coded mark of political interests and the buried trace of social fears. Magazine by magazine, *The Fateful Lightning* thereby seeks to correct the appealing limitations of reading unearthed stories closely by reading as well what they filtered out, which means tracking the local implications of editorial bias and the recollective significance of strategic blinders.

It might be argued that the immediate impact of these four regional magazines was slight; none surpassed a peak of fifteen thousand subscribers during their short runs. By contrast, the *Atlantic Monthly* claimed a circulation of thirty-five thousand by 1870, and *Harper's Weekly* was read by three hundred thousand (who read aloud to many more) during the early 1870s, when Thomas Nast's attacks on New York City's Tammany Hall, illustration by illustration, helped bring down the Democratic Ring's Boss Tweed.[16] Still, thousands across the country discovered peculiar regional challenges to Federal prerogatives that would never have appeared in the antislavery monthly or the Republican weekly. As a result, these four periodicals and the cities in which they arose offer varying gauges of continued political unrest, emerging social opportunity, and dickering regional agendas as Reconstruction first unfolded.

Here at the outset, both Grand Central Dépôt and its financier seem fitting and perhaps revelatory analogues. Cornelius Vanderbilt, dubbed "the first tycoon" by his recent biographer T. J. Stiles, was born and raised on Staten Island; he left school at eleven and remained a bad speller and sometime reader for the rest of his life.[17] His genius lay instead in accumulating transportation routes, first by water from Staten Island to Manhattan, then along the Atlantic coast and, with the discovery of gold in California, across Nicaragua to San Francisco. His shipping fleet further extended up the Hudson and across the Atlantic during the Civil War, when he quietly turned as well to railroad shares and to holdings that began with the New York and Harlem line in 1862, followed by the New York and New Haven line in 1863, and (after the war ended) the venerable New York Central in 1867. Commodore Vanderbilt did not build railroads; he acquired them, and in 1869 he merged his lines into the New York Central and Hudson River Railroad, at least in name. Through acquisition and lease during the postbellum years, his control would stretch to Boston

FIGURE 2. Edouard Baldus, *Louvre*. Albumen print. In the album *Paris et ses environs en photographies*, p. 15, no. 11. Courtesy of the Library of Congress, LC-USZ62-17876.

and Buffalo, Detroit and Chicago, and (crisscrossing the Midwest) to Toledo, Cleveland, Indianapolis, St. Louis, and plenty of stops in between. With the coalescing network and the growing domain of a railroad "king" for his contemporaries, it is no wonder that his tastes ran, as Kurt Schlichting has observed, to the "palatial."[18]

Of course, the Commodore did not act alone in building his network or in constructing Grand Central Dépôt. On 42nd Street, at least, he needed an architect—actually, an architect and two engineers—when the historic enterprise of the headhouse was joined to the structural moxie of the train shed's enclosed platforms. The architect designing the depot's public face was John Butler Snook, whose brief was to plan the facades and spaces that gave on to the "more affluent" parts of the city, as John Belle and Maxinne Leighton have noted.[19] For the headhouse that ran along 42nd Street and up the newly named Vanderbilt Avenue, Snook found his inspiration in the beautification of Paris and the additions to the Louvre undertaken during the 1850s by a recently elevated emperor (figure 2). What Christopher Mead has described as "a new monumentality of scale" was championed by Napoleon III and translated almost immediately into official buildings across Paris, especially buildings that were civic, commercial, or educational.[20] While Second Empire style could be adapted for residential use, its exuberant excess was particularly appropriate

FIGURE 3. Wartime title-page image. Wood engraving. *Atlantic Monthly*, January 1865. Courtesy of the University of Iowa Libraries.

for public buildings that displayed what Barbara Humphreys has called urban "wealth and dignity," the hallmarks of Grand Central Dépôt and an engaging twist on its metaphoric uses.[21]

With a similar élan in the United States, the *Atlantic Monthly* had become by the end of the Civil War a public sphere powerhouse. From its founding in 1857, the Boston magazine had opposed slavery with the kind of zeal that added a liberty cap to the title-page flutter of its iconic Stars and Stripes (figure 3). The magazine's New England pledge to individual freedoms was thereby urged in a nationalizing commitment to "Yankee humanism," as Ellery Sedgwick has formulated the *Atlantic*'s mission in his study of its nineteenth-century initiative. But even wartime emancipation and the postwar extension of civil rights did not abbreviate the magazine's certainty that the common good, figured in the nation's flag, required New England's leadership and the assistance of its educated elite. As Sedgwick observes, "This resistance to the democratic principle of majority rule in intellectual, aesthetic, and ethical issues and the attempt to reconcile social democracy with an authoritative hierarchy of cultural values were reflected in the *Atlantic* throughout the nineteenth century and beyond."[22] An antebellum allegiance to Old Glory, in other words, was an allegiance to Yankee oversight and to the literary mastery that gave the *Atlantic Monthly* unparalleled cultural capital.

It was an allegiance that periodicals elsewhere would resist, much as they resisted the engraving that initially graced the *Atlantic*'s title page: a portrait of John Winthrop, who founded the Puritan colony that became Boston. After the Civil War, such resistance flourished. One case study at a time, *The Fateful Lightning* demonstrates that taking issue with Boston's cultural preeminence created openings for alternate recollections of the war and, in turn, for a narrative inventiveness that defied the prescriptions of the *Atlantic*'s newly celebrated writers such as Henry James, Louisa May Alcott, and Rebecca Harding Davis. In fact, Davis's anticipation of slave initiative in "John Lamar," published in 1862 just two months after Howe's hymn, has become this book's springboard, its recurring point of departure in chapter after chapter as outlying periodicals reveal where resistant commemorative priorities and restless narrative maneuvers once lay. Although the *Atlantic Monthly* emerged from the war with what Sedgwick describes as "a prestige that drew young authors," such a quality journal was no more successful in choking off postwar magazine insurgencies than Federal forces had been during the war in blockading Southern ports.[23]

Here, too, what lay behind Grand Central's facades proves revealing, especially by analogy. Stiles has pointed out that red-brick masonry and painted ironwork effectively hid three separate depots.[24] In a surprisingly diplomatic fashion, Vanderbilt made sure that each line had its own ticket, baggage, and waiting rooms constructed so discretely that through passengers had to exit the building and come back in, the very reason the massive terminal had thirty-one doors. Roth has noted that "the compartmentalized Second Empire Baroque style was well suited to this kind of articulation," and certainly the depot's headhouse facades together encouraged an imperial sweep along 370 feet of 42nd Street and nearly 70 feet of Vanderbilt Avenue.[25] But the cumbersome repetition of essential services in separate pavilion spaces also suggests that this "union" of railroads was ad hoc, a reminder that postwar practices of incorporation developed slowly and sporadically in the United States for at least a decade.

During the 1860s and 1870s, compartmentalized separations and multiple entrances effectively suggest an alternative model of regional challenges to the *Atlantic*'s elitist facade, especially from more protean cities. Postwar Baltimore, for instance, could claim the economic vitality and diversifying neighborhoods—among them, German, Irish, and African American—to promote more than twenty literary journals, what Ray Atchison in his study of southern magazines has called "the largest number published in any city during the Reconstruction era."[26] Leading this phalanx, the *Southern Magazine* was the monthly of choice for ex-Confederates looking ahead to recovery, while issue after issue ignored the city's shifting demographics. Scorning emancipation, Baltimore's chief literary journal favored a competing narrative, one tied to resurgent white interests that could be bound locally to an antebellum past and an industrial future with little notice of Baltimore's ethnic neighborhoods.

Similarly, Charlotte was poised for quick growth in 1865. The city had long been built on the trade that multiple rail lines fostered and the business enterprise that also drew African Americans following the war, especially to one of the few commercial centers in the Carolinas that Union troops had not burned. As Hal Bridges has noted, however, *The Land We Love* was intent on becoming "the organ of the late Confederate army" and was endorsed by CSA generals like P. G. T. Beauregard, Joseph Johnston, and John Bell Hood.[27] Dedicated to putting his stamp on history in the making, its editor regularly solicited what he called "the *debris* of the bivouac fires," as long as those fires warmed the white South.[28] In the magazine's stories of the war, some of the first to arise from late Confederates, that priority created a tension between a vigorously commercial city hall and an orthodox slaveholding republic, a tension that was figured in the way narratives were structured and freedpeople were cast.

By comparison, Chicago in 1860 was the scene of the new Republican Party's national convention, its antislavery platform, and its western candidate, Abraham Lincoln. On the eve of the Civil War, the forward-looking city stood in the midst of proliferating tracks as a supremely crowded depot, particularly after immigrant numbers mushroomed and the hectic rail construction across Ohio, Indiana, and Illinois during the 1850s began filling local coffers. In 1860, however, Lincoln's opponent, Stephen Douglas, also knew Chicago well after moving to the city in 1847 and becoming active in creating the railway hub; as the Democratic presidential candidate, he drew much of his support from both city wards and downstate counties, where slavery had continued until the practice was officially banned by the state's constitution in 1848. The *Lakeside Monthly* was unwelcome there, and so were self-emancipated fugitives making their way north. Founded as the "Western Monthly" and bolstered by what Michael Hackenberg calls "a satisfactory frontier voice," the magazine would quietly negotiate the political crosswinds of Illinois.[29] Although abolitionist in tenor, the postwar monthly would not pause on the state's Black Laws or praise the state's black men.

Hundreds of miles farther west in San Francisco, the *Overland Monthly* emerged from a state that was just as politically divided and immigrant-rich. During the 1850s, proslavery Democrats ruled California. So extensive was their reach that whispers of Confederate plots persisted throughout the war. As C. Douglas Kroll observes, San Francisco was thought to be "a tempting prize for

FIGURE 4. *Grand Central Dépôt, New York.* Interior view of the train shed. Wood engraving. *Harper's Weekly*, February 3, 1872, 105. Courtesy of the University of Iowa Libraries.

the Confederacy"; in addition to a naval shipyard and a military arsenal, Kroll notes that "within the city itself were other prizes, among them the U.S. Mint, the Customhouse, and the Post Office, all likely to contain gold and silver that the Confederacy desperately needed."[30] Among San Francisco's postwar periodicals, however, the *Overland Monthly* revealed marked Union enthusiasms and little patience with Dixie's staunch advocates. Its well-heeled readers were not likely to be the newly vagrant gold panners displaced by land speculators and hydraulic engineers or the nearby farmers whose water was rerouted to meet soaring urban demand. Still, in recollecting the Civil War as the scene of racial opportunity, the city's principal literary monthly stood in for a polyglot western metropole where social relations were already unsettled.

A decidedly incomplete integration was the hallmark of all four magazines, just as Grand Central Dépôt made the most of unintegrated space yet again in joining Second Empire headhouse to revolutionary train shed, facade fuss to mechanical innovation, architect to engineer (figure 4). The vast interior that housed tracks and platforms was designed by Isaac C. Buckholt, and its breathtaking roof, which Schlichting calls a "lattice work of iron with glass panels," was designed by R. G. Hatfield.[31] Inspired by London's St. Pancras station and the earlier Crystal Palace, the train shed was roughly one hundred feet high, almost two hundred feet across, and more than six hundred feet long. Its vault was con-

FIGURE 5.
Cows grazing in a pasture at 45th Street and Lexington Avenue, Grand Central railyard in background, ca. 1872. Left half of a stereograph photo by G. W. Pach. PR 065-0476-0008, neg. #20573. Courtesy of the New-York Historical Society.

structed of thirty-two wrought-iron trusses imported from England and raised piecemeal in a near semicircular arch, whose cast-iron "shoes" (in Carl Condit's term) were hidden below ground.[32] Visitors could not figure out how the arches stayed up, and they were so amazed that the train shed soon became, as Belle and Leighton have pointed out, a postwar tourist site that was "second only to the U. S. Capitol" in popularity.[33] Tourists were further rewarded by the station's north facade, an ornamented rear wall reaching up to 112 feet and providing access to the twelve tracks and seven platforms that made the depot's train shed at the time the largest interior space in the United States.[34] On the other side of the tracks, cows foraged (figure 5).

In its visual retort to headhouse ornament, in the clean lines preferred by innovating engineers over the baroque clutter favored by historicizing architects, even in the bovine counter of Lexington Avenue to the upscale appurtenances just a few blocks away, Vanderbilt's looming train shed makes palpable both the postwar regional resistance to the *Atlantic Monthly*'s cultural hegemony and the commemorative work that other periodical platforms and diversifying tracks enabled. If the task of an antislavery virtuoso like Boston's foremost monthly was to summon a public for reconstructing liberty and reconceiving justice, especially in the wake of emancipation, then the commensurate function of more unusual postbellum venues was to distill the experience of war for those who contested the history of the victors. New periodicals in the South and West as-

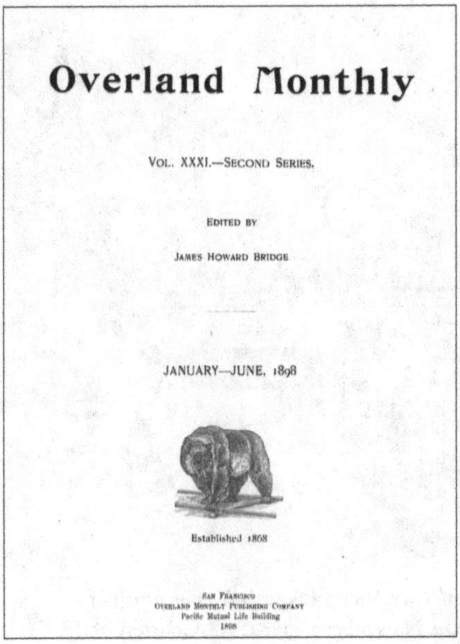

Overland Monthly

Vol. XXXI.—Second Series.

Edited by

James Howard Bridge

JANUARY—JUNE, 1898

Established 1868

San Francisco
Overland Monthly Publishing Company
Pacific Mutual Life Building
1898

FIGURE 6. First issue title page. Wood engraving. *Overland Monthly*, July 1868. Courtesy of the University of Iowa Libraries.

sembled what Michael Warner calls "counterpublics," which assailed the *Atlantic*'s national script as insistently as a raggedy David assailed a Goliath with subscribers. "Dominant publics," writes Warner, "are by definition those that can take their discourse pragmatics and their lifeworlds for granted, misrecognizing the indefinite scope of their expansive address as universality or normalcy. Counterpublics are spaces of circulation in which it is hoped that the poesis of scene making will be transformative, not replicative merely."[35] Substitute San Francisco for Boston, the title page of the *Overland Monthly* for that of the *Atlantic*, and a liberty cap on the flagpole gets replaced by a grizzly paw on the track (figure 6). In a similar fashion, the unfamiliar war stories of Baltimore and Charlotte, Chicago and San Francisco challenged the cultural zeal of New England as a counterempire of distant cities talked back.

The metaphoric handiness of Vanderbilt's depot takes a further useful turn since, even in cosmopolitan New York, local interests could become combative. When Grand Central began scheduling more than eighty trains a day, new residential neighbors objected. For decades, complaints about steam and soot had pushed railroad service farther north until, by the 1850s, steam locomotives were no longer allowed south of 42nd Street. When Vanderbilt constructed his terminal there, its success immediately spurred urban development—and then a returning clamor of complaints. Having just spent over $6 million to complete his project in 1871, Vanderbilt was reluctant to spend another $4 million

FIGURE 7. *The Underground Railway, New York City.* View of Fourth Avenue north of 59th Street. Wood engraving. *Scientific American*, November 28, 1874, 338. Courtesy of the HathiTrust.

until the city offered an innovative plan to split further construction costs.[36] In return for a wider, four-track arrangement to accommodate more trains, the Central and Hudson lowered its rails so that noise and vibrations were reduced, specifically in an open cut that became a tunnel with ventilation shafts as Fourth Avenue passed 59th Street and continued north (figure 7). Sinking the tracks also allowed the company to sell air rights after 1875 to what became Park Avenue, almost overnight one of the most expensive stretches of urban property in the world.

Hidden connections on underground lines provide a ready analogue to less familiar Civil War narratives in regional magazines, many of which do not enjoy air rights these days in tony scholarly neighborhoods or among the war's well-shod reenactors. The high road of familiar traffic still belongs to elite vehicles like the *Atlantic Monthly*, just as the control of cultural thoroughfares and literary intersections is still generally maintained by prominent writers like Rebecca Harding Davis. But less apparent circulation can suggest, as the chapters of this book reveal, the sunken resonance of Ina M. Porter's "Road-Side Story" from *The Land We Love* and Helen E. Harrington's "In the Palmy Days of Slaveholding" from the *Lakeside Monthly*, stories that begin to explain (as "John Lamar" does not) why Reconstruction faltered.

FIGURE 8. *Waiting for the Train*. Wood engraving. "The Boat and the Train," *Harper's Weekly*, July 17, 1858, 452. Courtesy of the University of Iowa Libraries.

Then, too, the way *Harper's Weekly* once imagined waiting for the train offers a revealing antebellum glimpse of depot culture, with its heterogeneous "company" and their inevitable maneuvers around the Refreshments stall and the Ladies Room, as well as their accumulating goods and a disputatious baggage master (figure 8). Indeed, the crowded station platform insinuates not only a witty glimpse of *Harper's Weekly* in the hands of the top-hatted reader on the right but also a more resourceful model for cultural recovery and Civil War stories, particularly when the inconvenient tracks out of Grand Central Dépôt led to multiplying stations like this one across the country. At a time when the national postal service was reorganizing and home delivery for most Americans was still decades away, contemporary periodicals and the early recollections of war they carried were regularly delivered to similar country depots, along low roads and high, via crowded platforms and growing networks. Indeed, the newsmagazine's use of an accented "dépôt" insinuates the Old French *depost* (and before that the Latin *depositum*), meaning a deposit or a storage site for deposits.[37] A few diacritical marks for absent letters, and it is easier to recall the U.S. mail delivery practice of depositing periodicals and the initial Civil War stories they carried in urban terminals and country stations, where they waited to be claimed.

To date, recurring periodical negotiations across gender, race, and class lines have generally been slighted by literary critics, at least as an entrée to understanding social crisis during and immediately after the Civil War. Over fifty years ago in *Patriotic Gore: Studies in the Literature of the American Civil War*, Edmund Wilson first drew attention to the memoirs, diaries, reports, and addresses that he substituted for the belles lettres he rarely found on either side of the Mason-Dixon Line. Famously preoccupied in 1961 with the sea-slug view of war, he nonetheless made his way, one diary or account at a time, to Oliver Wendell Holmes and the firm moral discipline that had become second nature in the *Atlantic Monthly*, though he did not notice Holmes's customary venue. More recently, Elizabeth Young in *Disarming the Nation: Women's Writing and the American Civil War* has augmented Wilson's scarce "ladies" by tracing the rich accounts of Harriet Beecher Stowe and Louisa May Alcott, Elizabeth Keckley and Loreta Janeta Velazquez, Frances Harper and Margaret Mitchell, who together assembled a "counter-genealogy" that for Young foregrounded abolition if not its magazine vehicles.[38] Just as resourcefully, Julia Stern has spoken for many studies of Civil War culture by focusing on a single barometric figure in *Mary Chesnut's Civil War Epic*, which turns a backward glance to Confederate defeat-in-the-making via the family papers of an elite and ironic "Cassandra."[39] While Stern includes few magazines, those early vehicles of commercial print memory, she offers a richer measure of the epic Southern drama that Edmund Wilson only briefly acknowledged.

On a much larger canvas, Jeremy Wells has been more attentive to the "cultural conquest" of well-read periodical pages in *Romances of the White Man's Burden: Race, Empire, and the Plantation in American Literature, 1880–1936*.[40] But he focuses on a later period and genteel heavyweights like the *Century Illustrated*, which for many readers replaced black liberty with white supervision after Reconstruction ended and the New South was on the rise. Looking to earlier and more vertiginous times, Randall Fuller in *From Battlefields Rising: How the Civil War Transformed American Literature* considers "a generation that had grown up in the shadow of the founding fathers."[41] His Northern cast favors illustrious writers who were stunned by the war's demands, though they often noted their consternation in personal letters and quotidian accounts not meant for the hands of strangers. The first stirrings of the war's print memory appear more regularly in the work of Coleman Hutchison, who has devoted *Apples and Ashes: Literature, Nationalism, and the Confederate States of America* to an equally sizable Southern cast and to more public broadsides, pamphlets, popular music, and periodicals like the *Southern Literary Messenger* in Richmond and *The Index* in London. His study thereby attends to the war's transnational repercussions and to a Confederate literary culture that left Lincoln's "house divided" in the dust. Among so many ambitious examinations of recovered Civil War texts, only Hutchison's auspicious project looks ahead in closing to the ready networks that periodical circulation engineered and to what their crowded print platforms revealed after the Confederacy was defeated and Reconstruction began.

That postwar interregnum of ex-states and ex-slaves still beckons, now more insistently thanks to several astute periodical studies. The most comprehensive of these is Alice Fahs's *The Imagined Civil War: Popular Literature of the North and South, 1861–1865*, which joins an array of Southern and Northern periodicals to an ambitious investigation of ephemera such as cartoons, comic valentines, and illustrated patriotic envelopes, some depicting the enslaved "contrabands" who are her book's recurring concern. But though she reaches into the 1880s and 1890s for the war's later echoes in juvenile fiction, Fahs does not extend her assessment of "commercial literary culture" to the magazine marketplace immediately after Appomattox or to the commemorative uncertainties of Reconstruction during the 1860s and 1870s.[42] Touching upon those "tumultuous" postbellum years in a larger portrait of developing print culture, Patricia Okker in *Social Stories: The Magazine Novel in Nineteenth-Century America* pauses on the battlefield concussions of John William De Forest and the home-front disquiet of Rebecca Harding Davis, while Linda Frost in *Never One Nation: Freaks, Savages, and Whiteness in U.S. Popular Culture, 1850–1877* calls upon a hefty archive of midcentury periodicals to discover the "racialized, nationalistic discourse" that the Civil War accelerated.[43] Even with their somewhat different lenses, both books encourage a more systematic attention to the saturated ways in which the experience of war was first remembered in popular magazines. So, too, does Christopher Hager's *Word by Word: Emancipation and the Act of Writing*, which discovers the "creative sparks" of black self-emancipation in periodicals like the *North American Review* and the *Christian Recorder*, the *New England Magazine* and *Douglass' Monthly*, as well as on board fences, clay pots, boot linings, and shipyard timbers.[44] As freedom shimmers in Hager's fugitive places, it is frankly hard to imagine how Reconstruction could have foundered, given the cresting wave of African American desire.

That is, until the varying agendas of regional magazines come into focus. Like Vanderbilt's depot rather than its radiating lines, this book was assembled from local encounters, from fistfuls of data and their intriguing patterns, from one unearthed story and then one disinterred magazine at a time. Like Grand Central's headhouse, with its unifying embellishments, a master narrative of emancipation and reckoning has coalesced, one that begins in chapter 1 with newly discovered stories about the fate of Confederate families after 1861 and ends in chapter 4 with the deployment of seasoned veterans in 1865 as regiments of United States Colored Troops were sent west to the plains. Pushing steadily into the immediate postwar years, when some of these magazine stories are set and all four primary periodicals were founded, this project has also benefited from innovative studies of postbellum literature, two in particular.

Sharon Kennedy-Nolle in *Writing Reconstruction: Race, Gender, and Citizenship in the Postwar South* has also investigated compartmentalized Reconstructive ventures, though she takes her cue from the redeployment of Federal troops in the truculent South during 1867, when five military districts were imposed. Alert to issues of labor, duty, reputation, and property, she focuses on "new and diverse notions of southern identity" that local stories and novels, white travel sketches, and black student periodicals delineated through the 1890s.[45] In pausing on their "imaginative vistas," Kennedy-Nolle raises the question of how Lincoln's "liberty" might be reconceived once the war broke ground for a "new nation," particularly following the chaotic years that have become my earlier, patchy terrain.[46]

Surveying an even more expansive period beyond the turn of the century, Brook Thomas in *The Literature of Reconstruction: Not in Plain Black and White* recognizes popular storytellers before moving on to more familiar writers, though often in their less heralded works. Grounding these in an enviable command of history and law, he makes the case for disentangling the snarled plots of Constance Fenimore Woolson and John William De Forest, George Washington Cable and Sutton Griggs, Thomas Nelson Page and Joel Chandler Harris in order to appreciate what postbellum witnesses once saw and rarely laid to rest. "Reconstruction will remain America's unfinished revolution," Thomas writes, "if we fail to acknowledge how complicated the situation was for the actors at the time."[47] Preoccupied with the construction of railroads and their success in bringing the West into the country's cultural orbit, he identifies a series of origin myths and "inheritance plots," along with a fundamental question for an eighteenth-century nation in decline: Who was the rightful heir?[48]

Both Kennedy-Nolle's "imaginative vistas" and Thomas's "inheritance plots" resonate across this book, which reveals what it was possible to imagine and who was likely to inherit on the way to the Centennial celebrations of 1876. In the *Southern Magazine* and *The Land We Love*, the "South" emerges from the war's loosed lightning as the site of Federal intrusion and ruined hearths, which could be replaced by makeshift cabins and substitute households. But the memory of loss persists for both the kin of white subscribers and so many Northern soldiers in other magazines, where they are restored to the dinner tables and parlors that embodied the Union as it was. Only fitfully is the dream of safe return exchanged, in the war stories of Northern periodicals, for a racially blended family and a larger household, whose new citizens found their place at the national table. That is what Davis's fierce slave plods north to secure. Yet it would most often be in the *Lakeside Monthly* and the *Overland Monthly* that a more capacious fireside was credibly imagined and the tug of old homesteads—inherited, restorative, beloved—gave way in the West at last.

Like the separate platforms of Vanderbilt's several lines, however, those larger narratives emerge piecemeal as case studies accumulate, while twelve other contentious periodicals worth enumerating provide an importunate chorus. From Boston, the prestigious *Atlantic Monthly* (1857–present) is joined by the more vituperative *Continental Monthly* (1862–64). From New York, the genteel *Harper's Monthly* (1850–present) and the more Republican *Harper's Weekly* (1857–1916) contend with the revived *Putnam's* (1868–70) and the newly founded *Galaxy* (1866–78), both staunch venues for American writers. From Philadelphia, the serene *Godey's Lady's Book* (1830–98) is augmented by *Lippincott's* (1868–1916) and its growing stable of Southern writers. From Richmond comes the dignified *Southern Literary Messenger* (1834–64) and the more contentious *Southern Illustrated News* (1862–65), which hoped to supplant *Harper's Weekly*. From Memphis, the short-lived but pugnacious *Southern Monthly* (1861–62) consorts in this archive with the *New National Era* (1870–74), a weekly paper that was designed in the District of Columbia to serve African American interests nationwide. Profiled at greater length in the opening pages of *Where My Heart Is Turning Ever*, this cache of periodicals has made it possible to revisit the neglected scenes of early Civil War stories, this time from peripheral metropoles linked to Grand Central's multiple platforms and the arching promise of its train shed roof. Each chapter then concludes with a single reprinted story and a closer look at the traces of one magazine's agenda, its dodges, and its positioning in a larger literary marketplace.

As a result, a latticework of intersecting print culture concerns materializes, one that helps to explain why particular stories appeared in the wake of war and why their narrative anatomy matters. This book's first chapter is grounded in Baltimore's *Southern Magazine* and links the postwar emergence of the International Copyright Association to greater marketplace support for regional American writers, who shifted the setting of Civil War conflict from the open battlefields of the East to the no man's land of border territory farther west. The second chapter demonstrates that the reorganization of a single national postal service descried by Charlotte's *The Land We Love* coincided with shifts in the fictional delivery of episodic events, a sign that both government and narrative

FIGURE 9. *Going on Board*. Wood engraving. "The Boat and the Train," *Harper's Weekly*, July 17, 1858, 452. Courtesy of the University of Iowa Libraries.

design were subject to breakdown, repair, and significant reinterpretation. The third chapter links Chicago's *Lakeside Monthly* to the extension of railroad lines during and after the war and to complaints about monopolistic control, just when the representation of Civil War time was similarly tugged by a storyteller's conventional omniscience and a soldier's battlefield dismay. The fourth chapter, which focuses on San Francisco's *Overland Monthly*, also considers the new functions of photography and magazine illustration as they jibed with changes in narrative distance and perspective to undermine traditional definitions of "truth." In light of such discussions, the book's coda then contemplates what became of Julia Ward Howe after the marching stopped and how Rebecca Harding Davis parlayed more venturesome roles for "the South" and African Americans outside the pages of the *Atlantic Monthly*, particularly at a time when new magazines supervised the heavy lifting of national recollection.

There was a prewar hint of both significant connections and instructive muscle in *Harper's Weekly*, whose engraved *Waiting for the Train* was coupled with *Going on Board* to portray the complications of nineteenth-century travel (figure 9). Where the train depot appears jam-packed with passengers and that "exasperating personage," the baggage master, the steamship platform crowds most passengers into the sketchier middistance and foregrounds instead the human apparatus of travel: the porters, haulers, fruit sellers, and deckhands, as well as, above them, the drivers and footmen representing the city hotels, coach owners, line magnates, luggage manufacturers, dressmakers, and even periodical editors who made travel work.[49] Surveying this scene, *Harper's Weekly* recalled "the throng, the noise, the reckless manner in which luggage is handled, the excitement about lost trunks, good berths, and misplaced keys" and finally the "*ensemble* which travelers do not readily forget."[50] For a wittily self-conscious newsmagazine, depot culture became the site of such intersections, the mirror space in which multiplying interests converged.

This is a book about recollective "*ensemble*," about the analogous intercession of not-so-transparent periodicals, the convergence of many hands when shared memory was created in print, and the need for thirty-one doors when recollecting the Civil War and its charged aftermath. More particularly, this book examines pavilion space, both the separate enterprises of four postwar magazines and the networks their labor facilitated, the dissemination that began for many with a Second Empire facade. Beyond filling a gap in American literary history, this book aims to provide a more rigorous method for taking the cultural pulse than literary studies and close reading alone have enabled. With an eye to the West, literary critics, as well as cultural historians and students of nineteenth-century media, may be drawn to this ongoing study of the short popular narratives that made the Civil War make sense to contemporary readers. So, too, would anyone interested in the fractured opportunity the Civil War provided for reckoning with "the South" and emancipation by reconceiving a Revolutionary era legacy, especially amid the yellowing pages of literary magazines with their flash of liberty and justice, of lightning and a terrible swift sword.

CHAPTER 1

Potshots

Border Traffic, International Copyright,
and Baltimore's *Southern Magazine*

To this day, the white mile markers once laid out by Charles Mason and Jeremiah Dixon carry the traces of an M on one side and a P on the other. Every fifth mile along the Mason-Dixon Line still sometimes reveals an aging "crown" stone, which displays the Baltimore coat of arms on its southern front and William Penn's family crest facing north. Across more than two hundred miles, the British astronomers laid these markers due west during the 1760s and thus settled at last the border dispute that had chafed the colonies of Maryland and Pennsylvania for more than eighty years. The line they surveyed a bare fifteen miles from Philadelphia later became the designated boundary between slave and free states in 1820, when Congress hammered out the Missouri Compromise to hold the Union together for a time. So in April 1861, when an ill-fated troop train left Philadelphia carrying one of the earliest Union regiments called up after Fort Sumter fell, the boys of the Sixth Massachusetts Volunteer Infantry were loading their rifles as they passed the stone markers and headed for rebellion to the south.

The first blood of the war was drawn on April 19 when those volunteers from Lowell and Lawrence made their way across Baltimore's city streets, a provocation that turned to tumult and brought the city under martial law.[1] For the next four years, Maryland remained a border state, tied to the South by sympathy and tobacco but bound to the North by rail networks and trade. Equally a crossroads after hostilities ended, Maryland surged with postwar capital, and Baltimore proved a haven for both Southern refugees and German immigrants. Many of the immigrants went west to farm the prairies, however, while many of the refugees remained to tug at the city's political compass and fortify its culture. "Baltimore, the frontier town of the Old South, spared by the ravages of war," wrote Basil Gildersleeve, "was the great hope and refuge of the shattered remnant of the young men of the Confederacy."² They were among the first to bolster the postwar magazine trade outside New England, and they welcomed a distinctly regional literature that would challenge the cultural ascendancy of the Northeast, consolidate interest in the local, and ultimately transform the "real" war that got into literary magazines.

These developments were facilitated in growing cities like Baltimore by the international copyright debates, which were insistently rejoined during the 1860s and produced informal agreements that stepped up royalty payments to foreign authors or their publishers. With cheap transatlantic fare ebbing as a result, literary magazines across the country sought more original contributions, among them short fiction that traded the side streets of London and the avenues of Paris for nearer settings while replacing distant cultural intrigue with ruder shocks closer to home. Indeed, the wider purview of regional editors as reprinting waned, together with the greater resourcefulness of American authors after the war, encouraged a backwater iconoclasm that would have striking consequences for new periodicals like Baltimore's *Southern Magazine* (1866–75). Founded as the *Richmond Eclectic* and initially filled with miscellaneous reprints from abroad, the literary monthly moved to Baltimore in 1868 and shortly thereafter to a new name and a new agenda, especially in recollecting the late rebellion.

Under editor William Hand Browne, the magazine's pages began to sketch unexpected sites in Civil War stories, spaces that were harder to read: an apartment in Richmond, a mountain village in North Carolina, a shop in Atlanta, a bluegrass home in Kentucky. Quite a few postwar monthlies reckoned with regional wartime disturbances, but in the *Southern Magazine* these seemingly random settings revealed an unexpected pattern: they tended to gravitate toward a Big House and its variants, which Patricia Yeager's sense of the "geography" of identity will complicate productively. In a further development, not only for Browne's monthly but sporadically for magazines in other regions as well, stories of the war that appeared while international fare was receding took a peculiar turn when they were set in Louisiana, a state that became (like Maryland) an occupied border territory where the imposition of Federal authority would have startling repercussions.

Browne was no more tolerant of local Unionists than Southern ladies in occupied New Orleans. In fact, he was frequently as outspoken as volatile wartime columnists and as dismissive as postwar editors like Daniel Harvey Hill in North Carolina.³ By the 1870s, however, the fate of the Confederacy had been decided, Federal troops had been redeployed to the South's military districts, and the best cause not yet lost lay for many in encouraging a distinctly Southern literature, still in the making. For Browne and his monthly, the catechism of despair that preoccupied other Southern monthlies was less insistent than the literature of protest, especially when the Civil War was the focus of seventeen idiosyncratic narratives. In place of the post-Appomattox mire of sagging Southern homesteads and failed cross-sectional romances in other periodicals, thirteen of these stories were adventurous tales of the ones who got away—from northern prisons, from Federal troops, from Petersburg under siege, from naval engagements on the Atlantic. They were thus stories of a second chance, narratively as protean as Baltimore itself, verbally as obstreperous as peculiar regional settings allowed, thematically as rebellious as Jefferson Davis without the bombast, and historically as far from the preoccupations of New England as a failed Confederate rebellion would permit. Unusual and diverse, these war stories anticipated a profound shift in national recollection toward border warfare, illegible residents, and their divisive allegiances, a later development that would spread from a handful of borderland stories and push the otherwise infrequent trope of divided kin toward the central position it occupies today.

At the outset of the war, just a week after Fort Sumter was bombarded, those in Baltimore who threw paving stones from the streets, hurled coal and dishes from nearby windows, and fired potshots at the Sixth Massachusetts from the porches of the Maltby House hotel were not working-class gangs, like the Plug Uglies and Blood Tubs of the 1850s, the period of the city's rising nativism. Generally, those earlier xenophobic groups were pugnacious Union men; as Frank Towers has pointed out, many would later join the city's Union Party despite their proslavery sentiments.[4] In 1861, by contrast, the April 19 attack was led by Southern sympathizers and Democratic merchants whose party was returning to municipal rule and whose leading citizens resented the intrusion of Federal troops.[5] Their resistance accelerated when General Benjamin Butler arrived in May and turned the heavy guns at Fort McHenry onto Baltimore's streets and squares. In addition, the writ of habeas corpus was suspended, the Democratic mayor was arrested, and thousands departed to enlist in Confederate regiments, an evacuation that ultimately strengthened the authority of the Union men left behind. Under close Federal surveillance, dissenting newspapers like the *Daily Exchange*, the *Daily Republican*, and *The South* were suppressed.[6] In their absence, the principal wartime challenge to the zeal of Boston's *Atlantic Monthly* and *Continental Monthly* came from Richmond, where the *Southern Illustrated News* quickened the pace and galvanized the politics of the baronial *Southern Literary Messenger*. Thereafter, once shortages, siege, and surrender had undone the Confederate capital, Baltimore would emerge as the North's best antagonist, specifically in setting the rhetorical terms upon which a version of "the South" might arise from Reconstruction to reenter the national lexicon.

Baltimore may seem like a ramshackle site for a literary capital with a commemorative agenda, but it was at Fort McHenry in this Chesapeake harbor that Francis Scott Key wrote "The Star-Spangled Banner" in 1814, more than a decade before the arrival of Edgar Allan Poe. During the years following the War of 1812, Baltimore stood poised to become the nation's leading port: its mills processed western grain and southern cotton, and its tall ships made the city the best purveyor of notions and dry goods, coffee and fertilizer for hundreds of miles.[7] In the 1790s, when the town was chartered, its population doubled and then doubled again during the next decade, while Boston fell behind. By the 1820s, the city had begun laying tracks for the pioneering Baltimore and Ohio Railroad as international trade escalated. Just a few years after the war that produced an anthem, Baltimore's imports exceeded $5 million, and trade reached Europe, South America, India, and China. So intermeshed were Baltimore's industrial concerns that the city began processing quantities of cotton duck for the tall masts that gave its distinctive clippers an exceptional canvas spread and extraordinary speed. Greater prosperity in turn bred the money for leisure among the city's elites and thus a demand for the books and booksellers, magazines, and printers that led Baltimore to crowd out Annapolis on Maryland's cultural stage.

As early as 1795, the city's circulating libraries were augmented by the more august Library Company, whose fifty-nine original shareholders grew to more than three hundred in less than five years.[8] By 1802 Baltimore had given rise to a typographical society and by 1806 a type foundry; only Philadelphia at the turn of the nineteenth century could claim as much. Where Annapolis echoed Britain's eighteenth-century coffee houses in founding the Tuesday Club of literary wags, Baltimore cut in with a Monday Club that first met on Wednesdays and then a Wednesday Club as the city's taste for music and drama grew.[9] Francis Scott Key was associated with the Delphian Club, which was so distinguished that only nine men could join at any one time, each partner to a muse.[10] In this fashion, the cultural ground and financial underpinning essential for magazine success were established.

John Neal, said to be James Fenimore Cooper's closest American rival, was a prominent Delphian and the mercurial editor of *The Portico*, a monthly magazine published as early as 1816 with the help of Delphian friends of friends such as lawyer William Wirt, artist Rembrandt Peale, and novelist John Pendleton Kennedy.[11] During the 1830s, Kennedy's plantation fiction would insinuate a southern edge to previously nationalistic fare; but even then, border tension dissipated when northern readers made a novelist like Kennedy popular and when the writer himself was inclined to be more urbane than the landed masters he described.[12] Besides, in the teens and twenties when the Delphians were active, the cultural adversary was British, *The Portico*'s aim was a native literature marked by true American variety, and the most vexing postcolonial praise came when London's *Monthly Magazine* called Baltimore's literary venture one of the best in the United States.[13]

By midcentury, the Delphians had faded, as had an early merchant class now invested, like Kennedy, in rural estates, while a new urban generation inherited an expanding economy. As Robert Brugger has observed, Maryland had been dividing since the eighteenth century along a line that ran at a slant through Baltimore, with areas to the south and east focused on tobacco and an enslaved labor system in decline, while areas to the north and west were increasingly committed to manufacturing, as well as raising more varied crops and livestock.[14] By 1853 the B&O Railroad had reached Wheeling and could begin consolidating the trans-Allegheny West, which supplied bituminous coal for city stoves, iron and copper for urban refineries, fruits and vegetables for Baltimore's canning industry, and heaping shipments of grain for the mills that were fueling international trade as never before. Backed by the security of state bonds, much like the Chesapeake and Ohio Canal, the B&O was essentially a municipal project helping to inaugurate the "public society" that Gary Lawson Browne sees replacing the private and aristocratic mercantilism favored by the state's tobacco plantations.[15] With the help of new rail lines, Baltimore on the eve of the Civil War had become the key port for what Browne calls "an interregional economy," and the city had seen sharp demographic shifts since 1840. As many as 170,000 new residents arrived during the 1840s and 1850s, almost 100,000 of them during the prewar decade alone, and they immediately became part of a kaleidoscopic cultural scene that would reveal who counted in the city's coalescing public order and whose interests the *Southern Magazine* would carefully advance or curb.[16]

In addition to those who relocated to Baltimore from the North, thousands of immigrants were the Germans fleeing revolutionary failure in 1848 and the Irish fleeing hunger and want. Just as their reasons for immigrating differed, so did their new social standing. Like George Peabody and Enoch Pratt, both from Massachusetts, the German Forty-Eighters came with sufficient skills and resources to make their way, often in the textile and shoe industries or, for German Jews, in banking and retail clothing. Because they joined an earlier generation of immigrant merchants who had customarily invested in tobacco, they quickly constituted one of the largest German communities in the country, with the merchant clubs, singing societies, libraries, mutual aid associations, newspapers, and *Schulen* that kept their language alive. Within their community, however, political affiliations shifted: where an older generation of prosperous merchants had established ties with the Democratic Party, more recent immigrants were often abolitionist, though they were wary of the Republican cry for government intervention.[17]

By comparison, the Irish arriving in Baltimore during the late 1840s and early 1850s were half as numerous, much less skilled, more likely to be Catholic, and thus more often the target of nativist violence, particularly when the pressure on wage-earning jobs increased.[18] As day laborers with little hope of German success, the Irish found themselves squeezed as well by the previous claims of Baltimore's black workers in a city with a large and largely free African American community, which Maryland's legislative priorities enabled. As Max Grivno observes, "Maryland's manumission laws remained quite liberal through the 1850s, and in the decade preceding the Civil War, free blacks outnumbered slaves in all of the state's northern counties."[19] Most worked at barbering, brick-making, and ship-caulking; alarmed by Know-Nothing attacks in the city's shipyards, they formed a black trade union and allied with wealthy Democratic patrons, who feared the voting clout of white workers more than the threat of black freedom.[20] Comparatively poor, black Baltimoreans nonetheless built churches, founded Sabbath schools, created literary societies, organized Masonic lodges, offered sanctuary to fugitive slaves, and counted themselves a large part of the city's beset labor force.[21]

During the years of civil war, Union regiments never decimated the city as they did Atlanta, Columbia, and Richmond because Maryland never seceded, border state that it was. In 1865, when Union armies were marching through the Carolinas and besieging the Confederate capital, Baltimore was still selling grain drills and guano and elliptic yoke shirts that guaranteed an exceptional fit while running new steamer lines to Havana and Liverpool and preparing to open the doors of the Peabody Institute as music academy, art gallery, library, and lecture hall.[22] No city south of the Mason-Dixon Line was better positioned to sponsor a literary resurgence or better able to shore up a southern alternative to Yankee boosterism and a cultural alternative to the "New South" that would eventually bring consumerism and Atlanta to the fore. Certainly no more southerly city in the wake of Appomattox could seize so expeditiously the communications network that magazines promised. At a time when the periodical trade was soaring in the Northeast and spreading nationwide, the vitality of Baltimore's many neighborhoods made the city "the most active of Southern postwar literary centers," as Ray Atchison in his study of southern magazines has documented.[23] Leading this counterattack, Browne's journal would become the self-proclaimed "exponent of the best thoughts and feelings of our Southern people" and thus, in 1871, the *Southern Magazine*.[24]

Yet Baltimore's diversifying neighborhoods were not equally visible in the city's foremost literary periodical. Buttressed by local capital and proliferating investments, the monthly began to pepper contemporary periodical debates with heated Southern rebuttal—potshots, in a sense. Etymologically, such blasts from hunters appeared fortuitous, meant to fill a cooking pot rather than a display case. From the porches of the Maltby House, they were fired at Union troops without careful aim, instances of resistance to authority that were later echoed in the editorial pages of the *Southern Magazine*. On paper, potshots could abruptly reorient memories of the Civil War, especially in the conflict's first anxious stories; John Winston's "An Escape from Johnston's Island" (November 1872), for example, supplied a bubbling Baltimore pot with Southern fare that was rarely offered in other venues. The emerging opportunism was arresting, especially when the random shots that Major Winston feared were recalled as an oppressive wartime threat.

Opening during the icy months of 1864, Winston's narrative chronicles the successful flight of several Confederate officers from a Union prison camp on Lake Erie. During the nighttime escape and the rugged Ohio days that follow, Northern suspicions are quick to surface, and sudden potshots are repeatedly feared—from a camp sentry when the Confederates scale the prison wall, from a Dutchman whose "vrow" refuses them supper, from an old man who notices their Southern accents, from an English hotelkeeper they cannot pay. Just as Confederate sympathizers in Baltimore grabbed paving stones, coal and dishes, or available weapons on ample porches, so those residing near the frigid prison camp seemed ready to fire damaging blasts without warning.

But in Winston's story, none of those blasts goes off. The sentry holds his fire because he thinks he sees a comrade returning from a henroost. The Dutchman's vrow settles for a "Nix!" later repeated by a series of Germans who speak little English—"Vocht dat?" "Nix."[25] An Irishman with his grandson simply refuses to provide board or bed, and a New Bedford down-easter worries the Confederates so much that they slip away. Everything changes when they cross the ice into Canada, where they are met with pies, pallets, a horse, and a sleigh, as well as an Englishman who accepts their labor in exchange for hotel rooms. With a little storytelling magic once Winston returned to North Carolina, the shots that are never heard become instead the slights that are always seen against the Germans, the Irish, and the down-easter. None of them deserves the praise allotted the English hotelkeeper, which comes as quickly as Richmond would have praised international recognition from London. In a similar manner, the *Southern Magazine* took other verbal potshots, often by describing border territory while dismissing immigrant neighborhoods, racial difference, and hazy allegiances with a bluster that masked steady purpose.

Even before arriving in Baltimore, the *Richmond Eclectic* had established an enviable reputation among ex-Confederates. Founded in the Virginia capital by two Presbyterian ministers, the monthly that initially reprinted British fare was drawn north by what former editor Moses Drury Hoge in December 1867 called "energy, fine literary culture, practical acquaintance with business, and, what I never possessed—*capital*."[26] Despite the loss of about $5,000, the rechristened *Southern Magazine* later served for several years as the official organ of the Southern Historical Society.[27] Under Browne, assisted at first by Fridge Murdoch and William L. Hill, the monthly increasingly provided original contributions from Southern writers like Paul Hamilton Hayne, Sidney Lanier, Margaret J. Preston, and John Esten Cooke. Prospering in Baltimore by 1869, the magazine claimed a circulation "larger than the *combined* circulations of all the other magazines in the South," according to publisher Henry C. Turnbull, though Browne privately lamented to Hayne in 1872 that his subscription list was still inadequate: "If we had but 10,000 circulation (and what is that out of 8,000,000 [Southern] people?) we could give such prices to contributors as would bring the best work of the best men."[28] When northern periodicals began paying southern writers in the mid-1870s, Browne's venture failed.

While it lasted, however, the *Southern Magazine* enthusiastically pursued the task of establishing a selective regional literature, one that contested the memorializing practices of other postwar venues. Wholly Southern stories such as Confederate Gray's "T.J.'s Cavalry Charge" (April 1870) and Max Marrowfat's "Seeking Dixie" (December 1872) rarely appeared in the years of the war or the magazines of the North, where the Southern taste for pseudonyms was also less pronounced. Accumulating in Browne's monthly, such stories suggest the experience of thwarting authority through artful dodging. Indeed, his magazine offered white nostalgia with a twist: reciting episodes in the Confederate epic of national defeat meant exploring the territory under Federal surveillance for avenues of resistance rather than discovering productive alliances with new neighbors across town.

Avenues of resistance? That was also the antislavery concern of the *Atlantic Monthly*'s "John Lamar" (April 1862), Rebecca Harding Davis's story that exchanges the plantation Virginia of John Pendleton Kennedy's *Swallow Barn* (1832) for the smaller farms of the state's northwestern recesses. Recollecting the intemperate politics that set Quaker friends in Pennsylvania against proslavery neighbors in Wheeling, Davis would observe years later, "My family lived on the border of Virginia. We were, so to speak, on the fence, and could see the great question from both sides."[29] Like the childhood companions from differing sections that her story follows, Davis sees in the borderland of Virginia's western hills a space for common ground, even as the "great question" of American liberty puts friends at odds. Arguably, the sensibilities of Southerners in occupied Baltimore might then encourage simply reallocating Davis's wartime cast, turning her abolitionist heroes into their zealous villains without tampering with the story's formal design or displacing her anger against unjust laws. Swap the watchful eyes of Federal troops on Baltimore streets for the monitoring gaze of a kindly plantation master, the potshots from the Maltby House hotel for the hidden knife of John Lamar's vengeful slave, and a prickly resistance to authority could become the war's recurring sectional hallmark, at least in periodicals from Baltimore and Boston. Even the unmindful friendship of Davis's upscale rivals in love jibes with a pattern of border reckonings between soldiers, ships, homesteads, and refugees in many of the war stories published by the *Southern Magazine*.

But the explosive violence that Davis imagined (and her readers then and now tend to see as borderland trait) was not customary in the *Southern Magazine*'s postwar stories, where potshots really were random and insurrection was less appealing than subterfuge or flight. Consider, for example, "Mrs. Spriggins, the Neutral" (February 1871), an anecdotal encounter between a discreet Confederate on a daily train to the city and a Northern nurse lamenting the loss of her scissors. While there is no more mention of slavery in this sketch by "Alcibiades Jones" than in other Southern stories that nod to "servants" or ignore domestic labor altogether, it is easy to notice the manly courtesy that produces a seat in Jones's "car," much like Davis's friendly toast to "Liberty," a few favors between his strangers much like a few memories between her friends.[30] Even the twang of colloquial talk, from Jones's "horspittle nuss" in Maryland or Davis's Illinois boatman serving as western Virginia sentry—"Heow many, neow, hes he like you, down to Georgy?"—emerges in both stories to mark the country's intersecting classes, the war's colliding interests, and the borderland's verbal traffic. But Civil War stories in the *Southern Magazine* regularly favored sites of containment—this railroad car near Baltimore, a ferry close to Tennessee, a steamer in New Orleans—where confrontations were as muted as a hushed prison break, and social revolution among the newly free was replaced by personal survival, whites only. While Davis makes sure her stubble-field shed is finally drenched in a master's blood, Jones makes sure his hobbled "nuss" can get off the train, a disquieting sign of a hobbled Reconstruction on the way.

That a regional literature of resistance coalesced in places like Baltimore and forums like the *Southern Magazine* is a consequence, at least in part, of the agitation for an international copyright law that was reinvigorated in the North after the war. Stretching back to 1790, when the First Congress passed a law protecting American authors for fourteen years before their work became public property, the pressure to respect the private rights of authors at home and abroad had long run afoul of a republican emphasis on educating distant citizens, which regional editors could insure with scissors and pastepot in hand. The result was oddly similar to a common practice in the digital age, as Peter Baldwin has noticed. "Except for being conducted on paper via post," Baldwin writes in *The Copyright Wars*, "their activities resembled nothing so much as today's blogs."[31] Encourage free circulation, the logic runs, and the proprietary rights of the few are engulfed by the restless curiosity of the many.

In addition, cheap book production and proliferating American periodicals had for decades secured the prosperity of homegrown publishing concerns that employed thousands of workers, many of whom owed their livelihood to the trade in transatlantic reprinting that an international copyright law would diminish. In their name, appeals to Congress from those who opposed rewarding well-heeled British authors or their fat London publishers multiplied. "Associating authors' rights with luxury and hereditary privilege," writes Meredith McGill, "these petitions argue that any extension of these rights would be an irresponsible sacrifice of public good to private interest. In equating international copyright with a threat to American industry, and locating national identity in the process of production, they make the powerful claim that manufacturing, and not literature, is America's true cultural product."[32] Even after the Civil War, "Philip Quilibet" (George E. Pond) in New York's *Galaxy* would cast the international copyright debates as "a scrimmage of booksellers, bookbinders, gold-beaters, big publishers, little publishers, type-founders, tariff-haters, paper-makers, printers, protectionists, authors, and importers."[33] Fearful of the British taste for fine printing, which few Americans could afford, U.S. manufacturers stymied major legislation by framing the international copyright issue as a contest between private ownership and public need.

Because many in the antebellum South were dismayed by the increasing consolidation of investment capital and fat publishing houses in cities like Boston, it is tempting to see their concerns aligned with those of "paper-makers, printers, [and] protectionists" against a common enemy with gatekeeping aims, whether in London or in Boston. Yet southerners had spoken out in favor of international copyright from the early years of the *Southern Literary Messenger*, founded in 1834; during the 1840s, William Gilmore Simms contributed several letters to the magazine on that subject. Taking up the case for "a native Literature" where *The Portico* had left off, Simms remonstrated against cheap British reprints and "the ancient wallow of colonial dependency" when he wrote: "As it is only through our own minds that we can be free, so, when these are surrendered to the tutelage of strangers, we are, to all intents and purposes, a people in bondage."[34] With the antebellum attacks on slavery increasing, however, it was not British fare that outspoken southerners most resented. By 1863 the *Southern Literary Messenger*'s "Editor's Table" spoke for many in seeking "our liberation from Yankee bondage," by then the hallmark of a familiar effort to lift the ban on British literary imports.[35] More to the point, perhaps, the *Southern Literary Messenger* congratulated a Richmond publishing firm on its effort to "remunerate English authors for their labours" and pay Southern authors over $15,000 in 1862 alone, while "Yankee swindlers" cut and ran.[36]

In an even shrewder move to encourage international recognition of the new government in Richmond, the Confederate Congress passed the Resolution in Relation to International Copyright on March 7, 1861, again at the urging of Simms. Though the statute established two months later was never tested because the Confederacy was never recognized as a sovereign nation with laws of its own, the Southern embrace of international copyright was a strategic means of resisting Northern cultural inroads while damning Northern business practices. As Melissa Homestead has put it, "This critique brings into sharp relief by way of contrast how international copyright participated in the articulation of the dominant version of Confederate nationalism, which represented the Confederate nation as commercially disinterested, agrarian, and aristocratic in opposition to the commercially motivated, industrialized, and plebian 'Yankee' North."[37] With few bookbinders, paper mills, or type foundries in the South to protect, as Alice Fahs has noted, the Confederacy that the *Southern Magazine* later championed could claim a ready audience for British books and an open hand for British authors without much financial risk and without compromising the "native Literature" that would celebrate a new nation among international peers.[38]

That position made for unforeseen alliances after the war, when the International Copyright Association was founded by northern men like publisher George Palmer Putnam and author James Parton in 1868. Failing in their attempt to secure immediate legislation, they continued their campaign into the 1870s, when debate came to the floor of Congress at last, after decades of petitions and memorials that died in committee or with a committee's report. Among popular northern magazines, as in Congress, the copyright issue turned on an author's right to the fruits of labor. In the *Atlantic Monthly*, Parton urged couching private recompense as public benefit, a solution he initiated by appealing to the interests of publishing houses as middlemen who could themselves secure good work through good wages. "Congress has passed patent laws which have called into exercise an amount of triumphant ingenuity that is one of the great wonders of the modern world," he wrote in "International Copyright" (October 1867); "but under the copyright laws, enacted with the same good intentions, our infant literature pines and dwindles."[39] In the event, Congress did not pass an act granting foreign authors copyright protection in the United States until 1891. But the energy with which the case was argued did shift the nature of informal agreements after the Civil War. "By the 1870s," Jeffrey Groves has observed, "the practice of purchasing advance sheets was largely replaced, at least in relation to popular works by well-known authors, by a voluntary royalty system."[40] The upshot was that foreign imports were curtailed, the American magazine trade was bolstered, and the way the Civil War would be recollected across the country shifted dramatically.

In San Francisco, the *Overland Monthly* was founded under Bret Harte's aegis in 1868 and, like the *Southern Magazine*, began almost immediately to publish Civil War stories that skewed the norms set by journals in the Northeast. When black soldiers stood watch in "A Dark Night on Picket" (July 1870) or a Kansas abolitionist defied bushwhackers in "The Cabin at Pharaoh's Ford" (October 1874), readers were reminded that along the border of what they knew best were soldiers who were not white and preachers who could be strung up for what they believed. In Chicago, the *Lakeside Monthly* began appearing in 1869, when editor Francis Fisher Browne encouraged a literary density and metropolitan skill that matched the offbeat vigor of the *Southern Magazine*. Subsequent *Lakeside Monthly* contributions about a more western war in "Two Only Sons" (December 1870), "Our Adjutant" (May 1873), and "In the Palmy Days of Slaveholding" (July 1870) complicated the glory of enlistment and the privilege of plantation households or the ease of their dismantlement when such stories were set in Ohio, Georgia, or Florida. Much closer to border skirmishing than to clear lines of attack, these able regional journals focused more often on the thickets and backwaters of war through the lens of their reconstructive moments, which brought out-of-the-way places into public view.

The career of the *Southern Magazine* and its principal editor might best be understood in such irregular western company. William Hand Browne's purpose, as he saw it, was to reinstate a selective "southern" culture; in his view, a literary monthly was peculiarly well situated to begin codifying southern memories of civil conflict and spurring the alternate future that his postwar readers would help construct. To poet and frequent contributor Paul Hamilton Hayne, Browne declared in 1870, "I want the new South, so far as it may be new, to be distinctly and especially the *South*, and not a bastard New England."[41] Nowhere was he more successful in mounting sectional resistance to what he called "Yankeeisation" than in the reconstructive pages of the *Southern Magazine*.

Regularly denouncing the spirit of "centralism" and the "club-law" of cliques, Browne advanced instead a vision of southern cum American civilization that scorned paramount national citizenship and promoted local white interests, equally bound to a revolutionary past and an industrial future. "The true policy of Conservatism," he observed in his monthly column "The Green Table" (December 1874), "is not (if that were possible) to blot out the past, but to lead the country, which has gone widely astray, back to the true paths, and to go forward in them."[42] What the Baltimore editor valued in his uninterrupted campaign for states' rights was what he often called "local self-government," whose guarantee of personal liberties thwarted the reach of Federal guns. "Every step towards empire on the part of the government," he declared, "is a step toward the enslavement of the citizens."[43] Unyielding in his editorial attacks on Reconstruction legislatures, which he dismissed in April 1873 because of "the domination of negroes and carpetbaggers," Browne feared by August not only the radical elevation of freedpeople but also the "taint of blood" that reunification would encourage and the "mongrel race" that would cost the white South its future by "fixing the savage element indelibly in the nerves and brain."[44] Even the bedroom thus seemed vulnerable to the congressional imposition of change, as public policy obliterated individual rights.

To combat the malignancies he saw arising, Browne joined contributing writers like Henry Ewbank, Edward V. Valentine, and G. W. Archer in fighting to preserve the heritage of Robert E. Lee and P. G. T. Beauregard. In his monthly column, he focused not only on the pages of the *Southern Magazine* but on the offices of the new Southern Historical Society, which took as its purpose "the vindication of Southern history from misrepresentation."[45] With one hand on the society's "Transactions," published as monthly addenda to the magazine beginning in July 1874, Browne reached with his free hand for a southern future conceived out of Baltimore's steady reliance on immigration and trade. "The South needs development," he declared in "The Green Table" (April 1873); "she requires railways, canals and public improvements of all sorts, which she has neither money nor credit to pay for, and without which she must languish and may die."[46] Not at all the agrarian model that southern apologists would consecrate amid the frenetic modernist heyday following World War I, Browne's conservative program looked instead to industrial development, foreign capital, immigrant labor, and a coalition with western interests to resist eastern monopolies and invite prosperity's return. "We must descend from the spectators' benches," he wrote in January 1874, "come down into the arena, and take our part in the world's great struggle," a typically Baltimorean maneuver for transforming the legacy of the country's forefathers into the coin of the realm.[47]

Browne's agenda for the South and his sense of the role that even a defeated Confederacy might play in a continuing national drama were underscored by the peculiar function of setting in the war stories he published. With surprising regularity, these seventeen narratives echoed Baltimore's border status by opening between places: at a window, on a ferry, in a harbor. Their characters, more often than not, seem poised for flight: on the Cumberland River in B. R. Forman's "A Confederate Prisoner's Experience" (April 1870), from that Federal prison on Lake Erie in "An Escape from Johnston's Island" (November 1872), or down the road out of town in R.S.R.'s "The Last Confederate Flag on the Atlantic" (July–August 1875). Like Confederate prisoners and wartime nurses, these were the Southerners and Northern fellow travelers Browne celebrated for rejecting Federal dictates. When such maneuvers led home for Confederate prisoners and wartime nurses, "home" was itself transformed from cloister to crossroads, as private refuge was charged in Browne's magazine with public purpose.

In this fashion, the political agenda and regional mandate of the *Southern Magazine* hovered over its stories and the imaginative spaces they carved out, much like the wartime occupation of Baltimore snatched many an "old homestead" from its rhetorical serenity. When wartime places became postbellum spaces in literary magazines, what was once constrained looked decidedly shifty. As Patricia Yeager has pointed out in "Narrating Space," her introduction to *The Geography of Identity*, "space must be recognized as a social product that relentlessly reproduces the social."[48] Simply put, refusing "Yankeeisation" in the magazine's editorial pages jibes with what author Caroline Marsdale would call "running like the mischief from about forty million Yankees" in "Cousin Jack" (December 1873), particularly in occupied Louisiana.[49] But Yeager's assessment takes an intriguing turn in positing an "encrypted" trace of less obvious social fear, a sense that regional place can turn into haunted space when narrative becomes, in her formulation, "the geographic equivalent of the ghost story."[50] As Yeager observes, "The physical world is also a site where unrequited desires, bizarre ideologies, and hidden productivities are encrypted, so that any narration of space must confront the dilemma of geographic enigmas head on, including the enigma of what gets forgotten, or hidden, or lost in the comforts of ordinary space."[51] It pays, then, to look with care at what gets haunted.

In the *Southern Magazine*, the ghostly trace of what must be escaped in Civil War stories is not usually the damn Yankees. It is the Big House in one guise or another: that snowbound Northern prison on the Great Lakes, houses like "huge sentinels" in the shelled city of Petersburg, or a torch-lit roadside hotel near New Orleans with "a marching army" of bedbugs.[52] All are invested with a deliberate authority, much like the nineteenth-century southern plantation that had come to represent more than increased family holdings. "No longer just a large farm with supervised captive labor," writes John Michael Vlach, "from the middle of the eighteenth century onward the ideal plantation was a large, tastefully appointed country estate belonging to a prominent gentleman."[53] Snatching this "old homestead" from its supposed serenity outside the sphere of war and loss suggests the regularity with which seemingly ordinary places, even the most private, were infused with political urgency when Baltimore's chief literary magazine told unpredictable stories of the war.

These Civil War outposts, all "homes" at once sizable and treacherous, are conceivably versions of Lincoln's White House in the Federal capital and thus the narrative embodiment of a dictatorial North. Even George Washington, who never lived on Pennsylvania Avenue, made it a point to invest the president's public home with the full weight of executive authority; as Rubil Morales-Vázquez has observed, "No one understood the relationship between place, space, and power better than the first president."[54] The outsized residence he envisioned was constructed during the eighteenth century as both domestic quarters and workplace (figure 10). Called the President's House or the President's Palace or (most frequently by 1860) the Executive Mansion, the building was completed with the classical porches or "porticos" that William Gleason notes were "legible chiefly as symbols of order and authority."[55] The plans for the Executive Mansion were actually drawn up by Irish architect James Hoban on an Old World model, what architectural historian William Seale has called "a gentleman's seat"; more specifically, Hoban's design evidently drawn from Mount Vernon.[56] Before the excesses of the Gilded Age, then, the Washington mansion as Yeager might see it actually recalled outsized planter authority and a southern social order founded on enslaved labor, which the *Southern Magazine*'s editorial columns approved but its war stories repeatedly aimed to escape. In these fictional versions of "the South," a patriarchal authority and the economic drag of a slave labor system in its last days prove to be the haunted space that almost every protagonist seeks to leave behind.

FIGURE 10. Theodore R. Davis, *"Reb" and "Billy Button" Carrying the President's Children to School*. Wood engraving. *Harper's Weekly*, April 17, 1869, 245. Courtesy of the University of Iowa Libraries.

For Civil War stories, the ghostly role of setting was to insinuate public need into personal space and to recast local households as public thoroughfares. As a result, Civil War settings promoted public households that could absorb wartime traffic and muffle the distinction between private property and public access. Domestic space was narratively reconceived in literary magazines nationwide so that private bedrooms, for instance, were on the decline as fictional spaces during Reconstruction, while slave quarters (which had rarely appeared in stories written while the war was fought) were showing up in literary magazines with greater frequency by the 1870s. Parlors were declining, but porches were holding their own; ballrooms were down, but gardens were more numerous, and docks were on the rise. Wartime sites like prisons, hospitals, and battlefields were less often invoked as the narrative itinerancy of the 1860s receded, but in their place hotels, boardinghouses, and offices gained a hold on narrative priorities to become more permanent and public "homes."

On a grander scale, too, Civil War stories frequently slipped out of settled spaces and into border territory by moving west, a relocation that complicated generic guarantees. As 1876 and Centennial celebrations approached, the Virginia locales that had characterized stories from Richmond's *Southern Literary Messenger* during the war and continued to appear in many northern monthlies occasionally gave way to more Louisiana settings in magazines published on both sides of the Mason-Dixon Line. Specifically, the open confrontation between North and South that ignited Big Bethel's "rifled howitzer" against "the invading foe" in the *Southern Literary Messenger*'s "Peninsular Sketches" (November–December 1862, July 1863) or "the rattle of musketry, the heavy boom of cannon, the fierce cry of onset" that commenced the Battle of Ball's Bluff in *Harper's Weekly*'s "The Revenge of a Goddess" (September 24, 1864) almost entirely disappeared.[57] In place of plain battle lines, postwar domestic relations wobbled strangely when a New Orleans family thought lost and a childhood sweetheart thought dead suddenly reappear in "The Young Priest" (December 1868) for *Lippincott's* or a Creole heiress turned servant is unmasked as a spy in "Mrs. F's Waiting Maid," for *Harper's Monthly* (June 1867). In an imagined Louisiana, a different and internecine war was fought, a war in which Virginia's open wheat fields and purple cockles, pitched battles and reliable sites for turning brothers into volunteers and husbands into recruits were nowhere to be found.

The distinct functions of Virginia and Louisiana as narrative spaces for rendering the personal more public, as the shiver of wartime clash and the pain of national reconstruction were destined to do, are clearest in two roughly contemporary stories about discontent in the ranks, one published in the North and the other along the war's western border. "The Story of a Mutiny," which was circulated by both the *Galaxy* (August 1870) in New York and the *New National Era* (August 11, 1870) in the nation's capital, is set near Yorktown during General George McClellan's siege of the city in April and May 1862, when the Peninsular Campaign was moving toward Richmond. The narrative centers on the army's failure to clothe and pay a regiment that then refuses to take arms, at least until the presiding general summons his artillery and a firing squad. An editorial note in the *Galaxy* reveals at the outset that the story is "undoubtedly true," since it came from an assistant surgeon who served in one of the regiments of General William H. Emory, praised as a "distinguished" commander and a "stern, faithful soldier."[58] The story's apparent purpose is thus to transform homeboys into citizens, citizens into soldiers, and soldiers into the disciplined regiment that creates its own deliberate space.

Indeed, "The Story of a Mutiny" ignores the irregular trenches dug around Richmond to favor the more orderly rows of an infantry camp, here described as "a canvas village with ten streets, each bounded by a row of tents on either side, and the parade-ground directly in front."[59] Eventually, the mutiny collapses, the men take arms, and the general leaves the parade ground with the hearts and minds of the soldiers in his pocket, ready confirmation that a Virginia home away from home will run with military precision on the nation's behalf. No wonder the story was published twice, both times in the North and both times at the end of the war decade while stern legislation was emerging from a radical Congress.

More ominous is a similar turn of events in "Sentenced and Shot," a story that appeared in Chicago's *Lakeside Monthly* (November 1870) and was set in central Louisiana during 1865. In this account of the war's western regiments, the issue is the questionable execution of a well-liked sergeant at the hands of a despised General Custer, later to die along the Little Bighorn. In the *Lakeside Monthly*, he is vilified as a "yellow-haired circus-rider from the Shenandoah" come to teach "Army of the Potomac notions" to the Second Cavalry Division of the Military Department of the Gulf after General Robert E. Lee in Virginia and even General Kirby Smith in Texas have surrendered.[60] As they have been ordered, troops form a hollow square, a fitting image of the alacrity with which private individuals are shown supporting public ends by filling holes with meaning. In Louisiana, however, the soldiers find themselves in a vacant sugarcane field edged round by "long festoons of Spanish moss," a "shallow" and "murky" river, a "dreary old tumble-down village" and a "dilapidated levee," the "long-haired, swarthy, ill-clad remnants of the late Confederate army," and a host of "distrustful, impoverished citizens moving about disconsolately" amid the stifling heat and the "*débris* of two armies scattered in every direction."[61] Once again the general prevails, this time by rescuing the offending sergeant within seconds of the execution volley that the blindfolded man hears as fatal and the general means as instructive, especially on the wilder periphery of the Virginia discipline he knows best.

But it is a sign of this border space that its instructive mission nearly fails. Across the devastated sugar plantations of Louisiana, the disgruntled soldiers have marched to this execution with loaded carbines and forty stored rounds in cartridge boxes. As the narrator observes, "To be shot by a rebel at Alexandria, Virginia, in 1861, is not at all like being shot by your friends at Alexandria, Louisiana, in 1865."[62] Assigned to occupy a defeated country while Virginia regiments were packing up and going home, the Second Cavalry resists the general's eastern authority, as well as the hollow square's disciplined design. Instead, this division gives in to a "reckless disregard of authority" by defying both the general and his guardhouse, an unexpected tack that frays the national purpose these soldiers enlisted to serve.[63] Particularly as reconstructing states and literary magazines moved away from the war, stories set in Louisiana like "Sentenced and Shot" revealed bayous of deception and chapels of Catholic ritual, the moss drapery of madness and the iron gates of decrepitude, where things were seldom what they seemed and never what they seemed in Virginia.

For the *Southern Magazine*, border territory like Louisiana might have been the site where divided sections came together, where longtime friends or fellow soldiers found common ground, as they do in Davis's "John Lamar" with a toast. Instead, borderland for Baltimore's literary monthly often proved to be the occupied space of surreptitious maneuver and hardening resolve. By 1901 even Davis understood how differently contested territory looked to shaken residents. "Recalling General Sherman's march through Georgia," biographer Jean Pfaelzer writes, "she warns that Americans too should be aware of the long hatred that follows brutal suppression."[64] It is therefore perturbing that Baltimore's journal associated Virginia with the older country of revolutionary days and Louisiana with the more tempestuous union that would emerge from Reconstruction. Richmond, in particular, stood most often for tidewater aspirations and what the Confederacy might have been, while upstate parishes suggested backwater hostility and what the South might yet become. As a comparison of representative stories reveals, Virginia and Louisiana could be used as spatial markers for a ruptured nation whose military districts were struggling toward the Centennial. With renegade insistence, the *Southern Magazine* thereby charted the difference between Confederate nationalism and Federal occupation, established order and ad hoc resistance, straight roads and mud.

How much was once riding on the orderly triumph of Richmond is perhaps clearest in a story that carries readers out of a besieged capital about to surrender. "A Midnight Ride from Petersburg" (December 1871) follows a late-night carriage quietly requisitioned by the quartermaster general for friends, a carriage that takes readers past surprisingly settled turf—civilian tent camps on the city's edge, Confederate breastworks, Beauregard's headquarters and Lee's distant flag, the "lonely, silent streets" of the shelled city, and a depot's sitting room turned into barracks—before arriving at the iron rails upon which the last train waits to depart.[65] Inside the carriage and then the railroad cars, characters turn into fugitives looking for a way out of a Confederate political experiment gone wrong, here described as the "citadel of a young nation's hope" that the fugitives and the monthly's readers relinquish.[66]

If Virginia becomes thereby the site of hope and loss in the *Southern Magazine*, Louisiana was more readily the site of loss and hope, however covert. Loss is initially foremost in "A Trying Journey" (November 1872) when a wagon loaded with cotton bales to be sold in Baton Rouge leaves the ill-supplied hospitals of New Orleans. Almost immediately, the wagon slips into ruts and a muddy quagmire; after prying the vehicle loose, the story's heroines endure three rain-swept miles in the woods and then a trudge into town so the wagon will not be confiscated, only to lose the cotton while Union soldiers pocket the proceeds. This misfortune is the last in a narrative series of transactions that begins in New Orleans, a city full of Northern occupiers as early as the spring of 1862 and thus a place where exploding shells were less common than entrepreneurial deals. The story's protagonists are repeatedly taken in, most importantly by the Federal authorities, who do not honor their bargain to meet hospital needs when the cotton is sold. Along the road outside New Orleans, the ladies subsequently stay in a chamber that is infested with vermin ("the beds, sheets, walls, floors were alive"), in a plantation manor that has been sacked, and in a hotel that fronts on the daily maneuvers of a black U.S. regiment.[67] In Louisiana's occupied territory, there seem to be no tent cities with bedroom furniture, no silent streets with houses standing guard, no waiting trains on iron roads.

Nevertheless, these resourceful ladies are taken in by their friends, as well as their enemies. On the road to market, they are repeatedly offered assistance and lodging by other Confederates who resent the Northern interlopers. The ladies are thereby portrayed less as fugitives finding a way out than as temporary refugees finding a way in, however meager, to a relocated "home." Robbed of their own "citadel" when New Orleans falls, they opt for the trade in cotton that Browne himself might have recommended and the home among strangers that, at least for them and for a while, replaces Northern occupation in New Orleans with Southern solidarity along the road. In the chamber, the plantation manor, and then the hotel, they discover progressively more public homes away from home along the border of a familiar road, homes that thereby become sites of sly Southern negotiation outside the trafficked intersections of occupied territory. Such local sites of resistance function differently from the Federal home grab par excellence in New Orleans, where General Benjamin Butler's "Woman Order" in May 1862 sought to bring belligerent ladies to heel by declaring them prostitutes for insulting Northern troops. In the *Southern Magazine* a decade later, New Orleans disappears almost immediately in the "trying journey" from public order to private escape and a competing public cause, a journey that would transform private homes into way stations haunted by a "long hatred" for border occupiers.

There were several reasons why riverine Louisiana struck authors of the Civil War era as a non-Virginia, a site that was less central to the country founded in 1776 because it was a more distant pocket along a national seam. Even before New Orleans surrendered to Admiral David Farragut on April 25, 1862, and General Butler arrived with the Union's occupying troops less than a week later, Louisiana was widely perceived as marking a series of key borders. Economically, the mouth of the Mississippi River had figured on the edge of international trade routes since the eighteenth century. As Scott Marler points out in

The Merchants' Capital, "like the South more generally, Louisiana was located on the nonindustrial periphery of the Atlantic world."[68] At one time a religious outpost governed by the Spanish and the French, the region and indeed the vast Louisiana Territory were overseen as early as 1806 from Baltimore, the oldest Roman Catholic archdiocese in the United States.

After statehood was gained by the territory's delta corner in 1812, an outpost's seeming homogeneity gave way across decades of immigration to proliferating boundaries, as Judith Kelleher Schafer has observed. In "Part Two" of *Louisiana: A History,* she describes the new nineteenth-century state as an emerging network of "opposing forces" creating one dividing line after another: "north Louisianians (including those in the Florida parishes) versus south Louisianians; Anglo versus Latin Americans; Catholics versus Protestants; sugar growers versus cotton farmers; city dwellers versus country folk; and plantation owners versus small farmers."[69] General Nathaniel Banks, who arrived with twenty thousand men in Cornelius Vanderbilt's transports to replace Butler during December 1862, eventually saw the political advantages of an obscure battleground in a border district, which Thomas Cutrer has incorporated into his "theater of a separate war" on the far side of the Mississippi River.[70] In Louisiana, sizable profits could readily be made.

For decades, thousands of immigrant farmers had agreed on the state's western appeal. Some journeyed overland from Alabama and Georgia, as well as exhausted acres farther east; others from Tennessee, Kentucky, and Mississippi drifted down the Mississippi River. Following these several routes across the South, immigrants and their enslaved laborers relocated in such numbers that, as Adam Rothman has noted in *Slave Country,* the Deep South consolidated as population surged in Alabama, Mississippi, and Louisiana from four hundred thousand in 1820 to more than two million in 1860, equally white and black. "From the 1820s to the 1850s," Rothman points out, "the demographic, economic, and political weight of plantation slavery in the United States continued to shift to the south and west."[71] On the far side of surging migration, New Orleans saw annual revenues soar, as Marler makes clear. "During the antebellum era, because of the city's location at the base of the enormous Mississippi River system," he writes, "half of all the South's cotton production routinely passed through the hands of New Orleans merchants on its way to textile manufacturers in the North and Europe."[72] The Mississippi River also transported considerable local freight in sugar and rice, along with foodstuffs from upriver farmers.

By 1861 the flow of western commercial traffic into New Orleans was substantial and, to some, unnerving. "Midwesterners," notes Cutrer, "seeing the means of marketing their produce threatened, seemed to be as ready to go to war for the river as for the Union."⁷³ Among Confederates, the far-off Department of the Trans-Mississippi West became an infrequent battleground but a vital source for eastern quartermasters, which helped make the Mississippi River what Cutrer has called "the most strategically important corridor of the war."⁷⁴ At Lincoln's urging, General Banks and his relocated regiments arrived in New Orleans with the aim of securing that trafficked corridor for the Union.

In Louisiana there were other wartime considerations almost as pressing. The state also bordered on Texas to the west. Sparsely settled in many places, Texas nonetheless enabled a lucrative Confederate trade in cheap cotton that had caught the eye of Massachusetts mill owners stranded by the Union embargo on Southern ports. As Ludwell Johnson has observed, "There seemed to be only one real chance to set the mills going again: the conquest of Texas."⁷⁵ With occupied Louisiana as a jumping-off point, Union forces could also hinder trade with the French, whose armies had long since left Louisiana but whose invasion of Mexico in 1861 had installed a puppet emperor and brought the imperial hungers of Napoleon III to the Rio Grande.⁷⁶ A Union expedition under General Banks left New Orleans for Galveston in October 1863 but achieved little of lasting value. Seeking a more effective point of departure for an overland assault into border country during 1864, the Union high command looked north to the Red River, to Natchitoches, and to Shreveport, the latest center of resisting Confederate forces and thus a tempting access point for a venture into Texas. But the waterways of upcountry Louisiana, unlike those of tidewater Virginia, proved treacherous to negotiate even for Confederates, as an unusual postwar story in the *Southern Magazine* would reveal.

CAROLINE MARSDALE

"Cousin Jack"

(*Southern Magazine*, December 1873)

The battle of Taylor's Ridge had been fought and won, and Cousin Jack, who had been reported among the wounded, was daily expected home on furlough. We hadn't seen him since the spring of '61; for hitherto he had escaped the bullets of the enemy, although he had gone through many a battle and skirmish. We promised ourselves much pleasure from his return, for in good old *ante-bellum* days Cousin Jack had ever been the light and life of our home, and we had missed him sorely when he left us for the theatre of war.

Alice and I nearly cried our eyes out when he went away, and we scolded Isabel severely because she was so quiet about it. We girls had no brother; but Cousin Jack, who was an orphan, had been living with us ever since any of us could remember, and Alice and I used to say that he was just the same as a brother. Isabel was not in the habit of saying much about him; the fact is, she was never much inclined to express an opinion about anything. During the third year of the war we had left our old home on Bayou Têche and taken refuge among the pine-forests of Sabine Parish, and we were still suffering from loneliness and nostalgia when the news of Cousin Jack's furlough came to cheer us. He was not badly wounded. He wrote that he was only *scratched*, but the surgeon told him that his wound must positively be nursed or it would not heal; and it was to this warning that we were to owe the pleasure of a visit from him.

"*I'll* nurse him!" exclaimed Alice, as she folded up the letter.

"No you won't; I'm going to do that myself!" exclaimed I. Isabel, as usual, said nothing.

"We'll have real coffee all the time he is at home," said Alice; "this ochra substitute is horrid." Alice was housekeeper.

"And I will practise some of my old songs," said I. "I haven't touched the piano in an age. It is very nice and patriotic, I dare say, to make soldier-jackets and knit soldier-socks, but I must confess I like singing and playing a great deal better, especially when Cousin Jack is here to listen and admire."

A few days after this, the gentleman in question, Captain John Harrington, made his appearance, very much be-whiskered, and rather seedy in uniform, but otherwise not much altered since we had seen him last. He carried his left arm in a sling, but he managed very well without its aid. He hadn't been with us a day before it seemed as if he never had been away from us, for he was petting Alice and teasing me just as he had done in old times. We were living in an old dilapidated log-cabin, and had brought very few of the luxuries of life with us from our home on the Têche; but I do not think there was a happier family than ours in all Louisiana, after Cousin Jack's arrival had made our household band complete. Even Isabel, the sedate and sombre, brightened up in the course of that first day and became quite lively— for *her*. Alice was not long in taking possession of her old seat on Cousin Jack's knee. She was fortunate in being exceedingly diminutive, and could sit where she pleased without let or hindrance. In the fervor of my welcome I had seated myself on Alice's old perch, but Cousin Jack immediately ordered me to get away, informing me that he would as soon hold a bale of cotton on his knee. As soon as I vacated the seat Alice took it, and commenced her old habit of rumpling Cousin Jack's hair. "As I live, the man has turned gray!" exclaimed she, jerking out a silver thread and holding it up for our inspection. "Why, Jack, the Federals must have been scaring you terribly! Now tell us truly, old fellow, *haven't* you been scared once or twice since we saw you last?"

"Scared as the mischief," replied Jack, "and with good reason too. If Julius Caesar had been where I was on the night of the twenty-second of last November, the old fellow would have trembled in his boots. I came very near going up on that occasion, as sure as you are a foot high."

"What were you doing then?" I asked.

"Doing! I was running like the mischief from about forty million Yankees, and getting shot at about every two seconds and a-half."

"Where were you?" asked Alice. "Begin at the beginning, and tell us all about it. Mollie and I are crazy to hear your adventures; and if your telling them interrupts Isabel's stitch-counting, she can go away if she wants to."

Isabel did not go away, but she continued to count stitches under her breath, and appeared nowise interested in what was going on. Jack gave one quick look at her, and then commenced his story.

"Well, you see," said he, "I was out scouting solus and alone up in Washington country, which if you know anything at all, you know is inhabited mostly by the strongest sort of Union people. There was a large body of Yankee cavalry perambulating about in that region, and I had been sent out by our boss to see what they were up to. That would have been easy enough if the natives had been the right kind of people; but as it was, with everybody against me, I dodged around all day like a thief, lost my way about fifty thousand times, and when night came on was about as tired and used-up a Rebel as ever you heard tell of. I didn't care so much for myself, but the critter I was riding had lost a shoe and was in a bad row for stumps; so I came to the conclusion that the sooner we came to a halt the better. I knew the Yankee troops were close by, and I knew that the natives would like no better fun than to hand me over to them; for if there is any one thing that a loyal citizen hates above all other it is a good Rebel. I was in disguise of course—had on a Yankee overcoat over my Confederate jacket— but somehow I felt that I had *Secesh* written in my face; and besides I doubted my ability to refrain from profanity if I should be obliged to listen to any loyal sentiments. But I could not ride on all night—my horse and I were of one opinion about that—and I was not prepared to camp out; so at last I made up my mind to ride boldly up to the next house I came in sight of and demand its hospitalities, and I acted upon this determination. It was now quite dark, but I saw two bright windows in the distance, and I was not long in making my way to the gate in front of them.

"'Halloo!' cried I, as I drew rein; and then I waited for an answer, but no answer came.

"'Halloo!' cried I again, but echo answered 'halloo,' and nothing else.

"Thereupon I dismounted and walked up to the house, which as well as I could make it out in the dark was a large and stately one. I was determined to make myself heard, so I seized the knocker and created a racket, which had the desired effect. The door was opened by a diminutive imp of darkness, and I was invited to enter.

"'Not yet, my friend,' said I. 'Bring out a light, if you please, and show me the way to the stable.'

"The boy disappeared, but soon returned armed with a lantern and key. He grew sociable as we went along, and informed me that his ole marster was dead, that Mas' Henry had jined the cavalry, and that there was nobody at home but old Miss' and Miss Calline. 'Maybe you know Mas' Henry,' continued he, giving a sidelong look at my overcoat.

"I gave him to understand that his Mas' Henry and I were rather more intimate than brothers, and then having seen that my horse was comfortable for the night, I wended my way to the house. This time I was met in the hall by the mistress of the house, who when I made known my necessities assured me that I was heartily welcome to a night's lodging. My sable friend showed me to a chamber, where I washed the dust out of my eyes, and then I went to join the ladies in the parlor, still wearing my overcoat, as I did not consider that a healthy locality to take it off in. I did not take the trouble to invent a name for old Miss' benefit, for we soldiers, you know, generally claim hospitality anonymously. When I entered the parlor I found my hostess comfortably reclining in an easy-chair in front of a most glorious fire, while at the piano was seated the prettiest girl—yes, I say it calmly and dispassionately—the prettiest girl I ever saw in all my life. I shall not take the trouble to describe her to you, for of course, being feminine yourselves, it would only bore you and make you envious. Suffice it to say that the prettiest thing *you* ever saw could not hold a candle to her. This was 'Miss Calline.' The parlor was handsomely furnished, and there were no end of books scattered about promiscuously; so it was easy to see, leaving politics out of the question, 'Old Miss' and 'Miss Calline' were the thing. The young lady was playing that lackadaisical thing that you play, Mollie, only she played it a thousand times better than you ever did. What in the thunder is the name of the thing? It is something in the pious line."

"Old Hundred?" suggested Alice.

"Oh no, Goosie. Let me alone, and I'll tell you directly. 'Maiden's Prayer,' that's it. Well, as I was saying, the young lady was playing—"

"Don't be so poetical!" interrupted I.

"Mollie, if you say another word I'll turn you out of the room. Isabel is the only one of you girls that can listen worth a cent."

"Oh, listening is Isabel's *forte*," said Alice. "She'd rather listen than talk, any day."

"Which can't be said of her sister Alice," observed Cousin Jack.

"That depends upon circumstances.

Go on with your story. The young lady was playing—"

"Well, the young lady stopped playing when I entered the room, and then—"

"'The dame made a courtsey, the dog made a bow,'" murmured I.

"Miss Mollie Harrington, I should like to know which of us is to tell this story!" exclaimed Cousin Jack.

"I only supplied you with an appropriate quotation, you ungrateful creature. But go on, and tell the story your own way."

"Shouldn't you like to know how she looked?" asked Cousin Jack.

"No we shouldn't," said Alice, shortly, while I shook my head.

"Perhaps Isabel might like to know," suggested Cousin Jack. But Isabel was absorbed in stitch-counting again, and appeared not to hear.

"I don't believe you are ever going to get past the young lady," said Alice.

Capt. Harrington sighed lugubriously. "Ah, but she was indeed hard to pass!" exclaimed he. "Such eyes!—"

"There, that will do," said Alice, impatiently. "I don't believe a word of what you are saying about her anyway."

"Yes," chimed in I, "in the language of Betsy Prig, 'I don't believe there's no sich person!'"

"Young ladies, will you allow me to proceed?" asked Capt. Harrington, meekly.

"Blaze away," said Alice, who, on account of her littleness, considered herself privileged to choose her own mode of expression.

"I made the young lady the most graceful bow that she had witnessed in many a day," continued the narrator, "and I flatter myself she made a note of it. Anyway, she welcomed me with the utmost suavity of manner, and invited me to come near the fire, which I was glad enough to do, for I was as cold as the deuce, having been riding in the face of a norther for the last two hours. Well, I seated myself on one side of the old lady, and Miss Calline seated herself on the other side. Before we had got through the meteorological observations necessary for the occasion, the supper-bell rang, and we adjourned to the dining-room forthwithly. I had had no dinner that day, and the way I did walk into old Miss's hominy and sausages ain't nothing to nobody. The old lady poured the coffee, and then commenced talking about the state of affairs in the country. You may bet your bottom dollar I never contradicted her, for although her sentiments were objectionable her sausages were not, and just about that time I was much more interested in the latter than the former. The lovely Caroline had nothing to say; she only ate wafers, and looked pretty. When I had at last got enough to eat, Caroline led the way to the parlor, the old lady very sensibly remaining in the dining-room. I soon found, upon examination, that my beauty hadn't much talk in her, so it wasn't long before I had her back at the piano.

"'Do you sing?' asked I, after she had finished rattling through a mazourka or two.

"She gave me the orthodox answer, 'A little.'

"'Then let us have a song, by all means,' said I.

"There was some loose music scattered around on the piano, and I recognised 'Ever of Thee' among it, by the picture on the back of it—a long-nosed, cadaverous-looking female, you know, with an expression like that of a dying calf. I placed the notes in front of the young lady, and intimated to her that she might blaze away."

"Did she sing well?" asked Alice.

"I should rather think she did," replied Cousin Jack; "just about fifty times as well as any one that ever *you* heard sing. Well, she finished 'Ever of Thee,' and then I called for 'Lorena,' and 'Her Bright Smile,' and about a dozen other songs, and then we were interrupted by an old mauma coming in with a waiter of egg-nogg. There was too much brandy in that egg-nogg, twice too much, but I didn't find it out till I had finished two tumblers of it. Caroline took only half a tumbler, but even that enlivened her no little. I proposed various equivocal toasts, and the innocent little traitor drank them all. Then she began letting me into her family history. Told me that she had lived all her life with her aunt, who was my present hostess; that her father was with Rosecrans' army in Kentucky, but that as soon as he could get a furlough he was going to take her aunt and herself to St. Louis, fearing to leave them any longer in such a locality. 'We have suffered nothing so far,' continued she, 'having been fortunate enough to have our brave defenders near us; but there is a rumor that Morrell is going to withdraw his forces before very long, and father has no idea of our being left to the tender mercies of those dreadful Rebels.'

"Here, instigated partly by the love of effect, but mostly by that infamous egg-nogg, I could refrain no longer. Springing up, and striking an attitude, I exclaimed, *a la* Hafed, 'Hold, hold—thy words are death!' and divesting myself of my overcoat in little less than no time, displayed the Confederate jacket to Miss Caroline's astonished gaze. I proceeded:

'Here, maiden, look, weep, blush to see
All that thy sire abhors in me!'

But before the quotation was completed, the young lady had gone glimmering, and what should I hear about this time but a tremendous commotion on the piazza, followed by a thundering knock at the door. I heard the door open, and then I went to the top of the spiral staircase (the parlor was on the second floor) and looked down to see what the racket was about. One look was enough. The hall was swarming with Yankee soldiers. 'Now I have done it!' thought I. You may be sure I ran back into the parlor and got into my overcoat again just a little faster than I had gotten out of it. But I knew that as matters then stood, the overcoat wouldn't save me. There was one tumbler of egg-nogg left. I drank that, and then looked around for a mode of escape. If there had been one tumbler more I dare say I should have faced the enemy; but as it was, I had prudence enough left to remember that discretion is the better part of valor, and to ask myself the question what could one slightly inebriated Rebel do among all those Federals. It was clear I should have to run for it, so I lost no time in making my way out of the window upon the roof of the front piazza. The wind had lulled, and the stars were shining brightly enough for me to see the outline of a tree at one end of the roof, and I immediately made for it. It was a holly, and you know the foliage of a holly is not pleasant to get among; but it wasn't the time for me to be particular. I counted ten thousand separate and distinct scratches, but I made my way down to the ground nevertheless. As soon as I landed, a voice from the piazza called out, 'Halt, or I fire!' but I had no idea of halting, so on I went, double-quick, my speed being slightly accelerated by a pistol-bullet whizzing past my ear. There was a crowd of horses fastened in the front yard, and I lost no time in putting myself on one of them; a second pistol-bullet from the piazza was accommodating enough to cut his halter, and then we tore down the road like a streak of lightning. It soon became evident that the Federals were after me, and then the race that followed was no joke, especially to me, for I was acting as spy, and therefore felt a delicacy in letting myself be captured. Away I went therefore, through woods and through clearings, in roads and out of roads, over fences and across ditches. I was barked at by at least a million different dogs that night, and shot at by my pursuers until I came to the conclusion that I was doing the Confederacy good service by causing the waste of so much Yankee ammunition. At length, between the pistol-shots, I could hear a tremendous roaring in front of me, and then I knew where I was going—right to the river, which, on account of the rains we had just had, was now a young flood, ripping and tearing around in every direction, entirely independent of its banks. The horse I was riding had got into the spirit of the thing, and the Atlantic Ocean couldn't have stopped him then, so on he went, straight ahead, with a scared Rebel on top of him. But when we reached the river I think he began to share the feelings of his rider, for there we were on a high bluff about three-quarters of a mile, it looked to me, above the surface of the water, which was rushing along as black as Erebus, and as rough as the mischief. However, the Yankees were close behind us, and this wasn't the time for reflection, so over we went. I thought we were never going to strike the water, and when we finally *did* strike, it seemed to me we never were going to stop going down. The water wasn't warm either, and before we rose to the surface again I began to wish I had faced the Yankees.

"My horse swam like a good fellow, but the current was almost too many for him, and more than once I thought I was a gone fawn-skin. However, after going goodness knows how far down the river (about fifty miles it seemed to me then) we at last managed to get out of the water. I had a shaking ague, and my horse wasn't much better off, but we kept a-going, and before long had the luck to strike on one of our pickets, who made me drink half a canteen of whiskey (which was all that saved my life), and then sent me on to camp, where I arrived safely, but very much the worse for wear. We were ordered away from that part of the country a few days afterwards, and I never saw the fair Caroline again, but nevertheless—

> Hers is a form of life and light,
> Once seen, becomes a part of sight—

"And—and—what comes next, girls?"

"Don't be foolish," said Alice, encouragingly. "See, you have already bored Isabel nearly to death with your nonsense, and she is about to leave the room to escape the rest of it."

"Where are you going, Isabel?" asked Jack.

"To walk," was the brief reply.

"May I go with you?"

"If you wish it." And Isabel did what

none of us had ever seen her do before—she blushed.

"What did that mean?" asked I, in astonishment, after Isabel and Jack had gone.

"What did *what* mean?" asked Alice in return.

"Isabel's blush."

"Why, Goosie, haven't you sense enough to see that Isabel dotes on Cousin Jack?"

"Well, what of that? I dote on him myself, but *I* don't blush when he talks to me."

"I see the matter is entirely beyond your limited comprehension, so I will say no more about it," said Alice, drily, and she left me to my own meditations.

Isabel and Cousin Jack were out late that afternoon, but Alice and I didn't miss them, for we had a call from Capt. Du Bois, of the ——-th regiment, and with him conversing we forgot all time. Beaux were few and far between in those wild woods, and Alice and I did all we could to make ourselves agreeable to the young officer. At length the pedestrians returned, and then we had tea (the sure-enough article that night—not sassafras, which was our usual beverage), and then Isabel said she had a headache, and went to her room; and Alice and Capt. Du Bois sat down to a game of chess, and then Cousin Jack came over to where I was sitting, and in a low voice claimed my congratulations.

"What am I to congratulate you for?" asked I.

"I am going to be married."

"To whom?" asked I, in surprise.

"To whom do you suppose, Goosie?"

"I haven't the slightest idea."

"Isabel."

"Isabel! Why I should as soon have thought of your marrying *me!*"

"*I* shouldn't as soon have thought of it—not by a long shot. Ain't you going to congratulate me?"

"Not until I have collected my ideas. You have scattered them all by your startling intelligence."

Alice and I talked the matter over after we went to our room that night, and then and there she informed me that she had suspected the attachment ever since Jack went away in '61.

"Well, you certainly have a great deal more penetration than I have," was my concluding observation.

"Of course I have," was the candid reply. And there being no more to say, we both went to sleep.

"Running Like the Mischief"

Much is hard to decipher in "Cousin Jack," like a book you can't judge by its jacket. As early as the story's first paragraphs, the furloughed captain turns out to be less injured than "*scratched*," which leaves him somewhere between an unnecessary sling and an unhealing wound. To quiet his family's misgivings, he tells the frothy tale of escaping a scare the previous November. On a midstate scout in 1863, he recalls, he found himself playing the spy near the contested town of Washington, north and west of occupied New Orleans, as well as the U.S. arsenal at Baton Rouge, but then south and east of the Confederate stronghold in Shreveport and the cotton country along the Texas border. In the tale Jack Harrington tells, he actually wears a semblance of Louisiana's murky allegiances, with his Confederate jacket hidden beneath a stolen Union overcoat. He thus appears like the flip side of the plantation Big House he stumbles across, the "large and stately" but deceptive Southern home that harbors Unionist sympathizers. Bone weary on enemy turf, the "Secesh" captain cannot gauge the holiday eggnog with "too much brandy," and soon he is "running like the mischief" (he says) "from about forty million Yankees" as he miscalculates his way back to Confederate lines through dumb luck. Froth indeed.

But a decade later in 1873, when Caroline Marsdale's story appeared in the *Southern Magazine*, Louisiana had seen Federal troops depart in 1865 only to return in 1867, when the postbellum South was divided into five military districts and reoccupied. Partisan tensions were therefore increasing even while commerce resumed.[77] As a story of Reconstruction, this exuberant tale reveals a deeper uneasiness through its contrasting locales, with three significant upshots. For one thing, Jack's dangerous scout and mad ride are set against the forest cabin of his female cousins in Sabine Parish, a cabin that serves as a refugee substitute for the Bayou Têche mansion they have all left behind. Apparently, wartime escape for every Harrington amounts to the kinder face of banishment across occupied territory. For another, the undertow of the story's Confederate removals, those successively abandoned Louisiana locales, is in turn contrasted with the well-appointed home and troubling allegiances midstate, where the Big House is treacherous and the holly prickly. If Jack's later "scratch" might still fester, according to his surgeon, the multitudinous scratches his escape produces do not suggest a quick and painless recovery for either the Confederate captain or a partisan Louisiana. Finally and against the odds, Jack is furloughed to his family's temporary household of relocated Southern women, who get busy singing his praises, mussing his hair, and knitting his future to their past, his light-footed energy to their family credentials. But at "home" on Louisiana's western border, the spirit of counterpoint in Marsdale's offbeat settings is amplified by sisterly rivalries, perpetual interruptions, and sharp skirmishes for the narrative floor. When these genial disputes are paired with a tale of escape that never quite masks threat and displacement, especially in its literary allusions, there appears to be a price to pay for seeming cheer, a price charged to a sister so adept at listening that she is silenced by the fearful things she hears.

Indeed, much about "Cousin Jack" is masked and perplexing. Even Caroline Marsdale, who contributed three other *Southern Magazine* stories about Louisiana, Texas, and Florida, has left no trace in nineteenth-century census records. What is almost certainly another Southern pseudonym likely belonged to Mary Edwards Bryan, who was born in the Florida panhandle in 1839 and moved to southern Georgia for schooling in 1850, before she eloped with Iredell Bryan at fourteen and journeyed to his immigrant family's upstate plantation in Louisiana's cotton country. When she arrived, her new in-laws were so alarmed by their son's youthful bride that they sent her to a Methodist boarding school in nearby Mansfield. Thus began a rocky marriage given to protracted separations, especially as a maturing wife started contributing to early Southern periodicals like the *Georgia Watchman*, the *Temperance Crusader*, *Southern Field and Fireside*, and (during and after the war) the *Natchitoches Union* and the *Semi-Weekly Natchitoches Times*, often as a literary or political assistant editor.[78]

When Mary's husband enlisted in what would become the Second Louisiana Cavalry during the first year of the war, her income helped offset the household expenses that would prove burdensome once severe leg wounds left Iredell partially crippled, as he would remain for the rest of his life.[79] Fortunately, Mary had long been able to modify her style, "from grave to gay, from lively to severe," as "Theodora Johnston" would put it in a postwar sketch of the author that also noted the "nonchalant gayety, dashed with picturesque humor," of her fiction.[80] To fill the many pages Bryan edited, she had a fondness for pseudonyms, what her most recent biographers have called a "routine recourse to pen names."[81] With increasing skill among what she termed Louisiana's "Border society," Mary prospered professionally in the northern reaches of her new state—and, arguably, in the pages of the *Southern Magazine*.[82]

From Florida to Georgia to Louisiana, Mary also understood the economic sway of the South's chief crop. As she would later write of her first years with the Bryan family, "We were living on Red River—the Paradise of Cotton, where people devote themselves soul and body to the fascinating staple and become as absorbed in it, as though they were veritable caterpillars."[83] So absorbed is "Cousin Jack" that a single reference to the caterpillar pride of northwestern Louisiana comes in a grace note when the captain tells the narrator to make way for her smaller sister, "informing me" (declares Mollie Harrington) "that he would as soon hold a bale of cotton on his knee." Until General Banks organized his expedition in 1864, cotton was the profitable mainstay of the upcountry Red River parishes and was just as likely to summon Northern interest, given the blockade-strapped mills of New England. In an illuminating backward glance immediately after the war, *Harper's Weekly* detailed the state's cotton output by bale during 1860, when the seven most productive parishes all lay north of Washington and Opelousas, Natchitoches among them.[84]

Accompanying the newsmagazine's profile of Louisiana was a state map that revealed why expeditioning Union forces would see the Red River as their way north—to the fields of Confederate cotton in Natchitoches, to the warehouses of Confederate bales in Shreveport, and to the trade routes that carried the Confederate export south through Texas (figure 11). Above the map was a composite image, an iconic tribute to Louisiana and its waterways that deserves a closer look. At the center of the engraved river scene is the seated figure of a Roman water god, identified by his draped command, his leafy crown, and his spilling jug.[85] On a white badge above are a judicial scale and the outspread wings of the pelican, which had long been identified with Louisiana and was part of the state seal, together with the motto "Union, Justice, Confidence."[86] On the left is a scene of harvest and on the right a plated alligator as dark as the enslaved workers in the fields. Fecundity is thus weighed against threat in the river's perennial floods, while daytime labor in the cane fields is balanced by moonlit anxieties in the waterways near New Orleans. During 1864 both the rich black dirt of Natchitoches Parish and the Red River's springtime water levels would beguile the Union regiments that General Banks led north, specifically toward a battle that Marsdale calls "Taylor's Ridge."

What Union troops sought in the fertile cotton fields to the north was not what they found, however. As John William De Forest (then a captain in the Twelfth Connecticut) saw for himself, the retreating Confederates and their general set fire to thousands of cotton bales that would not then fall into Union hands. "The smoke of burning cotton," he wrote, "streaked the day, and the flare

FIGURE 11. *Louisiana*. Wood engraving. *Harper's Weekly,* February 3, 1866, 77. Courtesy of the University of Iowa Libraries.

of it luridly starred the night; for even in his haste Mouton was determined that no fraction of the financial king should fall to the Yankees."[87] Scarcely filling the wagons that stretched for miles and frustrated as well by torrential rains at the outset and then low water on the Red River, forty thousand Union men made slow progress toward Shreveport, and joint operations with Federal gunboats were delayed. Seizing his opportunity, General Richard Taylor assembled Confederate forces near Mansfield, where a young Mary Edwards Bryan had attended school.[88] On April 8 they drove Union regiments from their ridge and toward the wagon train that was mired in a forced maneuver on a narrow road. "Their determined resolution to conquer gave an irresistible power to their advance," wrote Colonel Thomas Bonner of Texas in *The Land We Love*, "and the astonished and amazed Federals fled in confusion."[89] Bonner would declare the Confederate triumph "the greatest victory of the Trans-Mississippi Department," and Marsdale would open her story with Taylor's unanticipated success.[90]

The Confederate victory and Captain Harrington's wound at the Battle of Mansfield (or Sabine Crossroads) exemplify Louisiana's military resistance at its most effective, one of the reasons why the tone of "Cousin Jack" is exuberant. In addition, the leaps of the story from one setting to the next are sprightly turns, political loss redeemed by military hope after long months with invading troops. As early as the fall of 1863, so Confederate General John Walker later noted, the country around Washington and Opelousas had become a prowling ground for Union and Confederate forces alike, a wartime no-man's-land. Both armies had deployed what the general described as "a system of pickets and cavalry scouting into each other's lines."[91] In Marsdale's story, Jack Harrington is cast among them—"scouting solus," in his words, while he secretly reconnoiters. As he puts it, he "dodged around all day like a thief"; by nighttime, even his horse is spent and partly shoeless, "in a bad row for stumps." Despite his exhaustion, the Confederate captain in Miss Caroline's midstate parlor still manages to maintain his poise, a bravura performance that reveals a scout's inventiveness in occupied country where Baltimore's paving stones and potshots were ill-advised.

Unlike Confederate sympathizers on the porches of the Maltby House hotel, the jacketed spy is ready to be tactful in his own best interests. He keeps quiet while "old Miss" rattles on about political affairs because he hankers after her sausages. Her ample home with "bright windows" is nonetheless more danger zone than sanctuary and will soon be "swarming" with Yankees. It is therefore noteworthy that Marsdale's story further counters this parlor splendor with a western Louisiana home that smacks of the frontier and creative adaptation, "an old dilapidated log-cabin" with "very few of the luxuries of life." Against the lure of "Yankeeised" comfort and a parlor's "most glorious fire," Marsdale establishes a Confederate cabin remote from "many a battle and skirmish" but not from the ebullience of nattering sisters or the warmth of their family reassurances. From lonely scouting, to treacherous parlor pleasantries, to unguarded conversations in straitened border circumstances, "Cousin Jack" reveals the continuing allure of the Big House, as well as the muddy alternatives that were regularly more appealing in the *Southern Magazine*.

By 1873, however, the Red River Campaign was more clearly a limited Confederate success and a sore Union failure, one whose aftermath revealed what General Banks had been aiming to accomplish beyond fields of cotton. As Susan Dollar has cogently observed, "For the Union, the Red River represented a main inland route to Texas and the major inland waterway from the Mississippi. If the Federals could move up the river and take Shreveport, they would enjoy undisputed control of trade on the Mississippi by denying the Confederates western access to it. Once they occupied Shreveport, Union forces would also have easy access to Texas."[92] It would be as though they held a water god's gushing jug. Yet for Confederate households eluding a Union expedition across Louisiana's western border, Sabine Parish abruptly became a perilous place, which the battle at Mansfield demonstrated and Mary Edwards Bryan well knew. Figuratively, the crocodile of Egypt (or the alligator of southern Louisiana bayous) was creeping closer, not least when a "diminutive imp of darkness" informs the supposed Union officer that the family's women are unprotected.

"Cousin Jack" hints at Big House waywardness in the story's sketchy third site, the "old home on Bayou Têche," which the Harringtons have already abandoned before Marsdale's story begins. They have thereby escaped from the Têche's wartime service as what De Forest called "a sort of back alley, parallel to the main street, in which the heavy fighting must go on."[93] Having departed the marshes and bayous closer to New Orleans, the Harringtons have chosen the less inviting forests of northern Louisiana, what Johnson describes as a "brooding pine wasteland," where the war has found them nonetheless.[94] The precarious white privilege they relinquish in their cabin is thereby figured in the Big House twice over, first in the family home the Harringtons vacate and then in the Union home the Confederate captain exits with even greater haste. Intent on redefining "the South" as adaptable, Marsdale casts off the haunted "old home" space, apparently without regret.

But in "Cousin Jack," the Big House will not go away. In a more venturesome use of alternative locales, the shadowy Têche house uncannily anticipates the "large and stately" house in Washington country, as well as a more corrosive threat that Yeager would recognize as projected fear: namely, Southern collaboration with Union occupiers. For if the midstate "Miss Calline" is a teasing hint of the log-cabin Isabel, whom Jack will marry, then the covert allegiances of midstate "natives" come breathtakingly close to the adaptability of western refugees in Sabine Parish. When the "luxuries" of a house on the Têche are repeated in the "handsomely furnished" parlor of a house near Washington, each home full of women without men, the ghostly fear Yeager whispers appears to derive from the threat of divided Southern loyalties, as well as the border ability to adapt to a world in which Union soldiers seem to be everywhere.

The gravity of these multiplying threats produces a chase that is "no joke" for a spy who cannot afford to be captured and, by analogy, for impoverished postwar citizens who cannot afford to lose more cotton—or sugar, or rice. In this story of occupied Louisiana, the double fear is both the unrelenting tug of the Big House and the abetted power of the Union men who refuse to give up—during the long months of occupation, the long years of Reconstruction, or the long miles of Marsdale's race to the Atchafalaya River. Like Huckleberry Finn on the Mississippi a decade later, Jack Harrington can only dive into the roaring waters, particularly after Union troops with endless pistols, endless bullets, and endless vigor arrive at the duplicitous Big House, where they are invited in. For all his verbal wit and readiness to tear "down the road like a streak of lightning," the captain believes, like David Crockett, that he's "a gone fawn-skin" as his horse sinks beneath him.[95]

In the exuberance of 1863 and a story that is about to end with sisterly congratulations, the Yankee horse and the "Secesh" captain will rise again, shake off their "ague," and encounter a Confederate picket with a canteen of whiskey. Just as fortuitously, Jack's tale gets pieced together in the frontier cabin despite irrepressible interruptions. As he puts it in exasperation, "Miss Mollie Harrington, I should like to know which of us is to tell this story!" Cousin Jack fights for what is his, much as James Parton championed American authors and William Hand Browne argued for his version of "the South." With the same panache that leads a Confederate spy to throw off his borrowed overcoat and then exit a midstate parlor across the roof of the piazza, Gleason's "marker of white power and prestige," the prodigal captain also ducks swarming cousins to finish his story and take a walk, happily with the only sister that "can listen worth a cent." Put another way, the trickster captain skirts Big House privilege to take the leap of his life, thereby escaping both the potshots of the Yankees and, a little later, family skirmishing in another parlor. From his perspective, Isabel's few words—

six, by actual count—allow for exuberant progress even in courting, especially given a secret "attachment" that stretches back to 1861 and renders the war's dangers just so many interruptions.

From Isabel's perspective, however, every danger threatens the commitment to their "union" as it was. Perpetually counting her stitches, she is wary of the "mischief" Jack's story promises, the looks that make Miss Calline so engaging, and the river current that almost drowns her captain. In departing from the cabin with a maidenly blush, she leaves behind the eastern Caroline as uneasily as Louisiana would leave Virginia behind in magazine stories about the war. Yet her self-restraint is perturbing in at least two ways. For one thing, her comparative reserve costs her a character's heft in Marsdale's story; not only does she lose the chance to share her engagement news with her sisters thanks to "a headache," but her disappearance scarcely ripples the surface of household talk. For another thing, her restrained example of fending off threat with silence is lost on the loquacious Jack. Resourceful scout that he is, he cannot seem to hold his tongue once he has finished old Miss's sausage supper or mind his manners once he has tossed back too much eggnog. Isabel's lower profile might have served him better than an operatic outburst when he throws off his stolen overcoat, a clever lesson in reticence that others in a reconstructing Louisiana would learn with greater dispatch.

For Marsdale's readers with an eye for literary references or an ear for the implications that Isabel must hear while she knits, her continuing silence nonetheless becomes fraught. Some of this story's unnerving reversals are easy to catch. Fluffy eggnog, for instance, has historically suggested an upscale winter hospitality but here signals midstate betrayal. How else to explain the sudden arrival of Union troops and their "thundering knock" in the dark? Similarly, the swelling current of the Atchafalaya River would look like certain death to anyone on a riverbank bluff "about three-quarters of a mile" above it; but Christ was also baptized in the River Jordan, which was just as watery and consequential for turning certain death into new life. Besides, Jack Harrington describes the Atchafalaya as "rushing along as black as Erebus, and as rough as the mischief," a double reference to the dark primordial mists of an inchoate earth and the devilish misfortune that seems unchecked in Marsdale's colloquial phrasing.[96] While all of these familiar references would increase a sweetheart's worry, none of them in a thrilling account would stop her heart. In three instances, however, a referential nod is especially disquieting because especially brief, except for those who know how to listen.

The first allusion comes early, when one of the sisters asks the wounded Jack if he has ever been frightened as a cavalry scout. "'Scared as the mischief,' he replies, 'and with good reason too. If Julius Caesar had been where I was on the night of the twenty-second of last November, the old fellow would have trembled in his boots.'" The reference flutters by without explanation, in large measure because Julius Caesar was well-known to nineteenth-century American audiences; contemporary periodicals regularly reviewed histories of the Roman republic's first "king," and Shakespeare's play actually grew in popularity among American theatergoers after the Civil War, as Gay Smith has demonstrated. "A play about revolutionary senators attempting to restore their republic by assassinating their 'monarch,'" she writes, "had appealed to American audiences from the time American revolutionaries won their independence from England in 1783."[97] So familiar was the play on American stages that the Booth brothers—Junius Brutus Jr., Edwin, and John Wilkes—took up the roles of Cassius, Brutus, and Antony late in the war for a one-night benefit performance on New York City's traditional Evacuation Day—that is, on November 25, 1864.

Yet magazines with southern affiliations responded differently to the republican contest: Richmond's *Southern Literary Messenger* worried in "Observations on the 'Caesars,' of De Quincey" (October 1859) that "the ancient pure stock of Roman nobles and people had been cut off by the civil wars," while Richard B. Elder's "Servantgalism in Virginia" for Philadelphia's *Lippincott's* (June 1871) praised a Confederate soldier for being "brave as Julius Caesar."[98] In telling his tale, Captain Harrington invokes the military prowess of the "old fellow," but Isabel could easily have recalled that Caesar was stabbed by Roman senators, including his friend Brutus, as the price of an arrogance the inventive Jack shares. Contemporary histories may have abounded, but they did not end well for the would-be king.

Toward the conclusion of the Confederate captain's story within a story, he mentions the reason for the "ten thousand separate and distinct scratches" he suffers in his escape, namely, a speedy descent down the holly tree outside Miss Calline's second-floor parlor. During November, even midwar, holly would have reminded most Americans of Christmas or the winter solstice, since its evergreen leaves had sustained those weary of winter for centuries, back to the Druids. As Moncure D. Conway put it in "The Sacred Flora" for *Harper's Monthly* (October 1870), "The HOLLY (*i.e.*, holy) which invests our churches at Christmas was a sign of the life which preserved nature through all the desolations of winter to the ancient races of the North, and was gathered into pagan temples to comfort the sylvan spirits during the general death."[99]

But Harriet Beecher Stowe, in her continuing installments of "The First Christmas of New England" for the *Christian Union*, observed that Puritan memories of Christmas holly were supplanted in "Elder Brewster's Christmas

Sermon" (December 25, 1871) by the true "love-present" of the newborn Christ: "His cup... His baptism... the manger... the crown of thorns."[100] Indeed, R. A. Oakes would point out in *The Independent*'s "Dies Natalis" (December 22, 1887) that many believed holly was "the thorn woven into the crown placed on our Saviour's head at the crucifixion."[101] For a Christian listening to the impulsive Jack with more than half an ear, as Isabel does, birth in Bethlehem would have led inevitably to death on Calvary, with resurrection guaranteed only to the Son of God.

Between these two unsettling allusions is a third that seems histrionic, more than enough to make the silent Isabel chortle. When Jack reveals his true allegiance by dropping the Yankee overcoat, he strikes a pose "*a la* Hafed" and declares theatrically, "Hold, hold—thy words are death!" What appears laughably melodramatic, however, would dismay anyone who had read Irishman Thomas Moore's *Lalla Rookh* (1817), which Jeffrey Vail calls "one of the most successful, widely read, and frequently translated poems in the entire nineteenth century."[102] Divided unevenly into four tales sung to an Indian princess on her way to an arranged marriage in Kashmir, Moore's long poem allots much more than a quarter of its pages to "The Fire Worshippers," whose Hafed leads a doomed Persian revolt against seventh-century Arab invaders. Padma Rangarajan casts Hafed's fight as that of "liberty in the face of colonial oppression," a fight best understood against the backdrop of Britain's 1801 union with Ireland.[103] So similar are the circumstances of Hafed before his Arab princess and Jack before Miss Caroline that "thy words are death!" could serve for both. It is easy to miss their fateful sting when the reference goes unexplained, though a phrase without a gloss confirms that many readers did not require one. Like Isabel counting her stitches, they already knew that Hafed dies.

In Marsdale's story, the exuberance of 1863 nonetheless prevails. Eventually, the recuperating Jack accompanies Isabel on an afternoon walk that brings them home betrothed. Likewise, in *Lalla Rookh*'s frame story, the Indian princess who falls in love with her journey's minstrel poet discovers that he is Kashmir's prince in disguise. Both storytellers, in other words, cleverly seduce their prime audiences through an extended narrative tease; Moore himself aimed with *Lalla Rookh* to charm the English readers that Vail sees as largely female on behalf of Irish independence.[104] But just as Shelley Meagher reads "The Fire Worshippers" through the lens of a "growing British imperial interest" that made Ireland "Britain's original colony," so a wary Isabel might fear the designs of the troops old Miss summons in 1863.[105] A decade later, Marsdale could finger "*a la* Hafed" the occupying force that had been stationed for years across the once Confederate states.

Long gone are the open spaces and level battlefields of Virginia. In their place are the mysterious waterways and dark pine forests of Louisiana, where the imposition of Union command is both frustrated and sought. After all, Miss Calline's hall is "swarming" with Yankees like bees protecting a hive, substitutes for "Mas' Henry" and Miss Calline's father that "old Miss" must have summoned when she remained behind the parlor flirts. It is therefore revealing that Captain Harrington escapes from these enemy sympathizers as though on the edge of supposed sanctuary; that is, he bolts from a spiral staircase, climbs out a second-story window, runs across the roof of the front piazza, and struggles down the prickly trunk of that holly tree. His multitudinous scratches suggest the frightful expense of divided Southern loyalties, as well as a descent into hell—for a Confederate spy on the move, an apparent Union officer in the making, and a ragged nation on its way to 1876.

Reckoning more covertly with "about forty million Yankees" in a magazine that served as the official organ of the Southern Historical Society became a way of expunging Baltimore's less convenient postwar demographics: the sudden mobility of immigrants who go unnoticed, the defiance of planter authority that a large free black community would press, and the "Yankeeisation" of commercial traffic that stately homes should have refused. Relocating memories of upheaval from battlefield Virginia to occupied Louisiana and thus to a seemingly perpetual border territory also makes it easier to understand those tropes by which the Civil War would later become known: the emergence of mixed border loyalties as fictional embodiments of the "house divided" in Civil War novels of the 1880s and 1890s; the broad appeal of a wholly Southern romance of Reconstruction in *Gone with the Wind* decades later; and the continued contest between local affiliations and national allegiance that the outbreak of war sharpened and regional literature has complicated ever since. It is also true that beneath the verbal effervescence of "Cousin Jack" is Hafed's colder story of invasion and Ireland's epic tale of hinterland grudge just as a prickly national citizenship was getting redefined. In the Carolina vision of Charlotte's *The Land We Love*, there would be fewer lucky escapes from invading Federals and more tenacious Big Houses, whose ghosts were not so readily set aside.

CHAPTER 2

Old Times There

The Lost Cause, Charlotte's *The Land We Love*,
and Commemorative Stamps

During the final months of the Civil War in 1865, when General William Tecumseh Sherman and his foraging troops turned from the surrender of Savannah to the conquest of the Carolinas, the Confederate high command was in disarray. After a hurried council of war in Augusta, Georgia, where no one was certain about the path of Federal advance, General Daniel Harvey Hill was sent with a meager contingent north of Columbia, just before Union regiments arrived in a city packed with alarmed refugees, Charleston liquor, and baled cotton. Within hours, the state capital was on fire and General Hill retreated, as he and his fellow commanders would do for the rest of February and early March. In South Carolina, where Hill had been born, they fell back as homes and household goods went up in the flames of Union revenge for the loss of Fort Sumter; in North Carolina, where Hill had married, settled, and taught, they watched as homes were spared but not the endless pine forests and their turpentine factories. Surrounded by charred ruins after sixty thousand Union men had marched 425 miles to eventual resupply in Goldsboro, Hill took part in some of the last battles of a collapsing nation.

The postwar magazine he founded the next year in Charlotte would offer an uncommon witness to dashed hopes both in recollecting the war and in reconstructing the peace from North Carolina's chief Piedmont city and railway hub. Where trading partners like Charleston and Columbia had been decimated by previous siege or the Union advance, however, Charlotte had fared better. With access to financial support that flailing enterprises in other southern cities lacked, Hill's magazine proved attentive to commercial opportunities and agricultural developments, as well as the emphasis on education that Hill championed as a mathematics professor (1849–59), the antebellum superintendent of the North Carolina Military Institute (1859–61), and the later president of the University of Arkansas (1877–84). But Charlotte was also the old "hornet's nest" of revolutionary insurgency that British commander General Charles Cornwallis had once departed in haste, and more recently the city had shared the Confederate zeal that made Hill one of Lee's generals. In the immediate aftermath of defeat, *The Land We Love* (1866–69) would also become the magazine forum of choice for chronicling Confederate military action and kindling a fleeting nation's Lost Cause.

A curious set of tensions therefore arose and prompted several practices that would complicate emerging recollections of the Civil War. The first concerns the newly robust operations of the United States Postal Service, which was reorganized after 1865 to absorb the Confederate postal system. Institutionally, the post office thereby recovered its original postrevolutionary mandate: to deliver business correspondence, personal letters, and printed materials such as newspapers and magazines along the post roads springing up during the nineteenth century. As David Henkin declares at the outset of *The Postal Age*, "Before telephones, before recorded sound, before the transcontinental railroad, and even before the spread of commercial telegraphy, postal exchanges began habituating large groups of Americans to new expectations of contact with distant places."[1] The central government that Union troops would secure by force of arms and later redeployments to military districts in the South thus had a considerable prehistory in the long arm of the country's postal operations, which enabled both federal reach and local grasp. Inveigh as General Hill did against federal occupiers, the postal network he decried also carried his magazine as far west as San Francisco and as far north as Philadelphia with a local message of devastation that would echo nationwide.[2]

Second, the Confederate duty to remember while Northern victors were writing national histories was coupled in Hill's magazine with a New South summons to growth. Indeed, Charlotte's comparative postwar prosperity was crucial for funding *A New Monthly Magazine Devoted to Literature & the Fine Arts*, as Hill's first subtitle declared. That was particularly true in a defeated country starved for capital. Suturing sectional past to regional future with unusual skill, *The Land We Love* maintained a subtle emphasis on replacement in multiple registers. As a remedy for social, political, and even periodical difficulties, an emphasis on defiant substitution—for Northern histories, for antiquated pedagogies, for Reconstruction's occupiers, for Gilded Age priorities— became a pervasive strategy that Hill's magazine would quickly extend into northern and western parlors. *The Land We Love* even replaced its initial landscape cover with a composite set of images buttressing a commitment to patriarchal social relations, an enduring order that was fundamentally challenged by the abolition of slavery.

Third, the pull of a Revolutionary past in periodicals across the country as Reconstruction began suggested a national paradigm of breakdown and repair that was also mirrored in the sequence of events revealed by the war's first stories, even those whose industrious repair unraveled. Maps in prose, Civil War stories from the South, the North, and the West played out a similar economy of events where initial narrative action often reached back to a previous generation, where recurring actions confirmed the war's personal cost, and where discernible knots (especially the death of parents) demonstrated that old homestead values abided in a national imaginary even as the adventure of war became insistent and abolition became irreversible. For three postbellum years, in fact, *The Land We Love* foregrounded the American Revolution so regularly and even hyperbolically that it was impossible to miss the undercurrent of irreplaceable loss, a national trauma that Marianne Hirsch's sense of postmemory will both confirm and disturb. In their turn, readers of Hill's magazine, then and now, would be caught up in postmemory's uncertain reckoning with rage and despair.

Daniel Harvey Hill took up his editorial mission the year after defeat as a disciplined soldier who had been educated at West Point. He had served with valor in Mexico during the 1840s before resigning to teach at Washington College in Lexington, Virginia, and then Davidson College in Charlotte. From a Scotch Irish family of Revolutionary War veterans, he was as fierce a Presbyterian as his brother-in-law Thomas Jonathan "Stonewall" Jackson and as committed a Southern patriot.[3] In the first issues of his monthly magazine, he published his own biographical portrait of George Washington (June 1866) and welcomed Gabriel Manigault's history of the South Carolina Lowcountry before and after the Revolution (October and November 1866), as well as Fanny Fielding's sketches of homesteads in Virginia (October and November 1866).

For Hill, sectional loyalties grew out of marked differences in social priorities. He disdained the money-grubbing of the North and what his eulogist Alphonso Calhoun Avery would later call the "cant and hypocrisy" of those who drove "hard bargains" under "false pretenses."[4] As early as 1857 the Charlotte educator publicized his contempt in the most unlikely of places: a college mathematics text brought out by J. B. Lippincott and destined for a southern market. In Hill's *Elements of Algebra*, students discovered problems like this one: "A Yankee mixes a certain number of wooden nutmegs, which cost him ¼ cent apiece, with a quantity of real nutmegs, worth 4 cents apiece, and sells the whole assortment for $4.4; and gains $3.75 by the fraud. How many wooden nutmegs were there?"⁵ By replacing pedagogical banality with sectional venom and frankly dismissing sales in the North, Hill produced what Hal Bridges describes as "a document in Southern nationalism."⁶ He thereby laid the foundation in his mathematics text for a postwar strategy that would be similarly tied to section, social dynamics, and print.

For magazine editors like Hill, the intervention of the post office was crucial and had been since the U.S. Constitution was ratified in 1789. As Richard Kielbowicz has observed, "Far more than other government policies or actions touching the press, the routine operations of the post office shaped publications' contents, formats, and circulation."⁷ When magazine postage was determined by the number of sheets per issue following the Post Office Act of 1794, issues remained short, and so did general submission length. When newspapers could be mailed for a pittance, mammoth sheets appeared, story papers boomed, and so did serialized American novels. When page count and sheet dimension mattered less than bulk rates, especially once railroads proved able to handle bulkier mails without difficulty, the West moved quickly into the orbit of U.S. print culture, along with regional magazines and the lure of new territory to chart, as well as new subscribers to satisfy.

In this sense, the medium *was* the message, and, thanks to federally funded postal routes, the message spread. The early republic's first Congress, as Kielbowicz has pointed out, allotted sufficient funding to "forge, through a joint venture with private publishers, a system of mass communication indispensable for a growing nation."⁸ Decades later, *The Land We Love* would complain about subscription greenbacks lost in the mail and federal officials sniffing out the checks and post office orders that did not arrive. As Hill put it in November 1867, "A truly loyal man can tell by the odor through the fold of a letter the character of a bill. When the fragrance of the loyal greenback is wanting, the letter is never disturbed."⁹ But the editor relied upon the postal service's nationwide scope, even when he reviled its local transgressions.

As every magazine editor knew, the post office as an institution was simultaneously the creation of federal enterprise and the vehicle of local ambition. Like magazines in an expanding communications system, the post office was both network and node. On the one hand, writes Richard John of the country's early decades, "No other branch of the central government penetrated so deeply into the hinterland or played such a conspicuous role in shaping the pattern of everyday life. Indeed," John concludes, "it would hardly be an exaggeration to suggest that for the vast majority of Americans the postal system *was* the central government."¹⁰ On the other hand, post offices were more gathering places than governing places. As Milton Adkins's "In a Country Post-Office" revealed in *Godey's Lady's Book* (September 1876), the most eccentric residents, including "a general hanger-on and universal loafer," would stop by roughly once a week during small Plunketville's early years just to pass the time, "demolishing 'home twist' tobacco, whittling a soft pine board, and relating wonderful exploits of his more youthful days."[11] During the first half of the nineteenth century, local post offices were routinely set up in a wide variety of familiar locales, as John Wriston has discovered in Vermont: for example, the offices of lawyers and doctors, drugstores, harness shops, hatters' shops, kitchens, and railroad depots, as well as "the general store" and "the local inn or tavern."[12] In this regard, they became institutional lessons in the intersection of the federal and the local, what Michael Foley in his study of the early postal service in New England has called the "persistence of localism in the face of national market influences."[13] Kielbowicz similarly notes the "overlapping levels of community and the battle to shape the nation's culture," a battle in which magazines were likewise engaged and with peculiar results in early narratives of the war.[14]

Between 1861 and 1876, when cross-sectional romances might have multiplied to suggest the decline of the old Union or the determined success of Reconstruction, literary magazines across the country revealed that Civil War romances dwindled in number while the war's adventure stories never obliterated the persistent claims of old homesteads, most often the emblem of the Union as it was. If *Harper's Monthly* was right in 1874 that the purpose of the post office as the "far-reaching hand of civilization" was "to diffuse intelligence, whether private news in the form of letters, or public and general in the form of newspapers and magazines and books," then the message diffused would signify the continuing tug of home within an expanding federal purview that the post office institutionally embodied.[15]

In large cities and small towns across the country, post offices made it increasingly simple to serve local needs. As early as 1847, for instance, the scope of postal operations acquired a small, eye-catching, portable assist in new adhesive stamps, which Winifred Gallagher describes as "tiny receipts that turn letters and parcels into official mail."[16] Prepaid postage making the sender rather than the receiver responsible for costs had debuted in England during May 1840, when the Penny Black first appeared (figure 12). Replaced a year later by the Penny Red, which made the red cancellation cross more visible, the English penny stamp featured a bust of the youthful Queen Victoria, whose regal poise at thirteen would grace English adhesives of various denominations for the next sixty years. Small in size, the new "receipts" were large in consequence. "By virtue of its ubiquity, equity, stability, and longevity," writes Catherine Golden, "the 'Queen's head' stamp may be said to embody what today we

FIGURE 12. Early commemorative stamps: (*left*) the English "Penny Black" (1840), Queen Victoria, from a medal designed by William Wyon, steel engraving initially inked in black; (*center*) the first U.S. five-cent stamp (1847), Benjamin Franklin, from a painting by Jean-Baptiste Greuve, steel engraving initially inked in red brown; (*right*) the first Confederate ten-cent stamp (1861), Thomas Jefferson, from a hand drawing by Charles Ludwig, lithograph initially inked in blue. Courtesy of the National Postal Museum, Smithsonian Institution.

call Victorian values—moral propriety, domesticity and family affection, duty, and tradition."[17] No matter what values a nation advocates, adhesive stamps since the 1840s have offered regularly compact and circulating emblems, what Henio Hoyo describes as "ideal vehicles for diffusing an official national imaginary."[18] In the United States, postage stamps would serve other purposes during the Civil War; when specie was hard to come by and inflation climbed, in both the North and the South, stamps served as a substitute currency.[19] But even then their symbolic resonance (much like that of the Penny Black) was evident in the portraits each section chose to circulate, as well as the discrete traditions they invoked and *The Land We Love* would selectively honor.

When U.S. adhesives were first introduced, George Washington was chosen for the ten-cent stamp, his portrait already made famous by Gilbert Stuart and the one-dollar bill. For the five-cent stamp, Postmaster General Cave Johnson first settled on Andrew Jackson, from his native Tennessee. As Gallagher has noted, however, an alternative was urged due to "antebellum tensions," and the "fiery southern slaveholder" was replaced by Benjamin Franklin, the country's "universally beloved northern postmaster general."[20] Franklin was not so "beloved" before his death in 1790. But the many editions of his *Life* published during the nineteenth century remade his reputation—as John puts it, from "the consummate would-be English gentleman of leisure" to "the archetypal American self-made man."[21] On the country's first adhesives, Franklin and Washington stood in for the revolutionary promise of liberty and justice as founding fathers, public servants who were joined during 1851 by Thomas Jefferson as the earliest commemorative stamps proliferated.

In 1861, when Richmond suddenly needed to invent a usable past through adhesives, Confederate postmaster general John Henniger Reagan set aside George Washington and instead chose Jefferson Davis, also the first president of a new nation. For his second stamp, Reagan selected Thomas Jefferson, whose portrait was drawn by Charles Ludwig free style from the crisply executed U.S. stamp. Because Richmond did not have a well-established engraving firm, the Confederacy's first stamps were produced by lithographers Hoyer & Ludwig, whose stone impressions of Jefferson were considerably less crisp and less memorable. In the words of August Dietz, chronicler of the fledgling postal service, "Ludwig failed in all but the eyes."[22] Comparatively muddy and lifeless, Richmond's first ten-cent stamp made it easy to recall, as Devin Leonard has, that the first U.S. secretary of state had resisted the ambitious aims of President Washington's postal network. "Thomas Jefferson and his supporters," writes Leonard, "feared that the president was constructing a massive federal system that would be as oppressive as European monarchies."[23] In 1862 Postmaster Reagan added a lithographed two-cent adhesive that carried a portrait of Andrew Jackson, the stamp that would be used by periodicals. As a group, Davis—Jefferson—Jackson traded Victoria's expanding empire for the Confederacy's sovereign states; as a commemorative alternative to Washington—Franklin—Jefferson, Confederate portraits also submerged U.S. liberty and justice in a tribute to slaveowner paternalism and elite control. That alternative origin story was selected with care and renewed with stamps, not least on the parcels of periodicals arriving at local depots.

It is surprising, then, that a recurring preoccupation of the war stories the postal network reliably delivered was the mistaken report of battlefield death, the harsh listing that guaranteed homestead grief. Also circulated through the mail upon which so many relied, casualty reports were regularly assembled by newspaper correspondents from eyewitness accounts, hospital records, quartermaster rosters, and (eventually) the official reports of regimental commanders. None of these, however, escaped the miserable spelling and worse handwriting of overwhelmed clerks or the inattention of their commanders. The single rule that seemed to prevail, as Martha Reamy and William Reamy note in their *Index to the Roll of Honor*, was "if in doubt—scribble."[24] Errors multiplied in the wake of major battles, as Yael Sternhell has shown. "In the confusion of smoke, bodies and wounded soldiers that comprised the aftermath of a Civil War military engagement," Sternhell writes, "it was often not easy to determine the actual outcome of the event, and even harder to obtain authentic numbers of prisoners and dead. The chaos of the battlefield then trickled back to the home front in the form of mistaken reports and baseless rumours."[25] The resulting newspaper tallies, sent to faraway post offices and awaiting pickup by distant subscribers, were often misleading.

Indeed, anxiously awaited casualty lists could misinform in one of two ways: true losses did not appear and hometown shock was delayed, or false reports arrived with the village post and shock was needless, when someone who was thought "killed" might one day return. That was somewhat less likely after personal notification. Parlor grief was keenest when letters arrived from commanders or personal effects were returned. In his description of the "New York City Post-Office," published in *Harper's Monthly* (October 1871), T. B. Thorpe remarked on "the terrible significance in the hymn or prayer book *returned* 'from the front'" and the unclaimed mail marked "killed in battle."[26] No matter how reliable reports proved to be, the postal service in both the North and the South tended to spread wartime anguish, which only became more acute for Southern households as the Confederate Post Office Department began to collapse. "The mail facilities offered the only hope for news," Richard Ridgway has written in *Self-Sufficiency at All Costs*. "When these facilities were gone, fear, loneliness, and anxiety increased."[27] At once lifeline and death knell, postal networks linked those in camp to memories of home and those in parlors to the calamities of war.

At a time of home-front alarm, magazines helped right the balance in Civil War stories, where a narrative's plot could put a newspaper's information into perspective. Even the comparative brevity of stories in a newsmagazine like *Harper's Weekly* was sufficient to demonstrate how casualty lists went awry. In "'Fortune Favors the Brave'" (August 16, 1862), for instance, a Union soldier is listed as killed at the Battle of Fair Oaks, but that turns out to be another man in the regiment with the same name. In "Kate's Soldier" (October 4, 1862), a Union substitute is reported killed but is instead wounded, taken prisoner, and eventually exchanged. In "Alice Bankgrove's Soldier" (December 13, 1862), a Northern volunteer with near-fatal wounds is listed as killed but is instead captured and later escapes. In "Ralph Hazlitt, Soldier" (July 18, 1863), a Northern man who enlisted is reported killed but is instead found on the battlefield by a rebel surgeon, an old classmate who tends his wounds before he is paroled. All of these stories reveal how erroneous casualty reports could be, how corrective Civil War stories could prove or (alternately) how charged with forlorn illusion, and in any case how essential literary magazines were in chronicling the war's last best hope of home. In this regard, *The Land We Love* was in good company from its inception.

First appearing in May 1866, *The Land We Love* ran to roughly eighty pages of historical articles, agricultural essays, travel narratives, literary sketches, poetry, sporadic war fiction, battle accounts, editorials, and a column called "The Haversack," which was filled each month with the anecdotes of the rank and file. To essays with suggestive regional titles such as "The Minerals of North Carolina" (July 1866), "The Enterprise and Energy of the South" (February 1867), "The Female Writers of the South" (March 1867), "Peach Culture" (July 1867), and "Character of the Southern People as Established by the Events of the Late War" (January 1868), Hill added contributions from such poets as Henry Timrod, Margaret J. Preston, F. O. Ticknor, and Paul Hamilton Hayne. He also championed sectional periodicals, like Richmond's *Southern Planter* and Baltimore's *Southern Review*, Nashville's *Home Monthly* and Wilmington's the *Carolina Farmer*, as part of his effort to sustain what he termed "a native, Southern literature."[28] It was a fitting service for the magazine's twelve thousand subscribers, especially those in North Carolina, the "Rip Van Winkle" state.[29] Advocating manual labor and practical training over a gentlemanly emphasis on the ancient classics, Hill promoted the factories, foundries, ships, and machine-shops that would make the South less dependent on northern industry and more likely to replace goods imported from Massachusetts and New York with southern manufactures.

Even secession had not been self-sufficient, as Hill noted in his continuing thoughts on education published in August 1866 during the magazine's first summer. "State Conventions met for the purpose of separating from the old Union," he wrote, "in buildings planned by Northern architects, and erected by Northern mechanics out of Northern materials. The members took their seats upon Northern chairs, around a Northern table, and appended their signatures with Northern pens, and Northern ink, to the ordinance of secession, written upon Northern paper."[30] Insisting on greater attention to "scientific farming" and "labor-saving machines," Hill hoped southern dependence would no longer extend as well to carpets, chandeliers, lamps, candles, cords, knobs, grates, and andirons.[31] In the pages of *The Land We Love*, the Civil War was not always fought in North Carolina or won by Tar Heel contributors, but the magazine's emphasis on replacing northern production with southern enterprise drew its inspiration from Charlotte's wartime entrepreneurship and postwar prospects.

Hence, the tension between lamenting the dead Confederacy and celebrating postwar Charlotte. Historically, the city's development had relied upon commerce, initially after gold was discovered in 1799 and, more importantly, after the railroad arrived in 1852 and began transporting the region's wheat, corn, and cotton to markets farther south. The war years spurred the production of woolen goods, canteens, chemicals, and gunpowder, as well as a predictable boom for the Mecklenburg Iron Works and the relocation of the Confederate Naval Yard when Norfolk faced capture in 1862. By the late 1860s, *The Land We*

Love was advertising Charlotte's banks and insurance agents, candy manufacturers and washing machines, local stationers and institutions like the Mecklenburg Female College, the Bingham School near Mebaneville Dépôt, and Davidson College in Mecklenburg County. The rapid ascendance of cotton after the war and the municipal purchase of a cotton press during the early 1870s made Charlotte what Thomas Hanchett in *Sorting Out the New South City* has called "the busiest inland cotton market in both Carolinas."[32] That development was encouraged by a major postwar railroad expansion through the region's inland cities rather than its decimated Atlantic ports.

In addition, a growing African American population more than doubled after emancipation and continued to increase as commercial opportunities multiplied across a city too small for ghettoes. Hanchett points to Charlotte's "salt-and-pepper racial mixing" prior to 1876, when a downtown business district was only beginning to consolidate.[33] During the Reconstructive years, he observes, "the houses of prosperous professionals and businessmen such as Zebulon Vance and Jonas Rudisill comfortably coexisted with the small cottage of workman John Moore, the African American church, and . . . two wagon-manufacturing operations."[34] As *The Land We Love* began reorienting the postbellum South in print, Charlotte was diversifying its business and industry, yet the growing town was still nearly a decade away from the kind of commercial density that fostered the first city directory in 1875–76.

The South that Hill's magazine celebrated looked less like Charlotte's salt-and-pepper wards, however, and more like the tilled lands of Mecklenburg County, where farmers were white and the American Revolution was a recent memory. When North Carolina seceded from the Union on May 20, 1861, according to state historian Milton Ready, the date was meant to honor an earlier devotion to self-government in the Mecklenburg Declaration of Independence, which was reportedly signed on May 20, 1775. Although documented evidence is scarce, Ready notes, it appears that the "Mecklenburg Resolves" on May 31, 1775, denied both "the authority of Parliament" and "the sovereignty of the king."[35] By popular account and more than a year before the Second Continental Congress acted in Philadelphia, the radicals in western North Carolina declared themselves free of distant rule, an independence their descendants continued to recall.

The Land We Love drew attention to that heritage repeatedly but most noticeably during its first year in the "Sketch of Mecklenburg County" (December 1866), which traced a "careful vigilance for *right*, *conscience*, and *liberty*" to the declaration of a "free and independent government" in May 1775 and thereafter up through Jefferson Davis as he held the last meeting of the Confederate

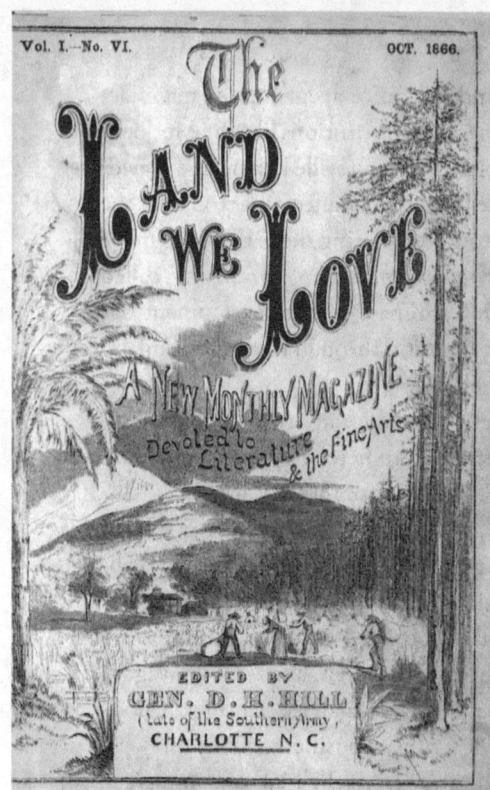

FIGURE 13. First cover on buff paper. Wood engraving. *The Land We Love*, July 1866. Courtesy of the HathiTrust.

FIGURE 14. Second cover on blue paper. Wood engraving. *The Land We Love*, May 1868. Courtesy of the University of Iowa Libraries.

Cabinet in his flight through Charlotte.[36] "The old hornet's nest," readers were told, "was yet intact and game to the last moment, the whole swarm buzzing."[37] Where Janette Thomas Greenwood has pointed in *Bittersweet Legacy* to the region's Colored Union Leagues, to the rising generation of black teachers and preachers, and to what she describes as the "cross-racial coalition of the black and white better classes" that was on the way in the 1880s, *The Land We Love* favored instead what Hill in 1867 called "being reconstructed on the true basis, the white man taking the lead in work" while abandoning what he dubbed the "whistle of negro equality."[38] By replacing city labor with county work and steam locomotives with steam ploughs, the magazine replaced the city's freedmen with the county's farmers to demonstrate who inherited "*right, conscience,* and *liberty*" from patriotic sires.

Nowhere is Hill's replacement strategy clearer at a glance than in his monthly's two covers. *The Land We Love* was initially published in 1866 with a buff cover that portrayed fields of cotton and once-enslaved laborers still at work (figure 13). This image was soon discarded, however, for a blue cover and a more benign invocation of an elite social order, one the earlier image renders more complex (figure 14). As Lorraine Hale Robinson has shrewdly observed, postwar magazine covers mattered because they amounted to "'icons' of a South triumphantly redefining itself."[39] In this case, it matters what carried over from one cover to the next. Besides the hills and forests that replace Charlotte's urban enterprise, it is most conspicuously the tiny image of a plantation house with a curious tower. Too distinctive an architectural detail for a generic Big House, the tower recalls nearby Blandwood, one of the earliest genuinely "Italian" villas constructed in the United States (figure 15).

First employed there in Greensboro during the 1840s for North Carolina's governor, John Motley Morehead, the Tuscan design arrived in Charlotte a decade later in the home built for the governor's son, John Lindsay Morehead (figure 16). As architectural historian Catherine W. Bishir has observed, "Italian" villas relied upon an imported style that replaced laborious handcrafting, vernacular models, and local artisan arrangements with steam-powered materials, ornate crafting, and "the contract mode of building," which began with a Northern architect.[40] Governor Morehead commissioned Alexander Jackson Davis of New York, a sure sign of what Bishir calls "a national rather than local arena... not only in the building... but in the money, materials, and men it required."[41] Awaken Rip Van Winkle, it seems, and the burghers of Manhattan were ready, even for business hundreds of miles south.

Both Moreheads were committed to education, business ventures, and (above all) the spread of railroads. As Bishir has noted, it was a program de-

FIGURE 15. A. J. Davis, *Residence of Gov. Morehead, North-Carolina. Blandwood in Greensboro, North Carolina.* Wood engraving. In Andrew Jackson Downing, *A Treatise on the Theory and Practice of Landscape Gardening, Adapted to North America* (New York: A. O. Moore and Co., 1859), 335. Courtesy of Preservation Greensboro Incorporated.

FIGURE 16. Sketch by Samuel Sloan of the home of Governor Morehead's son, John Lindsay Morehead, on the northeast corner of Tryon and Moreland Streets, Charlotte, North Carolina (around 1855). Courtesy of Preservation Greensboro Incorporated.

signed to develop North Carolina's western counties with the help of planter interests statewide, interests to which those favoring "improvements" in the once-sleepy state were beholden. "They sought thereby," writes Bishir, "to expand North Carolina's participation in the market economy, credit systems, industrial development, and slavery-based commercial plantation agriculture to supplant old-fashioned subsistence farming."⁴² As she further notes, these "improvements" in most of the counties the railroads served did tend to inspire a bigger appetite for northern commodities. Such a hunger would later give General Hill pause, but he would also encourage a program of regional growth through local development that Governor Morehead had already promoted. As the first cover of *The Land We Love* revealed, the unfettered "we" in his magazine's title may have loved the land but had not traditionally worked the fields.

In Hill's second cover, the villa has been turned around for a view of the tower's front windows, which obscure the cotton crop to the rear and are dwarfed by a considerably more elaborate paternal authority. Here, the landscape's towered "mansion" in the bottom panel is visually reduced by an iconographic cadre that begins with "THE PATRIOT," George Washington, whom Robinson sees as both "landowner and slaveholder."⁴³ The presidential nod to American independence and the rightful inheritors of American liberty is confirmed by "THE JURIST," Roger B. Taney, who authored the *Dred Scott* decision in 1857 and therefore its unforgettable claim that Negroes "had no rights which a white man was bound to respect."⁴⁴ Such a claim becomes almost divine mandate through the pious intercession of "THE SOLDIER," General T. J. Jackson, and the constitutional defense of slaveholding proclaimed by "THE STATESMEN," Daniel Webster, John C. Calhoun, and Henry Clay. Their patriotic legacy is visually supported from below by the landed South and visually centered on the task of *The Land We Love*, which is confirmed by the laurel wreath and the classical putti, who seem to be reading magazines.

Indeed, it could be said that Hill's enterprise in codifying southern history replaces the diminished though picturesque appeal of "Charlotte N.C." just below, as that landscape replaced the first cover's larger claims for the plantation South. It is not simply fields of cotton or even enslaved labor but Mecklenburg's "spirit of '75" transformed into Governor Morehead's "improvements" that Hill's South, belaureled as "the land we love," shores up against northern ruin. More precisely, it is a continuing patriarchal tradition, already anachronistic elsewhere, a "distinctive" southern republicanism that Peter Bardaglio sees deriving from coverture and the domestic dependency of white women, white children, and enslaved people.⁴⁵ That masculine tradition is exemplified at Blandwood in a commanding belltower and two outbuildings (or "dependencies") devoted to kitchen and office that complete Hill's ideal plantation home.

Yet the Civil War created a growing number of southern homes without men, sometimes by choice. Postbellum North Carolina, for instance, saw an increase in petitions for divorce, cases that were eventually taken up by the official delegates to the state's constitutional convention in 1868. Often lodged by abandoned wives, some twenty-seven divorce petitions struck at the heart of coverture—that is, at the pervasive patriarchal assumption that married women were mastered by their husbands, enough to lose their independent reason and consent. Those twenty-seven cases, fifteen of which were honored in 1868, sapped both husbandly authority and the divine luster of the marriage contract. "Granted a will of her own," writes Karin Zipf, "a wife violated the natural principles of marriage and gender relations, thus presenting a threat to social harmony."[46] Zipf, who has examined North Carolina's postwar divorce petitions, goes on to observe that "by recognizing women's equal contract rights in marriage, American courts and legislatures would emancipate women as the Civil War had emancipated slaves."[47] Abandonment, contract, divorce? None of that seems to touch Hill's magazine covers with their assurance that home endured, that crops deserved tending, and that an African American labor force (whether foregrounded or hidden) was permanently bound to house, master, and land.

Two further postwar developments roiled Hill's prospects, however, and shook the continuing appeal of his magazine's covers, with their steady tribute to the antebellum social norms of the plantation South. In 1866 Edward A. Pollard published *The Lost Cause: A New Southern History of the War of the Confederates*, which launched a polemic for southern nationalism that an ex-general might have shared but that Hill assailed. A year later in 1867 the United States Congress passed the Reconstruction Acts, which divided the ex-Confederacy into five military districts, promoted the political authority of African American citizens, and returned federal troops as district occupiers. Both developments were to reveal the agendas that lurked in the emerging rhetoric of the Lost Cause, which was not initially as monochromatic as it has since become.

For one thing, Hill's celebration of battlefield valor would highlight how much Confederate nationalism could be grounded in a southern masculinity and a white paternalism that was nonnegotiable, even as factories and foundries multiplied. For another, the political ascendancy of African Americans in Reconstruction Charlotte revealed how thoroughly Confederate "patriotism" in *The Land We Love* was bound to the "spirit of '75" and the constitutional blueprint for a slave republic, which offered the racial and cultural homogeneity that had historically spurred the rise of nation-states. Finally, the iconic southern homestead that exemplified Lost Cause mainstays for both Hill and Pollard was repeatedly imperiled in *The Land We Love* by General Sherman's march through the Carolinas in 1865 and then obliquely rescued by the fiction Hill grudgingly printed, stories submitted not by the war's white soldiers but by the war's white women, who persevered and adeptly rewrote Hill's patriarchal script. For them, the task of remembrance was unrelenting but empowering, enough to turn them for a postbellum moment into the American Revolution's true heirs.

That is not exactly what Pollard's *The Lost Cause* preached, despite its considerable heft and what Coleman Hutchison in *Apples and Ashes* has called "a 752-page harangue."[48] Drawing upon his wartime contributions to the *Richmond Daily Examiner* as a writer and sometime editor, Pollard initially cast the Civil War as a contest between alternative civilizations, the North bound to "Consolidation" and the South to the state sovereignty that assured what the Articles of Confederation had originally promised, "freedom and independence."[49] More than seven hundred pages later, Pollard concluded that the "war closed on a spectacle of ruin" not only for the defeated Confederacy but also for the country's founding principles.[50] Yet he looked ahead with Henry A. Wise, former governor of Virginia, to the honorable battle Confederate armies had lost but the South might still win, what Pollard called the "great struggle of constitutional liberty" that "yet remains."[51] Notably, questions of "negro equality" and "negro suffrage" had not been decided, another hint of the epic scope that Pollard imagined for a commemorative southern literature.[52] As Alan Nolan has observed, "The Lost Cause is therefore an American legend, an American version of great sagas like *Beowulf* and the *Song of Roland*."[53] For Pollard, at least, it was a saga that could still end nobly, if white southerners would only remain loyal to constitutional principles and shun the acquisitive practices of the voracious North that had left him stranded. "After the Confederacy died in 1865," Jack Maddex has written, "Pollard found himself living in a foreign land—a slaveless, Northern-dominated United States."[54] In *The Lost Cause*, which he revised and augmented in 1867, Pollard's portrait of competing nationalisms transformed defeat into triumph, desolation into integrity, and a reckless northern imperialism into an abiding southern domesticity that promoted the "peculiar institution" as stabilizing, an antidote to marketplace greed.

It has been customary in recent scholarly accounts, beginning in 2001 with David Blight's *Race and Reunion*, to gloss *The Land We Love* as ground zero for the Lost Cause, the literary incorporation of Pollard's principles. As early as the new magazine's opening article, Hill's first essay on education (May 1866), the editor wrote of the "dear old homestead" and the homogeneous "colony" in which "the worship and customs of . . . fathers will ever be preserved" in a "mighty Republic."[55] But in the face of severe wartime losses, Hill shifted almost immediately to the need for "a total radical change," beginning with education and thus forcing the reassessment that Pollard refused in his purported "new southern history."[56] It was also a personal affront to a battlefield general that a hasty journalist like Pollard got his facts wrong.

At Sharpsburg along Antietam Creek, Pollard had asserted, a copy of General Lee's orders had been sent to Hill, a commanding general he characterized as a "vain and petulant officer" who threw down the unwelcome directives.[57] They were discovered on the ground by a Union soldier, who then passed the intelligence up the line of command to General George B. McClellan. Thus, Lee's Maryland invasion failed. Hill spent the rest of his life denying that charge, beginning with an article in *The Land We Love* titled "The Lost Dispatch" (February 1868), which impugned Pollard's "gross slander" and lack of evidence.[58] The next month he editorialized about Pollard's refusal to visit the battlefields of "heroic daring," even those near Richmond; four months later, in July 1868, he railed about the "blunders" and "misrepresentations" of Pollard's "so-called history."[59] That December he declared: "There was not a drummer boy or colored servant in Lee's army, who had not more accurate knowledge of the battles of the late war than the bomb-proof penny-a-liner, who set himself up as their chronicler."[60] General Hill had plenty of company among Confederate officers in maligning the newsman's battlefield reports, as Pollard biographer Maddex reveals, but few others were as spiteful, since few others had so much personal reputation at stake.

Hill's larger issue, however, concerned the authenticity of postwar accounts, the credentialing of historians, and the burden that scurrilous volumes placed on what was widely called "the truth of Southern history." Scarcely diligent and never impartial, as Hill saw it, Pollard also jeopardized the legitimacy of his project by refusing to fight—refusing, that is, to exercise the valor that a martial culture demanded of its men. The impassioned Hill wrote in July 1868: "The American people will despise the zealous advocate of the war, who crept into a bomb-proof when the bullets began to fly, snarled and snapped while there, alternately at Mr. Davis and Mr. Lincoln, at Confederates and Federals, and then crawled out when the firing was over, to make money, by stealing the property and defaming the character of Confederate soldiers."[61] Even for Pollard, one of the defining axioms of the Lost Cause was the battlefield honor of Confederate troops against the Union's heaping numbers and purchasing power, what Gary Gallagher has described as "inexhaustible reserves of men and materiel."[62] But for Confederate officers like Hill, Pollard exacerbated a postwar domestic crisis: in defeat, honorable men born into a patriarchal society often felt crippled, a development that Anne Sarah Rubin notes has been of increasing interest to social historians. "Their manhood and valor had been tested and had fallen short on the battlefield," she writes. "Consequently, it would need to be reasserted at home."⁶³ For Rubin, as well as Hill, it was bombs, not bomb-proofs, witness, not shelter, that defined the ground on which postwar historians could stand, the ground on which the uses of memory could be tested.

In *The Land We Love*, that test was more sharply engaged in 1867, when recovering North Carolina became part of Military District #2. Now once seceding states would be required to ratify the constitutional amendments abolishing slavery and safeguarding the civil rights of African Americans before returning to the Union and sending representatives to Congress. For the editorializing Hill in August 1868, it was proof of Reconstruction's imperial purpose, a sure sign that a willingness to work would not prevail against "the will of the conqueror."⁶⁴ In September 1868 he warned that the North would obliterate "the manhood, the independence, the integrity" of recent enemies.⁶⁵ Hill had already protested the creation of the Freedmen's Bureau and the "odeur d'Afrique" its operations encouraged.⁶⁶ He cried out against the Reconstruction Bill and then southern "Scallawags, those "thievish whites engaged in beastly negro-worship."⁶⁷ In the developing drama of Reconstruction as *The Land We Love* limned it, freedpeople would nonetheless prove as crucial as singing laborers had been to antebellum plantation verities. In this, Hill's magazine was not alone. "It is telling to observe," David Blight has written, "that virtually all major spokespersons for the Lost Cause could not develop their story of a heroic, victimized South without the images of faithful slaves and benevolent masters."⁶⁸ When those images faltered, when the plantation tradition collided in print with a new social order, the result was not simply that African Americans moved into positions of power that onetime Confederates had lost.

For Hill, as for many white southerners in their military districts, the abolition of slavery and the Reconstruction Acts of 1867 doomed the Revolutionary project that the Constitution had seemingly assured and the white South had steadfastly safeguarded, even at grave expense. In Hill's circles, the Confederacy was widely portrayed as a defensive enterprise as early as the assault on Fort Sumter. Examining the aspirations of Jefferson Davis's government, Stephanie McCurry observes, "The Confederate States of America would represent a new birth of liberty: theirs was to be a proslavery nation and a white man's republic . . . simply, as many claimed, the original republic of the United States redeemed and perfected."⁶⁹ In that spirit, Hill indicted "New England fanaticism" and predicted the failure of another "grand experiment at sudden emancipation," a reminder not only of white southern stewardship but also of white northern peril now that the country's founding blueprint was to be emended.⁷⁰ Withering in his scorn for Pollard's "slanders" and certain that "the truth of Southern history" lay with "old army friends," Hill insisted in April 1868 that "a native, Southern literature" would help sustain "the Union and the Constitution" as surely as the Democratic Party.[71]

The fatal disruption that was imagined in postwar magazines such as *The Land We Love* and the Civil War stories they circulated ultimately helped to reconceive "the South" and to engage emancipation by way of rebuttal, more or less through the commemorative practice understood as "postmemory." The term comes from Marianne Hirsch, whose attention to the Holocaust in *The Generation of Postmemory* begins with the inherited suffering of the next generation that was coming of age as survivors began to die. Postmemory, writes Hirsch, invokes "the relationship that the 'generation after' bears to the personal, collective, and cultural trauma of those who came before." And she adds, "Postmemory's connection to the past is thus actually mediated not by recall but by imaginative investment, projection, and creation," the skills that Civil War stories fostered in the magazines of the 1860s and 1870s.[72]

Because Hirsch acknowledges other traumas and their corrosive aftermath around the world, the potency of belated witness has stretched across time and into the Americas. Arlene Keizer has written about "African American postmemory" in the dark cutouts of artist Kara Walker.[73] Sinéad McDermott has examined postmemory's "ethics" in Bobbie Ann Mason's *In Country* (1985), where the daughter of a dead Vietnam veteran lives with transgressions and misfortunes she never experienced.[74] Like Hirsch, Sari Edelstein points to family photographs, most insistently in Katherine Anne Porter's *Old Mortality* (1937), and she examines what she describes as "the problematic politics of postmemory for southerners who struggle to make peace with the legacy of slavery, civil war, and perhaps most of all, the loss of a culture that was both vaunted and vexed."[75] Joycelyn Moody recounts thorny discussions of slave narratives in her undergraduate classrooms, where African American female students are "deeply connected to a horrific past they did not endure but nonetheless embody, remember, and sustain."[76] They too are legatees of Civil War trauma.

During the 1860s and 1870s, the fraught terrain of postmemory coalesced almost immediately at a time of widespread reckoning, when accomplished magazinists and untrained contributors were drawn to what Hirsch calls elsewhere "an aesthetics of the aftermath."[77] Generally, such writers were geographically or temporally distant from the events they described as they fictionalized firsthand experiences, retold the accounts of others, or simply concocted a series of events—all mediated endeavors. Rebecca Harding Davis in western Virginia's Wheeling, for instance, invented "John Lamar" while she was herself in border country, which she would later compare to "the flanks of Vesuvius after the red-hot flood of lava had passed over them."[78] Still, her war in the *Atlantic*

Monthly was imagined rather than reported, akin to Hirsch's "imaginative investment" or Kennedy-Nolle's "imaginative vistas" and thus closer to what Argentine writer Carlos Gamerro describes as the response of witnesses at a remove. "A more suitable term," Gamerro writes, "might be bystanders, a word that refers more to the witness-observer than to the witness-participant."[79] The Civil War stories that magazines like *The Land We Love* delivered shortly after the war were most often discovered by readers as bystanders and most often written on a spectrum from participants to observers to could-be witnesses, at least across the mediated terrain of the "vulnerable times" Hirsch describes.[80] By 1866, when *The Land We Love* was founded, not only had an increasingly vulnerable Confederacy surrendered, but the Thirteenth Amendment abolishing slavery had been ratified, confirmation that the conservative demand for "the Union as it was, the Constitution as it is" had been superseded by a more radical project, a revolution in social relations that stories of the war were then beginning to portray.

The occasional fiction in Hill's magazine animated that project, though republican fervor generally gave way in eight Civil War stories to "vulnerable times" and a recurring emphasis on traumatic replacement that only began with the magazine's two covers. "Home on Furlough" (November 1866), for instance, chronicles Federal raids and an amputation; yet replacement is signaled not by a prosthetic arm but by a substitute labor force and the therapeutic virtues of farming. As the soldier-hero puts it, "They did worse things than to take our darkies from us."[81] "The Texas Soldier" (March 1867) casts General Sherman's march as "the great human Juggernaut" ("Fire, fire, blood and smoke, plundering men, shrieking women") before replacing a ruined Georgia homestead with marriage and removal to Texas.[82] "Elmsville and Its Hospital" (June and July 1866) seems headed for recuperation in South Carolina until brother Frank Barton unexpectedly dies and is replaced in his sister's heart by lover Phil Bradford, just as sister Lily is replaced by nurse Lula, each name echoing the replaceable one before.[83] In all these stories and more, the Southern home and family sustain damage, as though the picturesque invitation of the magazine's iconic landscape were stolen by raiders, its mansion invaded, and its field transformed into Hill's "waste and desolate places—the habitation, it may be, of reptiles and wild beasts."[84] From a daughter's gown on the snow to the pearl handles of dessert knives, from the walls of a family cottage to the tombstones of a family graveyard, the homes and ghosts of *The Land We Love* were inevitably and insistently white.

Therein lies a postmemory shiver—that is, a reasonable charge that the term is misapplied to the Lost Cause. Because Hirsch seeks a recollective space for annihilation and its lengthening aftermath, specifically for Holocaust survivors, enlisting the moral high ground of postmemory for patriarchal slaveowners and their fellow travelers in print can seem like privileging the sorrows of the Third Reich and its horrific and persistent appeal. That is especially true when the terrain of postmemory, where the tremors of the past continue to shake the present, is extended to the families of Vietnam veterans and the agitated discussions of slave narratives among African American students. Still, casting the Lost Cause and its multiplying commemorative ventures as postmemory reanimates an anguish that Hill would recognize while revealing the country's eighteenth-century vision of liberty and justice as perpetually redefined through contest. During 1869, for example, as Hill's magazine flailed, congressional debates about the extension of voting rights included not only African Americans but also white women, Native peoples, the gypsies in Pennsylvania, and the Chinese farther west. As transplant senator Willard Warner of Alabama put it, "The question before us is not one of negro suffrage. It is the question of suffrage in itself. It is the broad question who shall be the voters of this country, in whose hands shall rest the political power."[85] Widening the purview of postmemory risks moral censure but opens a fraught political moment, a cascade of charged events, to competition among history's legatees.

It is therefore significant that during Reconstruction the delivery of episodic events in short magazine fiction across the country shifted noticeably as postmemory's competing engagements with recent trauma multiplied. In the unfolding of any story, events may be said to count narratively in several different ways: they establish how far back an instructive chronology reaches, they reveal patterns across stories when similar action recurs, and they suggest knots in any given story when a single moment is repeated, told twice. During the 1860s and 1870s, many magazine stories of the recent rebellion reached back in time—for instance, to when a father flees France or leaves Ireland behind, when he loses money or marries for it, when a family immigrates to Virginia, lands on the Potomac, or settles in Tennessee. When Civil War stories initiate events, more than one father fights in the United States Army, and more than one family recalls the Crimea or early Indian attacks.

But stories published in Southern magazines were unusually caught up in a wider scope for a shared national past. In the *Southern Literary Messenger*'s "Peninsular Sketches" (November/December 1862, July 1863), for example, the narrative begins with the fall of Fort Sumter in 1861 and then looks back beyond the British surrender of Yorktown in 1781 to the moment when John Smith met Powhatan in 1607. In "My Uncle Flatback's Plantation" (October 1863), again for the *Southern Literary Messenger*, George William Bagby profiles an old Virginian whose father fought in the American Revolution before he himself marched through the War of 1812. In "The First Campaign of a Fat Volunteer," which appeared in the *Southern Illustrated News* (January 10 and January 17, 1863), Louise Manheim's Confederate private opens his tale with the memory of John Brown but concludes with the recent war in Mexico and the exemplary service of Thomas J. Jackson, later to find his stone wall at First Manassas. The South's local heroes, in other words, were deeply invested in the country's martial past, whose long narrative trajectory encompassed the Confederacy's struggle for independence.

Conversely, it is noticeable how much Rebecca Harding Davis's "John Lamar" differs, especially in selecting for Boston's *Atlantic Monthly* (April 1862) which events would resonate. Where Manheim recalls the "terrible and unabated fury" of John Brown and his "diabolical conspiracy" at Harpers Ferry, Davis describes the lifted knife of the enslaved Ben as striking "a blow for freedom" in the same western Virginia hills.[86] Where Bagby references the family's "Patriarch of the Hill" who fought in the Revolution, "John Lamar" invokes Jeremiah and a "God of Vengeance" descending on Babylon.[87] Where "Peninsular Sketches" links Confederate forces in Virginia to Cornwallis's "forts" and Powhatan's "Werowocomoco" during the early days of the country's southern past, Davis's story imagines Ben's past stretching only as far back as his father's escape from a Georgia swamp to the free North, a "heroic dream" that will be realized for Ben "just beyond the ridge."[88] Selecting an originating event in Civil War stories, like selecting portraits for commemorative stamps, amounts to selecting whose past will carry weight. Where Davis reaches a generation back for an intuition of freedom that Ben will pursue, southern magazines like *The Land We Love* routinely saw war narratives rooted in colonial memory and white America's origin stories.

It is therefore remarkable how many of the war's first stories from Boston to Philadelphia, Richmond to Memphis, and Charlotte to San Francisco reached farthest back to the death of parents, mothers slightly more than fathers: a dying mother leaves a girl in her brother's care, for instance, or an octoroon flees New Orleans when her father passes away. These are not generally a story's opening events; they are simply the earliest moments recalled as narrators assemble their tales. Deaths in fictional families were scarcely new and often proved central to nineteenth-century plots; but as the fleeting inauguration of a new history, they seem especially resonant. Positing an originating moment in the death of a parent means structuring the narrative out of familial loss. In fact, dying is predictably one of the five most frequent events across Civil War stories, along with declaring love and marrying (most often in wartime romances), plus volunteering and fighting or skirmishing. Put another way, Civil War stories in one magazine after another were about securing home, leaving home, and losing home, or at least losing the way "home" was once defined. Rather than suggesting a national "house divided," in Lincoln's familiar biblical phrase, the war's first stories generally suggested a home invaded, sometimes by the casualty lists that arrived with the nearest newspaper.

When stories in some sixteen war-era periodicals got stuck on one insistent event, as though postmemory's trauma needed to be recollected more than once, it is often a fateful loss: an old Southern mistress dies, a fellow sergeant is killed, roughriders massacre hundreds of black soldiers at Fort Pillow. Returning to such a scene in a story that can only repeat it underlines both which consternating differences resonated as the events of the war entered a national imaginary and how high the personal cost of Union or Confederate repair might be. While Anne C. Rose has rightly pointed out in *Victorian America and the Civil War* that soldiers returned home to the same "social and intellectual trends" they left, at least in the North, it does not follow that they returned to the same lives or that social upheaval scarcely frayed the fabric of daily life, as Rose has claimed.[89] Grounding postmemory so repeatedly in the death of parents also meant structuring the imagined Civil War out of a severed link to the nation's past, together with an inherited certainty about whose liberty and justice would signify for the distant subscribers of any magazine, including *The Land We Love*.

As the Civil War spurred the "imaginative investment, project, and creation" that postmemory delivered in midcentury literary magazines, it might be expected that a wartime preoccupation with shrinking families and ruined homes would be overtaken in print by romances, which often favored the recurring tropes of enlistment and combat as a context for the next generation's renewal through marriage. Davis's Ben, for instance, remembers that the house servant he loved has disappeared into the beckoning North. In *The Land We Love*, however, a similarly momentous gravity seems to tug even minor characters into the past, and a concluding marriage can actually rescind its promise: "In an Old Drawer" (December 1868) reveals a Confederate girl rummaging among past keepsakes, only to find that her future marriage prospects are narratively replaced by the story of her grandmother's cottage wedding sixty years earlier. True happiness, it seems, was secured decades before secession, before "murderous, marauding" Union troops arrived.[90] How to sustain the "union" as it was in the midst of sad rupture becomes the task of postmemory's bystanders in a "Road-Side Story," and it is not a task that Ina M. Porter leaves to her story's men.

INA M. PORTER

"Road-Side Story"

(*The Land We Love*, August 1866)

The reception-room where I awaited the cars was lonely, and I was glad to hear steps in the hall coming that way. Traveling arouses all the curiosity in my nature; I lose myself in vague wanderings about this or that person; not idle prying, I trust, but an expanding interest in the joys and sorrows of my fellow-creatures. The footsteps were those of a woman, and I straightway fell to wondering what manner of creature would appear. Fantasias in verse and song to the unseen flocked to my busy brain, to fly like frightened birds before the presence of the odd-looking little old woman, who stood in the entrance for a few seconds with that hesitating air of untraveled persons, and quickly found for herself and bundles the most unobtrusive spot in the room. A thin, sallow boy followed with an idiotic air and odd maneuvers. I am a polite man by nature as well as training, so I stirred the fire, and invited her nearer it, as I marked an occasional shiver under a threadbare shawl. "Thank you, sir; come, Davy!" The tone was pleasant, the fire likewise, for her timid manner fled before its sparkle, and my companion proved rather agreeable than otherwise to look upon, with her restless eyes, under a white ruffled cap, surmounted by a well taken care of, but exceedingly worse for the wear bonnet, and a clean checked, homespun dress, just meeting the tops of a pair of stout shoes. Even the threadbare shawl had an air of doing its best, however little that might be. Several remarks passed relative to the belated trains, dreadful state of the roads, etc. Traveling seemed a new thing; and from the brisk manner in which its disadvantages were set forth for my edification, a fear arose that I was going to be bored. Now, if there is one kind of bore who possesses superior qualifications to another in this particular, it is the ungrammatical bore; the difference is as marked as between a well-polished gimlet and a rusty auger. The tidy old lady was very intelligent by nature, but several errors had struck my sensitive ear, and brought conviction that the weather and cars might be enlarged upon disagreeably; thereon I grew communicative myself, and after a roundabout dissertation on these already exhausted subjects, remarked that I was affected by an uncomfortable drowsiness, rose with a yawn, drew on my army overcoat, settled myself for the night, and advised her to do the same. The two left to themselves talked in a low tone; the boy was evidently her son, and I was touched by her tenderness in many simple ways. She made him take off his jacket, turn it round and round before the fire, took sewing materials from an emaciated pocket-book, darned a place here and there holding it up with an air of satisfaction. It was one of the gray jackets we were all wearing then, like the one I had on, only his was worn almost white with faded blue trimmings, while mine was so much better I could not resist holding up an arm by way of contrast, breathing a blessing on the mother who made it, and the sister who had so cheerfully given up her pretty opera-cloak for the facings of brother's new uniform; but the contrast was painful unless I had owned another jacket to give the boy, so I pulled my cape over the bright red cuff, and wished I had on my old one. Watching the faces before me, hearing her suppressed tones and his silly chuckle, I dozed away and could have slept had it not been for steps sounding again in the hall. The clerk of the house came in with such a flourish, confound him! that Morpheus fled amazed from my couch. I wanted to collar and choke him, not for waking me up solely—that was an aggravating circumstance, but not the exciting cause of my indignation. I remembered the shabby old lady found her way in alone, while a fashionable, handsomely-attired young lady was ushered in with all that parade and needless ceremony so annoying to real gentility. I argued, the one is rich, the other poor—sometimes I hate wealth, it narrows so many hearts and cracks so many brains! Resentment against the younger, in behalf of the elder lady, filled my breast. I hated the former before I looked at her; indeed I would not vouchsafe a glance from under my old slouched hat to one who had suddenly grown rich, and fancied herself in position by possession of a few dollars. I knew she was one of that class by the rustle of her sweeping dress. Bah! the fool! I muttered in my chivalric defense of the silent representative of poverty, who, I fancied, was already enduring heroically the arrogance of a "parvenu." A ripple of a laugh fell among my thoughts, a pleasant sound of itself, and for another reason—in the solemn earnestness of warfare men and women laughed seldom, it was chiefly little children who could laugh as in the olden time. Before I was quite aware of my intentions, I raised the brim of my hat to look at that face, while the shine of a laugh lay on it. A glance was enough to remove all preconceived ideas of the lovely woman before me. I called myself a fool as heartily as I had called her one. "Parvenu," indeed! How refined in style, how delicate in manner! Had the other been wife and heir at law to Croesus, she could not have found a more attentive listener. My aforesaid curiosity manifested itself in the most vehement manner—what if the train came before I divined whether that soul was as fair as the body! Were those eyes as honest as bright? Was that hair God's glorious crowning, or a "switch," held on with curious frettings of spikes and pins? Was it a dimple or shadow on that faultless chin? Were those roses on lip and cheek to the manor born, or parasites? At this juncture I wondered if she was married or single; strangely enough, the conversation grew suddenly interesting and important. I found myself wide awake at the next remark, which, singularly too, replied to my speculations. "Yes, ma'am; my husband," said the red lips proudly. It was a sweet word, sweetly spoken; I never thought so before, nevertheless it ruffled my composure; this may have risen from a commendable fear that she may not have been happily married; however, a resolution was offered and adopted to hate her husband, modified only by a providing clause that the man could give satisfactory evidence of his fitness to stand in that relation. This was a cool, sensible proceeding, and I gave myself due credit for disinterestedness in my devotion to the sex; at the same time acknowledging my capacity for hating or loving, men or women, suddenly and fervently, on the slightest provocation. That I was just to the lady's husband was evident to any observer. Why was she traveling alone? He was doubtless an idle, drunken skulker from the army; or why that wistful sadness that flitted now and then from those lustrous eyes? Possibly she might think well of the scapegrace, or might not; in either event it was furthermore resolved, that if he intruded himself in our midst, and offered the slightest indignity, stranger as I was it should be resented. I might restrain my rage until I whirled him out of her presence, but it was doubtful, very doubtful indeed! Don Quixote could not have been by half so crestfallen in his famous retreat from the windmills, as I after this desperate onslaught against the missing husband. I discovered myself a fool beyond a shadow of disputation when I heard her say: "We have all suffered, but my husband still lives, thank God!" It occurred to me at that moment more might be said than either lady would desire me to hear; and, with all my interest in others, I wish to know nothing of the penetralia of a human soul, which is not voluntarily given to my keeping.

I arose, and replenished the dying fire, for which I was repaid by looks of gratification from my companions; even the boy giggled in his sleep, and carried his hands to and from the fire to his mouth, as if the flames were food. Naturally, as it came to us all in those days, the war was our theme. Men and women could not sit silently together then, when all held hands in the game whose stake was life or death! The devotion of our women, especially, and their heroic sacrifices, I enlarged upon. "Still," I continued, "there are instances rare, I grant, where avarice has laid violent hands on the hearts of women as well as men." "There are dreadful necessities forced on us now," returned the young lady.

"Necessities? Would you call selling a draught of water to a thirsty man a necessity? Would you think water could be bartered and sold?" queried I.

"No, there's no excuse for that, none!" she added warmly. The old lady began to speak and checked herself, laying her wrinkled hand on Davy's restless fingers.

"It *has been done*, I bought it, and I grieve to say, a woman sold it," I repeated sorrowfully.

"What? Where?" ejaculated both voices simultaneously.

"Ten miles from Corinth, Miss., at a cabin-door." The old lady interrupted me with a deprecatory gesture and a flood of tears. "Pardon me, dear madam," said I eagerly.

"Forgive me, O forgive me!" she pleaded. "It was all along of poor Davy, all for poor, hungry Davy!"

The other lady joined me in entreaties that she would spare herself the recital of such unhappy memories, but she would speak, and this was the way she told her story.

"I must tell you why I sold the water, it does me good here," putting her hand to her throat. "I wanted to tell when the soldiers took it from my hand, but the words choked me and would never come. I was afraid they'd judge me hard and am glad to tell. It is not very long, sir, in words, but some days would stretch themselves out into years, just like I've seen the little saplings throw long shadows across my yard when the sun was sinking down. My old man was dead, I was a widow when my Davy here was a bit of a shaver, toddling around alone. I lived in a nice little home, not fine as yours, ma'am, but you know the old saying, 'A rich man's castle's no dearer than the poor man's cot.' He was handy with his hammer and plane, and we knocked about it inside and out, until when fine folks passed that way, they'd say, 'What a snug little cottage!' And little it was to be sure, but then it was mine, and it's the best of all good feelings to know a thing is a body's own; then again, after my husband died, it was all the dearer for the sake of him that built it. We three lived there then, Matty, Davy and me. Well, after a while Matty grew up and married, left me and her brother until when the war came, she come back to us, saying, 'I've come back home, mother, it's so dark over at my house when John is gone.' Poor thing! It never got light again, for John never set foot in the door any more! Two widows lived and worked together, bearing the same hard pain. We didn't have time to sit down and cry in idleness, for if there was no more soldier clothes to make for John, there was plenty more, who had no mother, sister, nor wife to work for 'em, and we hadn't the heart to stand by and see 'em go off, without helping them on. Most of my work was spinning and knitting, on account of failing eyes; but Matty's tears fell day after day over as many a pretty web of cloth as you ever laid your eyes on; they was none the uglier for that.

Davy stirred in the large chair, but lay back again docile as an infant under her touch, and her oft-repeated whisper of 'Hush, Davy dear!' I saw something was the matter with him, the great eyes across the hearth exchanged glances with mine and rested on him pityingly. Well, we worked on, every body was working, rich and poor, and we wouldn't be outdone by nobody, if we did have heavy hearts; for that manner, every body's hung heavy, but it was all for duty, and you know there's no choice in that. My Matty was brave as any body. When John went off, he looked back and saw her smiling, and kissing her little brown hands at him; but when he was clear out of her sight, she fell down as still as the dead. Then she come home next day, light of tongue and hands and feet to hide the aching for my sake, like she hid it for his. Ah me! It's the first lesson and the last, and it comes easy to us all to hide the hardest achings from them we love, and laugh when they step on the hiding-place, to keep 'em from finding it.

"Old folks take no notice of how time slips off. When I wasn't thinking of Davy as nothing but a stripling he comes to me one day and tells me the 'Time was come for him to go.' 'Where,' says I, 'my son?' 'To fight for you and Matty.' My old heart fell, for he was my baby, but I just said, 'Davy, you are too young.' 'But, mother,' he kept on, 'who learnt me we was never too young to do right, when we knew the right way?' He didn't look then like he does now, poor Davy! And I was so proud of my boy, he was a mighty child for learning, and found so many better ways of saying things than I did, that he worked me up to thinking his way; but it was pitiful to see him go, he was so young and tender. When he walked out of the door in his proud way of stepping, with his musket on his shoulder, I got old all of a sudden, and it come to my mind how Abraham laid his Isaac on the altar, and I prayed it might go well with me and my baby as it went with him and his; but with all the hoping and praying, I went weak and tottering the whole winter long. Then another aching come for Matty's sake. Her father died of a cough, and folks used to say she looked like him; but I never thought so, until she took to coughing the same hollow way. I tried to make her careful of it, but she loved to work; since John was dead and Davy gone, she loved it more and more. She used to say, 'Young hands is fitter for work than old ones, mother, and it makes trouble lay lighter for them that's gone, to work for them that's here.' Then again she'd say, 'Let me work, it feels like I was standing guard in his place.' I knew what she meant, and she'd work with all her might, like she stood at the head of a regiment, leading our boys to glory! We got along very well, thank God, until the cavalry got to dashing round. The stock, gardens, fields, barns, and houses suffered where they went, people got to leaving their homes, for homes wasn't homes any more and women wasn't safe to stay at 'em. There was a running to and fro like the prophet said would come, but, eh Lord! I couldn't make my mind to leave my home until I was called to the Father's mansion in the skies. The way they did would make me mighty mad, but I never said much until they killed my cows, then I give 'em a piece of my mind. 'Matty,' I'd say, 'that's what I call stealing.' 'Why, mother,' she'd say, 'it's capturing!' Sometimes when I couldn't laugh with her, she'd tell me, 'Never fret, mother dear, if Davy comes back safe they can't make us poor.' And then the tender-hearted thing would speak up for the raiders, saying, 'They must be hungry men, and may be they don't know it's widows they are taking from.' 'Hungry, indeed!' says I, 'do you reckon they'll eat that dress of yours, and my shawl, and the coffee-mill, and the saddle, and—' She'd put her hand over my mouth, and I'd quiet down and say, 'If they'd come and ask me, I'd give and welcome, according to the Scripture, and for Him that tells us to love our enemies.' 'But mother,' she'd keep on, 'we'll try to think kinder of 'em; there's men that's mad and blind rushing 'em on us, and it an't one half that knows what for.' Not that she hadn't as much pluck as me, for when she saw a wrong done, her cheeks would turn like sun-red peaches, and her eyes flash sparks like my old man's anvil, but she'd grown so serious and forgiving in her ways. She'd often say, 'Ah! mother, it an't for long any how. I'll go to father and John, and Davy will come back a man to take care of you.' I'd try to keep dark, but my fears was great, there used to be stains under her eyes for two or three hours every day, and then they'd fade out white as lint, leaving my heart aching and aching, worse and worse for the day that was sure to come. I thought she worked too much, and took to doing all I could in her place, she'd cry, and say, 'It hurts me worse than weaving to see you work, mother.' One day I went off to look up work, and get her physic from the hospital, when I come back she was lying on the trundle-bed, so tired she didn't even know the sun was shining through the window on her shut-up eyes. My Matty was likely, and likelier than ever when she was sleeping. I laid my bundle down and sat watching her while I rested, we was growing closer and closer to each other in them sad days. I begun to feel gentle and watchful over her as though she was a little one at my breast. I knew she was going fast, and I felt like every minute away from her was wasting time, she'd so soon be gone. I crept close and kissed her soft, thinking not to wake her; but she started up scared and laughed at her weak trembly ways, and her sleeping like a grand lady in the daytime, until she coughed so hard, I made out I was too serious to hear her pretty voice, and talked myself to keep her quiet, in my anxious way, about the times being so hard, and every thing getting from bad to worse over the country. I was fearing we'd have to leave the old place after all, or suffer for our bread. I was low-hearted in my ways, and she was hoping in hers, like her father was. She put her arm round me and talked on, while she smoothed my hair away under my cap with her little fingers, making me ashamed that an old woman like me, should be learning faith in God out of her own child's mouth, when it ought to have been me teaching and she learning. Long weeks went by in the same way of working and talking light for each other's sakes, when a day come that looked a little brighter than the rest, and we thanked God for the sun and the blue sky. Matty had got so she could not stand about much, and the old chair sat by the window every day, holding her in its ragged arms. She always had a pretty way of talking and she sat there with her eyes looking a long way off, as if she learnt all her sweet words from the sky. This time she said softly, 'Mother, I don't blame the boys for fighting for Dixie, it is such a beautiful land! I used to think it was prettier than heaven when John was here.' The sun was shining, and I thought when I followed her eyes out of the window, that if all the blood that was flowing was to flow in vain, the living would be slaves and only the dead men free! A shadow fell across the door and I knew it was Davy's. Matty sprang past me, and turned back. I stopped and looked, then we fell into each other's arms like two dead women! It was Davy, but not the Davy that went away, he was a boy, and this was an old man's face that laughed in ours, and threw his bony arms about, crying, 'I'm so hungry! so hungry!' We kissed each other, and then rose to kiss him, but he bit my face until I screamed and fell back shuddering with pain, and afraid to look that way again. Matty led him to the hearth; the old chair and the clock and my wheel seemed to stir his heart, for he wasn't so wild, and looked around laughing as if he knew it was home, but it was a foolish laughing that hurt our hearts, and we knew he never was to be right-minded any more. I needn't name the place where he had been, for Davy can hear it in his sleep, and then there's no calming my poor daft boy, and when I see him in his worst ways, I think I lose myself and say too bitter things of them I'm trying hard to forgive. He's forever dreaming he's hungry, waking or sleeping, and never knows he's got enough. It's a hard thing for a mother to look on, and know it will never pass away! Matty and I couldn't smile any more, we'd look at each other with wet faces and still tongues, sometimes there wouldn't be a word spoke in that house all day long, but, 'I'm so hungry! so hungry!' We didn't look up often, it was so hard to see a skeleton sitting on the floor, laughing at the specks floating through his fingers to the light, or eating forever and ever, whether any thing lay before him or not; you think it's a sad sight now, but it was a sadder one then for I had nothing but bread some days to put in his hands. I was afraid he'd eat the flesh off mine or Matty's when we'd give it to him. I couldn't leave them by themselves to hunt for work, and it was only the little I had hid from the raiders that was left to live on. God knows how long it was, for we lost the count of weeks and months, and knew nothing but day and night until Davy's words seemed to eat our lives away! To pray and sleep was all the comfort we had, except loving each other more and more every day. One night I woke smelling fire, and Matty was coughing like she'd choke to death. O my God! I had a hard shaking ague with the hot flames leaping round me, and not a minute to save any thing but our lives, that was awful; but when I saw the black savages yelling outside, I'm an old woman and a strong one, but I fell against the wall with the horror on me! Matty led me and Davy out like children, the weak was strong in them days, and she knelt down with the flames flashing on her face and prayed to God to save us, and He did, for when they came near her, more than mortal strength was in her hands, and they shrunk off afraid she was so death-like and beautiful! We never asked black nor white for any thing; we was too proud, and we walked away, glad to leave the horrible sights and sounds and to get Davy where he wouldn't laugh so wild in our ears. The weather had turned bitter cold and though the sun had shone on the snow the day before, it lay sharp and white under our bare feet. I can shut my eyes now and see Matty leading the way in her white gown like a spirit. We walked awhile and rested awhile all night and the next day, and the next night we huddled together by a fallen tree and slept. Next morning we come to the cabin you told of, sir, and felt safe when we found it was close to our own soldiers. I got something to eat and work to pay for it from them, many a one helped me along by a kind word when he'd nothing else to give, but my poor girl never got over that night's sleep in the snow. Her eyes sunk deeper and deeper, the blood stole up from her heart and down from her cheeks, and one night I heard it gurgling through her lips, and rose up to see my darling die. I held her close to the fire, and tried to warm her cold hands in my bosom. She smiled and raised 'em up slow and tried to smooth my hair down, in her old way, but they fell round my neck and I leaned my face down to hers, it hung so heavy with the aching. I couldn't wake Davy, he'd a laughed, and I'd never heard her whispering, 'Mother, mother! There's no more hunger nor thirst, nor any more sorrow there!' It was 'mother! mother!' to the last, till I felt Death unlock her slender fingers from my neck and we fell back in the darkness. Davy woke me up in the morning, laughing and running his bony hands over his dead sister's face. I couldn't leave her there with him, I was afraid he'd bite her white cheeks, so I buried her without a coffin, and dug the grave myself. If her sweet lips could have spoke, I knew she'd say, 'Never mind, mother, it's only Matty's old dress you are laying by, she's got a new one up in heaven!' Thinking of the things she used to say, I took comfort from her silent face, laid the earth on it soft as any kisses, and come away to live for Davy. I knew there was many a one willing to help, but I couldn't go to find 'em, and there was no passing in and out of Corinth until orders was given to leave. When the soldiers scattered from the main body, hunting for water, they found me in my door, weak and sick of starvation; there was a few handfulls of parched corn left, but I couldn't eat a grain, fearing my boy'd go wild for the want of it, any more than I could beg the men for their bread. To them that had the money I sold water, and give it to the next that come for part of their rations. It was all I could do until we eat enough to get strength to come away. The well give out in a short time and then we staggered off and left Matty all alone by the road-side. It's there I'm going now, for we found friends to help us along, and God has dealt kindly with me and Davy, he an't so wild-like since he's got better to eat than bread. A heap of the old settlers has gone back I hear, and if I can earn enough to build a cabin by the side of Matty's grave, I'll stay there until we're called to meet father and Matty and John."

I sat still in the dim light of morning, and saw a fair, smooth hand, and a wrinkled hard one clasped together in sisterhood of grief and tenderness. The boy gazed about vacantly, eating an imaginary meal with claw-like fingers, and muttering in painful childishness, "I'm so hungry! so hungry!" These were the only sounds, until we three bowed our heads and wept together. The trains came at last—the old lady was going westward, and as the cars moved slowly past under the shed, I saw another handkerchief beside mine wave a blessing. Something flew in my eyes just then, it may have been a cinder, for it passed away as I raised my hat in answer to a smile of recognition from the beautiful face that had been my "*vis-a-vis*" across the hearth in the wayside hotel. We all have our stories, she had hers, but you are tired, my friend.

Good night!

"Dreadful Necessities"

Set in a stretch of northeastern Mississippi that endured stiff fighting, growing shortages, and withering disease, this "Road-Side Story" seems oddly overpopulated. Not the dilapidated family outside Corinth that loses husband, daughter, and daughter's husband; even son Davy returns home less than he once was, as though the war's privations were figured in this one family's diminishments. Rather, it is the way their tale is told that seems crowded. If this is a story about grief, about a homespun female "Abraham" whose son and the generation he embodies are sacrificed, then there is no real need for the frame story's railroad reception room or the depot fire that is "replenished" more than once. Alternately, if this is more surely a wartime account of Southern destitution, of cabin water sold, and of an army man's recognition that those at home also suffered, then the richly jacketed officer by the depot fire makes sense but not the fashionable lady, or her fawning clerk, or her whispered husband. So large a cast for so small a room is excessive, unless the story shares the perspective of the fashionable lady herself, quietly reproving the pompous officer who must reckon with the damage that regiments leave behind. Indeed, when this story's Abraham wears an old woman's bonnet and sturdy boots, the Bible's quintessential patriarch dissolves into a western woman with a frayed sewing kit, a gendered transformation that makes the jacketed officer recalling a sister's opera cloak seem altogether slight.

Written by Ina Marie Porter in Alabama but published anonymously in *The Land We Love*, "Road-Side Story" reveals more than a stubborn Southern patriarchy and the emerging strains of the Lost Cause. That is only one of several discreet adjustments engineered by a narrative whose shifting social order, depot setting, and Reconstructive calculus replace the puffed prose and masculine assertiveness of its opening lines. In their stead, as the train finally leaves the station, are several revisionist tallies that invite a gentler "reception," especially in the muscular *Land We Love*. For one thing, the patriarchal social order promoted by the magazine's two covers and its editor's repeated endorsements ends abruptly for the old woman prewar, when her husband's death becomes this story's originating event and makes the old woman a female head of household even before Mississippi seceded. For another, the frame story's railroad setting makes its chief narrator the figure of a newly mobile household order, a traveling old homestead that unsettles both domestic dependencies and masculine priorities. Finally, a surprising depot "sisterhood" that brings a handsome lady and a blacksmith's wife together effectively joins Old South privilege and New South endeavor, an eastern rustle and a western hardihood that render a Confederate officer's "chivalric defense" at once laughable and inept. For a story that appears to favor a shriveled household and a womanly lament, it is as though Governor Morehouse's Blandwood kitchen rises up against his Italianate tower.

Part of the reason for such covert insurgency in *The Land We Love* could be the distance from North Carolina's Mecklenburg traditions to Mississippi's Tishomingo County, where Corinth had been incorporated as recently as 1856. Yet Charlotte and Corinth had much in common on the eve of the war. Both were thriving cities where railroad lines intersected; Corinth was founded as "Cross City" in 1853, when it became clear that the tracks of the Memphis and Charleston Railroad were destined to cross those of the Mobile and Ohio. Both cities were thereby centers of commercial enterprise rather than plantation resistance; as Kristy Armstrong White has noted of Corinth, "Its population consisted mainly of small planters who did not own very many slaves, the land not being rich enough to support large-scale farming."[91] That population stood at 1,200 in 1860, just over half of the 2,265 reported the same year in Charlotte.[92] But the Mississippi town already supported the Corona Female College, which was founded in 1857, the same year the Charlotte Female Institute opened its doors. On the upswing thanks to significant rail access, Corinth could claim even more than Charlotte when war was declared. As Steven Nathaniel Dossman has observed in *Campaign for Corinth*, the well-positioned town became "the most strategic three feet of dirt in the entire Western Theater"—namely, the heart of the lower Mississippi River Valley where rail lines finally crossed.[93] As the first year of fighting drew to a close in early April 1862, both Union and Confederate armies fatefully converged just over twenty miles north in Tennessee for the onslaught that Charlotte managed to avoid, the horrific engagement that drives Davy mad.

Winston Groom has called the Battle of Shiloh "the first great and terrible battle of the Civil War," an unforeseen exercise in "ruthless battlefield butchery."[94] Napoleonic assaults in a new era of improved weaponry and unimproved medicine drove up casualty rates on April 6 and 7; Shelby Foote puts the two-day tally of deaths at 23,741, more than the losses of the Revolution, the War of 1812, and the Mexican War combined.[95] No wonder Davy babbles. Because he enlisted after Matty's husband, John, he seems to have joined the Corinth Rifles; that local regiment returned at the end of 1861 as part of the Ninth Mississippi, which filled its ranks with volunteers like Davy during the war's first winter. The motto of the Corinth Rifles was "This We Will Defend"; in a whispered reference from Porter's story, Davy tells his mother that he's leaving "to fight for you and Matty."[96] In the event, the newly created Ninth Mississippi Infantry was the only local regiment that saw action at Shiloh, deployed for what Groom calls "an instant bloodbath from buck and ball" on the battle's first day.[97] That could be where Davy's hunger begins: because the Confederate attack was delayed, all provisions were consumed at once. "It was a Confederate belief that rations carried lighter in the stomach than in a haversack," Foote writes, "and they had consumed their three days' rations at the outset."[98] Defeated Confederate soldiers may well have paused for water on their way back to Corinth, where conditions were quickly deteriorating.

The story of their thirst, of Davy's abject craving, and of his family's grim misfortunes was published alongside two further "Road-Side Stories" in *The Land We Love* (December 1866, January 1867). Alabama archivist Judy Atkins Taylor has confirmed that all three accounts came from Ina Marie Porter, a discovery that "Ida Raymond" (Mary T. Tardy) first documented soon after the stories appeared.[99] In *The Living Female Writers of the South*, she described this clutch of stories as "truly excellent pictures of 'life in Dixie.'" And she added, "Few, to read them, would think they were written under adverse circumstances—written during that period of desolation which followed the surrender of the 'Confederate cause.'"[100] Born in Tuscaloosa around 1845, Ina M. Porter had moved with her family to Greenville in southern Alabama to avoid Union troops. Jefferson Davis had appointed her father commandant of the camp of instruction for the region; he and his wife soon founded the wartime hospital in which the town's women regularly served. Their numbers thinned after Confederate surrender, however, and the Porter home was equally hard-pressed. As Raymond reported, "A friend tells me that Miss Ina Porter and her mother were the only available workers on the place—all the others sick, and the servants all left, except one, a girl, who had the small-pox, and was of no assistance. Mrs. Porter was physician and nurse, and Miss Ina cook and maid of all work."[101] A collaborative domestic partnership thus developed between Greenville mother and daughter, much like that between the widow and her Matty.

For them, the war's "dreadful necessities" soon mean caring for a "skeleton" Davy and charging for water to pay for food. Ten miles outside Corinth, they manage to avoid the order for all citizens to depart on April 9, when the city was turned into what local historian Margaret Greene Rogers describes as "a vast hospital center."[102] Kate Cumming, who served in the city as a nurse, reported that the Tishomingo Hotel and every other sizable building took in Shiloh's wounded Confederates, who were starving. When the regiments of General P. G. T. Beauregard's Army of Mississippi evacuated at the end of May, they left behind what Cumming called "a desolate place," with bad water and men "begging for a mouthful to eat."[103] As Dossman notes, drinking water was scarce and sanitation inadequate, which led to typhoid, dysentery, and measles, even for the Federal troops that occupied the city after the Battle of Corinth on October 3–4.[104] During the months to come, Union raids for food and supplies stripped Mississippi households that had already been scavenged, first by Confederate stragglers and local guerrillas seeking Union sympathizers and then by cavalry and deserters from both sides. "Homes wasn't homes any more," the old woman reports. She calls the raids "stealing," while Matty insists the raiders are "capturing." Either way, the acute losses of the battlefield become in Porter's story the acute hunger of roadside cottages, where a ravenous Davy bites his mother's bending face.

In the absence of protection and coverture's patriarchal guarantees, what Joan Cashin has termed "the antebellum bargain between men and women," the roadside family falls back on the "autonomy" Cashin's "bargain" had reserved for men.[105] The old woman spins and knits, then looks for work and for the hospital "physic" that Matty's growing cough requires. Matty weaves and sews; as she puts it, thinking of her husband, "Let me work, it feels like I was standing guard in his place." The two women labor in a struggling Corinth world where "every body was working." Without father, husband, or brother, Matty and her mother substitute a collaborative domestic economy: "Two widows lived and worked together" even to provide "soldier clothes" to Corinth men without women, an offer of substitute protection rather than substitute sanctuary. As McCurry has pointed out, white Southern women no longer clung to being "outside war," what she terms "Antigone's claim."[106] Instead, the old woman has seen Davy off to war as an Abraham sacrificing an Isaac now that her husband is gone.

Arguably, the transformative potential of a woman in patriarchal shoes is abbreviated by the loss of her "snug little cottage" and the family's sudden itinerancy. As George Rable has noted in *Civil Wars: Women and the Crisis of Southern Nationalism*, at least a quarter of a million wartime Southerners left their homes behind.[107] "Women headed most refugee families," Rable has written before concluding, "Their experiences and the inevitable clashes with new neighbors sorely tested the capacity of Southerners not only to make sacrifices for the Confederacy but also to give up outmoded social practices."[108] In the "bitter cold" of 1864 and one of the worst Mississippi winters on record, the snug cottage catches fire, and the family departs with nothing: "We never asked black nor white for any thing," Porter writes; "we was too proud, and we walked away, glad to leave the horrible sights and sounds." In this "Road-Side Story," like so many other stories in *The Land We Love*, the Southern home and family are fatally damaged. By the time the cottage catches fire, the widow and her ailing daughter have surrendered their standing among sheltered women and become McCurry's "new political constituency," since they undertake the work of unprotected women and approach what McCurry calls "political personhood."[109] Because of the war's deprivations, Matty and her mother are suddenly seen, suddenly heard, suddenly counted.

Ina Marie was no Matty. She survived the war and remained at home in one of Greenville's first families. As a result, she was neither mobile nor abandoned, but like this story's "refined" young lady she met refugee women who were. In her "Interesting Reminiscences of Greenville in the 60's," she commented that, at the hospital, "a widow, a poor wife whose husband was in the army was sometimes employed there and the 'leftovers' helped to support her little children."[110] This story could belong to that stranded woman, whom Porter found significant enough years later to recall. But neither in her "Reminiscences" nor in her story did Ina Marie fully reconceive Southern social relations. As another Jefferson Davis or Thomas Jefferson or Andrew Jackson might have predicted, it is escaping contrabands who set fire to the cottage and "the black savages yelling outside" who finally threaten the shrinking white family's survival. In part, that is an acknowledgment of the enslaved people who left Alabama plantations by the hundreds and made for Union lines in Mississippi, especially after Lincoln announced the Preliminary Emancipation Proclamation in September 1862. In short order, occupied Corinth included one of the largest contraband camps of the war, with streets, wards, a school, a church, a hospital, and a commissary, as Cam Walker has documented.[111] In this "Road-Side Story," however, the promotion of independent white women and children marks the limit of imagined social transformation, at least for wartime Mississippi and for *The Land We Love* thereafter. Here contraband camp order is recast as black roadside assault, a dependent uprising made "savage" as an antebellum social order gives way.

It is thus one of the hidden functions of this story's framing depot to contain black male threat while bearing witness to white female emancipation, at least in travel. As Cashin notes, "Before the Civil War, many women had never even been on board a train."[112] Laura Edwards elaborates in declaring that antebellum white women were homebound, "subject to the governance of a household head. They could move in the physical space outside the household's borders, but they could not claim the requisite civil and political rights that would allow them to assume the same independent public personas that white male household heads did."[113] The result is a story of circumspect revolt, a story in which the simple prose of an old woman literally replaces the fussy syntax of a Confederate officer whose "busy brain" reveals an impatience with the "ungrammatical." At first, his self-important spiel crowds everything, given his "expanding interest in the joys and sorrows of my fellow-creatures" and his "roundabout dissertation on . . . already exhausted subjects." For his replacement narrator, however, rail travel may be a "new thing," but she already has the wit to declare of her story that "it is not very long, sir, in words, but some days would stretch themselves out into years, just like I've seen the little saplings throw long shadows across my yard when the sun was sinking down." In the nighttime depot, the old woman finds an adept public voice for harsh domestic matters, noticeably in a public "reception-room."

The richly jacketed officer relies on class prerogatives, which historians have found hard to confirm in wartime depots and railroad cars. Rable observes that "even on the railroads the social hierarchy broke down as women and children of all classes rubbed elbows."[114] That sounds like the reception-room conversation in "Road-Side Story," though Cashin is more cautious. "While it is risky to generalize about so many transient meetings under such duress," she writes, "it seems clear that the war did not erase all social distinctions among refugees. The once-affluent felt contempt and pity, sometimes mixed together, for women who had absolutely nothing as their households fell apart."[115] It is therefore intriguing that the old woman, when she tells her story, puts her hand to her throat rather than her heart. "I must tell you why I sold the water, it does me good here," she says, as though it were more important to find her voice in public than to sequester her woes at home. Hers is the gesture of a citizen rather than a citizen's wife, and it turns this story into a virtual petition, like those arising across the South from hard-pressed women crippling the legal fiction of coverture. In "Road-Side Story," the old woman is already a widow but one speaking out, hand to throat, for reasons of her own.

So did Ina Marie Porter, well beyond this story. After the Civil War, she joined the Ladies' Society for the Burial of Deceased Alabama Soldiers, which complicates a reading of her old woman. When the society's name changed to the Alabama Ladies' Memorial Association (LMA) with annual dues of "one dollar," it seems unlikely that the blacksmith's widow would become a member or that she would be as committed as Ina Marie to the first stirrings of the Lost Cause.[116] Notably, Caroline Janney has argued in *Remembering the Civil War* that "LMAs had embraced the name 'ladies' in 1866–67 to reclaim their position as ranking members of society in the wake of emancipation."[117] The depth of their polite rancor can also be gauged in *The Land We Love*, when contrabands set fire to the roadside cottage. In an unsettling narrative economy, it is the eviction of white women and children that provokes the story's gendered insurgency but then ensures its conservative aims; even earlier, it is the "rustle" of a well-bred lady's dress that awakens a Confederate officer's willingness to reconsider depot possibilities. In Porter's story, the old woman will never take up quite as much space on Confederate platforms as the smartly dressed lady, which Porter's obsequious station clerk could verify.

But the "dim light of morning" nevertheless finds "a fair, smooth hand, and a wrinkled hard one clasped together in sisterhood of grief and tenderness," as a returning male narrator discovers. It therefore seems wise to recall that, for Laura Edwards, the Civil War fatefully transformed the status of domestic premises: "War and emancipation shook the antebellum household to its foundations, destabilizing the configuration of private and public power it supported" and turning "household" into "a highly contested political issue."[118] In her view, "household" had historically produced in the South a "discourse that revolved around the interests of propertied white men and silenced those of everyone else."[119] It is thus worth looking more closely at an old woman who is no longer "silenced," especially as a narrator.

For her, the war becomes an accelerating experience of family misfortune. In Kara Walker's terms, the old woman is a version of the dark cutout, a depot silhouette in "dim light" of someone who hasn't previously mattered. She is Bobbie Ann Mason's Vietnam vet, Katherine Anne Porter's vexed photograph, Joycelyn Moody's unwelcome storyteller with a message for recent students of color. But the Confederate officer and the fashionable lady? In the nighttime depot, they are bystanders, those ushered into "vulnerable times" like so many magazine readers. Caught in postmemory's troubled aftermath, they imagine both frontier woe and western fortitude, while the old woman inherits the "*right, conscience,* and *liberty*" of revolutionary Southerners. She may not be a Mrs. George Washington, fit for a latter-day postage stamp, but she's almost a Mrs. Benjamin Franklin, here a wife who has lost her man but not her "pocket-book" or her skill in stitching things together and bringing depot bystanders to tears.

Admittedly, her story's reception room is a transitory public stage. The waiting rail lines are also a mixed blessing, one that historically brought both Corinth's wartime trauma and Charlotte's postwar surge. As the story concludes, its remaining characters also part ways, the widow and Davy heading toward hardships to the west and the better-dressed travelers boarding a train heading east. In Charlotte's short-lived literary venture, editor Daniel Harvey

FIGURE 17. The Confederate Monument at the north side of Montgomery's historic capitol, erected in memory of the Confederate dead by the Ladies' Memorial Association, 1890. Photograph. Courtesy of Michael W. Panhorst.

Hill would warmly support female education and reluctantly publish women's fiction. But Martha Washington would never grace his cover, although she was the first First Lady, and neither would Mary Anna Jackson, although she was Hill's sister-in-law and one of the most celebrated Confederate widows of the postbellum years. Where they failed to command his attention, it is easy to see a nameless old woman getting lost.

Yet the "dreadful necessities" of her tale together with her resilience do not simply fade, even as the Confederate officer concludes "Road-Side Story." In its final scene, he and the handsome lady are visibly reduced to a raised hat and a waving handkerchief, a final tribute to the increased stature of the old woman and her boy. Unnamed to the very end, she effectively steals their scene with the "bundles" she carries and the "emaciated pocket-book" she opens for its "sewing-materials," the very sign of a self-reliant domesticity on the move. "It was not so much that white women emerged voluntarily out of the recesses of the household into public life during the war," writes McCurry, "as that the state came barging in their front door, catapulting them into a relationship they had never sought but could hardly refuse."[120] In the worst of times, the old woman steps up. Like the saplings she recalls, the Confederacy's poor petitioning women were beginning to throw long shadows.

With a similar resourcefulness, the Ladies' Memorial Association and its many local chapters would be instrumental in soliciting donations for a monument to the Confederate dead in Montgomery. The fundraising drive began in 1865, just before "Road-Side Story" appeared, though the LMA campaign was interrupted by the need to rebury Alabama soldiers tossed hastily into shallow Northern graves. It would be decades before their memorial was dedicated on December 7, 1898, when crowds would gather on Montgomery's Capitol Hill within yards of the spot where Jefferson Davis took the oath of office (figure 17). In 1900 Ina Marie Porter Henry Ockenden would edit a history of the Confederate Monument's protracted construction and would announce that "the noble shaft commemorates the heroism of man and of woman. It is the exquisite title page to the history of the Ladies' Memorial Association."[121] The monument would include four white granite figures representing the infantry, the cavalry, the navy, and the artillery—all suitably male.

But Michael Panhorst, former curator at the Montgomery Museum of Fine Arts, has also paused as Ockenden did on the monument's limestone shaft, topped by the bronze figure of *Patriotism*, notably female. "There is a consensus of opinion," Panhorst declares, "that southern white women carried the torch of remembrance for their lost husbands, sons, and fathers—especially during Reconstruction when Confederate veterans could not legally assemble lest they be charged with treason."[122] In her history, Ockenden reveres that elite contribution. She could afford the annual dues of the Ladies' Memorial Association, in which she was long active, and so could the rustling "lady" of her story. There, as later in Montgomery, it was the lady's role to stand as witness, to lend a sisterly hand, and to demonstrate even fictively who was included in McCurry's new political "we." A younger Porter's "Road-Side Story" thereby acknowledges the stature of white women too poor to wear petticoated silk and yet too capable to hide a willing needle. The visible authority of such Antigones in *The Land We Love* came, however, at the expense of imagining Alabama's Bens or the racial advances that could rededicate a revolutionary nation. Those left to witness a reconstructing order's social damage in the South would play decidedly different roles as postwar Chicago stitched together a separate peace.

CHAPTER 3

Railroaded

The Western War, Railroad Sprawl, and Chicago's *Lakeside Monthly*

During the 1860s and beyond, the quickening circulation of nineteenth-century magazines owed much to the wartime spread of railroads, enough for innovative delivery practices to give the Civil War's first stories a head of steam and thus a new narrative urgency. Amid the upheaval of civil crisis, newly circulating periodicals could well have seen in the railroad's iron path and thundering power something of President Lincoln's stern purpose in proclaiming emancipation or General Grant's tenacity in approaching the gates of Richmond. Long associated with gathering speed, the railroad could offer a visible sign of the northern zeal that would soon claim the postwar territories to the west and a ruined South hungry for "improvements." Just as importantly, a developing rail network had already encouraged the widening markets, swift dissemination, and keen demand for periodicals in which the experience of civil cataclysm was first imaginatively distilled. Between the fall of Fort Sumter in 1861 and the Centennial celebrations in 1876, railroad lines helped engineer both the invasion of troops and the spread of literary magazines, so it should come as no surprise that railroads might take their place in early Civil War stories with all the impact of newsmagazine pages thrown from passing mail cars (figure 18).

But among hundreds of short war fictions published before Centennial festivities ended, railroads actually figure much less often as hurtling machines in the garden than as accessible public lobbies—that is, as platforms, stations, and depots. Instead of standing in for imperial appetite, such spaces recall the persisting claims of the local, even in a postwar nation bound together by newly laid ties. Curiously, recollected depots insinuated less of an iron grip and more of a deliberate pause, the site at which competing narrative priorities would gather. Because that pause to consider then became the unexpected hallmark of railroad scenes in the war's first fictions, both for Chicago's *Lakeside Monthly*

FIGURE 18. Winslow Homer, *News from the War*, detail. Wood engraving. *Harper's Weekly*, June 14, 1862, 376–77. Courtesy of the University of Iowa Libraries.

and for magazines founded elsewhere, expanding rail technologies proved consequential, especially for examining how memories of the war took shape after 1861 and how far their narrative rumbles could be carried.

In magazine after magazine, story after story, unexpected patterns soon developed. Most plainly, the fictional platforms from which local heroes depart, the remembered stations in which furloughed veterans check their baggage, and the sheltering depots at which refugee heroines dodge the artillery blasts of siege guns were almost always cast as hurried and heterogeneous, crammed like Grand Central with a hodgepodge of strangers. Insistently, travelers are seen together in public space that must be negotiated and that becomes a metaphoric alternative to the more settled places that many characters leave behind, places such as Boston and Chicago but also Virginia and Louisiana, Ohio and Florida. In fact, travel makes even settled places exotic, especially for traveling Northerners who could see the past become spatialized. That whiff of modernity eventually turns an imagined railroad depot into a crowded hiatus, a temporal gap that produces the growing disruption of story breaks, flashbacks, and multiple storytellers whose control of narrative time is negotiated in the blink of an eye, the opportunity of a pause. So the advent of new rail lines for writers both north and south of the Mason-Dixon Line seemingly invited the kindness of strangers, nowhere more so than in Chicago as the country's preeminent rail hub.

In addition and more specifically, the war stories that appeared in Chicago's *Lakeside Monthly* (1869–74) were uncommonly attentive to something broken and then replaced—a father's blessing, an engagement, the regiment's commitment, planter authority. What arose as a result was a peculiar double vision of the new nation about to emerge, a distinctly western vision of early allegiances regrafted when binding ties to family (white and black, native and foreign-born) were pulled loose. For a magazine that would devote a full issue and more to the catastrophic fire that swept across the city in October 1871, the singe of civil war would be keenly felt as both rupture and repair, especially in a state such as Illinois, which had long been as politically divided as the country would become. In the tumultuous weeks after Lincoln's election in 1860 and then later when the war was recalled in the *Lakeside Monthly*, Chicago's unusual dependence upon available labor and urban workers, who generally arrived from somewhere else, would help redefine the postwar case for emancipation, most pointedly by extending claims on liberty and justice to wage slaves.

In the end, what railroads imaginatively provided to those recollecting the war were sites of intersection, which means that the war figured for a significant number of stories as social traffic rather than perpetual motion. In a depot crowd that could suggest newly emerging relations among strangers, there was also a selective emphasis, and the *Lakeside Monthly* helps to reveal why. Arguing stoutly for emancipation, the magazine rarely imagined those once enslaved with much dimension, at least not as the war's protagonists and chief legatees. Yet because the Union's Illinois regiments were generally posted to remote Southern locales, Illinois men often returned with unconventional stories. As a result, the *Lakeside Monthly* fitfully queried the country's social foundations—family, home, property—and a reunited nation's abrupt evolution. In place of the Union as it was, however, the magazine's stories recalled a more unsettling war that Dana Luciano helps link to the American Revolution, as well as to the countermonumental sway of remembered bids for social justice that go far toward explaining the gathering crosswinds of Reconstruction.

When tracing such patterns while war stories, literary magazines, and new tracks multiplied beyond Chicago, it is also worth recalling the shadow network and deliberate pauses of the Underground Railroad. As Larry Gara has pointed out in *The Liberty Line*, the channels of self-emancipated escape became a "railroad" in contemporary reports because of their local "stations," regional "conductors," and interstate "tracks."[1] Underground transactions described in literary accounts of the 1860s and 1870s also placed less emphasis on the momentum of national will than on the assistance of local hands, aid that enslaved people would seemingly reciprocate in Northern stories of escape from Confederate prisons. By contrast, the stories of escaping soldiers had a good deal to say about the daily hardships of the journey north, unlike the tales of those escaping slavery. When magazines with varying agendas conspicuously made black journey less important than white reception, made slave "travelers" count for less than abolitionist "conductors," and made federal jurisdiction less compelling than local help, it would not be enough that resolute fugitives secured a mute or ventriloquized place on the "train," especially a place that Homer Plessy in 1896 would eventually lose. The "stations" that brought so many Civil War characters together often left silent African Americans fundamentally amorphous, and their hazy future became a matter of local color rather than federal proclamation.

This underground tug on the national imaginary was admittedly sporadic and noticeably diminished after 1862, when freedpeople could escape languishing plantations by traveling more openly, by migrating to Union camps, and by enlisting in the U.S. Army. Yet before the Emancipation Proclamation went into effect on January 1, 1863, there was at least one story of underground movement worth examining, a story that was published by Boston's *Continental Monthly* and set, importantly, on the Ohio River. The "mysterious agency" that a Cincinnati heroine joins in "Fugitives at the West" (May 1862) underlines the political gravity of a more clandestine and still crowded hiatus, a western "station" where a Christian minister's daughter, a hobbled black gardener, a mixed-blood seamstress, and a white man with a covered cart could work together to turn local aid into quiet speed.[2] Ultimately, Miss S. C. Blackwell's story underscores their intersection and its transformative potential by centering on a white girl's political awakening as an escaping slave holds out her hand for food. After being fed and bonneted, the anonymous fugitive is guided "from point to point and friend to friend" on a covert "railway" whose stations function less as interludes than as reveilles, wake-up calls for western "agents" and eastern readers alike.[3]

In its preoccupation with a "wide and deep" sympathy for broken slave families, this story aims for the sentimental clutch of Harriet Beecher Stowe's *Uncle Tom's Cabin*, which Blackwell references at the outset and Dana Luciano has probed in *Arranging Grief*, her study of nineteenth-century loss and its weight on narrative time.[4] For Luciano, tears shared over Stowe's best-selling novel rehabilitated the mythic tug of the country's originating trauma in 1776. "That appeal," she writes, "refounds the nation itself as a collection of familially oriented subjects seeking a millennial and fundamentally maternal regeneration of damaged national time," a universalizing appeal Luciano describes as "monumental."[5] In a rush of brief accounts that exemplify the need for underground "tracks" through Cincinnati, Blackwell repeats Stowe's model by including another Eliza with her child in her arms, another aging Tom and his Phillis, another Mrs. Bird and her empty nest. All serve to confirm the potency of the maternal and what Luciano calls "the natural time of affection" and its broad appeal, the "restorative feeling-in-common of sympathy."[6] So familiar was that narrative summons by 1862 that, just as Luciano might have predicted, Blackwell's story initially seems less a contrived fiction than a chronicle of observed events, all steadily intended to make converts of *Continental Monthly* subscribers as Blackwell's Ohio matron is converted by her preacher's daughter.

Against Luciano's entrée to feminized national time, Rebecca Harding Davis's "John Lamar" (also published in Boston during the same year) appears both masculine and rude, its women made peripheral to a callow bonhomie and a field hand's revolt. In a bolder and far brisker fashion, Davis's three flashbacks allow an impersonal narrator to recall the earlier days of her three men, timely gestures that tie family bonds to differing definitions of liberty for an idealistic Union captain, his Confederate cousin, and the Southerner's resentful slave. Just as their remembered childhoods fade, however, their older allegiances give way to three reconceptions of revolutionary pledges and a founding American covenant's legitimate heirs. Most receptive to a boatman preacher's "shrill voice" and a panting slave's "melancholy cry," Davis's story pointedly exchanges a young wife's muffled sobs and a young sister's ready tears for slave blood that "throbbed," a narrative achronology that picks up speed thanks to a deft storyteller who inhabits all three perspectives without losing a command of clear-eyed questions.[7] While the country's mythic origins are variously reinterpreted, Davis's narrative velocity and her sure-footed conclusion are no more in doubt than her slave's northerly progress. With a near balance of scenes (twenty-six), pauses (twenty-five), summaries (twenty-seven), and ellipses (twenty), the pace of narrative time in "John Lamar" is modulated to guarantee that "manly" souls prevail and that the judgment of the Lord is left for readers to determine.[8]

By comparison, "Fugitives at the West" is familiar in its maternal focus, predictable in its sentimental underpinnings, untidy in its lengthy pauses, but unexpectedly daring in its delivery, especially its embedded stories. Unlike Davis's agile narrator, who intervenes to examine the perspective of her principals each in turn, Blackwell's narrating matron welcomes the nested stories of others. The hungry fugitive tells of her escape with her "old man," their brutal capture ("down on the ground like beeves"), and their renewed escape, though her husband still "shakes like a leaf" and her face is so bruised that she can scarcely see.[9] The student of theology (and antislavery beliefs) reports their passage farther north in the covered cart. The mixed-blood seamstress seizes the narrative for so long that she gets named: Sallie Smith also narrates the story's earliest events, when her daughter is claimed by her white husband's creditors as property to cover his debts. Unlike Davis's avenging slave, Blackwell's Sallie challenges Virginia's large corner of the country's mythic past as surely as she shakes a fist in the face of an "ole slaveholder"—and then joins Cincinnati's "negro church" to become an eloquent speaker for the Lord.[10] As she declares, "He will shake and shake the nations, and will say: 'Let my people go free.'"[11] In this story's comparatively sloppy pacing—with two scenes, thirteen pauses, thirty-six summaries, and twenty ellipses—Sallie almost makes an embedded narrator of God, and she anticipates the time of divine deliverance. Where Davis's narrator creates a new "North" as her slave sees it, Blackwell creates slave narrators, the time of deliverance along the Ohio River, and thus a crowded "railway" hiatus whose self-emancipated fugitives speak their mind.

Yet against this fleeting Cincinnati way station are more than thirty stories in which imagined platforms were not underground in any sense. Instead of negotiating a geographical divide like Miss Blackwell's Ohio River, which lay between slavery in the South and freedom in Canada, stations in various stories from various magazines were positioned between a settled past and an uncharted future. In a narrative economy where time and space could become entangled, the railway station then functions as a hiatus whose transformative capacities are less certain and whose "whirling" or "rushing" or "rattling" locomotive suggests what Wolfgang Schivelbusch has called "the railroad's continuous evolution toward ever greater speed, regularity, and uniformity."[12] Often in these imagined accounts, the railroad setting is naturalized and distinctly local: William Sikes in "One of My Scholars" for *Harper's Monthly* (October 1865) describes the "unwonted bustle and confusion" of the platform, where a neighboring regiment pours out "like a swarm of gay-colored bees" as families say goodbye.[13] In other stories, the station is more unruly and yet more reconstructively charged: Margaret Vane Hastings sees bustling hackmen and irritable baggage masters, "choking dust" and "the usual mêlée of leave-takings and greetings" in "Lois Pearl Berkeley" for the *Continental Monthly* (November 1864); her story thereby neglects the restorative "visions of cool, green forest depths" to which her sick veteran would like to return, his version of home as it was.[14] Instead, Hastings substitutes the mêlée of camp life, what she calls "this commingling on one level of all ranks and conditions of men in the same broad glare of every-day trial."[15] It is a "commingling" that will upset local order and produce national heroes, likely at the expense of the girls they leave behind. In the imagined war of literary magazines, a crowded hiatus could help initiate national citizens by uprooting neighborhood boys as regiment after regiment was transported to the front.

The cost of commingling, often obscured in the war's first narratives, was easier to glimpse in later stories if military service proved disruptive, if families found it harder to part. That was particularly true for the white boys who had rarely left home and for their girls who refused to stay put. When an addled sister tries to follow an Ohio regiment in Rebecca Harding Davis's "Ellen" for the *Atlantic Monthly* (July 1865), it is hard to dismiss the "great innocence and purity" of her love for her brother, hard to cheer the boisterous "crowd of men, with whips, calling out" and "plucking" on her shawl when the railroad cars stop, and hard to approve the "shrill cry" of the wartime train that is "rushing thus into a world that opened suddenly wider and darker before her."[16] In the Civil War's first stories, trains almost always rush offstage, or the characters on them jostle each other when they might have looked out the window, or they look out the window only to see the "unwonted bustle and confusion" of recurring platforms when they had hoped, like sick veterans, for "cool, green forest depths." Ellen's unfailing innocence suggests that, for the *Atlantic Monthly*, old village ties were harder to surrender and not necessarily lost when wartime engines picked up speed. Family affection simply rode the rails.

On other fictive platforms of the 1860s and 1870s, negotiating with strangers proved to be both promising and fraught. Historically, yoking local interests to distant cities had been the stated aim of early railroad construction for decades, when funding for new lines was often solicited from the farmers and merchants that the lines would serve and thus from local interests seeking wider markets for freight. While northern capitalists would come to see postwar trunk lines (or main routes) as "their new standard of union and social order," in Sarah Gordon's brisk phrase from *Passage to Union*, the "local conflicts" out of which financial backing and antebellum legislation first arose would persist.[17] After all, the rural routes and differing gauges of many lines were purposefully designed to buttress local control; the normative time zones of a more integrated rail network would not arrive until 1883.[18] In 1861, by contrast, local concerns often prevailed: through travelers had to change trains eight times between Charleston and Philadelphia, for example, and not simply from want of railway planning. As John Stover has observed in *American Railroads*, "Tavern keepers, teamsters, and porters were happy that not a single rail line entering either Richmond or Philadelphia made a direct physical connection with any other railroad entering the city."[19] Since rail lines had not previously favored through traffic beyond the cities whose growing orbits they had traditionally served, their fraught promise was creatively registered during the Civil War and Reconstruction in narrative returns to one packed depot after another.

Just as creatively, the several postal reforms that would dramatically affect the distribution of Civil War stories and the magazines in which they appeared were increasingly made between depots, often to assure better city service once railroads became responsible for most postal transport (figure 19). Because expanding rail technologies could handle bulkier mails, magazines in the North

FIGURE 19. *The Lightning Postal Train from New York to Chicago*. Wood engraving. "The Fast Mail to Chicago," *Harper's Weekly*, October 9, 1875, 816. Courtesy of the University of Iowa Libraries.

found a surer berth with newspapers after the Postal Law of 1863 abolished the distinction between them, thereby creating second-class mail for all periodicals. That legislation in turn provided a boost to the periodical club system, which rewarded groups of subscribers who received bulk deliveries at a single post office. Because delays in routing bundles were often exacerbated by the practice of sorting mail upon arrival, magazines and their stories would reach subscribers more quickly after railway mail cars, which James Bruns in *Mail on the Move* has called "rolling redistribution centers," were fully in place with special fittings and trained clerks by 1864.[20] Because rail lines were extended and beginning to merge by 1869, when the Ward mail-bag catcher was adopted, the "on the fly" pickups that were illustrated in *Harper's Weekly* promised "a progress of vast proportions."[21] Fast trains sorting mail en route for every postal station along the way eventually abbreviated delivery time without fully abandoning smaller depots, though their local connections were more sharply limited, more often "on the fly." As vehicles for promoting reliable mail service and what Carlene Stephens has described as "lucrative postal contracts," railroads regularly aimed for greater speed and thus faster delivery.[22] But their schedules also reckoned, in the immediate aftermath of the Civil War, with the wayside depots and local concerns that lingered when the war's first stories were told.

Such developments were still in the offing as antebellum Illinois and its enviable port on Lake Michigan attracted immigrants, settlement opportunities, and booming trade. In *Nature's Metropolis*, William Cronon argues that Chicago was positioned "like an artificial spider suspended at the center of a great steel web."[23] Indeed, the city itself looked like a web, as an early aerial view in *Harper's Weekly* revealed and an early contributor to New York's *Putnam's* confirmed (figure 20). Observing in "Chicago in 1856" (June 1856) that the city's growth was "conspicuous" and its motto was "ONWARD," this visitor described the urban scheme that the Harper art department later drew: "Take the letter H; call the upright column on the right hand the lake shore; let the crossbar represent Chicago River, the left hand column will stand for the two branches, and you have a plan of the water lines of the city of Chicago."[24] The result, quickly noted, was a city with three divisions—the North Side on the right, the South Side on the left, and the West Side to the rear along the horizon. Once a trading post on the lake's muddy shore and then, from 1803, the frontier site of Fort Dearborn, the city was incorporated in 1837. Thereafter, each river-bound city division would assume its own character as settlement patterns differed markedly.

What Bessie Louise Pierce has described as a "continuing stream of newcomers" in her three-volume history of Chicago was encouraged by work on

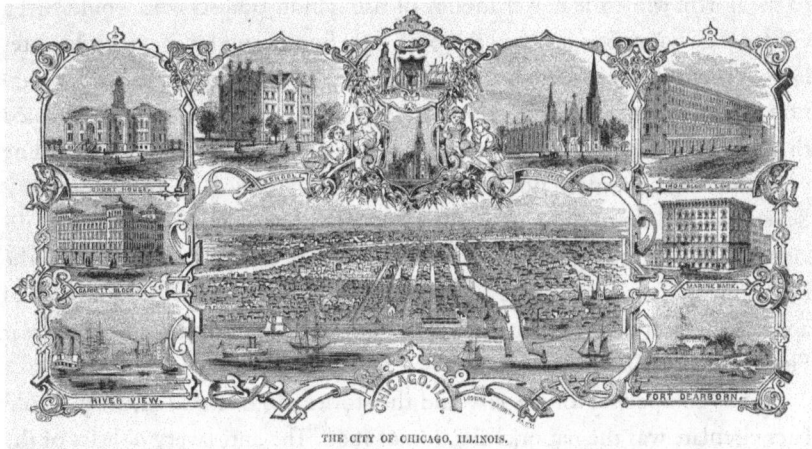

FIGURE 20. *The City of Chicago, Illinois*. Wood engraving. *Harper's Weekly*, September 10, 1859, 580. Courtesy of the University of Iowa Libraries.

the Illinois and Michigan Canal beginning in the 1830s, by the construction of plank roads during the 1840s, and by the Illinois Central as railroad tracks were laid into the South during the 1850s, while steamships and Conestoga wagons brought entrepreneurs, shopkeepers, and unskilled laborers to Chicago's growing commerce in grain and lumber, cattle and hogs.[25] By 1860, as Theodore Karamanski has noted in *Rally 'Round the Flag: Chicago and the Civil War*, German artisans and shopkeepers represented approximately 20 percent of Chicago's population; they lived across the city but tended to dominate in the middle-class neighborhoods of the "Nord Seite," along with a sprinkling of Scots and Scandinavians in wood-frame cottages and the Irish in the shabbier streets of Kilgubbin.[26] The South Side had become a business district filled with hotels, boardinghouses, shops, banks, and docks, with the homes of prosperous businessmen along Michigan Avenue and, farther inland, those of the Irish stevedores, teamsters, and factory workers who made up roughly 18 percent of the city's residents. On the West Side were small numbers of unassuming bourgeois homes, plus the working-class "cabins"—German, Irish, and Bohemian—that Pierce sees mushrooming by 1865.[27]

During the postwar years before the Great Chicago Fire of 1871, settlement patterns shifted somewhat, due in large measure to what John Jentz and Richard Schneirov have described as a fundamental economic reorientation. Their *Chicago in the Age of Capital* documents the lapse of "the old producers' republic" when prewar boosting gave way to a "class-divided capitalist social order."[28] By 1870 the "boosters" with the deepest pockets had long since built mansions to the north, while the newer money of rising industrialists who would fuel a Gilded Age boom was invested in South Side homes and businesses, which relied on the labor of those most often to the west.[29] "No matter what their national origins," Jentz and Schneirov observe, "artisan entrepreneurs transformed themselves into employers, not masters of a craft, and their employees became permanent wage earners, not journeymen and apprentices on their way to independence."[30] From the muddy earth of early Indian paths to the watery divisions of a developing city, from the airy promises of western wealth to the fire that would consume entire postwar neighborhoods, Chicago was elemental and raw, preoccupied with commerce, wealth, and labor in ways that the Great Fire would both destroy and resurrect.

Just as compelling for the city and the stories the *Lakeside Monthly* would later circulate was the national election of 1860. The antislavery politics of the previous decade found willing champions in Chicago, where the newly organized Republican Party met to choose a presidential candidate. As Karamanski has observed, "It is doubtful Lincoln would have been president had the convention been held in another city."[31] When Chicago votes were counted on November 6, Lincoln garnered ten thousand, as Pierce details, thanks to Wide Awake clubs, torchlight parades, North Side enthusiasm, and the vigorous support of the *Chicago Tribune*. But the election's Democratic candidate, Stephen A. Douglas, was himself a Chicagoan and polled eight thousand votes from the city's South Side businessmen and its outspoken Irish laborers, groups that read the reactionary *Chicago Times* and benefited from the land grants and federal funding Douglas secured to put railroads at the center of Cronon's "steel web."[32] Pierce points out that Southern sympathizers known as Copperheads elected a Democrat as the city's mayor in 1863, before Lincoln was reelected to higher office by fewer than two thousand local votes in 1864.[33] While some in the city were fervently devoted to antislavery politics as either a moral imperative or a ready shield against "Slave Power" interests spreading into the western territories, others refused to abandon older Democratic allegiances during or after the war.

Both factions prospered during the Civil War as Chicago's rail system expanded and the demand for war matériel intensified. Pierce observes that the city became one of the Union's chief military suppliers, specifically of "guns, bullets, and field ambulances, tents and uniforms, saddles and harnesses for horses," as well as quartermaster essentials like "oats, salt, pork, beef, bread, and lumber."[34] Given Chicago's ready access to rail transport, notes Karamanski, the city also became "the natural funnel through which Union forces in the West were provisioned."[35] During the war years, Chicago had good reason to recognize what William Thomas in *The Iron Way* calls "the importance of networks," which led a western general like William Tecumseh Sherman to revolutionize warfare through "fighting aimed at routes, bases of supply, communication, and transportation."[36] Those networks proved to be crucial in the war's Western Theater; many Illinois regiments marched with General Sherman across Georgia in 1864, just as they supported General Grant at Vicksburg in 1863 or, as Victor Hicken has demonstrated, saw early service in Illinois and Missouri, Kentucky and Tennessee.[37] The less familiar war they fought, often far from the pitched battles of Virginia, joined "networks" to heavy casualties and tied hinterland bivouacs to more rugged terrain. The later recollections of those in Illinois regiments, like those of largely forgotten observers in western parlors and parlor cars, would be deployed in narratives that rarely appeared in the *Atlantic Monthly* but did find a postwar outlet closer to home.

A crowded hiatus then and now, Chicago was alert to the railroad opportunities that literally helped fuel the *Lakeside Monthly*. Just two years after the Thirteenth Amendment abolishing slavery was ratified in 1865, newspaperman Francis Fisher Browne arrived in Illinois by way of Michigan, New York, Massachusetts, and Vermont, where he was born. In 1869 he acquired an interest in the new *Western Monthly*, which he would go on to edit and then rechristen the *Lakeside Monthly* in 1871. That year, as Michael Hackenberg has shown, the magazine's circulation reached nine thousand and then climbed to a high of fourteen thousand in 1873, a year before the venture failed.[38] Hackenberg notes that the *Lakeside Monthly* would provide "a satisfactory frontier voice and publishing forum for scores of local writers, whose literary works had little or no chance in the then established Eastern magazines."[39] Similarly, Frank Luther Mott describes the new monthly as "a distinctly sectional periodical," one that billed itself as "Devoted to Literature, Biography, and the Interests of the West" from the outset.[40] Shortly after its launch, the magazine in "Our Field" (April 1869) was touting a widening scope, "not the city of Chicago alone, but the entire West, from Minnesota to Texas, from Ohio to the Mountains."[41] Over the course of its extended run, the *Lakeside Monthly* would circulate essays on topics such as the "sable singers," Chinese labor, the free library movement, Civil Service reform, the Indian Territory, and moving the national capital west.

Instructively, Chicago's abolitionist priorities marked the magazine as early as its second issue. In an article titled "Suffrage" (February 1869), published just as the Fifteenth Amendment extending voting rights to African Americans was proposed in Congress, Sherman Booth declared with a western edge: "Surely dark-skinned loyalists are better citizens, and more deserving of trust, than white-livered traitors."[42] Yet the magazine's twelve Civil War stories were oddly ambivalent and quirky, set as they were in noticeably more western locales. In the pages of the *Lakeside Monthly*, the imagined war began for some on a farm in Ohio or aboard a railroad car in Illinois, while other contributors favored the war's Western Theater: eastern Tennessee or a Nashville cavern, the Kentucky springs or Kennesaw Mountain in northwest Georgia. Such narratives also featured odd casts, like an Ohio farmer and a soldier's sister, or a Northern colonel on an Illinois train and the Virginia hostess he recalls. Their preoccupations were unthinkable elsewhere: pagan rites and Far Eastern salaams, or mutiny at a Union camp in Louisiana some two months after Appomattox.

In the pages of the *Lakeside Monthly*, the railroad might have figured as a site of intersection because Chicago had long styled itself as the place where East met West—geographically, demographically, politically, culturally—and sometimes with the sting of Charlotte's "swarm." Protesting eastern elitism in "Current Notes" at the end of its first year (December 1869), the magazine queried with a snort, "What Western citizen has ever sat as a regent of the Smithsonian Institution?"[43] But such swipes generally subsided into a call for "reciprocity," which Browne's magazine was quick to foster.[44] In "East and West" (March 1869), G. Nelson Smith cast the East as "age, maturity, permanency, finish, wealth, intelligence, refinement and art" leavened with "a certain timidity," which "the great, broad, free West" as a "rude phantasmagoria" would challenge—not because East and West were "antagonists" or "rivals" but because, intersecting in Chicago, they served as "complements" with ambitions worth intertwining.[45] "If the sun does rise in the East," Smith wrote, "it spends at least half the day in the West."[46] On a national canvas, that diurnal model of reciprocity could work an entrepreneurial magic.

The city was already known for both outsized growth and self-promotion, what London's *Saturday Review* in "New Chicago" (December 27, 1873) called with a sniff "a continual supply of brag."[47] Growth and brag had actually been plentiful for decades as frontier Chicago sought eastern investment, especially amid recurring monetary alarms. Pierce has detailed the shortage of funds when the city incorporated during the 1830s and then the rush of "wildcat currency" before banks were established and steadier financing was assured.[48] As Cronon has pointed out, "Capital held one of the most important keys to metropolitan empire, which was why boosters wrote so many tracts making their case to potential investors."[49] Chicago's self-promotional maneuvering suggests a readiness to pitch western interests to eastern audiences even when recollecting the Civil War fictively, another exercise in reciprocity that would offer both a "rude phantasmagoria" and a subtler if suspect gentility.

Where Charlotte's *The Land We Love* ducked that city's postwar urban heterogeneity to foreground instead the nearby cotton fields, their enslaved labor force, and their barbed caste hierarchies, Chicago's *Lakeside Monthly* radiated the muscle, networks, and contending classes of a hungry city with more steel than soil and more explicit social friction than apparent social ease. Where Civil War stories in *The Land We Love* tarried in a white man's republic that never fully lapsed for D. H. Hill, despite multiple replacements and fiction's gendered challenge, recollections of the war in the *Lakeside Monthly* embraced racial politics but rarely dismissed the appeal of supposed antebellum homogeneity. One story suggested building a connecting passage between Northern and Southern homes, while another jockeyed between a Florida slave wife, a neighboring plantation mistress, and a marveling visitor from New England.

Closer to Baltimore's *Southern Magazine* in its characteristic vitality, the *Lakeside Monthly* was even more decidedly urban, particularly in the "Fire-Proof" issue (January 1872), which included multiple parts ("Before the Fire," "Burning of the City," "After the Fire," and "The Losses") before concluding with contributions from William Alvin Bartlett ("What Remains") and J. W. Foster ("New Chicago").[50] With a supplementary section as well, the *Lakeside Monthly* documented plenty of midwestern fortitude but refused the *Southern Magazine*'s tongue-lashings, as well as the regular escapes of the Baltimore periodical's war stories. Surprisingly attuned to the vulnerabilities of *The Land We Love*, the short war fiction that Francis Fisher Browne published refused to let go of a backwater past in chapels or caverns, around cottage hearths or on hotel verandahs. Even railroad scenes, whether underground or bound for the West, favored a crowded hiatus as a site of perpetual negotiation, which effectively postponed the frontier futures of both a Cousin Jack and an aging widow with needle and thread.

In the *Lakeside Monthly*, whose editor was trained in Massachusetts but whose initial backers came from Chicago's commercial sector, the best early indication of a municipal booster pitch aimed across half a continent was a series of tributes to the city's self-made men. For almost two years, each new issue opened with what the magazine described in "Current Notes" (December 1869) as "a biographical sketch of some *Western* man," a portrait meant to foreground the "go-aheaditiveness of Western people" as celebrated in the magazine's first "Editorial" (January 1869).[51] In his study of Chicago's early literary venues, Fredric John Mosher has noted that these *Lakeside* sketches were cash cows devoted to "some wealthy business man who was willing to pay for his portrait and biography."[52] It is true that subsidized biographies apparently produced an uptick in printed copies to be circulated among local acquaintances, until Browne finally "rescued" the *Lakeside Monthly* (as Frank Luther Mott put it) from "those vices of local magazines—indiscriminate 'boosting' and 'selections.'"⁵³ Nevertheless, the frontispiece engravings in these issues were handsome additions and the magazine's only early illustrations. More importantly, these sketches of local success reveal what version of "the West" the new magazine preferred and how wide a spectrum of Illinois "brag" was regularly featured. Even more insistently, the other pages of these early issues also suggest what the sketches of old settlers, new money men, and urban labor would repeatedly leave out.

The magazine's founding issue (January 1869) commenced with a portrait of the city's first mayor, one of Chicago's most resourceful immigrants (figure 21). In the *Lakeside Monthly*, the story of William B. Ogden proves to be one of "untiring energy," from his hunting and fishing in western New York, through his "diversified business pursuits" in Chicago during 1835, and, thereafter, to "the first floating swing bridge" across the Chicago River, "the first reaper sent to England," "the preservation of the public credit" during the panic of 1837, and "the great struggle with slavery" two decades later.⁵⁴ The redoubtable Ogden was the first president of Chicago's Rush Medical College, as well as president of the State Bank of Illinois–Chicago Branch and of the early University of Chicago's board of trustees. He was also heralded as the "Railway King of the West": the first president of the Union Pacific Railroad Company, he would also superintend a series of more local companies, including a "grand trunk line" from Chicago to Pittsburgh that would eventually provide a daily link to New York.⁵⁵ In this inaugural tribute to one of the city's oldest settlers, Chicago itself becomes a heterogeneous depot for freight, especially the lumber, iron ore, and coal that became Ogden's principal investments. The ebullient city's premier representative, he emerges from this sketch as a man of "unyielding will," as well as "cultivated tastes" and "large-hearted hospitality," just the man to carry Chicago's "go-aheaditive" banner across the country.⁵⁶

Ogden remained single until he was seventy. He would finally marry in 1875, just two years before he died and six years after the monthly's high praise appeared. In its enthusiastic portrait, his bachelorhood until late in life smoothly buttressed the magazine's gendered back-slapping and pointed to one assumption the profile casually endorses. As historian Pierce has observed, "In the eyes of the world, building a city on the marsh was man's work."⁵⁷ Even decades after the marsh vanished, the biographical sketches leading off each monthly issue were all of men, and their twenty-two portraits regularly cast the "untiring energy" and "unyielding will" of the West as conspicuously masculine.

But if muscle predominated in the first pages most readers saw, subsequent pages demurred. G. M. Kellogg, for instance, in "Self-Made Men" (July 1869) set aside masculine initiative to champion social exchange. "The key-stone

FIGURE 21. *Very Truly Yours W. B. Ogden.* Steel engraving. *Lakeside Monthly,* January 1869, frontispiece. Courtesy of the HathiTrust.

of civilization," Kellogg insisted, "is the domestic, social and national interdependence of man upon man."[58] He cheered the well-tutored while scorning autodidacts: "Self-taught men! Ridiculous pretense." He further stipulated that home schooling would be a collaborative effort from another "Mr. and Mrs. Noah" rather than an exercise in self-reliance.[59] Two issues later, the magazine's unillustrated profile of Harriet Beecher Stowe (September 1869), which was tucked between Frank Gilbert's "Chinese Ethics" and A. T. Freed's poem about the land of dreams, celebrated the author of *Uncle Tom's Cabin* as "the greatest of the great family" of Beechers and the "acknowledged queen" of a "brilliant" literary circle in antebellum Cincinnati, where her home served as the "active station" of the city's underground railroad. In the *Lakeside Monthly*, it was a small step from Stowe's conversations with hurried fugitives to an international best seller, the new Republican Party, and the more recent Emancipation Proclamation, all "betwixt the turning of griddle-cakes and the washing of dishes."[60]

Even more vigorously, Lawrence Leslie's "The Wife of Garibaldi" (June 1870) saluted a "dauntless" woman for accompanying her husband, "sharing the toils of the march, the dangers of the battle, the perils of the camp often pitched amid death-breeding marshes, fording rivers, crossing almost impenetrable forests, or fighting by his side."[61] No wonder Sherman Booth's "Suffrage" (February 1869) encouraged votes for women as "the next great reform," and Mat.

Hawthorn's "The Citizen as a Voter" (April 1869) confirmed a woman's "right to equal protection with man under the laws, her right to own and dispose of her personal property and income."[62] For Hawthorn specifically and for others tacitly in the magazine's most "self-made" issues, the key to "brilliance" or "dauntless" courage or "great reform" was work, widening contributions by "the laboring classes, the producers, the working, thinking PEOPLE" upon whom "republican institutions" could rely.[63]

Amid such gender play, it is noteworthy that Anna De Quincey's single *Lakeside* recollection of the Civil War, "A New Story of Lee's Surrender" (May 1871), revolves around hidden labor, first in Virginia as the war concluded and then on a Chicago-bound train where a Union colonel from the West shares the Virginia anecdote. In this story within a story, a plantation mistress welcomes General Lee and his retreating officers before playing a more reluctant hostess to General Grant and his staff. Ostensibly, De Quincey's point is a Union officer's discovery that Lee's army is heading toward Lynchburg instead of Danville, a timely revelation that the western colonel will share with the story's traveling narrator. But from this Virginia mistress's ill-timed boast, to the officer's wee-hours initiative (cajoling, listening, checking the "soft earth" outside for Confederate traces), and then to the framing narrator's self-sufficiency (insisting as she does on "the 'right' to secure my own checks and find my own seat in a crowded train"), each character works and eventually works in secret not only within the story but also to get the story told.[64] Just as assuredly as William B. Ogden in the Chicago marsh, this story passes from parlor to camp, to car, to print.

In the course of that extended effort, each narrator transforms ready confrontation (with a spiteful Confederate, a high-level subaltern, a seat-stealing madam) into reciprocated cordiality, a loosening of tongues that finally ushers De Quincey's narrative onto the pages of this Chicago magazine. Because male and female protagonists share Ogden's "untiring energy" and "large-hearted hospitality," General Lee's true destination is first hidden and then revealed—by his rebel hostess, that resourceful Union officer, his awakened commander, a storytelling western colonel on a train, and a married woman traveling alone in this complex "told-to" narrative. Each narrator suggests an ungendered will and resourceful action in unusually crowded circumstances, one storytelling hiatus after another that also models reading itself for magazine subscribers who learn to stay alert.

This complicated narrative structure amounts to a paradigm shift in social relations via narrative sleight of hand. As early as her story's title, De Quincey seems to make the most of male celebrity draw in "Lee's Surrender." Indeed, she substantiates elite sparkle and military authority by attributing her account to Union general Orville E. Babcock, the wee-hours officer who cajoles his Confederate hostess, listens to her imprudent tale, and checks the Virginia mud for hoofprints. But De Quincey's elaborate narrative frame—the railroad car, the absent passenger, his stolen seat, the frame narrator as an assertive wife who is ready to hear a story she will later publish—insinuates an upstart challenge to masculine privilege on that train, a peculiarly American setting. As Schivelbusch has observed, nineteenth-century American railroad cars did not share the European fondness for compartments, which were modeled on the earlier coaches of traveling elites. Instead, the longer American cars recalled riverboat cabins and steamer saloons, which offered ampler space and greater mobility to all and sundry. "The classless open car," writes Schivelbusch, "was economically, politically, psychologically and culturally the appropriate travel container for a democratic pioneer society."[65] Grafted onto a story about generals and their entourages in late-war Virginia, De Quincey's railroad car as mobile parlor slyly makes room for the extra woman on the train.

Her narrative task is to offset Virginia plantation boast with Illinois railway wit, to correct high-toned misstep with plucky enterprise, to cap masculine discovery with a feminine public sphere (stolen seat, stolen story), and, lastly, to place a female author's name on General Babcock's reported anecdote. In the story of a crowded plantation mansion (too many guests), its crowded mud (too many hoofprints), and a no-less-crowded train (too many travelers for limited seating), the anecdotal leap back in time that this story requires produces a self-made woman, perhaps even two (hostess, passenger), each with an agenda of her own. Recalling the war in Chicago thus makes for a "new story" and an unforeseen "surrender" as one storyteller replaces another in the "democratic pioneer society" of a western railroad car, a mobile setting forever preoccupied like a Chicago anecdote with usable brag, as well as unstinting labor.

The imaginative latitude of Civil War fiction in the *Lakeside Monthly* meant that jiggling gender in the self-made West was as simple as inventing a "Mrs. Noah," one of the "working, thinking PEOPLE" whose story would enlarge the postwar world of the emancipated as readily as a woman traveler finds her seat on a crowded train. In Illinois it should have been almost as simple to jiggle the assumption that the self-made were generally white; historically, the state's abolitionists had begun organizing "lines" and "stations" of another sort in the late 1830s, following the death of editor Elijah Lovejoy in southerly Alton at the hands of a proslavery mob in 1837. Thereafter, several underground lines began converging on Chicago, where a small community of free blacks and self-emancipated fugitives joined with white abolitionists during the 1840s to create a comparative safe haven. With the passage of the Fugitive Slave Law in 1850, however, the city's port became critical; according to Verna Cooley, "The work of the Chicago Underground Railroad conductors was to help the fugitives secure passage on Canada bound vessels."[66] So widely known was the conductors' success by 1859 that John Brown was said to have stopped in Chicago with the armed abolitionists who accompanied him to Harpers Ferry.[67] Led by Chicago's progressive activists, Illinois would soon become the first state to ratify the Thirteenth Amendment abolishing slavery in 1865, and the *Lakeside Monthly* would echo allegiances to Union, liberty, and abolition.[68]

But in the magazine's inaugural "Word to the Public," it appeared that the "leading Western men" soon to serve as contributors were intent on appealing to the city's Ogdens rather than its African Americans.[69] As Richard Digby-Junger has noted, the magazine's first issue promised to attract "all intelligent businessmen of the West"—hence the early focus on William B. Ogden.[70] When the liberating "train" relied on work that remained secret and self-made opportunities less bragged about than whispered, it becomes clearer what the abolitionist politics of the *Lakeside Monthly* left out, particularly as its geographical scope grew. A broader lens reveals that Illinois fostered a more moderate Republicanism midstate, as well as a zealous challenge from the southern counties, where slavecatchers made underground "conductors" uneasy and alarmed their neighbors.

In reckoning with the presumptions of Browne's subscribers and the Civil War stories his magazines circulated, it is worth considering the variegated politics of Illinois, which sharply differing demographic patterns did much to explain. Northern parts of the state, such as Chicago, had been settled mainly by those who arrived on Great Lakes steamers from the East, often native-born immigrants like Browne who helped to create what historian Kevin Phillips has called "greater New England."[71] By contrast, southern sections had attracted settlers from states such as Kentucky and Tennessee, enough to align that area with what Phillips calls the "Border and Upper South." Between them, and drawing on out-migration from the mid-Atlantic, was a belt that Phillips designates as the "Lower North," where the state capital was finally located in 1839, two years after Springfield attracted Abraham Lincoln. Two decades earlier in 1818, however, both the first governor of Illinois and his lieutenant governor were slaveholders. As Fergus Bordewich has pointed out in *Bound for Canaan*, "Slaves could be freely brought into the state as long as they were registered at a county clerk's office."[72] Even after Illinois abolished slavery in 1848, the southern counties remained politically unmistakable across a region that Cheryl Janifer Laroche describes as "an extremely dangerous area for freedom seekers and abolitionists alike," particularly after 1850.[73] The *Lakeside Monthly* would acknowledge as much. An early sketch of William Bross (June 1869), lieutenant governor from 1864 to 1869 and a firm abolitionist, alluded to the "darkness of Egypt" in southern Illinois and praised Bross for delivering the only speech that supported the newly Republican Fremont in far southern Cairo.[74] In that part of the state, the Democratic Party prevailed.

Nevertheless, routes for slaves escaping from Kentucky, Tennessee, and Missouri were quietly arranged, and the "depots" and "passengers" of a surreptitious railroad began to appear in the state's southern woods. As LaRoche documents, those on the run were hidden in "tree hollows, caves, precipices and sinkholes, high ground and lookout points, forests, thickets, and southern swamps."[75] Turner further notes that food and warm clothing were provided at secret "stations."[76] But she also acknowledges the high cost to "conductors" of getting caught: a fine of $1,000 or six months in jail, in addition to the confiscation of freedom papers if the helping hands were black.[77] After 1850 the Fugitive Slave Law would nonetheless hurry escaping fugitives north to Lake Michigan and a more solicitous Chicago while also complicating the legal stakes for emerging Republicans. As Eric Foner recalls in *Gateway to Freedom*, Massachusetts abolitionist Wendell Phillips branded Lincoln "the Slave-Hound of Illinois" because the young politician was intent on enforcing the new federal constraints in free territory.[78] Those "Black Laws" from the early days of statehood remained on the books through the 1850s. Indeed, the *Lakeside Monthly*'s extended profile of the Honorable Anson S. Miller (April 1869) would confirm that he was the first to press the Illinois legislature for repeal, a move that finally succeeded a year after the Fugitive Slave Law was itself repealed in 1865.[79]

As the magazine's fourth "go-aheaditive" sketch, the portrait of Miller was designed to celebrate one of the "distinguished men of the West," a true "representative of its spirit of progress, freedom of thought and independence of speech."[80] Thanks to Revolutionary ancestors in Massachusetts, Miller emerges as a blend of the Bunker Hill his family leaves behind and the judicial bench he claims in Illinois, along with a seat in the Illinois House (figure 22). After 1844, this profile declares, his "eloquent and powerful speech" would call attention to the state's troubling curbs on African American emigration and freedoms—for example, the right to testify in court, to be educated, to sign a contract, or to own property.[81]

But the magazine's extended tribute to Miller's accomplishments never mentions those of John Jones, the free black man who emigrated from Tennessee during the 1840s and went on to become a prosperous tailor, an intercessor with white activists, and a Mason who authored *The Black Laws of Illinois and a Few*

FIGURE 22.
Hon. Anson S. Miller, LLD. Steel engraving. *Lakeside Monthly*, April 1869, frontispiece. Courtesy of the University of Iowa Libraries.

Reasons Why They Should Be Repealed (1864). In 1871 Jones would be the first African American in Chicago elected to public office as Cook County commissioner. For achieving by the 1870s the kind of political position that Miller won in the 1840s, Jones would become the hero of a competing narrative about social justice and black agency: the home he shared with his wife, Mary Jane, was one of the most active underground "stations" in Illinois after 1850 and reportedly the Chicago sanctuary where John Brown stopped on his way to Harpers Ferry. Karamanski calls Jones "the political father of black Chicago," the man who "led the fight to repeal the black laws and restore integrated schools."[82] His absence from the pages of the *Lakeside Monthly* is not surprising, given its audience. Yet the magazine's editorial enthusiasm for marshland individualism suffers from the neglect of self-made African Americans intent on a bracing rupture with the past, those black entrepreneurs who did as much to advance an abolitionist agenda and postwar civil rights as the Ogdens and Millers the magazine so ardently commended.

A similar preference for white generosity over black justice came to bear in "Jack Dessart" (October 1871), a Civil War story that was published eight years after its chief midwar action. Burdett Nash's recollected struggle is a border romance set in "the slaty hills of Kentucky" amid reports of horrific casualties at the Battle of Chickamauga in northwestern Georgia.[83] Although the eastern confrontation at Gettysburg would be long remembered after July 1863, particularly in magazines from Philadelphia, New York, and Boston, the Civil War was also hard-fought on the battlefields of the West, and Union forces were no less engaged during July 1863 in the siege of Vicksburg. Two months later, as that midwar summer ended, the Union's western armies were struggling to command Tennessee's crucial rail junction at Chattanooga before moving on to Atlanta and the sea. "Jack Dessart" hinges on the Chattanooga campaign that included Chickamauga's "desecrated Sabbath" on September 20, when the story's Union hero kills a Southern officer who proves to be the brother of his border sweetheart.[84]

Curiously, railroads do not figure in Nash's story, although Union and Confederate armies each traveled nearly a thousand roundabout miles to Chickamauga and repeatedly changed trains to accommodate lines. But few stories in the illustrated weeklies or the literary monthlies of the East lingered on the "horror undone" of Nash's western battlefield, which is first anticipated and then recollected by a female friend who recognizes the "cross-providences" of warring sections and the peculiar difficulty of gauging a national future as the "shadows of memory" and nine interruptions gather.[85] For Jack Dessart, "God's will" in a new era means his loss of the girl he met at a Kentucky resort; but for the story's narrator, the "light divine" that flickers after Appomattox touches both the Northern lieutenant she loves and the Southern freedmen she teaches.[86] While Jack, his intended, and her narrating friend jostle story time each in turn, just as they unexpectedly meet in the first place at the Kentucky springs before the war, "God's will" ultimately banishes the placid site where their paths first crossed in favor of a second chance postwar, specifically in a politically crowded South.

What these characters all forfeit for their "commingling" are the restorative visions of home, here embodied in "a pleasant secluded bend of the creek" where political allegiances nonetheless intrude.[87] In Civil War stories, the advent of the railroad consistently makes such quiet places shimmer when they lapse into the eternal calm of a receding local past or become the peopled sites where onetime strangers meet, as they do at leisurely watering holes. For that reason, the depot as crowded hiatus recalls the "secluded bend of the creek" that it displaces as surely as American railroads and their cars recalled the commercial enterprise of earlier river traffic while displacing canal boats and laden canoes forever. Like Miss Blackwell's anonymous fugitive and her Cincinnati heroine, one headed for future freedom and the other at home in settled habits, many other western characters find themselves near a "secluded bend of the creek," even after the railroad and its depots intercede. When the whistle of a new era sounded and platform babble grew, there was apparently still time in the 1860s and 1870s to negotiate both more "secluded" western places and the go-aheaditiveness of a "steel web."

Negotiating positions were hardening, however, particularly as Chicago's differing neighborhoods became ever more distinct social classes. During the Civil War, only some men could afford to buy a substitute and thereby avoid military service, as Pierce has noted, while others saw the cost of living soar beyond their means.[88] The result, as Theodore Karamanski and Eileen M. McMahon have pointed out, was violent unrest, "wildcat strikes by workers struggling to keep up with the price of necessities."[89] In addition, the German immigrants who welcomed emancipation as the essential underpinning of "democratic ideals," in Karamanski's phrase, were increasingly at odds with the Irish who instead saw Karamanski's "potential economic threat" in the competition for unskilled jobs, the same friction that was on the rise in Baltimore.[90] The city's workforce was changing in other ways as well—for example, with the measureable uptick of women laboring in the wartime garment industry. As Jentz and Schneirov observe, "The explosion of female employment in the 1860s was shocking, even by Chicago standards."[91] A negligible factor before the war began, working women soon amounted to 18 percent of the city's laborers and 60 percent of those in the wartime garment industry, which had quickly come to rely upon the inexpensive sewing machines that were operated at large clothing firms.[92] "The employment of women," write Jentz and Schneirov, "was an integral part of the formation of a wage-earning working class in Chicago," what was quickly becoming "a permanent wage-earning working class."[93] The Great Fire in 1871 hurried that development, especially among those with few skills.

Chicago in the Age of Capital examines the city's deepening economic dilemma, "an enormous labor shortage in Chicago's booming economy that could only be met by immigrants," especially when nearby farmers preferred to stay on fertile midwestern land.[94] In the wartime meatpacking, manufacturing, and garment industries, as well as Union regiments, immigrant laborers stepped up; often they gravitated toward the Democratic Party or, in 1873, combined to inspire Chicago's short-lived People's Party. As Jentz and Schneirov observe, "The transformation of the public sphere occasioned by the end of slavery made the

FIGURE 23. *Lieut. Governor of Illinois, William Bross.* Steel engraving. *Lakeside Monthly,* June 1869, frontispiece. Courtesy of the University of Iowa Libraries.

cooperation of foreign-born workers in the labor movement possible, and this interethnic movement brought the labor question and labor unrest into Chicago politics for the first time."[95] Even a literary magazine like the *Lakeside Monthly* took note, with articles such as "A Solution of the Eight-Hour Question" (September 1869), "The 'Labor Reform Party'" (December 1870), "Political Communism" (July 1871), and "Political Economy of the Fire" (January 1872), as well as ad upon ad for sewing machines. The political tenets of the magazine's western contributors were not often radical, but few other monthlies reckoned with emancipation so broadly conceived.

Neither did William Bross when he first came to Chicago in 1848. Born in New Jersey, the son of a deacon with business interests in lumbering and canal-building, Bross assisted his father from an early age with his axe in hand, the picture of muscular and ambitious labor in the *Lakeside Monthly*'s avid profile (figure 23). On the magazine's pages, lumbering and rafting carried him through distinguished studies at Williams College that made him a "thorough classical scholar," a "great lover of the natural sciences," an "ardent student of natural history"—and ultimately a newspaper editor.[96] In 1849 he began work with the Presbyterian *Prairie Herald*; in 1852 he founded the *Democratic Press*, which the *Lakeside Monthly* would cast as "a political paper" with "a commercial object," namely, boosting Chicago among eastern investors as "the great railroad and commercial focus of the Northwest."[97] In 1854 he wrote his first proselytizing pamphlet, which promoted the city's "extensive manufactures" and the "radiating lines from Chicago to every point of the compass except those lying lakeward."[98] In 1858 his daily paper was consolidated with the *Chicago Tribune*, which shared Bross's devotion to the city, to the new Republican Party, and to the cause of abolition.

During the Civil War, as the *Lakeside Monthly* noted, William Bross was foremost in raising and financing an African American regiment, the Twenty-Ninth United States Colored Troops (USCT), and "one of the first to recognize the liberation of the bondsmen as the result of the war."[99] He would go on to become the sitting lieutenant governor of Illinois when this boostering profile was published. In yet another sketch of a local titan, the self-made Bross was praised for dismissing "genius" and substituting the "hard work, energy, industry, honesty and economy" that were the "true elements of greatness," though he never seems to have reckoned with a rising proletariat whose labors would leave new wage earners subordinate and restless, a permanent underclass.[100]

The magazine's subscribers eventually negotiated a similar chasm between the haves and the have-nots in Egbert Phelps's "Our Adjutant" (May 1873), this time the sizable gap between army brass and "we sojers," embodied in an immigrant who has spent more than a decade as a sergeant in the Regular Army out west.[101] Like James Fenimore Cooper's Natty Bumppo on the prairie, Sandy MacIntosh first appears against "the dying sunset light," here in wartime Georgia, though he sounds like he would still be at home in the Scottish Highlands.[102] Doubly doomed by clan hardship and sad personal loss, absorbed in the solitary melodies he sings ("Auld Robin Gray," "Bonnie Doon"), he is nonetheless a figure of laboring challenge, even to the romantic captain who tells his story. "There's mony a mon wha has little o' happiness to luik back upon i' his past, an' still less to hope for i' the future," he insists.[103] Like those that General Sherman's troops unhoused and *The Land We Love* lamented, he discovers that "hame was hame to me nae langer"; but like so many immigrant laborers in Chicago, he acknowledges that even a "stalwart form" and a spirit of "resolve and stern determination" cannot offset the "hopelessness" of the future, especially in his embedded narrative.[104] Instead, he sets himself against the privileged in Scotland ("thievin', rievin', murtherin' loons") and the "saft-headed fule" of an officer on the dusty road to Atlanta, a road that in Phelps's story is full of marches and skirmishes, "weary miles" and "formidable breastworks."[105] For the storytelling captain in 1864 Georgia, his is a "blighted life" marked by "withered hopes" that lead to a fatal fever before the war ends.[106]

Yet in refusing history's romance, Sandy MacIntosh reveals the captain's willful blindness and insinuates doubt about the story's poetic grace—for example, the way in which the captain describes Union progress through the mountains of northern Georgia. Beside the embers of a campfire on a "crag" near Kennesaw Mountain, the captain indulges in "a beautiful and romantic view" of the army's pitched tents: "A thousand feet below us, stretched out to the right and left as far as we could see, the long lines of Sherman's army, marked by the twinkling camp-fires which, dwindled to mere points of light, sparkled through the valley like reflections of the stars which studded the sky above."[107] Few other contributors to postwar magazines described army encampments from such a vantage point, yet the sparkling vision is one that MacIntosh softly derides for its "double" or "half" truth, so often "entirely fause."[108]

In this story's measured revisionism, Phelps's Scottish adjutant anticipates the judgment of historian William Thomas, who argues in *The Iron Way* that General Sherman's aim as he approached Atlanta was to eradicate what MacIntosh would deem "fause" hope—that is, according to Thomas, "to wipe a place from the map, to render it dead or worthless, to irrevocably alter the geographic connections that sustained the Confederacy and its claims to progress."[109] In relying on railroads for resupply, General Sherman also coordinated an assault on both Confederate forces and Confederate civilians that made his regiments the fearsome engine of Union triumph. "More than any battle," Thomas argues, "Sherman's Atlanta Campaign and the subsequent March to the Sea demonstrated to the South that its driving economic vision of the Confederacy, based as it was on railroads, slavery, and agricultural wealth, was obliterated."[110] One-time sergeant Sandy MacIntosh does not claim as much on a Georgia "crag," but his willingness to perforate the captain's engaging panorama, and Egbert Phelps's willingness to let him, insinuates the kind of "exhaustion" that Chicago's laborers were beginning to share.[111] For them, as for this adjutant, recollections of the war were more "callous," even in a magazine whose William Bross could not abide unions and would not accept the emergence of an outspoken proletariat.[112]

It is nonetheless true that Phelps's story persists in setting romantic memory against revisionist lampoon, beauty against exhaustion, timeless appeal against time cut short. His insistence on unrelieved tensions suited a magazine that saw itself at the intersection of East and West. But a similar willingness to weigh conflicting perspectives could create unmistakable slippages, especially as the *Lakeside Monthly* looked South to antebellum Florida and other "twinkling" pictures rendered "fause" by hard experience.

HELEN E. HARRINGTON

"In the Palmy Days of Slaveholding"

(*Lakeside Monthly*, August 1870)

There lived in New England, in eighteen hundred and thirty-something, a pale little Puritan about thirteen years old, who seems, as I think of her, half strange and half familiar—not unknown, and yet scarcely to be called well-known or intimate—whose surroundings nevertheless rise very distinctly before my memory. This little girl was myself.

The child had so little life that she was called by Aunt Achsa, her schoolteacher, incorrigibly lazy. Madame Pérault "have névare see some young ladies so not try to play ze piano." By her doting mother, she was said to be "a little delicate, though of course not alarmingly so." But by the wise old family doctor she was pronounced upon in more serious phrases. He lapped the skirts of his surtout over his sleek knees, adjusted his glasses to the right focus for a close inspection of the wan little phiz, and said with kind cruelty:

"Well, ma'am, she looks as though next spring's *easters* might blow her away so far that all next summer's breezes could never bring her back to you."

Close following on my mother's faith in the Divine Revelation was her faith in the medical revelation. Dr. Barstowe's *dictum* was in her eyes scarcely less to be regarded than holy writ itself.

"Oh, Doctor!" she cried, in those agonized tones that must be so familiar to the ears of all "family physicians" of long standing. And the Doctor, having thus by a mere threat or show of force annulled any opposition he might have looked to encounter in carrying out his wise plans, drew me to him, and with sundry endearments—(at which I shuddered a little, because they were associated in my memory with a "slight portion of castor oil") he asked me if I would like to pick roses from the bushes and oranges from the trees at Christmas time, and have a lovely summer instead of the approaching dreary winter. I made no reply, probably through fear that he might be describing the plains of heaven and promising me a transfer to that blissful realm which I much preferred contemplating from a distance.

"How would you like to go down to Florida and stay with Aunt Anna, while the frost is nipping the little Yankee girls' noses?"

A light broke over my mind, and probably my face, too. And I have reason to suppose that the illumination reached my mother. Her eyes were opened, and she saw how weak I was and how sage the Doctor's advice, and how foolish and short-sighted her natural shrinking from the parting with her one darling for a time, and committing her treasure to other hands and hearts than the tried and loving ones of home. The Doctor never swerved from his text, nor my mother from her allegiance; and so it fell out that, under the protection of my Aunt Anna, going South to resume her place as governess, and of a gentleman returning to his plantation after the cool delights of a Northern summer, I set sail from New York. It was November, and the frosts were just sweeping away the last traces of autumnal glory, and the footsteps of the advancing winter-monarch were making themselves visible on the earth and audible in the air.

There were bright days and starry nights, cruel sea-sickness and hungry convalescence, and all the strange experience that makes up the memory of everyone's first sea voyage, I suppose. There was a storm off Cape Hatteras, when I wished I had stayed at home and died decently in my own little bed that did not toss about, and then a glorious day with a fair wind when I was glad I had not stayed anywhere and died anyhow. Then came the first view of the quaint old town of St. Augustine over the bare, dazzling sand-hills—the ancient fort frowning toward the bay—the strange Spanish pilot—the long wharf—the curious medley of buildings, from the ruinous mansion of departed Spanish glory to the white-painted and green-blinded American "residence;" all looking then very much as they look now after a lapse of almost forty years.

We met with a cordial Southern welcome, and the "little invalid" was made to feel that *home* was ready for her in the kind hearts of the new friends.

To me the novelty was like a fairy tale. As Dr. Barstowe had promised, roses and jasmines were plenty, with myriads of other flowers of which the very names were strange to me. Oranges hung from the trees that shaded the second story windows, as plentiful as apples in the dear old home orchard. All sorts of strange and luscious fruits abounded. There were crowds of black servants, and many little dark creatures always under foot and in the way. The whole made up a scene in bewildering contrast to the simplicity of my Northern home.

For a week we rioted at will. Then my Aunt Anna, the governess, installed herself in the school-room with the rather reluctant candidates for scholarship, and I either took my place among them, or disported myself in the garden, or on the piazza, or down by the sparkling waters of the bay which washed a beach not fifty yards from the house. Beyond the low island lying in front of this beach I could watch the breaking waves of the Atlantic. The fairy hours passed quickly by, and I studied the new picture of life presented to me—especially the new pages in the book of human nature opened to my view in the conversation and habits of the negro servants who swarmed on the premises of Mr. Lawton, our host.

At home, freedom of intercourse with servants was out of the question, but here nothing interfered to prevent the utmost familiarity with the black members of the household; for members they were, having no individual existence (one might say), but shining only in the reflected light of their master's glory.

Among them I had my favorites, and they in their turn esteemed me differently. To old "Mauma Liddy," the nurse, I was "de young lady from de Norf," and as such treated with reverence and attention. Liddy was, like St. Paul, "free born;" but she had married a slave, and when her husband's master died, poor Sam was sold in the settlement of the estate, taken to Cuba, and Liddy never heard of him again. She was a dignified, portly woman of about sixty-five, with a bland face and a protuberant nether lip that folded over her chin with an expanse sufficient to form half a dozen ordinary lips. Her wool was nearly white, and was always covered with a bandanna tower of marvellous construction.

Mauma was the soul of patience and good humor, and I used to marvel at her fortitude as, morning after morning, "Maas Alfred," her especial care (a boy four years of age), used to prance up and down the nursery, keeping just beyond her grasp, while she followed him with his clothes, repeating in persuasive tones, "There, now, be a good boy! Come, now, Maas Alfred, git on yer close, honey, dere's a good chile," until finally the young scapegrace would deign to allow the patient creature to button him into his trousers and jacket. There was never any attempt at authority on her part. She carried her point by stratagem and coaxing with wonderful persistence and success. This seems to have been a good system to produce young rebels.

After Mauma Liddy, Primus excited my most amused interest. He was a boy ten years of age, under training as assistant to Thomas, the waiter. The latter was tall, finely built, and handsome in form and face, and possessed of a wonderful professional aptitude. Primus kept his eye on his model throughout the meals, his left foot in advance and firmly planted, his small tray flat against his breast, ready for presentation with the same slight flourish that Thomas gave his, and the same imperturbable gravity of countenance, no matter how funny the talk at table might be. But woe to Primus if he inadvertently dropped a fork or spilled the water! Mercy was no part of Thomas's code of discipline, as Primus's ears could testify.

Like most young negro slaves, this embryo waiter had no very firmly rooted regard for the principles of *meum* and *tuum*. He was, of course, inordinately fond of sweets, and was ingenious both in procuring surreptitious supplies and in evading the merited penalties for so doing. The eldest daughter of the family, Margaret, was housekeeper, and charged with the duty of giving out the daily modicum of tea, sugar, rice, hominy, molasses, etc., for family consumption, and after each meal she locked up the residue, which might tempt the black servants if left unsecured.

One morning we had just finished breakfast when some noise in the street called us all to the piazza, and Margaret forgot for a moment the sugary treasures in her charge. Suddenly recollecting them, she returned to the breakfast room, and—there was Primus with his hand up to the wrist in the sugar-bowl, scooping up the delicious stuff, and carrying it with great haste and relish to his mouth. The rustling of Margaret's dress made him look up, start, replace the cover, and then turning his back, he began again assiduously folding napkins.

"Primus!" said Margaret, sternly, looking from him to the scattered relics of his theft and back again, "Primus, you've been taking sugar!"

"Oh, no, Miss Margaret!"

"Don't tell an untruth, Primus; that will only make your fault worse!"

"'Deed I neber, Miss Margaret! I neber been tech dat bowl!"

"What, then, is that on your nose and around your mouth?" and the young housekeeper gave him a look of clinching and withering severity, and pointed to his face, which was sparkling all over its black surface with the shining crystals.

"Dat, Miss," answered the unblushing thief, "*Oh, dat's praspration, Miss!*"

Of course, Margaret was surprised quite out of her dignity by this obstreperous lie, and Primus was saved from punishment by her love of fun, although she threatened him severely "next time." He departed to the kitchen with a penitential aspect and a portentous demureness of countenance which, to the inexperienced eyes of the truthful little Puritan spectator, bespoke a sincere and lasting reform—an impression somewhat shaken by seeing Primus, on his way to the kitchen, execute a series of back somersaults, with the triumphant chuckle:

"Didn't ketch it dis time!"

If Primus fell short of saintship, it was not for want of conscientious painstaking by his mother Amelia to instil religious instruction into his hard sconce. From my window I once saw Amelia seated on the door-step, in no very amiable mood, waiting for her young scapegrace to perform his devotions, which duty she exacted with great punctuality and small gentleness.

"Come heah, sar, and say you praah, sar!"

Very reluctantly Primus complied as far as posture was concerned, dropping on his knees and putting up his little brown hands with their white palms prayer-fashion in her lap; but his mind was slow to concentrate itself on the opening clause of this act of worship. As he paused and hesitated, Amelia's hand came down heavily upon his ear, warning him not to trifle with religion, but to go on with "Our Fader." Seizing the cue, he advanced with tolerable glibness; but, his memory failing, he was brought to a sudden stand at the end of "kingdom come." After that his case was one of special religious difficulty, Amelia deaconing out the prayer, and emphasizing each sentence with a hearty cuff, first with one hand and then with the other— illustrating it with cuts it might be called. Of course, by the time Primus had arrived at what he pronounced "deliver a smeazel" and "devil and devil, amen," his ideas on spiritual subjects were beginning to be very diffuse.

This poor slave mother, who was so hard a teacher of gospel truth, was at the same time suffering a daily martyrdom. One evening, when reading in the parlor, I heard Amelia approach her master, who was smoking on the piazza. From my position just inside the window I heard her piteous request and the hard answer of her owner. She and her son had been bought some three months before from a man whose pecuniary necessities compelled him to sell the mother and son away from the husband and father, who was too valuable a field hand to be spared. Amelia was devotedly attached to her husband, and this forced separation developed a temper soured and violent; so that, in fact, she proved an almost worthless purchase. Her obstinacy was untamable. She quarreled with her fellow servants, and, in short, seemed the personification of all evil to those who were ignorant of or indifferent to the despair which consumed her.

In the present instance, Amelia approached her master, and, with a low courtesy, said she hoped Massa would do her a great favor. She prayed God He would put it into Massa's heart to do what she asked. And her request was to be sold back again!

"Why, Amelia," said her master, "why do you wish to be sold back? Aren't you kindly treated here? Don't you like your Mistress and the family?"

"Oh, yes, Massa!" sobbed the wretched slave, "yer all good and I likes yer; but, Massa—*my husband!* William and me we allus cared so much for each oder, and we aint contented nudder of us. Sell me back, Massa, for de lub of God, or I shall die!" and she threw her check apron over her head and writhed in the agony of her supplication.

"That is impossible, Amelia. You can't be sold back. You must try to become contented, and after a while you will forget William and get another husband. You'll be as happy as ever then."

And, as if to put an end to the scene, he rose and walked the piazza.

But the woman was desperate. She followed him, imploring him with the pertinacity of despair, till at last he forbade her uttering another word.

Crushed by the failure of her humble hopes, the poor creature crept slowly down the steps, and, bowed nearly double, shuffled off to her garret over the kitchen, whence I heard her sobs and moans for hours.

A few days afterwards she met me and said:

"Miss Ella, enty you kin write a letter?"

"To be sure I can. Shall I write one for you?"

With a shower of thanks she placed herself on her knees by the side of my desk and began to dictate. After much and vague information about her health and that of the boy, she stopped a moment, and then, trembling with emotion, added, "Tell him, Miss Ella, nebber to forgit his promise and I nebber forgit mine." And after this artless renewal of their plighted troth, the letter closed with messages of remembrance to old friends in the usual negro form: "Tell Aunt Mimy" or "Uncle Jerry, howdy for me."

After sealing and directing this letter, to be given in charge to "Mr. Marland's Caesar," who was going over in the morning, I asked Amelia what that promise was she had spoken of.

"Oh, Miss Ella, you don't care for heah poo' nigger's promise to one oder."

"Yes, I do," I replied; "and I am very sorry for you Amelia," and the tears of sympathy filled my eyes to prove my words.

Taking my hand in hers, so huge that it was entirely hidden, and fixing her grief-wild eyes on mine, she said solemnly:

"Yer see, Miss Ella, William and me we keers for one oder better dan some white folks, and we promise 'fore God nebber hab no oder wife nor no oder husband while we lib in dis worle!"

No wonder I sobbed on my desk for half an hour after Amelia left me for the daily routine along which she bore her heavily laden spirit. No law recognized their union, no minister solemnized it; but it was "till death do us part" to them, nevertheless.

Unable to control the proud spirit of the woman forever chafing under the sense of her wrongs, Mr. Lawton sold her to a Captain Derby, where we shall hear of her again.

It was a peculiar feature of St. Augustine society for very young misses to attend balls and parties, and it would have been considered great neglect if a child of my age had been overlooked in the invitations. Thus it came to pass that on a certain occasion I accompanied my Aunt Anna and the Lawtons to "The Hall," where I took my initiatory sip from the cup of dissipation.

The Spanish dance, in all its perfection, was danced in that old city at that time, where the old Spanish customs had not yet given way to the innovations of modern times. We were threading its beautiful and graceful figures, when all at once the music jangled and then stopped entirely. High words were heard from the vicinity of the musicians, and the gentlemen rushed to the scene of the disturbance, while the ladies, pale and terrified, grouped themselves at the opposite side of the room.

"Let him learn to behave himself!" "Served him right!" "Ungovernable temper!" and other angry exclamations reached our ears, as our partners returned with apologies for the interruption, and we re-formed the sets. The music recommenced. But we had not danced over ten minutes, when suddenly the leading violin failed, then the other pieces gave out and the dance ceased; and between the crowding figures I saw several of the players carrying out the leader, Marcellino, the blood flowing from a great gash in his head and staining his shirt front. Ladies screamed, universal agitation prevailed, and the ball broke up in confusion.

I learned afterward that the whole trouble arose from an order given by Captain Derby, a gentleman of fashion and standing, to the band leader, Marcellino, to play a certain dance. This order conflicted with the previous instructions of the dancing committee; but, unaccustomed to being thwarted by a negro, Captain Derby seized the triangle from its terrified player, and with it gave the leader the blow which led to the disturbance already described.

Great blame was attached to Captain Derby, and overwhelming was his own chagrin and mortification. For what? That he had allowed his temper to get the better of him in the presence of ladies. There was the rub! He had no remorse for his brutality to the unoffending musician—only apologies to the ladies! To them he apologized humbly and frankly; and, as they considered that he had "acted nobly" by so doing, they readily forgave him, and never wounded his exquisitely tender sensibilities by referring to the affair again.

This was the drawing-room version of the affair. But from nursery and yard gossip I learned that a demand had been made on Marcellino's master to punish his servant for disrespectful conduct to one of the first gentlemen of the place. But the master was a just man (for a slaveholder), and the poor fiddler escaped further ill-usage; but thereby a feud was established between his owner's family and Captain Derby's which lasted for years.

One afternoon my Aunt Anna and I set out to pay a visit to Mrs. Derby, an old lady of high position, mother of the Captain Derby already mentioned. She was at home, quite invalided by an attack of the asthma, to which disease she was subject. We found her in her easy chair, before a cheerful wood fire, and her bland, cordial reception of us quite conquered my young heart. As she and Aunt Anna carried on their conversation, I became lost in admiration of the gentle, winning sweetness of voice and manner which characterized the old lady.

Soon the "fore-log" of our beautiful fire parted, and the live coals were scattered over the hearth.

"Let me trouble you, Miss Ella, to touch that bell," said our graceful hostess.

When the bell was answered, it was by my old friend Amelia. She seemed not to notice me, but knelt to clear up the hearth; and as she did so, her gown of blue check (made in the common fashion of servants, which we called "half high") displayed her neck and shoulders sufficiently to show them to be scarred in a shocking manner by the recent application of a whip.

"Put on your handkerchief, Amelia," said her mistress; and, probably feeling an apology to be necessary, she remarked, as the woman left the room:

"Amelia has been out of temper ever since she came here, and yesterday she brought in an armful of wood and threw it down in a passion, and when I told Edward he punished her very severely. I am sorry he was so severe, for it makes her look so badly."

I had no more admiration for the Southern grace and loveliness of our entertainer! By a sudden transformation she grew hideous and repulsive in my eyes; and when my aunt rose to go, I could scarcely contain myself sufficiently to take a civil leave of her.

In the hall Amelia was standing with a sullen expression, waiting to open the door for us. It was the work of a moment for me, as I passed, to empty my purse of the little money it contained into the poor creature's hand; putting my finger on my lips and doing it without Aunt Anna's knowledge, for my young perceptions had found out that she had but little sympathy with my pity for slaves.

Within a week of these occurrences, I was sitting in the nursery, benefiting by Maum Liddy's experience in making a patchwork quilt, when I heard her say to the seamstress, in answer to some low remark:

"Oh, no! 'Melia ain't gwine to steal now if she nebber been tief before."

"What are you talking about Mauma?" said I, with a feeling of sickening apprehension.

"Oh, nuttin, Miss Ella," was her cautious answer.

On my insisting further, almost in tears, Liddy said:

"Well, well; sit down again, honey, and don't be so 'strep'rous. I'll tell ye, but don't say nuttin 'bout it. Dey say 'Melia done gone to de sto' and buy herself hankercher an' timble, an' got money ter pay for um an' more lef'; an' Massa Armistead dat keeps de sto' he done gone tell ole Miss Derby dat he spec de gal steal from somebody; but 'Melia she won't tell no how whar she done git de money, an' she gwine for to be sen' to de fort to be locked up an' licked tel she willin tell whar she got it, dat's all."

"All!" It was enough. My heart stood still. The blood left my face, and chancing to glance toward a mirror, I thought I saw a ghost. Liddy was frightened at my looks, and even turned pale—the purple hue that fright brings to the negro face.

"Lord, honey! I's sorry I telled ye. Dat's happenin' every day. Dat aint nuttin new."

I slipped out of the house, and in a few seconds was flying along the red-hot road, under a noon-day sun, toward Mrs. Derby's. On the way I met Captain Derby, with a repulsive looking man, leaving the house, and behind them, with hopeless mien, walked my poor friend Amelia.

Amelia was saved for that time, and I was saved, too, from the strange loss of natural anti-slavery principles which changed so many "birthright" Northerners into slaveholders or apologists for slavery. From that day to this, hatred of the system which made such horrors possible as that which threatened poor Amelia has been a part of my nature.

This brings me to a part of my narrative which I shall have to dismiss with a bare statement of the fact, because, to my girlish mind, it was an incomprehensible phenomenon, and even to my more mature apprehension is scarcely to be accounted for.

Miss Margaret Lawton, born and brought up a slaveholder, had been engaged to Captain Derby. In consequence of the incidents connected with him which I have narrated, Margaret dismissed her lover, and firmly withstood the efforts of all about her to change her mind. Whereupon the Captain consoled himself by turning his devoted attentions to my Aunt Anna; and she, a New England girl who had never seen a slave until a year before, on her first visit to the South, accepted him, temper, slaves, and all.

It was "all a muddle" to me. I began to be homesick, and to long for my own dear bracing Northern atmosphere—moral and material. My dear friend, Miss Margaret Lawton—a kind of angel or goddess I remember she appeared to me then—was my constant companion, my solace, my *confidante*, my guide, philosopher, and friend, and all the more when Aunt Anna had gone off from her old standards of character and married Captain Derby. Margaret and I, between us, concocted a notable plan, the results of which you shall soon see.

"Is it true, Aunt Anna, that you think of selling Amelia?"

"Yes, Ella. Captain Derby finds her so troublesome that he will only keep her till he finds a purchaser."

"How much will he take for her?"

As I asked the question I started to hear Captain Derby's voice in high amusement behind us.

"Angels and ministers of grace defend us! The pretty little Puritan is going to buy a nigger! She is going to become a trader!"

"You are right, Captain Derby; I am going to set up in that business at once. Will you sell Amelia? How much will you take for Amelia?"

"Yes, indeed, Mademoiselle, and for much less than I gave for her, too; or I'll swap her for a horse, cow, pig, or even a yellow dog, if I cannot do better. I could scarcely lose by the exchange." And the gay Captain laughed at my shocked expression and at his own sorry predicament as the owner of a chattel worth less than a "yaller dog."

"Captain Derby, let me have Amelia for my own, and Aunt Anna shall have my little mare Pattie that she knows and likes so well. The horse is my own, and she can come down just as Mr. Lawton's carriage horses do every season."

"But suppose your horse should die on the way down South."

"Well, sir, suppose your slave should die on her way up North."

"Waal, Miss," replied the Captain, imperfectly imitating the down-east twang and patois, "I will dicker my gaal for your haws."

"Well, sah," replied I, mimicking the Southern drawl, "I will exchange my hawse fo' youah blagyirl!"

And so the bargain was concluded.

"Remember, little Ella," said the Captain, "you are a wicked slaveholder."

No need to bid me remember; my delight was unbounded, and it only seemed that the sacrifice of my pony was too small for the great end I had attained.

It was a season of sad parting when the time came for me to go North once more. Amelia was given reason to hope that her separation from Primus would be only temporary, and that even happier reunions might be hoped for in the future. But I knew I should probably never see the dear sunny and flowery land again. I kissed dear Margaret in a passion of sorrow, and clung to every one till the last moment. Mauma Liddy walked with me to the wharf, holding "Maas Alfred" by the hand, to "git de las' look." Primus walked beside, to carry what he called my "umbruther." Thomas, the efficient, did everything about my baggage, overloaded with *souvenirs* for the North. Hester and Maryanne and March blubbered at the gate. On the whole, my most alluring view of slavery was my last—perhaps because it was the slaves and not the slaveholders who formed the mass of the picture.

There was a festival in our little town when the wandering lamb came back—restored to health and home, and presenting Amelia as the spoils of the expedition. The occasion was improved by the formation of a Relief and Abolition Society. Scarcely a year passed afterward without the purchase and liberation of some poor slave. First came Primus, the hero, one would judge from his airs, of a voyage at least around the world by his own prowess. Then Amelia's "o' man"—and what a meeting there was between husband and wife! Then came others, Margaret acting as our Southern agent to report cases of special hardship and desert. And I here record my belief that a negro baby is the "cunningest" thing in the world, perhaps excepting a white baby.

In one of the last battles of the war died the rebel General Derby, son of Aunt Anna. He was reported by our soldiers as spurring his horse directly up to and over a breastwork which his men were hopelessly assaulting, seeming to feel, as many of his brother officers seemed to feel, that the cause being lost they had nothing to live for.

With them passed away a whole race, a whole generation, a whole system, a whole great social epoch of luxury and elegant leisure, of patriarchal kindness and protection of a weak race mixed with tyrannical oppression of the same,—a strange and beautiful picture of light and shade. The place that knew it shall know it no more forever. Let us preserve its memory while we can.

"Deliver a Smeazel"

In a story set mainly along Florida's Atlantic coast during the 1830s, the most intriguing character might appear forgettable, yet another rascal with his fingers in the sugar bowl. Spotted swiping the "delicious stuff" by the handfuls, Primus is caught in a lie because the stolen sweet sticks to his face, which is "sparkling all over its black surface with the shining crystals" amid the "scattered relics of his theft." Primus is as much a "scapegrace" as his master's four-year-old son, but only the enslaved boy is required in the next scene to say his prayers publicly. He dawdles through the "Our Fader" and comes to a dead stop before "Thy will be done," aptly enough. His mother's impatient prodding gets him through his last lines, which unabashedly turn "deliver us from evil" into "deliver a smeazel" and "forever and ever" into "devil and devil, amen," despite Amelia's stern intentions. Less a devout petitioner than a Topsy redux, Primus is disciplined, punished, and rendered comic.

The scene could so easily be a flash of heartland hokum in the *Lakeside Monthly*. But the sparkling image that almost makes a white mistress laugh is also a reminder that the sugar industry gained a foothold on plantations south of St. Augustine during the late eighteenth century. Aggressively labor-intensive as a crop, particularly at harvest time, sugarcane provides an unusual lens for evaluating Harrington's slaveocracy and her story's anticipation of the Civil War. Noticeably, the society parties and balls to which Miss Ella is invited, the visits and gossips in which she gets absorbed, claim far less of her account than Mr. Lawton's household, where nearly everybody labors. Then, too, the absence of a St. Augustine railroad depot hides the growing presence, after Miss Ella's winter recovery, of a surreptitious "station" that sends Amelia's slave family north, though Florida's own underground railroad generally ran south and ran historically on black initiative rather than white kindness. Most importantly, the Indian attacks that overwhelmed East Florida's young sugar industry were often prompted by Black Seminoles, who turned upon planter authority with all of Amelia's gathering resentment. By setting her story in "palmy" St. Augustine during the 1830s, Harrington creates a local version of the breastwork war later insuring that the South's General Derbys would finally be gone with the wind.

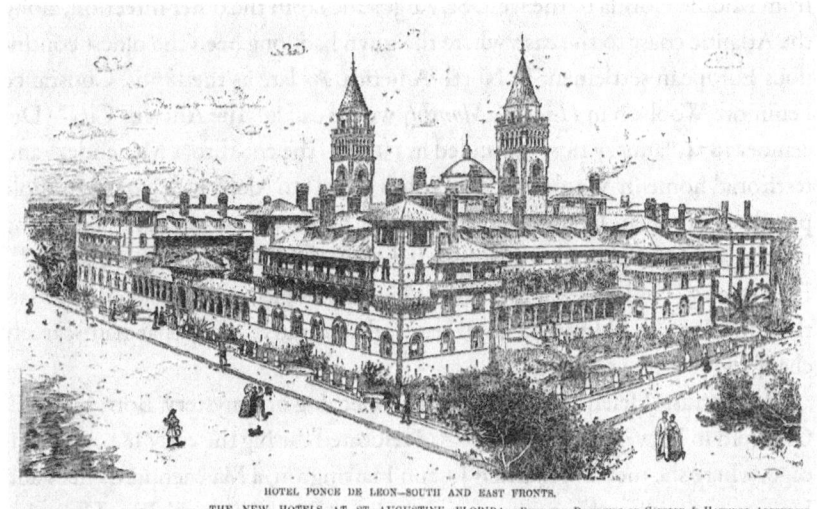

FIGURE 24. *Hotel Ponce de Leon.* Wood engraving. *Harper's Weekly*, November 26, 1887, 860. Courtesy of the University of Iowa Libraries.

During the gilded years that followed the Civil War, railroads would transform nineteenth-century Florida. Indeed, Standard Oil magnate Henry Flagler first visited St. Augustine toward the end of the 1870s as John D. Rockefeller's "ruthless" wizard with rail transport and rock-bottom freight rates, according to biographer Thomas Graham. "When Flagler began his operations in Florida," Graham continues, "he understood very well the vital role that railroad connections with the North would play in the success of his plan to turn St. Augustine into a winter Newport."[113] So began what Susan Braden in *The Architecture of Leisure* has called "the Flagler System of railroads"; by 1912 the Florida East Coast Railway would extend past a series of Flagler hotels to Key West, a network that commenced in 1885 with the small line connecting St. Augustine to Jacksonville, some thirty miles farther north.[114] By the late 1880s *Harper's Weekly* was celebrating "our American Italy" and naming St. Augustine's Hotel Ponce de Leon "one of the great American hotels" (figure 24).[115] As the newsmagazine observed, "The Florida of twenty-five years ago had all the natural advantages of a health resort, but only these."[116] For St. Augustine's new wintering elite in 1887, it was apparently difficult to scrape by without porticos and rotundas, electric lights and Turkish baths.

During the 1830s, however, midway between the Spanish cession in 1821 and statehood in 1845, Florida was a frontier. Although tracks were being laid for the territory's first steam-powered line, the Tallahassee Railroad, it would run from Middle Florida to the west. St. Augustine lay in the other direction, along the Atlantic coast to the east, where the town had long been the oldest continuous European settlement in North America. As late as the 1870s, Constance Fenimore Woolson in *Harper's Monthly* would call it "The Ancient City" (December 1874, January 1875), founded in 1565 by "the cut-throat Menendez" and territorial home in Woolson's "The South Devil" to "dead hidalgos," Seminole peoples, Minorcan laborers, Africans both free and enslaved, and a growing number of Americans after Spain ceded the territory to the United States.[117] Even during Woolson's sojourn in the 1870s, St. Augustine still looked like Harrington's "quaint old town," an exotic and restorative place that had scarcely changed for forty years.

By contrast, Helen E. Harrington is something of a mystery. Born Helen E. Griswold in New York in 1819, she had relocated during the early 1840s to Chicago, where she met and married Joseph Harrington, a Massachusetts man and Unitarian minister who was serving as a missionary to Chicago's First Unitarian Society. He had been educated at Harvard and gone on to teach before he was ordained in 1840. The couple would be sent in 1845 to Hartford and in 1852 to San Francisco, where the clergyman died suddenly of Panama fever. With her only surviving child, Helen returned to the East and supported her small family until her death in New York City in 1872. A warm obituary notice in San Francisco's *Daily Evening Bulletin* praised "her winning address, her bright conversational powers, her uncommon talent and skill as a musician, and her personal amiability," which helps to explain the engaging curiosity of Miss Ella in Florida.[118] More significantly for the *Lakeside Monthly* and this story, the Harringtons departed from Chicago during the spring of 1844 for an extended trip to the East and South—to visit and preach in Baltimore, among other places. Their further itinerary is now in doubt, but Helen had remained in touch with a childhood friend who moved to St. Augustine with her family during the 1820s. When Frances Smith married there in 1837, Helen helped secure her wedding clothes in the North.[119] She was familiar with St. Augustine, in other words, because a friend worth visiting knew the city well.

Certainly her story's narrator remembers "the quaint old town" with a traveler's appreciation of the harbor, "the ancient fort frowning toward the bay—the strange Spanish pilot—the long wharf—the curious medley of buildings, from the ruinous mansion of departed Spanish glory to the white-painted and green-blinded American 'residence.'" Once landed, the "little invalid" gazes with a tourist's eye at southern exotica: roses, jasmines, oranges, and the enslaved. In memory, she casts such "novelty" as a "fairy tale," with the makings of a "scene" that those in southern Illinois might have recognized. Just off the boat, she describes "the black members of the household" as accoutrements, stage props "having no individual existence (one might say) but shining only in the reflected light of their master's glory." Both the appeal of a family's "master" and the booster preoccupation with self-made men would help Harrington's story find its place in the *Lakeside Monthly*, especially when the master and his household were seen through thirteen-year-old eyes.

From that perspective, it is remarkable that nearly everybody in this "cordial" home visibly labors. Miss Margaret carries the keys as the family's housekeeper. Aunt Anna schools the family's white children as governess. Maum Liddy supervises the nursery. Thomas instructs Primus on how to wait table with "a wonderful professional aptitude." Meanwhile, the black scapegrace busies himself folding napkins, a convenient cover for his "unblushing" theft. It thus seems a small step to the labor required to produce the sugar that catches his eye. There is even a slight nod in Harrington's story to the zenith of sugar production in East Florida, just before the Second Seminole War began in 1835. Her St. Augustine mansion is presided over by Mr. Lawton, whose name recalls the Charleston land agents (Joseph and Charles Lawton) who bought and sold regional properties like Dunlawton, then a thriving coastal sugar plantation.

Until the displaced Seminoles attacked the numerous works up and down Florida's Atlantic coast, sugarcane was a cash crop whose processing was eventually steam-powered, a striking development that Patricia Griffin has called "mechanized agriculture."[120] If larger plantations amounted to slave "villages," as John Michael Vlach has noted, sugar plantations were slave factories, what Lucy Wayne in *Sweet Cane* describes as "industrial complexes" that crushed, clarified, boiled, and crystallized around the clock when the cane was harvested.[121] Wayne declares that sugar was "the ideal plantation product for East Florida" during the 1820s, but increasing competition from Cuba and Louisiana meant that the ruined works were not often rebuilt after Seminole attacks.[122] At once labor-intensive and deeply dependent on slavery's unpaid workforce, the sugar industry's demands on harvest workers were "horrendous," as Sidney Mintz's puts it, what amounted to the theft of labor for sprawling capitalist markets.[123]

Chicago was certainly in that orbit, and the *Lakeside Monthly* was committed to work as the hallmark of western endeavor. Given the magazine's antislavery principles as well, it was possible in its pages to reconstitute abolition's rhetorical priorities by demoting Luciano's play on sentiment and substituting a less customary respect for labor. In "A Glance at Florida" (October 1869), for example, Kate Doggett sustains Browne's gospel of labor by praising the "wondrous springs of this flowery land" but deploring the "spirit of injustice" that animates its "governing class."[124] When that "oppression" of "red men ... black ...

the poor of their own color" is overcome, Doggett argues, "fishermen and mariners will utilize the waters, farmers will till the now desolate wastes, lumbermen will cut from the pathless forests woods beautiful as those brought from the Indies." Only the "truly free," for Doggett, will seize the opportunity to work, a spirited summons to reform without tears.[125] Hers is the kind of rhetorical strategy that Dana Luciano has called "countermonumental," a tack that offsets abolition's more customary appeal to "maternal" sentiment. Aiming instead to disorient would, in Luciano's deft phrase, "force the sentimental heart to skip a beat," thereby engaging readers more actively, less conventionally.[126] While the sugarcane harvest and the South's overburdened workforce were not widely discussed in Chicago's literary venues, how to deal fairly with enslaved laborers does redirect the narrative economy of Harrington's scenes, where respect prevails while sentimental tears fall short.

That is pointedly true after Amelia is punished by Captain Derby for dumping an armload of wood. As Miss Ella discovers in Mrs. Derby's parlor, the slave mother was beaten so severely that her neck and shoulders were "scarred in a shocking manner by the recent application of a whip." Seeing something so "hideous and repulsive" converts the youthful narrator to abolition, just as seeing yet another image in this story's ongoing volley converts the reader into a montage maker, a creator of meaning from Harrington's "strange and beautiful picture of light and shade." For Luciano, more active reading becomes the most stirring consequence of countermonumental dialogue. As the reader's stand-in, Miss Ella finally recognizes Amelia's misfortune, not with a hug for an ailing Christian or tears for a separated wife but with all the change in her purse, what amounts to surreptitious pay for honest labor. If the lash marks confirm a master's power, they also expose Amelia's growing challenge to Captain Derby and the patriarchal arrogance his temper reveals.

Because Harrington's story is intent on how Miss Ella becomes an abolitionist, it is eventually up to her to "deliver" Amelia into an emancipated life in New England. But Florida's slaves had historically found their own way by heading in the other direction, south. After the practice of slavery was abolished across the British Empire in 1833, Florida's escaping fugitives in growing numbers made for Nassau, roughly one hundred miles offshore. What Irvin Winsboro and Joe Knetsch describe as a "saltwater railroad" ran through British ships from St. Augustine or through Seminole country to the Florida Keys and Bahamanian assistance there. Although records are scarce and research on this alternative route has only recently begun, enough enslaved people made their escape in this fashion to create a considerable population in the Bahamas and to alarm Florida's slaveholders, the Lawtons and Derbys of the territorial years. "Put simply," write

Winsboro and Knetsch, "the principle that slaves could escape forced servitude via a short saltwater route to the British Bahamas was one that continued to frighten masters and planters in the South and to complicate Anglo-American affairs until the firing on Fort Sumter."[127] Like the freedpeople taught by Nash's narrator in "Jack Dessart," other Amelias and their families discovered a second chance that was closer than New England and easy to reach without the North Star.

Just not for Harrington's "cordial" household. "In the Palmy Days of Slaveholding" is a tale of slave rescue that is finally less attentive to black resistance than to white tutorial. As Toni Morrison has observed, "The subject of the dream is the dreamer. The fabrication of an Africanist persona is reflexive... an astonishing revelation of longing, of terror, of perplexity, of shame, of magnanimity."[128] Unlike Amelia or Maum Liddy, Miss Ella actually tries on different roles through the series of women she might soon resemble: the New England aunt who marries an intemperate slaveholder, the slave mother who refuses to leave her husband despite a master's cruelty, the resident belle who secretly enables slave escape. As her story concludes, Miss Ella confronts the troubling grace of plantation manners that foster both "patriarchal kindness" and "tyrannical oppression."

These qualities figure in Harrington's portrait of Mrs. Derby, the brutal captain's gracious mother who never lifts a finger. Her "gentle, winning sweetness of voice and manner" undergoes a "sudden transformation" for Miss Ella when her hostess reveals a complicity in violence; for Mrs. Derby, Amelia's scars seem unsightly rather than unjust. That casual cruelty reappears in her son, particularly when the captain's "ungovernable temper" disrupts the dancing at "The Hall." What might have been a family stain then becomes a shared habit of deflection: the ladies avert their eyes to accept Captain Derby's apology. But his verbal screen fails to hide the bandleader's bloody gash, just as Amelia's handkerchief fails to cover her shocking scars. At the heart of Harrington's "quaint old town," in the kind of hinterland that serves so often as an enticing past, lies a ferocity that curdles Southern manners and abbreviates the restorative salve of days gone by.

As though to mirror such unrestrained violence, St. Augustine's apparent somnolence was also about to erupt. Harrington sets her story just before the Second Seminole War, the time during the 1830s when U.S. officers and their troops poured into town. The historical tremor of racial assault thus lurks behind this story's "shining crystals." In late 1835 and early 1836, after American settlers had been arriving for more than a decade, the Seminoles set fire to the sugar plantations along the coast, a conflagration that drew attention as far north as Baltimore. Collating accounts of "The Seminole War" from Florida papers, *Niles' Weekly Register* quoted a February 11 report as declaring: "The whole of the country, south of St. Augustine, has been laid waste during the past week, and not a building of any value left standing. There is not a single house now remaining, between this city and Cape Florida, a distance of 250 miles, *all, all, have been burnt to the ground*."[129] With the assistance of the region's self-emancipating slaves, who had long taken refuge on Native lands and encouraged Native resistance, the "desperate Seminoles and their black allies" (in Jane Landers's revealing phrase) swept through sugar plantations that, in most cases, would never recover.[130]

Harrington's story postpones that uprising, but her narrator also creates the gap that the Second and Third Seminole Wars and then the rebel General Derby would fill. Delivered as an extended flashback, "In the Palmy Days of Slaveholding" effectively invents a Florida past for a postwar nation and a western magazine in the midst of Reconstruction. It is therefore instructive that the Seminoles who torched East Florida's sugar works had long offered safety and then a new social order to black fugitives. As Landers points out, "The Seminoles had been incorporating escaped slaves into their society for at least a half-century."[131] The fugitives who remained on Native lands affiliated with the Seminoles, built their own Florida villages, cleared their own wilderness plots away from Native outposts, and paid an annual tribute as latter-day vassals rather than slaves. They became Black Seminoles during a territorial period when they could not become "African Americans," which the Supreme Court's *Dred Scott* decision confirmed as late as 1857. Until 1838, in the judgment of Larry Eugene Rivers, the Seminole alternative in Florida made for a mutually beneficial arrangement: "The Seminoles required blacks to help them keep their lands, and blacks allied with the Seminoles to enable them to preserve their freedom."[132] Black Seminoles embodied an alternative to scars and gashes, a social consolidation that slips into the temporal gap produced by Harrington's play with narrative time.

Closing that gap in a handful of paragraphs leads to a protracted denouement in a story that, oddly, ends three times. First, the "festival" that greets Miss Ella's return to New England also embraces Amelia, whose "o' man" and son Primus soon join her. The joy of their reunion outstrips the earlier "passion of sorrow" when Miss Ella leaves Florida and "the black members of the household," no longer props. "On the whole," Miss Ella confesses, "my most alluring view of slavery was my last—perhaps because it was the slaves and not the slaveholders who formed the mass of the picture." Even in the midst of farewell tears, labor continues: Mauma Liddy holds "Maas Alfred," Primus carries Miss Ella's "umbruther," and Thomas stows her considerable baggage. A second ending emerges when the "hardship" of the South turns into the "liberation" of the North, as Harrington's coming-of-age tale subsides into a coming-of-justice narrative that Miss Margaret commences and Miss Ella concludes. It is a steady advance: Miss Margaret spirits a slave away, Primus arrives, and then his father arrives to be greeted by Amelia thanks to Miss Ella, who is ready to welcome the new stories ("a negro baby is the 'cunningest' thing") that are about to be told. With narrative time moving unimpeded and countermonumentally toward social justice rather than sentimental tears, Harrington has little reason to mourn a cankered past and reverse the millennium.

But the story's last two paragraphs insist upon a third ending, one that sounds a note of lament for General Derby's "lost" cause and "a whole great social epoch of luxury and elegant leisure." The appeal of planter ease seemingly continued in New England as well as Florida, in downstate Illinois as well as Chicago and the first fictive reckonings with the Civil War. Harrington even catches slaveholding's appealing malice in her title, where "palmy" suggests both flourishing plantation beauty and the slap of a hand, both honorable poise and quick brutality. With more verbal wit than political resolution, that double image in the *Lakeside Monthly* recalls the stereograph's heyday in San Francisco, where more than landscape scenery would come into play. Meanwhile, Florida's sugar crystals sparkled, the double sign of privilege and labor for *Lakeside Monthly* subscribers on the way to a conflagration of their own.

CHAPTER 4

Emancipation and Grizzly Reckoning

The Advent of Photography, San Francisco's
Overland Monthly, and the Model of Parallax

The principle of parallax is older than the nineteenth century, older than Copernicus, older than Ptolemy. Even Aristotle, who believed the earth stood still, knew that a stellar body seemed to move when observed from different vantage points. That apparent shift does not have to be Greek to anybody: just hold a finger out at arm's length, cover one eye, then cover the other. Any pair of eyes provides two slightly different points of view, which help to place what is observed and to secure a depth of field as the stereo camera once did in the nineteenth century (figure 25). On a larger scale, the parallax of heavenly bodies can be determined from at least two different sites more than a few miles apart, or from the same site more than a few weeks apart and therefore at different stages of the earth's yearlong revolution around the sun. Adept at such measurements, Asaph Hall at the U.S. Naval Observatory determined, between August and October 1877, that the planet Mars had two undiscovered moons, which he named Phobos and Deimos, or Fear and Terror, after the *Iliad*'s two minions of the god of war.

In a similar fashion, the United States, which only slowly began taking a singular verb after the principle of a looser confederacy was defeated, coalesced during the nineteenth century. Out of differing points of view and then the invocation of war, a powerful General Government emerged in 1865 together with a newly paramount national citizenship as the jurisdiction of postwar states receded. At this apprehensive moment of political consolidation and cultural opportunity, what quite a few Americans had in hand as they tried to define a reconstructing union were battlefield pictures—most provocatively, the first stereo views of Antietam soldiers where they fell on September 17, 1862. Indeed, what the *New York Times* called "dripping bodies" with "a terrible distinctness" were made both more familiar and more unnerving by the fact that

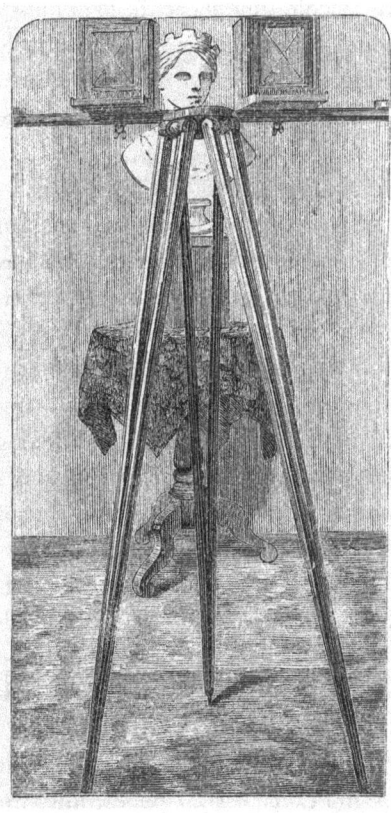

FIGURE 25. *Taking Stereoscopic Picture of Near Objects*. Wood engraving. Austin Abbott, "The Eye and Camera," *Harper's Monthly*, September 1869, 480. Courtesy of the University of Iowa Libraries.

Mathew Brady had been marketing these Maryland pictures to Northern parlors, while operator Alexander Gardner had anticipated Brady's gallery business by taking most of his Antietam photographs as stereo views.[1]

From photography's wartime advances, as well as from Asaph Hall's heavenly spectacle, three points follow for understanding how many Americans first made the Civil War coherent, points grounded like binocular vision in the principle of parallax. First, the irregular double image of the stereo view, which is constructed of two photographs taken roughly two and a half inches apart, like a pair of eyes, may serve as a model for the irregular double vision of the Civil War that would emerge after Antietam's horrific casualties. In late 1862 battlefield photographs were suddenly compared in record numbers to the artistic drawings made for new illustrated magazines, which often celebrated the regiments with which special artists traveled. Also made on the spot, such drawings contrasted sharply with the "dripping bodies" that Gardner discovered and Brady displayed. Even more insistently, these new visual technologies clashed at the very moment that Abraham Lincoln announced the Preliminary Emancipation Proclamation on September 22. The stereo model of "fraternally twinned images," in Miles Orvell's apt phrase, thus offered an available cultural logic across representational mediums that were at odds and across civil rupture to the emancipated postwar nation, not at all the Union as it was.[2]

Second, the stereo model can also be extended to Civil War stories as exercises in commemoration from decidedly different sites, such as Boston and San Francisco. In fact, postwar California and Bret Harte's new literary magazine, the *Overland Monthly* (1868–75), took advantage of an unusual distance from the East and its parochial perspective to cast San Francisco as exotically polyglot, truly Olympian Boston's fraternal twin and the country's demographic future. In issue after issue, the magazine's booster agenda favored a keen sense of otherness that proved receptive to the claims of new black citizens. Looking back to the war years, the *Overland Monthly* also published a clutch of stories so idiosyncratic that they can be explained in part by the earlier crowding of the forty-niners and the continuing enticement of San Francisco for so many from so many other places, even years after gold was first discovered. Repeatedly, the Civil War narratives circulated by the *Overland Monthly* directly challenged eastern priorities through their unusual witness, which intensified the competition of visual logics with a further dissonance in perspective that readers were left to resolve.

Finally, the emerging habit of seeing stereoscopically, like our more recent hankering for instant replay, created a significant postwar opportunity for imagining how new African American citizens might augment the body politic. Again, the stereo view is pertinent because its illusory depth bespoke the necessary ascendancy of the viewer, who alone could contrive a merging of images and a "virtual reality" whose three-dimensional field was nowhere visible on a pasteboard card. By analogy, it was up to magazine readers to envision a parallactic postwar nation, one whose imagined dimension and reconstructive audacity might spring in part from perusing regional magazines. In the culture wars that actually intensified after 1865, when the Thirteenth Amendment unlocked slavery's chains without defining emancipation's freedoms, magazines like the *Overland Monthly* published surprising Civil War stories whose commemorative peculiarities have remained largely unexplored. A cultural moon of sorts with any new satellite's unexamined trajectory, Bret Harte's magazine was both captured by and separate from the eastern periodical behemoths that students of Reconstruction have been slow to set aside.

Like other regional venues for bringing civil clash into focus, the *Overland Monthly* emerged from an idiosyncratic site of production, especially as memories of the war began to coalesce. By 1868, when the magazine was founded, San Francisco had become a moon of many hues thanks to soaring immigration and the glittering "come hither" of California. For decades, the lure of instant wealth and a widely touted city had attracted what Barbara Berglund describes as a "promiscuous mixture of peoples and cultures," the hallmark of Berglund's *Making San Francisco American*.[3] As early as the 1850s, Michael Kowaleski has noted, "the novelty of California was largely emphasized for an audience in the East, or at least for an audience with eastern sensibilities."[4] Courting immigrants, sojourners, and tourists of all sorts, California in general and San Francisco in particular had opted to become a scene worthy of any gaze, a piece of what Martha Sandweiss has called "the imagined West."[5]

Many arrived by sea and could therefore recall the unusual contours of the California coast and the spectacle of the bay city that M. G. Upton later portrayed for the *Overland Monthly* in "The Plan of San Francisco" (February 1869). From the nighttime steamer, Upton would write, Telegraph and Rincon Hills rose up like "luminous cones" beneath Russian Hill, towering "in stories of light."[6] By 1869, when the first transcontinental railroad was completed, the city was on the cusp of a new tourist boom that would reward the well-established "light" of self-promotion and the appeal of California's photogenic splendor. With the West suddenly accessible and captivating, another way of seeing, as well as unpredictable things to see, made stereo views and their viewers ever more the model for how to read the social revolution produced by the Civil War, particularly when African Americans began exercising their rights as citizens and war stories with abrupt leaps in narrative distance and perspective made their way into regional print.

Such developments had yet to crest the national horizon as negotiations surrounding the Emancipation Proclamation began during the summer of 1862, when Abraham Lincoln willingly linked the extension of civil liberties to elusive battlefield success. The Union victory in mid-September at the Battle of Antietam allowed the president to tie the rights of enslaved people in rebellious territory to the force that new social relations would require. "Thenceforward and forever," as Stephen Sears has written, "the United States would be a very different nation."[7] As James M. McPherson has added, "The symbolic power of the Proclamation changed the war from one to restore the Union into one to destroy the old Union and build a new one purged of human bondage."[8] Unfortunately for Lincoln and the "new birth of freedom" he would invoke at Gettysburg, what the Army of the Potomac found along Antietam Creek in the midst of a warm Indian summer was a bloodbath, as Mathew Brady's photographic exhibition would soon reveal.[9] More than 150 years later, September 17, 1862,

FIGURE 26. Alexander Gardner, *The "Sunken Road" at Antietam*. Stereo view. Courtesy of the Library of Congress, LC-DIG-ppmsca-07751.

remains the single bloodiest day in American battlefield history, a day on which more than twenty-two thousand men were reported dead, wounded, captured, or missing in action.

Yet the threat of military disaster little more than sixty miles from Washington produced another opportunity, even before the Preliminary Emancipation Proclamation was issued less than a week later. Fortuitously, Antietam Creek and the town of Sharpsburg lay close enough to Brady's Washington gallery for Alexander Gardner and his assistant James Gibson to make their way into Maryland with armloads of photographic supplies right after the smoke cleared.[10] The Army of Northern Virginia refused to retire following the long afternoon's losses, and the Battle of Antietam remained a standoff for another hot September day, while intermittent truces were declared so the wounded could be moved. On the field that General Lee and his army finally left behind, Brady's operators discovered burial parties just setting out and bloated bodies beginning to decompose, like those photographed along the sunken mill road soon to be known as Bloody Lane (figure 26).

The raw force of such stereo views, even in distant San Francisco, can best be understood by way of the visual norms these images defied. In the immediate wake of battle, anxious readers generally looked to the new illustrated weeklies, whose wood engravings quickly augmented battlefield dispatches and casualty reports. By the fall of 1862, special artists (or "specials") such as Edwin Forbes had been traveling with the Army of the Potomac for months. They were thus on the spot for what he called "the most picturesque battle of the war," by which he meant that specials at Antietam could see the battle unfold across

FIGURE 27. Edwin Forbes, *Brilliant and Decisive Bayonet Charge of Hawkins's Zouaves.* Wood engraving. *Frank Leslie's Illustrated Newspaper,* October 11, 1862, 40–41. Courtesy of the University of Iowa Libraries.

open fields from the comparative safety of reserve batteries.[11] What Forbes witnessed and then drew that September afternoon was printed in *Frank Leslie's Illustrated Newspaper* as *Brilliant and Decisive Bayonet Charge of Hawkins's Zouaves,* a double-page engraving of the moment when the Ninth New York poured across fields and meadows, then up over a stone wall and into the roar of Confederate artillery and the flash of rebel muskets (figure 27). Their charge was to cost the larger brigade of 940 some 455 men, but the cheering New Yorkers would see rebels running through the streets of Sharpsburg.[12]

In the drawing that *Leslie's* engraved, some of the New York volunteers have already fallen, but Forbes's composition takes its visual excitement from those still standing: from the distinctive uniforms of the Zouaves, as well as the muzzles they load and the bayonets they hoist to give the illustration its title. Significantly, the flag the soldiers raise in the left foreground has not yet been struck down, as it would be repeatedly when Confederate guns opened fire. Instead, those batteries are consigned to the engraving's sketchy background, an arrangement that translates the shallow field of the medium into the sketchy inadequacy of the Southern cause. Special artists like Forbes, who traveled at the pleasure of Union generals and the army they accompanied, had every reason to align their political loyalties with their professional interests as they drew for the woodblock, especially since the newsmagazines they supplied were serving largely Northern audiences by 1862.

As a result, the "picturesque" moments that subscribers discovered usually gave greater dimension and weight to foregrounded Union regiments, which were often filled from the ranks of weekly readers.[13] In both Northern par-

FIGURE 28. Edwin Forbes, *The Battle of Antietam—Charge of Burnside's 9th Corps, on the Right Flank of the Confederate Army, 3:30 p.m., Sept. 17th, 1862*. Sketch in pencil and Chinese white. Courtesy of the Library of Congress, LC-DIG-ppmsca-22526.

lors and Union camps, it was thus reassuring to peruse New York's *Leslie's Illustrated*, which had been founded in 1852 and generally relied for its war coverage on artistic drawings begun hastily near the field. No matter what special artists chose to portray, they started with a blank sheet that invited quick lines, like those in the pencil sketch that Forbes made of the Zouave charge (figure 28). In the scribbled notes added to his subsequent drawing to guide the New York art department, Forbes numbered the points of interest he had decided to include, such as "2—The old Lutheran church" and "5—Rebel line of battle." From blank sheet to sketch and from drawing to engraving, specials thereby articulated a logic of constructed space.

No wonder, then, that Brady's October exhibition of Antietam photographs brought New York gallery visitors up short, while the battlefield photographs stirred local journals to consider an unpicturesque war stripped of apparent design. Noting the difference between the morning casualty lists and the startling images Brady displayed, like a view of Antietam's vicious early fighting, the *New York Times* spoke of their "dull, dead, remorseless weight" on breaking hearts and of "the horrible significance that dwells amid the jumble of type" (figure 29).[14] Where the dead in Forbes's drawing amounted to battlefield obstacles and visual litter, Alexander Gardner's views for Brady took such obstacles as central, and the litter of battlefield concussion became Gardner's recurring visual theme.

Routinely, photographic operators were confronted with a scene that was always already there, always already what Peter Galassi has called "the intractably three-dimensional stuff of the world."[15] Particularly when taken along the

FIGURE 29. Alexander Gardner, *Antietam, Maryland. Bodies of Dead, Louisiana Regiment.* Stereo view, right half. Courtesy of the Library of Congress, LC-DIG-cwpb-01105.

fence line of the Hagerstown Pike, Gardner's photographs from Maryland suggested a logic of irrelevant detail: among the rotting bodies of the Confederate dead, it scarcely mattered whose arm was raised or which rail was down. Instead of Forbes's converging lines of battle, Gardner's stereo view of Antietam's "contest" favored endless detritus; William Frassanito speculates, in fact, that Gardner could identify General William Edwin Starke's Louisiana Brigade by the insignia on one soldier's knapsack, which gallery visitors could inspect with a magnifying glass.[16] But when growing numbers of viewers recalled what they had seen in illustrated weeklies, the divergences of the new mediums were difficult to reconcile.

In negotiating the clash between Forbes's boundless glory and Gardner's boundless litter, the very task of seeing stereoscopically, wartime Americans were assisted by the many discreet adjustments that artistic drawings and battlefield photographs might undergo, adjustments that brought both sorts of pictures closer to Orvell's "fraternally twinned images." Photographs could be staged on the battlefield, for example, just as portraits had been staged in the studio; at Gettysburg almost a year later, Gardner would rearrange bodies, insert props, and fudge his captions.[17] Mathew Brady had also been accustomed to retouching portraits during the developing process, a practice that gave photographs some of the creative play of artistic drawings. Indeed, the antebellum popularity of portrait photography bequeathed to wartime operators a recur-

FIGURE 30. Alfred R. Waud, *The Battle of Antietam—Carrying off the Wounded after the Battle*. Wood engraving. *Harper's Weekly*, October 11, 1862, 649. Courtesy of the University of Iowa Libraries.

ring visual syntax; as Joel Snyder has pointed out, Civil War photographs were consistently taken at eye level, straight ahead without tilt, and from a "respectable" distance rather than up close.[18] Like drawings made on the spot, photographs also borrowed occasionally from picturesque conventions, most notably in the use of cloud negatives, which allowed operators like George M. Barnard to create the moody skies of his composite images. Prevalent as such landscape conventions were, they could also be manipulated by special artists in the field, sometimes for the battlefield jolt more often associated with photographic views. At Antietam, for example, Alfred Waud sketched a field hospital amputation that would have brought "dripping bodies" with "a terrible distinctness" to readers of *Harper's Weekly*, if the Harper art department had not rearranged the patient on the left head-first and tucked the lifted soldier's sawed leg snugly before the drawing was published nearly a month later (figure 30).

Still, the logical tension between the order of constructed space and the sprawl of irrelevant detail was hard to miss, and the difficulty of bringing a disquieting double vision into focus was likewise apparent in the illustrated pages of *Harper's Weekly*, while the *Overland Monthly* of the 1860s and 1870s was unadorned. During the war, the illustrated weeklies often purchased Brady's

FIGURE 31. *Scenes on the Battlefield of Antietam. From Photographs by Mr. M. B. Brady.* Wood engraving. *Harper's Weekly*, October 18, 1862, 664–65. Courtesy of the University of Iowa Libraries.

gallery photographs, especially his portraits, and turned them into wood engravings. A process that worked reasonably well for staged likenesses, however, miscarried noticeably when Brady's *The Dead of Antietam* became the engraved *Scenes on the Battlefield of Antietam* in the newsmagazine (figure 31). With images in hand, Harper artists in New York first organized individual photographs into a composite view, which was designed to frame the picturesque arches of Burnside's Bridge and thus looked less like battlefield witness than art department intercession. More importantly, the sharp details in Gardner's photographs gave way to the receding lines in several of the newsmagazine's assembled drawings, as staff artists employed rows of the dead to create the illusion of pictorial depth rather than the shock of recognized insignia.

Consider Gardner's *Gathered Together for Burial: After the Battle of Antietam* (figure 32). Comparatively, the related "scene" in the newsmagazine sacrificed motley clothing and gaping flesh for the gentle curve of battlefield death, which carried the eye past tufts of grass to the midground trees and the distant ridge, all beneath conventionally striated skies (figure 33). Gone were the vacant faces and what Keith Davis has called "the brutal inertness of death."[19] In their place, readers of *Harper's Weekly* saw death's quiet order in a row of awkward smudges that resisted scrutiny and missed the "actual expression" of "last agonies," as the *New York Herald* (October 5, 1862) had described them.[20] Instead

FIGURE 32. Alexander Gardner, *Gathered Together for Burial: After the Battle of Antietam*. Stereo view, left half. For Mathew Brady, *The Dead of Antietam*. Courtesy of the Library of Congress, LC-DIG-stereo-1s02944.

FIGURE 33. *Scenes on the Battlefield of Antietam. From Photographs by Mr. M. B. Brady*. Wood engraving, detail. *Harper's Weekly*, October 18, 1862, 664. Courtesy of the University of Iowa Libraries.

of providing in wood engraving a genuine integration of constructed space and proliferating detail, illustrated weeklies revealed how antithetical the mediums were in 1862 and how much readers were left with a troubling tension between flattened glory and pointless litter.

If baffled Americans needed help in reconciling the war's disparate images, they were likeliest to get it from other pages of newsmagazines and from other periodicals that carried war stories. Particularly in the aftermath of Antietam's losses, the stories circulated in literary monthlies revealed a similar dissonance when they began fluctuating between the familiar and the unconventional in their narrative design. Sentences in Antietam stories started to fall apart with the "whir" of chance bullets, the broken mutterings of rough soldiers, and the abrupt emergence of dialect. Customary past-tense narration could falter when present-tense interruptions became more acute. More broadly, the formal tension between narrators in their summaries and characters in their scenes accelerated as authoritative narrators lost verbal ground to a vernacular litter. In Antietam stories from magazines across the country, the rounded perspective that narrative omniscience shared with artistic drawing was increasingly fractured by the rude details, irrelevant and obtrusive, that surfaced in dialogue and photograph alike, as the insurgency of characters with things to say challenged the directing hand of a narrator and the assurances of a stable order. In place of photographic sprawl, however, stories about Antietam repeatedly favored the ascent of a minor character, one able to read a divided dramatis personae and teach magazine readers how to discover depth by bringing disparities into focus.

Like Melville's Ishmael and Hawthorne's Surveyor Pue, these minor characters often describe scenes they never saw and conversations they never heard, but the stories they piece together do not arrive in due course at *Moby-Dick*'s floating coffin or the enigmatic tombstone of *The Scarlet Letter*. Instead, these "told to" stories are often as broken as their sources, a narrative strategy that makes ways of seeing part of the point. For example, in Elizabeth Stuart Phelps's "A Sacrifice Consumed" for *Harper's Monthly* (January 1864), a small-town neighbor leaves much to the reader by offering the "truthful" story of a drudging seamstress in several ill-fitting pieces: the sentence fragments of the opening "picture" ("a low room, scanty but neat furniture"), the pointed observations that slowly tug the reader into the story's apparatus ("you would not wish to see her in a brighter dress"), the artful tweaks to readerly anticipation ("you must not expect excitement or change of scene"), the fumble of the soldier who tells the girl that her lover has died ("and—and I come to tell you that—to tell you—well, he's gone"), even the visible breaks in the story's delivery and the recurring use of the word "broken."[21] Repeatedly in such stories, a character in the wings observes events or their recital as a stand-in for the reader, who knows little, rather than the author, who knows much.

The quiet mediation of these nameless narrators suggests not only the synthetic task of a midwar reader but also the growing importance of a midcentury "observer," Jonathan Crary's term for marking the nineteenth-century shift away from the status of things seen and toward the dynamics of seeing. For Crary, the stereoscope serves as the representative medium of that shift, while the camera obscura embodies the certainties of perspective that were fast dissolving. As he points out, the stereoscope imitated human vision by achieving depth through reconciling disparities; in Crary's formulation, the apparatus presupposes perceptual experience to be essentially an "apprehension of differences" when images are inexact.[22] But reconciling disparities could be a dangerous undertaking during and after the Civil War, as George Ward Nichols revealed in "The General's Story" (*Harper's Monthly*, June 1867), where narrative complications provide a disturbing example. Years after the shock of casualty lists, it was not the standoff between glory and litter that frayed his account but the terrifying possibility of becoming stereoscopic, of playing different parts long enough that identity itself became malleable across an ever deepening field.

In "The General's Story," doubling is so rampant (the double identity of the narrator as spy, the double spy he meets in prison, the double narrative generated by the frame story) that observation repeatedly invites "metamorphosis" until the Antietam captain retreats into himself. Indeed, the postwar general he becomes finally drops the narrative reins for the safety of the frame story's fireside. Returning home to Washington, the general declares: "With the name of Peters I shook off that terrible nightmare of suspense. I awoke, as it were, from a horrible dream where I had been playing a part, where I had been a helpless actor to my own personality. A restful, thankful, happy consciousness was it, when I was free, when I came to know myself again."[23] The "horrible significance" of the general's "dream" is that personal freedom for a spy depended on acting the helpless twin, the hapless citizen of Baltimore instead of the resourceful Pennsylvania captain, the "careless *flaneur*" of Richmond instead of Secretary Seward's agent.[24] It was an unsettling lesson in binocular vision, a lesson the country's enslaved workers and freedpeople already knew. Even before *The Souls of Black Folk* appeared in 1903, W. E. B. Du Bois wrote in "Strivings of the Negro People" for the *Atlantic Monthly* (August 1897) about how "being a problem" felt.[25] "It is a peculiar sensation," he observed, "this double consciousness, this sense of always looking at one's self through the eyes of others."[26] As "The General's Story" reveals, something akin to double consciousness was a wartime lesson that many white Americans were only beginning to learn.

By January 1863, when the Emancipation Proclamation went into effect, the habit of seeing stereoscopically was spreading almost as rapidly as the handheld stereoscope, which was invented by Oliver Wendell Holmes in 1861 and quickly became commonplace on parlor tables. Holmes himself wrote of the eye's uneasy balance in "The Professor's Story," which was serialized in the *Atlantic Monthly* beginning in December 1859 and would later be retitled *Elsie Venner*, Holmes's first novel. Taking up the real and the ideal that the infatuated lover "blended" in one installment, Holmes declared: "The heart's vision cannot unite them stereoscopically into a single image, if the divergence passes certain limits."[27] Still, the *Atlantic Monthly* kept the possibility alive years later when responding in "Recent Literature" to Thomas Wentworth Higginson's essay collection *Oldport Days* (January 1874), with its poetic capacity to combine the "literal" and the ideal "in one stereoscopic view"; similarly, Asa Gray's earlier comments on Charles Darwin's *Origin of Species* (August 1860) played the radical claims of Darwin against those of the more conservative Charles Lyell "like the two counterpart pictures for the stereoscope" that together made "one apparently solid whole."[28] Such a reasoned venture, the making of "one apparently solid whole," eluded the domestic Holmes when he looked at Brady's views of Antietam. In "Doings of the Sunbeam" (July 1863), he admitted that he shoved the photographs of "fragments and tatters" into the far corners of his cabinet, where "mutilated remains" belonged.[29] Like so many other viewers who recalled illustrated periodicals, Holmes and the *Atlantic Monthly* were left with litter, glory, and their unresolved tension.

It is therefore noteworthy that the *Overland Monthly* was founded in a decidedly plural San Francisco as an alternative register, a fundamental challenge, a fraternal twin. Its very name was coined to defy the cultural hegemony of the Northeast. Writing his first "ETC." column for the magazine's debut in July 1868, editor Bret Harte began his two-and-a-half-year tenure by declaring: "'Pacific Monthly' is hackneyed, mild in suggestion, and at best but a feeble echo of the Boston 'Atlantic.'"[30] Harte further dismissed possibilities like the "Wide West" as "threadbare," the "Occidental" as "cheap pedantry," and the "Sunset" as "cheaper sentiment." Instead, it was the railroad, "the highway of our thought," as he put it, that would deliver western "breadth and liberality" in one direction and eastern "refinement" in the other, a transaction that was important enough to put the railroad track on the magazine's title page (figure 6). Astutely, Harte sketched the track's twin lines beneath California's grizzly bear and its "primitive" defiance, a sign that the *Overland Monthly* would not take backwater status kindly when the "Development of the Country" was uppermost.[31]

By the time the San Francisco magazine was founded, the *Atlantic Monthly* had sustained its growing cultural authority for a decade. With the help of Davis's deft hand in "John Lamar" (April 1862), Boston's smug prestige had already inflected narrative priorities in stories of the war. But emancipation complicated the stories that less elite magazines would tell, particularly if they followed the lead of Abraham Lincoln as his views on race and national citizenship shifted over time.[32] That was particularly true for a polyglot western metropole where social relations were already unsettled. In *The Public City: The Political Construction of Urban Life in San Francisco, 1850–1900*, Philip Ethington points to what he calls "the climate of the social revolution unleashed by the Emancipation Proclamation," which made race rather than republican virtue a determining priority and thereby countered an antebellum sense of the common good.[33] Beginning in 1863, Ethington argues, the country's prevailing political model would derive instead from social groups and their competing interests. That proved to be the case for San Francisco's chief postwar literary magazine. In the ten eccentric Civil War stories that the *Overland Monthly* circulated and particularly in the four that reckoned with race, a fundamental shift from individual initiative to group dynamics, from personal liberty to public service, and from established consensus to social contention defied Boston's high-toned example and helped reorient the play of postwar storytelling.

San Francisco's rough iconoclasm and the *Overland*'s journeyman challenge produced a Davis "twin" in the lesser-known, unfamous Freeman S. Bowley. As Keith Wilson has reported, Freeman Sparks Bowley was a seventeen-year-old from Maine when he enlisted as a white officer in the Thirtieth United States Colored Infantry (USCT) during the war's final year, before he immigrated to San Francisco in 1868 for work as a fireman on the Southern Pacific Railroad and began publishing stories drawn from his wartime experience.[34] His "A Dark Night on Picket" (July 1870) in the *Overland* depicts black military service with none of Davis's verbal audacity, none of her narrative finesse, none of her slave Ben's vengeful muscle. Instead, Bowley's recollection of colored troops near Richmond offers a "groan of superstitious horror" and faceless voices in the dark, especially when contrasted with his well-spoken division officer of the day.[35] What Bowley describes as the "maniac laugh" of a great horned owl is actually more memorable than his black men in the ranks ("a Sergeant," "my reserve," "the vidette"), who come and go in a less accomplished narrative without names, without features, pretty much without character.[36] Against Davis's sharp portraits, they are a blur.

Yet they can handle musket barrels as well as bayonets, and they capture rebel prisoners armed with carbines while fending off "large, ferocious, yellow dogs."[37] Narratively inexact, they nonetheless register the African American claim to the perquisites of citizenship via military service. Bowley's black soldiers on picket do not talk much, and when they do it is in the practiced dialect of "good Lordy hab mussey!"[38] But where Davis casts the fight for freedom as an exercise in bold initiative, personal and daring, Bowley's narrative fumbles treat the black claim to civil liberties en masse, not only an undifferentiated group effort but an effort by the only group—the USCT—that historically counted. Davis could not have served Boston's *Atlantic* better than in her slave master's parting tribute: "When we stand where New England does, Ben's son will be ready for his freedom."[39] Even in its irony, her delineation of black power amounts to single-handed combat and a commitment to the founding ideals that rippled on the magazine's title page. But Bowley's submergence of character in crowd, of fetching talk in silent obedience, of Ben's "glittering knife" in the musket barrels of disciplined troops is a reminder that slave revolts were far less numerous than black enlistments, which the *Overland Monthly* was almost the only postwar magazine to imagine.[40]

More than the right side of history, that amounts to the right side of emancipation's social logic, the fundamental postwar shift to "class and group identities" that Ethington sees replacing "the republican assumption of an indivisible public interest."[41] Arguably, that new social paradigm was emerging more quickly in the *Overland Monthly* and San Francisco because the city was, in Glenna Matthews's phrase, "born cosmopolitan."[42] The California coast had long attracted Spanish explorers and then Mexican settlers, European traffickers in fur and then New England traders in hides and tallow. But the discovery of gold at Sutter's Fort in 1848 provoked what Kevin Starr describes as "an ecumenical challenge of unprecedented magnitude," thanks to an international rush of Anglo and African Americans, Chinese and Polynesians, Britons and Frenchmen, Germans and Australians, as well as thousands arriving from Mexico, Chile, and Peru.[43] The extraordinary mélange, which converging routes made possible, the city then rendered competitive, especially when new residents crowded hotels and shanties, boardinghouses and tents. As Matthews puts it, "San Francisco was not born enlightened—far from it—but it was born in such a way that many groups could contend in its public sphere."[44] After the Civil War, there was no better city in the country for interest groups to contend and for Freeman S. Bowley to make his home.

By 1870 local interest groups were already becoming socially tiered in ways that would infuse recollections of the Civil War in the *Overland Monthly*. San Francisco's African Americans, for example, were not the city's laborers but its household staff—domestic servants, porters, chambermaids, cooks, and waiters, as Douglas Henry Daniels has shown. In the midst of the war and its immediate aftermath, they were vocal enough to bring about significant political challenges to disenfranchisement, court prohibitions, and segregated public schools. "During the 1860s," Daniels points out, "one color bar after another fell, and San Francisco's Negroes waxed optimistic as they shared the enthusiasm of slaves in the south and freedmen throughout the nation."[45] Arguably, their success was due to their comparatively small numbers, spread throughout the city. According to Najia Aarim-Heriot, Chinese immigration was surging in the 1860s, but African American demographics scarcely budged. "While African Americans constituted only 0.8% of the state population," she writes, "the Chinese amounted to about 8.8%."[46] As local historian John S. Hittell put it as early as 1878, "about ninety people in a hundred were white, nine Asiatic, and one African."[47] The region's growing push to exclude competitive labor during the economic contractions of the 1870s therefore targeted the Chinese as the greater threat. On this score, Barbara Berglund has observed that "the hostility directed at the Chinese actually made San Francisco a relatively friendly environment for African Americans throughout the nineteenth century."[48] Both Ethington's "class and group identities" and Bowley's colored troops would prosper in a city whose multiplying perspectives meant that, in the years preceding the Chinese Exclusion Act of 1882, resident "Africans" were not widely maligned.

Among San Francisco's periodicals, the *Overland Monthly* did not solicit the Chinese and Irish immigrants whose cheap postwar labor fueled foundries and machine shops, railroads and mines. Instead, the city's new literary magazine was financed by German-born entrepreneur Anton Roman from his bookstore on Montgomery Street, a business district thoroughfare that had long been San Francisco's "fashionable promenade," according to Hittell.[49] Despite Harte's satiric forays, the magazine's tenor owed much to merchant interests and the commercial brashness of an overnight city. "The one purpose of her existence is to transact business for others," wrote James F. Watkins in "San Francisco" (January 1870); "the amount of that business is the limit of her development; and the amount of population gives the limit of the business."[50] Peddling benign social difference as booster lure, the *Overland* cast San Francisco as far more "poly" than the cities of the East, enough so that Noah Brooks's "Restaurant Life in San Francisco" (November 1868) could point to the tantalizing culinary spread the city's neighborhoods laid out, including "Russian caviar, Italian macaroni, German pretzels, Swiss cheese, Yankee codfish-balls, English roast beef, Spanish omelettes, French kickshaws and Mexican ollas and Asiatic nameless things."[51] Despite the monthly's instant success in both the East and the West, editor Harte still railed politically, but by 1870 the magazine's ten thousand readers had grown accustomed to the diverging agendas that postwar tables of contents reveal.[52]

The economic hardihood of San Francisco proved to be a case in point. On the self-congratulatory pages of the *Overland Monthly*, the city that had been built with gold in the 1850s had, by the late 1860s, been refurbished with silver after Nevada's Comstock Lode was discovered in 1859. By March 1874 Benjamin P. Avery was reporting in the "ETC." column he inherited that the western "*entrepot*" could boast a gold and silver yield in 1873 of $82 million.[53] The result was an imperial gaze that the magazine turned into an appreciation of social difference and a vendable regionalism, especially when the *Overland Monthly*'s "Pacific slope" reached north to the Oregon Territory and British Columbia, south to Mexico and the hemispheric Americas of immigrant crossings, and west across the Pacific to ancient kingdoms. With a sweeping gesture toward an "immense seacoast," as well as toward Asian shores an ocean away, founder Anton Roman would later write: "Here I saw an opportunity for a magazine that would furnish information for the development of our new State and all this great territory, to make itself of such value that it could not fail to impress not alone the people of the West Coast, but the East as well."[54]

That link to the culturally dominant Northeast was cannily pursued. When Harte's western stories, like "The Luck of Roaring Camp" (August 1868) and "Miggles" (June 1869), appeared in print, the response from eastern audiences was overwhelming. Associate editor William C. Bartlett would note that "a single news company in New York gave a standing order for twelve hundred copies."[55] For the ailing and departing Roman, that was sufficient proof of western development's wide appeal. For the more literary Harte, the magazine's very success buttressed what Ernest May has called his "profound contempt for commercialism," and the magazine's first readers might have wondered at its decidedly mixed messages as Crary's "apprehension of differences" collided with imperial designs.[56]

Such divergences recall San Francisco's midcentury political allegiances, which had been sharply divided ever since California entered the Union in 1850 as a free state. Despite the local celebrity of John Charles Frémont as Bear Flag insurgent and vigorous Free-Soiler, California had been led during the 1850s by Senator William Gwin, previously from Mississippi and publicly committed to the proslavery policies and state domination of the "Chivalry" Democrats. Their influence continued after Gwin left office during the war's early months, even after Democratic newspapers were suppressed during 1862. In wartime San Francisco, there were still residential pockets of wealthy Confederates; Sandra Hansen has noted that Southern women in "brownstone houses" were "fingering Dixie melodies (not too loudly) on the pianos on Rincon Hill."[57] But with the election of Republican Leland Stanford as governor in 1861, San Francisco became ever more firmly pro-Union; historian Hittell would describe the night the city learned of Lincoln's reelection in 1864 as caught up in "a grand celebration," with "numerous bonfires, illuminated windows, torches, roman candles and rockets" that lit a procession of thousands.[58] Small wonder that during the Civil War years the California Board of the U.S. Sanitary Commission collected $1.2 million of the $4.8 million the organization raised countrywide.[59] Even on Rincon Hill, Gary Scharnhorst has noted, Bret Harte and his sister made an outsized Stars and Stripes to fly over the home they shared.[60] The magazine he edited would later echo the city's political priorities and his own local defiance.

Coupling such politics with a feverish enthusiasm for "the West" in the war's aftermath, the *Overland Monthly* did not pause for long on the postbellum South. A few early military accounts recalled Southern battlefields: General Alexander McDowell McCook's Shiloh in "Six Weeks in the Mud" (March 1869), Freeman S. Bowley's black troops at Petersburg in "The Battle of the Mine" (April 1870), and a series by General John Ames that began with "Under Fire" (November 1869), an account of the Battle of Fredericksburg and its immediate aftermath. In addition, occasional grace notes touched on Southern social practices: for instance, J. McCormick's "'Dead Broke'" (November 1869) examined the suspicion of strangers in antebellum Southern towns. But the states of the failed Confederacy were most thoughtfully evoked by an Ohio-born Union journalist named Stephen Powers, who left Raleigh on January 1, 1868, and walked 3,556 miles by the southern route to San Francisco, where he arrived ten months later on November 3. A classics scholar, Powers penned numerous anecdotal accounts of his trek that would be compiled as *Afoot and Alone* (1872), many chapters first appearing in the *Overland Monthly* under the fanciful pseudonym Socrates Hyacinth.

During the war, Powers accompanied Union troops as a correspondent for the *Cincinnati Daily Appeal*; he intended on his postwar expedition to make an observer's careful record of ordinary conditions across the country. As he put it in the prefatory to his book, this new venture would be a "personal and ocular study of the most diverse races of the Republic."[61] While Powers had joined General Sherman's army on its demolishing march through Georgia and had accompanied President Lincoln's funeral train on its solemn journey to Illinois, his postwar account of the defeated Confederacy was often solitary and slowed to a walker's ambling pace. When Harte recommended the manuscript Powers assembled for publication, he would call the hefty collection "a volume of travel and observation," precisely what a correspondent's eye for detail encouraged.[62]

FIGURE 34.
A Southern Mansion and *A Home in Ruins*. Wood engraving. In Stephen Powers, *Afoot and Alone: A Walk from Sea to Sea by the Southern Route* (Hartford, Conn.: Columbian Book Company, 1872), facing 41. Courtesy of the University of Iowa Libraries.

In "A Ruined State" (July 1869), for example, Powers notes the "carpetless halls" and the "sad and lonesome sound" of "naked floors" in South Carolina's plantation homes, and he lingers on their "rank and noisome jungle of weeds," as well as their "tepid and sickly stillness . . . as if a corpse breathed a breath upon our faces."[63] When *Afoot and Alone* appeared three years later, that image of South Carolina became an uncanny visual double, the once proud home sunk into a deserted wreck (figure 34). But in "A Ruined State," Powers twins such wartime devastation with the quicker pace of Reconstruction and a lively racial interplay near Raleigh. "In North Carolina," Powers wrote, "a man grubbed in his own field; and whites and blacks often labored together, chopping, firing brushwood, composting heaps in the fence corners, and what other things thrifty farmers can do in winter. But in South Carolina the land-owners sat in fives and tens in the corner groceries . . . while squalid and tattered land-workers wandered in the roads, searching for employment they did not wish to find."[64]

What he would note in "Some Pine-Knots" (January 1872) several installments later with a "sad, sad, and piteous" requiem was the infected traces of a dying plantation order, one that energetic "farmers" elsewhere in the South were already eradicating.[65]

Just as revealing are his prose portraits of African Americans, who are less a part of the local scenery than a part of the local conversation. In Raleigh he describes the "colored factotum" named Robert who helps him decide what to carry on his trek, though in a roundabout fashion.[66] Robert opts for neckties, collars, and socks, which Powers then replaces with books (Longfellow, Horace), a few personal items, and a sewing kit, "my mother's little housewife."[67] He and Robert have different ideas about what makes the man, but they do confer. In this same account, Powers meets a freedman proud of his Union League badge, a "dusky" cooper explaining the Constitution ("life, liberty, and de 'suit ob property"), and a black giant ferrying travelers across the Cape Fear River, where he takes Powers for a Yankee peddler.[68] By the time the Ohio man has walked through Charleston, Savannah, Macon, Montgomery, Selma, Vicksburg, Shreveport, and Comanche, past the Brazos River and into the landscape he describes in "Solid Days in Texas" (June 1871), he has seen a well-born family's "poor, Black wench" transformed into a "Black Belle" by the "dusky warriors" posted at desert stations along the frontier.[69] For Socrates Hyacinth on his curiously social journey, progress toward the West hinges on acknowledging the newly free people of the South, before Texas becomes the gateway to the Indians of the Southwest.

Powers was intent during his trip on a simple purpose, as Harwood P. Hinton has observed: "to describe the attitudes and conditions of the common man along a highway that stretched from a land of despair in the South to one of golden dreams in California."[70] What he found along the Pacific, however, was the nearly systematic extermination of the state's Native peoples. Kevin Starr has observed that no other state during the nineteenth century could claim as many independent tribes, as many linguistic families, as many separate languages, or as many sustained losses when the Native population plummeted from roughly 150,000 in 1845 to fewer than 30,000 in 1870.[71] Beginning in 1872 and writing under his own name, Powers would also publish in the *Overland Monthly* a lengthy series of articles on Native peoples and their cultures, articles that were collected as *Tribes of California* (1877) and that noted ethnologist Alfred Kroeber would later call the "best introduction to the subject."[72] Even on his tramp across the South and Southwest, Powers had noticed the Apaches in "Solid Days in Texas," the Comanches in "On the Texan Prairies" (April 1869), the Diggers in "A Flock of Wool" (February 1870), and the Pimos in "Adventures in Arizona" (January 1871), accounts that likewise appeared in the receptive pages of the *Overland Monthly*. Indeed, Harte had earlier shared a sense of white aggression and Native disaster in the California town of Union, where he was so outspoken in his newspaper editorials that he was forced in 1860 to decamp for San Francisco.[73]

He discovered there a wartime city in which thousands of Chinese men were both inveterate laborers and unwelcome immigrants whose numbers were about to soar. David Wyatt notes that three thousand Chinese in 1860 became twelve thousand in 1870, far outstripping the African American immigrants on the way.[74] In San Francisco, according to Ethington, one in twelve urbanites was Chinese, more than ten times the density of African Americans.[75] The result, writes Linda Frost, was that the California press made the Chinese "the region's central racialized other and the best illustration of the dilemma of American freedom and economic possibility."[76] The *Overland Monthly* would thus emerge in a postwar city whose political battles were decidedly multiracial, a Pacific slope city where seeing stereoscopically was at once unusually difficult and unusually revealing.[77]

Nowhere were San Francisco's contending groups and the *Overland*'s literary editor more decidedly at odds than in Harte's "Plain Language from Truthful James" (September 1870), a narrative poem that concerns cheating in a frontier game of euchre. Almost everyone has noticed, as Harte biographer Gary Scharnhorst has, that the departing editor's final contribution to the magazine was a "sensation," one almost immediately dubbed "The Heathen Chinee."[78] As Harte's opening stanza puts it, "For ways that are dark / And for tricks that are vain, / The heathen Chinee is peculiar."[79] Fewer commentators have acknowledged, as Scharnhorst persuasively argues, that the satiric poem about the threat of "Chinese cheap labor" was open to appropriation, specifically by anti-Chinese demagogues whose purposes the editor was quietly mocking.[80]

Yet Harte's subtle deployment of tale-teller Truthful James, a frontier narrator of sorts, suited the *Overland Monthly*'s political kaleidoscope, as several of the engravings made for hurried reprints reveal. One of Joseph Hull's illustrations for a quickly pirated Chicago edition in 1870 portrays, for instance, the social differences that Truthful James is not so plainly negotiating, seated as he is between Irishman Bill Nye and Chinaman Ah Sin (figure 35). Like a narrator turned stereo viewer, Harte's central figure discovers that it is his job to read a racialized West, particularly during an inevitable game of cards. A year later in the Boston edition that Harte approved, one of Solomon Eytinge's illustrations suggests how combustible both frontier euchre and national politics could become without much narrative intercession (figure 36). Because Truthful James

FIGURE 35.
Joseph Hull, *Which we had small game, / And Ah Sin took a hand*. Lithographed card in envelope. In Bret Harte, *Plain Language from Truthful James* (Chicago: Western News Company, 1870). Courtesy of the University of Iowa Libraries.

FIGURE 36. Solomon Eytinge, *In the scene that ensued / I did not take a hand*. Wood engraving. In Bret Harte, *Plain Language from Truthful James* (Boston: James R. Osgood & Co., 1871), 16. Courtesy of the University of Iowa Libraries.

"did not take a hand" in Nye's attack, the precarious balance of two racially "fraternal twins" disintegrates.[81] Each of these illustrations demonstrates how essential and yet hard-pressed a seemingly minor character might prove, especially in *Overland Monthly* narratives that looked back to the Civil War. For Harte, Truthful James is at once this poem's speaker and its wayward negotiator, at once exotic entrée and crumbling binocular hope.

Two decades after the discovery of gold and the California dream of instant wealth, readers who encountered Bowley's "A Dark Night on Picket" were accustomed to the western habit of self-promotion and what Wyatt describes as "the peculiarly overdeveloped ability of Californians to frame experience as spectacle."[82] Almost without exception, the Civil War stories that appeared in the *Overland Monthly* ran like Bowley's on a kind of theatricality similar to the nineteenth century's tableaux vivants. Arguably, all stories are portals to another place and an imagined sequence of events. But *Overland Monthly* stories of the war were repeatedly and consciously staged, like the later illustrations for Harte's "The Heathen Chinee," with surreptitious winks to readers as spectators. Sometimes fictional street scenes looked like theater sets; in G. T. Shipley's "Saint Saviour of the Bay" (October 1868), a Federal naval officer entering Bahia compares street scenes to the stage flats he saw as a child, "doors opening into nowhere; columns carrying nothing; windows giving light to nobody; stairways ending in vacancy; red walls, green walls, blue walls, yellow walls, all jumbled together."[83] Elsewhere, Californian theatricality meant phantasmagoric vision; in Henry King's "The Cabin at Pharaoh's Ford" (December 1874), the addled daughter of an abolitionist parson is chained to her Kansas bed when he departs for his midnight errands, and it is her "fever of madness" that includes a "monster harp of gold" and a "chorus of many voices" in a scene of orchestrated glory.[84]

More generally in Harte's literary monthly, there was a tendency toward roles, masks, costumes, and disguises, often noted by minor characters. The magazine's most conventional story about race, written by later kindergarten activist Sarah B. Cooper and titled "Old Uncle Hampshire" (November 1872), easily recalls Stowe's Uncle Tom in an aging slave's convenient loyalty to a plantation home. But in San Francisco's postwar magazine, he fends off local bushwhackers through the "outward meekness that served as an opportune disguise for a burning indignation."[85] In the drama that Uncle Hampshire stages on Cooper's wide verandah, even a stereotype understands both strategic role-playing and how to ad lib.

The fragile mediation of such characters suggests not only the synthetic task of any commemorative venture but also the growing importance of Crary's midcentury "observer." Writing of the paradigmatic stereoscope, its cards, and their viewers, Crary has argued that "the illusion of relief or depth was thus a subjective event and the observer coupled with the apparatus was the agent of synthesis or fusion."[86] In Crary's sense, a minor character who "did not take a hand," like Truthful James or a Kansas parson's feverish daughter, can become the vehicle of a new fusion, what Asa Gray called "one apparently solid whole." That character's mediation, their synthetic way of seeing, can effectively become the unacknowledged center of their narrative, which art historian Wendy Bellion describes in a similar vein as "artifacts of spectatorship as well as of place."[87] Because the mobilization of spectators is key to any commemorative project, the hovering shadow of a narrator recollecting the Civil War can become the hovering summons to readers in a parallactic national project. Scratch a Civil War story, in short, and notice "who sees," in Gérard Genette's crisp formulation.[88] Scratch a Civil War story in the *Overland Monthly* and notice interest groups proliferating as "truthful" negotiators struggle to keep their spectacles intact.

That was a particular problem for the westering narrator of "An Episode of 'Fort Desolation,'" the *Overland Monthly*'s most peculiar venture in charting emancipation. Unheralded and largely unremembered, Josephine Clifford provides the chance to read the Civil War's imaginative legacy parallactically, which means seeing past the *Atlantic Monthly* to the continuing service of the United States Colored Troops in Socrates Hyacinth country, the remote territorial forts of the West.

JOSEPHINE CLIFFORD

"An Episode of 'Fort Desolation'"

(*Overland Monthly*, March 1871)

"How much you resemble Mrs. Arnold!" exclaimed the Doctor's wife, after an hour's acquaintance, the day we reached Fort ——. It was not the first time I had heard my resemblance to this, to me, unknown lady remarked on. A portion of the regiment of Colored troops to which Doctor Kline belonged, and which we met on their way in to the States, as we were coming out, had been camped near us one night; and a colored laundress, who had good-naturedly come over to our tent to take the place of my girl, who was sick, had broken into the same exclamation on first beholding me. Captain Arnold belonged to the same regiment, and was expecting, like all the Volunteers then in the Territory, to be ordered home and mustered out of service, as soon as the body of Regular troops to which my husband belonged, could be assigned their respective posts. Their expectations were not to be realized for some time yet; and when I left the Territory, a year later, a part of these troops were still on the frontier.

Fort —— was not our destination; to reach it, we should be obliged to pass through, and stop for a day or two, at the very post of which Captain Arnold had command—which would afford me excellent and ample opportunity for judging of the asserted likeness between this lady and myself. I must explain why we were, in a measure, compelled to stop at Fort Desolation (we will call it so). It was located in the midst of a desert—the most desolate and inhospitable that can be imagined—in the heart of an Indian country, and just so far removed from the direct route across the desert as to make it impracticable to turn in there with a command, or large number of soldiers; for which reason, troops crossing here always carried water-barrels filled, with them. A small party, however, such as ours was then, could not with any safety camp out the one night they must, despite the best ambulance-mules, pass on the desert.

With most pardonable curiosity, I endeavored to learn something more of the woman who was so much like me in appearance; and I began straightway to question Mrs. Kline about her. The impression of a frank, open character, which this lady had made on me at first, vanished at once when she found that Mrs. Arnold was to be made the subject of conversation between us.

"Is she pretty?"

"Yes—quite so." Ahem! and looked like me. But my mother's saying, that there might be a striking resemblance between a very handsome and a very plain person, presented itself to my memory like an uninvited guest, and I concluded not to fall to imagining vain things on so slight a support.

171

"What kind of man is Captain Arnold?"

"The most good-natured man in the world."

"Oh!" Something in the manner of her saying this in praise of Captain Arnold made me think she wanted to say nothing further; so I stopped questioning.

We left the Doctor and his wife early the next morning, and reached Fort Desolation at night-fall. The Orderly had preceded us a short distance, and, when the ambulance stopped at the Captain's quarters, Mrs. Arnold appeared on the threshold, holding a lantern in her hand. She raised it, to let the light fall into the ambulance; and as the rays fell on her own face, I could see that she looked like—a sister I had. The Captain was absent, inspecting the picket-posts he had established along the river, and would return by morning, Mrs. Arnold said; and she busied herself with me in a pleasant, pretty manner. She could not resemble me in height or figure, I said to myself, for she was smaller and more delicately made; nor had any one in our family such deep-blue eyes, save mother—we children had to content ourselves with gray ones.

The night outside was dark and chilly; but in the Captain's house, there were light and warmth, and it was bright with the fires that burned in the fireplaces of the different rooms—all opening one into the other. I was forcibly struck with the difference between the quarters at Fort —— and Mrs. Arnold's home at Fort Desolation. Comforts (luxuries, in this country) of all kinds made it attractive: bright carpets were on the floors here; while at the Doctor's quarters at Fort ——, one was always reminded of cold feet and centipedes, when looking at the naked *adobe* floors. Embroidered covers were spread on the tables, and white coverlets on the beds; while at the Doctor's all these things were made hideous by hospital-linen and gray blankets. Easy-chairs and lounges, manufactured from flour-barrels, saw-bucks, and candle-boxes, were made gorgeous and comfortable with red calico and sheep's-wool; but the crowning glory of parlor, bed-room, and sitting-room was a dazzling toilet-set of China—gilt-edged, and sprinkled with delicate bouquets of moss-roses and foliage.

"Where *did* you get it?" I asked, in astonishment—*not* envy.

"Isn't it pretty?" she asked, triumphantly. "The Captain's Quartermaster, Lieutenant Rockdale, brought it from Santa Fé for me, and paid a mint of money for it, no doubt."

At the supper-table I saw Lieutenant Rockdale, who commanded the post in the Captain's absence, being the only officer there besides the Captain; and, as he messed with them altogether, I need not say that the table was well supplied with all the delicacies that New York and Baltimore send out to less highly favored portions of the universe, in tin cans. Lieutenant Rockdale was a handsome man—a trifle effeminate, perhaps, with languishing, brown eyes and a soft voice. He seemed delighted with our visit, and took my husband off to his own quarters, while Mrs. Arnold and I looked over pictures of her friends, over albums, and at all the hundred little curiosities which she had accumulated while in the Territory. The cares of the household seemed to sit very lightly on her; a Negro woman, Constantia, and a Mulatto boy, of twelve or thirteen, sharing the labor between them. The boy seemed to be a favorite with Mrs. Arnold, though she tantalized and tormented him, as I afterward found she tormented and tantalized every living creature over which she had the power.

I had noticed, while Constantia and Fred were clearing off the table, that she had cut him a slice from a very choice cake, toward which the child had cast longing looks. Placing it carefully on a plate, when he had to leave it for a moment to do something his mistress had bidden him, in the twinkling of an eye she had hidden it; and when the boy missed it, she expressed her regret at his carelessness, and artfully led his suspicions toward Constantia. Hearing him whimpering and sniffling as he went back and forth between dining-room and kitchen, his childish distress at losing the cake seemed to afford her the same amusement that a stage-play would, and she laughed till the tears rolled down her cheeks. Later, he was summoned to replenish the fire; and, knowing the little darky's aversion for going out of the house bare-headed (he had an idea that his cap could prevent the Indian arrows from penetrating his skull), she hid the cap he had left in the adjoining room, and then laughed immoderately at his terror on leaving the house without it. The next morning, she led me out to the stables to show me her horse—a magnificent, black animal, wild-eyed, with a restless, fretful air. Crossing the space in front of the house, she called to a soldier with sergeant-chevrons on his arms—a man with just enough of Negro blood in his veins to stamp him with the curse of his race.

"Harry!" she called to him, "Harry, come hold Black for me; I want to give him a piece of sugar." She opened her hand to let him see the pieces, and he touched his cap and followed us. He loosened the halter and led the horse up to us, but the animal started back when he saw Mrs. Arnold, and would not let her approach him. Harry patted his neck and soothed him, and Mrs. Arnold holding the sugar up to his view, the horse came to take it from her hand; but she quickly clutched his lip with her fingers, and blew into his face till the horse reared and plunged so that Harry could hold him no longer. Laughing like an imp, she called to Harry:

"Get on him and hold him, if you can not manage him in that way: get on him anyhow, and let Mrs. —— see him dance."

The Mulatto's flashing black eyes were bent on her with a singularly reproachful look; but the next moment he was on the horse's back, the horse snorting and jumping in a perfectly frantic manner.

When Mrs. Arnold had sufficiently recovered from her merriment, she explained that the horse had not been ridden for a month; the last time she had ridden him he had thrown her—she had pricked him with a pin to urge him on faster.

About noon the Captain arrived; and I found him, as Mrs. Kline had described, "the most good-natured man in the world," and, to all appearances, loving his wife with the whole of his big heart. He was big in stature, too, with broad shoulders, pleasant face, and cheerful, ringing voice. The shaggy dog, who had slunk away from Mrs. Arnold, came leaping up on his master when he saw him; the horse he had ridden rubbed his nose against his master's shoulder before turning to go into his stable, and

Constantia and Fred beamed on him with their white teeth and laughing eyes from the kitchen door. Later in the afternoon, he asked what I thought of his quarters, and told me how hard his Colored soldiers had worked to build the really pretty *adobe* house in strict accordance with his wishes and directions. But I could not quite decide whether he was more proud of the house or of the affection his men all had for him. Then he told me the story of almost every piece of furniture in the house; and, moving from room to room, we came to where their bed stood. Resting beside it was his carbine which the Orderly had brought in. Taking it in his hand to examine it, he pointed it at his wife's head with the air of a brigand, and uttered, in unearthly tones:

"Your money, or your life."

With a quick, cat-like spring, she was by the bed, had thrust her hands under the pillow, and the next instant was holding two Derringers close to his breast. Throwing back her head, like a heroine in velvet trowsers on the stage, she returned, in the same strain:

"I can play a hand at that game, too, and go you one better!"

She laughed as she said it—the laugh that she laughed with her white teeth clenched—but there was a "glint" in her eye that I had never seen in a blue eye before.

When once more on the way, my husband asked me how I liked Mrs. Arnold. "Very well," said I; "but ——," and I did not hesitate to tell him of the peculiarities I had noticed about her. He himself was charmed with her sprightliness, so he only responded with "Pshaw! women!" after which I maintained an offended (he said, offensive) silence on the subject.

Not quite four months later, my husband was recalled to Santa Fé, and we again crossed the desert, with only three men as escort. I had heard nothing from either Mrs. Arnold or the Captain in all this time, for our post was farther out than theirs; indeed, so far out that nothing belonging to the same Military Department passed by that way. It was midsummer, and the dreary hills shutting in Fort Desolation, and running down toward the river some distance back of the place, were baked hard and black in the sun; the little stream that had meandered along through the low inclosure of the fort in winter time, was now a mere bed of slime, and the plateaus, which had been leveled for the purpose of erecting the Captain's house and the Commissary buildings on them, could not boast of a single spear of grass or any other sign of vegetation. The Captain's house lay on the highest of these plateaus; lower down, across the creek, were the Quartermaster and Commissary buildings (here, too, were Lieutenant Rockdale's quarters); and to the left, on the other side of the men's quarters, was the guard-house—part *jacal*, part tent-cloth.

How *could* any one live here and be happy? Black and bald the earth, as far as the eye could reach; black and dingy the tents and the huts that strewed the flat; murky and dark the ridge of fog that rose on the unseen river; murky and silent the clefts in the rocks where the sun left darkness forever.

It might have been the fading light of the waning day that cast the peculiarly sombre shadow on the Captain's house as we drew up to it; but I thought the same shadow must have fallen on the Captain's face, when he appeared in the door to greet us. Presently Mrs. Arnold fluttered up in white muslin and blue ribbons; and both did their best to make us comfortable. How my husband felt, I don't know; but they did not succeed in making me feel comfortable. Perhaps the absence of the bright fire made the rooms look so dark, even after the lights had been brought in—there was certainly a change. Supper was placed on the table, but I missed Constantia's round face in the dining-room. In answer to my question regarding her, I was told she had expressed so strong a desire to return to the States that she had been sent to Fort ——, there to await an opportunity to go in. Lieutenant Rockdale's absence I noticed also. He did not mess with them any more, I was informed.

My attention was attracted to a conversation between Captain Arnold and my husband. The guard-house, he told him, was at present occupied by two individuals who had made their appearance at Fort Desolation several days ago, and had tried to prevail on the Captain to sell them some of the Government horses, and arms and ammunition, offering liberal payment, and promising secrecy. They were Americans; but as the number of American settlers, or White settlers, in this country is so small, it was easy for the Captain to determine that these were not of them, and their dress and general appearance led him to suspect that they belonged to that despicable class of White Men who make common cause with the Indian, in order to rob and plunder, and, if need be, murder, those of their own race. Of course they had not made these proposals directly and openly to the Captain—at first representing themselves as members of a party of miners going to Pinos Altos; but they soon betrayed a familiarity with the country which only years of roaming through it could have given them. He had felt it his duty to arrest them at once, but had handcuffed them only to-day, and meant to send them, under strong escort, to Fort ——, where their Regimental Commander was stationed, as soon as some of the men from the picket-posts could be called in.

It was late when we arose from the supper-table, and the Captain and my husband left us, to go down to the guardhouse, while Mrs. Arnold led me into the room where their bed stood. This room had but one window—of which window the Captain was very proud: it was a *French* window, opening down to the ground. Throwing it open, Mrs. Arnold said:

"What a beautiful moon we have to-night; let us put out the candle and enjoy the moonshine"—with which she laughingly extinguished the light, and drew my chair to the window.

From where I sat I could just see the men's quarters and the guard-house, though it might have been difficult from there to see the window. We had not been seated long when I fancied I heard a noise, as though of some one stealthily approaching from somewhere in the direction to which my back was turned; then some one seemed to brush or scrape against the outside wall of the house, behind me. "What's that?" I asked, in quick alarm. It had not remained a secret to Mrs. Arnold that I was an unmitigated coward; so she arose, and saying, "How timid you are!—it is the dog; but I will go and look," she stepped from the low window to the ground outside, and vanished around the corner of the house. Some time passed before she returned, and with a little shudder, sprang to light the candle.

"How chilly it is getting," she exclaimed; and then continued, "It was the dog we heard out there. Poor fellow; perhaps the cook had forgotten him, so I gave him his supper."

Rising from my seat to close the window on her remark about the cold, I stepped to the opposite side from where I had been sitting; and there, crossing the planks that lay over the slimy creek, and going toward the Commissary buildings, was a man whose figure seemed familiar: I could not be mistaken—it was Lieutenant Rockdale. No doubt the man had a right to walk in any place he might choose; but, somehow, I could not help bringing him in connection with "the dog, poor fellow," for whom Mrs. Arnold had all at once felt such concern.

Soon the gentlemen returned, and we repaired to the parlor, where a game of chess quickly made them inaccessible to our conversation. The game was interrupted by a rap at the front-door, and Harry, the Sergeant whom Mrs. Arnold had compelled to mount her black horse that day, appeared on the threshold. In his face there was a change, too; his eyes flashed with an unsteady light, as he opened the door, and ever and again, while addressing the Captain—whose thoughts were still half with the game—his looks wandered over to where Mrs. Arnold sat. We were so seated that the Captain's back was partly toward her when he turned to the Sergeant; and he could not see the quick gesture of impatience, or interrogation, that Mrs. Arnold made as she caught the Mulatto's eye. Involuntarily, I glanced toward him—and saw the nod of assent, or intelligence, he gave in return.

The Sergeant had come to report that the prisoners in the guard-house had suddenly asked to see the Captain: they had disclosures to make to him. When Captain Arnold returned, his face was flushed.

"The villains!" he burst out. "They had managed to hide about $5,000 in United States bank-notes about them, when they were searched for concealed weapons, and they just now offered it to me, if I would let them escape. Not only that, but from something one of them said, I have gained the certainty that they are implicated in the massacre of the party of civilians that passed through here about two months ago: you remember, the General ordered out a part of K Company, to rescue the one man who was supposed to have been taken prisoner. The wretches! But I'll go myself, in the morning, to relieve the men from picket-duty, and select the best from among them to take the scoundrels to Santa Fé!"

When about to begin my toilet the next morning I gave a start of surprise. Was *that* what had made the house look so dark and changed? Before me stood a large, tin wash-basin—of the kind that all common mortals used out here—and the beautiful toilet-set of China, with its splendors of gilt-edge and moss-roses, had all disappeared—all save the soap-dish and hot-water pitcher, which were both defective, and looked as though they had gone through a hard struggle for existence.

When our ambulance made the ascent of the little steep hill that hides Fort Desolation from view, I saw three horses led from the stable to the Captain's house—the Captain's horse and two others. He was as good as his word; and before another day had passed, the two men penned up in that tent there would be well on their way to meet justice and retribution. A solitary guard, with ebony face and bayonet flashing in the morning sun, was pacing back and forth by the tent; and walking briskly from the Commissary buildings toward the men's quarters, was Harry, the Mulatto Sergeant.

From the first glance I had at Mrs. Kline's face, when we reached Fort ——, I knew that the mystery of the change at Fort Desolation would be solved here. Constantia was there, and acting as cook in Dr. Kline's family. She was an excellent cook, and we did ample justice to her skill, at supper-time. The gentlemen leaving the table to smoke their cigars, Mrs. Kline and I settled down to another cup of tea and *médisance*. From what Constantia had stated on coming to Fort ——, it would seem that in some way Captain Arnold's suspicions had been aroused in regard to the friendship of Lieutenant Rockdale for his wife. About two months ago, he one day pretended to start off on a tour of inspection to the picket-posts; but returned, late the same night, by a different road. Stealing into the house through the kitchen, he had, rather unceremoniously, entered the bed-room, where he found Lieutenant Rockdale, toasting his bare feet before the fire. Raising his carbine to shoot the man, Mrs. Arnold had sprung forward, seized his arms and torn the gun from him. In the confusion that followed, the toilet-set referred to, and other articles of furniture, were demolished: but Constantia, who had crept in after the Captain, to prevent mischief, if possible, gave it as her opinion that Mrs. Arnold "had grit enough for ten such men as him an' de Leftenant."

"If you did but know the ingratitude of the creature," continued Mrs. Kline, "and the devotion her husband has always shown her!" And she gave me a brief sketch of her career: Married to Arnold just at the breaking out of the war, and of poor parents, she had driven him almost to distraction by her treatment, when thrown out of employment some time after. At last, he went into the Union forces as substitute—giving every cent of the few hundred dollars he received to his wife, who spent it on herself, for finery. Later, when for bravery and good conduct he was made Lieutenant in a Negro regiment, she joined her husband, and finally came to the Territory with him. In their regiment, it was well known that he had always blindly worshiped his wife; and that she had always ruled him, his purse, and his company, with absolute power.

Before retiring for the night, we debated the question: Should we remain the next day at Fort ——, or proceed on our journey? The mules needed rest, as well as the horses, for the Quartermaster could not furnish fresh mules, which we had rather expected; still, my husband was anxious to reach Santa Fé as soon as possible—and we left the question of our departure where it was, to settle it the next morning, at breakfast.

The news that came to Fort ——, before the next morning, made us forget our journey—for that day, at least. Captain Arnold had been murdered! The big, true-hearted man was lying at Fort Desolation—dead—with his broken eyes staring up to the heaven that had not had pity on him—his broad breast pierced with the bullet that a woman's treachery had sped!

Before daybreak, a detachment of six men had come in from Fort Desolation to Fort ——, to report to the Commander of their regiment that Captain Arnold had been assassinated, and Sergeant Henry Tulliver had deserted, taking with him one horse, two revolvers, and a carbine. Captain Arnold had started out the morning before, with only two men, to call in the picket-posts. An hour later, the two men had come dashing back to the fort, stating that they had been attacked, and Captain Arnold killed, by the two White Men who had been confined in the guard-house. It was ascertained then, for the first time, that the prisoners had made their escape. A detachment of men was sent out with a wagon, and the Captain's body brought in—the men with their black faces and simple hearts gathering around it, with tears and lamentations—heaping curses on the villains who had slain their kind Commander.

Suddenly a rumor had been spread among them that Harry, the Sergeant, had set the prisoners free; and instantly, a hundred hoarse voices were shouting the Mulatto's name—a hundred hands ready to take the traitor's life. Vainly Lieutenant Rockdale—who, after the Captain's departure, had at once repaired to his house—tried to check the confusion, that was quickly ripening into mutiny: the excitement only increased, and soon a crowd of black soldiers moved toward the men's quarters, with any thing but peaceful intentions. Perhaps Harry's conscience had warned him of what would come, for while the mob were searching the quarters, a lithe figure sprang over the planks across the creek, ran to the stables below the Captain's house, and the next moment dashed over the road, mounted on a wild-looking, black horse.

Could they but have reached him—the infuriated men, who sent yells and carbine-balls after the fugitive—he would have been sacrificed by them to the *manes* of the murdered man: and perhaps this effect had been calculated on, when the fact of his having loosed the prisoners had been brought to their ears.

"How did it come to their ears?" I asked of the Doctor, under whose care one of the six men, overcome with fatigue and excitement, had been placed. It seems that Mrs. Arnold had expressed her conviction of the Sergeant's having liberated the prisoners, to Lieutenant Rockdale, in little Fred's hearing; and the boy had innocently repeated the tale to the men. In the afternoon of the same day, the detail had been made of the men who brought the news to Fort ——; but when the detachment had been only an hour or two on the way, they found the trail of the escaped prisoners. The men could not withstand the temptation to make an effort, at least, to recapture them. They knew them to be mounted, for the two horses which Sergeant Tulliver had that morning separated from the herd were missing; but the trail they followed showed the tracks of *three* horses, which led them to suppose that Harry had found the men and joined them.

But the trail led farther and farther from the road, and fearing to be ambushed, they turned back, leaving the man who had been driven from the companionship of his brethren by a woman's treachery, to become one of the vultures that prey on their own kind.

"Like—a Sister"

In 1866, as Union armies were demobilizing and their state regiments mustering out, the volunteers of the 125th United States Colored Troops were posted to the New Mexico Territory. Enlisting in Kentucky during 1865 and thus the war's final spring, black volunteers were obligated for three years rather than the duration of the war, while white veterans were on their way home. Clifford sets her account of New Mexico's frontier forts and simmering antagonisms in the midst of these diverging fates, and she structures the story her narrator tells around noticeable contrasts that only begin with regimental postings. In a series of seeming alternatives, she opens narratively with the odd physical resemblance between Mrs. Arnold and the lieutenant's wife who tells her tale, two women who look similar enough to be sisters. The story they share then moves from a fort with centipedes and gray blankets to a fort with bright carpets and red calico, from a big-hearted captain to a handsome lieutenant, and from a delicate toilet set to a battered soap dish and pitcher. Yet "An Episode of 'Fort Desolation'" is also about converging emancipations—of those Lincoln proclaimed free, of those the army obligated, of those constrained by marriage, and of those sent to the guardhouse. As the insistent patriarchal social relations of army life collapse at frontier forts and along western trails, Clifford's story reveals domestic dependents in revolt and a predatory competition coming into focus as postwar futures go awry.

Her "episode" concerns the military shift after Appomattox from sectional civil war to a western assault on Native peoples. Unlike tales of homecoming in the East, the *Overland Monthly* here stages Reconstruction's harsh politics in stereo view, with surrender in Virginia superseded by uprisings along the frontier, liberty's ripples set against Bret Harte's grizzly snarl. In fact, several startling developments at Clifford's fort recall both the play of theatricality in the *Overland Monthly*'s Civil War stories and the "horrible significance" of Antietam. The first of these is Mrs. Arnold's fondness for display, which is suggested by her toilet set, as well as by her own insistent posing. Hers is a perverse self-indulgence that creates a disturbing view of postwar outrages, here the seeming result of U.S. Army privilege. In addition, the black characters she torments return such treatment with a covert defiance—flashing eyes, a request for transfer. As a result, a sergeant's domestic resourcefulness and the fleeting vision of a makeshift black "family" are abruptly ruined. Most importantly, the unnerving physical resemblance between one post mistress and another gnaws at the distance between spectacle and spectator, view and viewer, with chilling consequences for Clifford's own readers and the nation's once comfortable armchairs. While the *Atlantic*'s Oliver Wendell Holmes shoved the stereo views of Antietam back into his cabinet as the best way to contain their horror, the *Overland*'s frontier wife cannot so easily sidestep a look-alike "desolation" or a black sergeant's silent reproach.

Neither could Clifford, a veteran of New Mexico's postwar garrisons. Born during 1838 in a Prussian castle to a patrician officer and his aristocratic wife, Josephine Woempner was raised in St. Louis after her family emigrated in 1846. As she would later recall, her father was drawn by the dream of "liberty" and land for his young family, as well as by "the families of the poor black slaves whom he meant to buy of their cruel master."[89] Unfortunately, Georg Heinrich Ernst Woempner died in 1854, and Josephine married (probably in November 1863) a captain in the First Missouri Cavalry named James Clifford. He went on to secure a postwar commission as a lieutenant in the Third U.S. Cavalry and an immediate posting to the plains. During the spring of 1866, both Cliffords joined a large wagon train of army men, mules, horses, and guns that set out from Fort Leavenworth in Kansas.

Cheryl Foote has written of how "enjoyable" the young officer's wife found an overland journey that took months but offered "new places and customs."[90] In "Marching with a Command," published in Chicago's *Lakeside Monthly* (April and May 1873), Clifford herself wrote of leaving the Kansas plains and the lower peaks of Colorado as she traveled through the Raton Pass to Fort Union in New Mexico. From there, the wagons moved south along the Rio Grande to Fort Craig and Fort Selden before heading west across the desert, with its "rocky hills" and "Indian hostility," to Fort Cummings and, at last, Camp Bayard, soon to become another fort.[91] "A clear brook—so clear," wrote Clifford, "that it was rightly baptized Minne-ha-ha—gambolled and leaped and flashed among the green trees and the white tents they overhung."[92] All the more reason to notice the "desolate and inhospitable" terrain that surrounds Mrs. Arnold.

Admittedly, Clifford's frontier quarters were not amiable for long. As Foote documents and George Wharton James elaborated in his 1913 profile of Clifford, her husband was a hard drinker who revealed to her after their trek ended that he had killed a man in Texas. He soon feared the army had discovered his secret from his wife. His paranoia mounting, he began threatening her in what

James describes as "a series of midnight terrorizings."[93] After repeated instances of near strangulation, he tried a pistol and a kind of Russian roulette, then a hatchet and the promise of cutting her up for roasting. Clifford would later detail how he brought her back from an attempted escape by riding her beloved white horse to death and then fatally beating her little dog as a lesson. In the spring of 1867, a year after the wagon train had left Kansas, Clifford finally eluded her husband, who was arrested on other charges and declared insane. But the domestic terror of remote New Mexico remained with her well into her new life in San Francisco, where she arrived later in 1867.[94] When Harte invited her to write for the *Overland Monthly* and she looked back to garrison life for her "episode," she paused less on Indian menace and more on what festered inside the fort's adobe walls.

That included the continuing presence of black troops. As Elizabeth Leonard points out, some 180,000 black men volunteered once the Bureau of Colored Troops was formed in May 1863, just months after the Emancipation Proclamation went into effect.[95] Michael Meier notes that more than twenty thousand of those black volunteers came from Kentucky, a border state where Confederate loyalties were strong and the Union's enlistment quotas were going unmet toward the end of 1864.[96] Recruiting officers themselves needed an armed escort, not least when they turned to black volunteers in a slave state that Lincoln's proclamation strategically exempted. By March 1865, as John David Smith has demonstrated, Union recruiters were offering freedom to black volunteers and their families, despite Washington's uneasiness about local allegiances. "Because of President Lincoln's concern for the sensitivities of Kentuckians," Smith has written, "the Commonwealth was the last loyal slave state to become a recruiting ground for blacks."[97] The 125th USCT was thus organized in Louisville from February to June 1865, and the regiment left Kentucky for the New Mexico Territory at a postwar moment when mustering in was far less common than mustering out.

By the time Josephine Clifford arrived in 1866 with the Regular Army's Third Cavalry and Fifth Infantry, the companies of the 125th USCT had been dispersed to Camp Bayard, Fort Craig, and Fort Cummings. While the Cliffords would discover at Bayard a tented camp and thus the need for a more permanent installation to protect nearby copper mines from Indian attack, Forts Craig and Cummings were more substantial because they had been established before and during the war. According to Monroe Lee Billington, Fort Craig was constructed in 1854 to protect those traveling the north–south road along the Rio Grande, while Fort Cummings was built in 1863—as Billington puts it, "to restrain the Apache Indians and guard the most dangerous point on the

FIGURE 37. *Fort Cummings, New Mexico, 1867*. Photograph. In William Thornton Parker, *Annals of Old Fort Cummings, New Mexico, 1867–8* (Northampton, Mass.: self-published, 1916), opposite 8. Courtesy of the Hathi Trust.

southern route to California, with the exception of the Apache Pass, Arizona."[98] Given the function of each post at which the 125th USCT was stationed, it is likely that Clifford's story recalls Fort Cummings, which was served by Cook's Spring but otherwise lay far from the nearest river, some twenty miles away.

In his *Annals of Old Fort Cummings*, William Thornton Parker described the fort as "lonely" in its isolation. "To the west and south-west stretched the limitless prairie, dreary and desolate," he wrote, while elsewhere were "a few stunted trees" and "the everlasting mesquite bushes."[99] The painting he commissioned of Fort Cummings in 1867 confirmed the "dreary prison-like abode" he detailed, which in the late 1860s was hundreds of miles from the closest railroad station at Fort Hayes in Kansas (figure 37).[100] Where Clifford remembered the brook that "gambolled and leaped and flashed" at Camp Bayard, Parker kept returning to the frontier's "vast solitudes," and he noted that all of the windows at Fort Cummings faced the parade ground.[101] When Mrs. Arnold snuffs the bedroom candle, then, the moonlight she welcomes never touches the horizon, only the "men's quarters and the guard-house" nearby.

In a defensive stronghold where all views necessarily turn inward and few events disrupt daily routines, even in Clifford's story, the extravagances of Mrs. Arnold replace the dreary landscape no window actually reveals. The visiting narrator notices the "embroidered covers" on the tables and the "white coverlets" on the beds, the "easy-chairs and lounges" contrived from "flour-barrels" and "saw-bucks," and, above all, the "dazzling" toilet set with its "bouquets of moss-roses and foliage." Not only is the set "gilt-edged," as the fort's prospects are not, but its delicacy also bespeaks Santa Fe and the larger world of New York and Baltimore that the fort's quartermaster can access. If the fragile china were the only sign of Mrs. Arnold's flash and transgression, it would still be enough to suggest her outsized ambitions, which fort life cannot finally suppress.

Yet the display the captain's wife most favors is the spectacle she makes of herself. When her husband picks up his carbine and points it at his wife with the playful demand of a "brigand," Mrs. Arnold grabs a couple of hidden derringers as though scripted, Clifford writes, "like a heroine in velvet trowsers on the stage." Just as she plays at posing, she also toys with her husband's dog and her own plunging horse to "see him dance." She laughs "like an imp" at the horse's groom and takes her amusement from the "stage-play" of a houseboy's small losses, usually thefts she engineers. If she is the "better half" of the Arnolds' western union, the "Mrs. Captain" of a reconstructing household, it is at least troubling that she stages disaster both in her home with the steady captain and in a marriage about to be smashed along with her imported china.

More provocatively, the boy she torments and the groom she teases are black, and so is the captain's cook, Constantia, who is more constant in her service than her mistress in her marriage. The boy, Fred, shares the household work, despite whimpering over his disappearing cake and stolen cap. The groom is a mulatto sergeant named Henry Tulliver, his rank a reminder of the army's insistence on white officers in USCT regiments. As Leonard has pointed out, black soldiers generally rose no higher than sergeant; as Thomas Mays has added, even USCT sergeants were sometimes white, since their duties required the ability to read.[102] The groom's rank and his "flashing black eyes" therefore indicate his unusual skill and self-possession, which will survive both Mrs. Arnold's mistreatment and his own criminal conduct in freeing the two "White Men" who kill the captain. Where Fred's tears suggest the dismay of newly free African Americans who saw emancipation's promises evaporate in Reconstruction's failures, Sergeant Tulliver's dexterity on the rearing black horse suggests the self-emancipation of Kentucky's African American volunteers, as well as a familiarity with the "snorting and jumping" of black rage.

Even in deserting, Clifford's sergeant lends a grizzly stature to the story's semblance of a black family, while the cook brings constancy and the boy an innocent devotion. Among other things, Constantia keeps an eye out for Fred; she cuts the slice of cake for him that Mrs. Arnold then hides. That cake is "very choice" because the cook is very accomplished in the kitchen, any kitchen; as the narrator notes later at Dr. Kline's table, "We did ample justice to her skill, at supper-time." More importantly, Constantia sustains Clifford's narrative progress by bringing the story of white trespass to a crisis. It is Constantia who tells Mrs. Kline what the captain finally discovers: Lieutenant Rockdale "toasting his bare feet" in the captain's bedroom. The shattered toilet set is one result of the mêlée that ensues, but so is the cook's effort "to prevent mischief" and her final comment, that Mrs. Arnold "had grit enough for ten such men as him an' de Leftenant." Her steady eye posits yet another seeming contrast between mistress and servant, who nonetheless share a discernible "grit." If the cook and the houseboy and the sergeant approximate an evanescent family and therefore a second story of "desolation" as Civil War upshot, it is a Reconstructive tale of black service and white theft.

What is worse, it is a story with troubling personal implications, a third development that comes as early as the first sentence. The story is narrated by a version of Josephine Clifford in 1866, when she was a dutiful lieutenant's wife who had recently arrived with the Regular Army. In this twilight "episode," the narrator sees what she might become when military barracks have been completed, domestic luxuries have been imported, and a wartime marriage has run aground. She is more than a captain's wife in the making; she actually looks like *this* captain's wife, as one character after another exclaims. The story's opening line is an outburst that becomes a refrain: "How much you resemble Mrs. Arnold!" In a twinkling, the seer melds with the scene, the viewer becomes part of the view. As the narrator puts it when she first meets the captain's wife, "I could see that she looked like—a sister." A gendered reminder of Miles Orvell's "fraternally twinned images," Clifford's narrator negotiates both the awkwardness of her own future shock and the burden of a disintegrating national household. She is a Truthful James amid competing races, an army wife and frontier witness amid race war.

More to the point, she is the reader's representative, the viewer embodied, a minor character writ large. She thereby transforms bystander witness into stereoscopic agency, since it is her quick eye that catches what her husband has missed and enables her performance as western spectacle. Another nameless narrator, it is she who provides the depth of field in uncharted postwar territory, which ends in a trail "farther and farther from the road," where ambush and the "flashing black eyes" of the sergeant lurk. No Captain Peters who stages his own helpless twin after Antietam, she nonetheless implicates Clifford's readers in an eerie scene of frontier assassination while postwar vultures seek their prey. Where Sergeant Tulliver might have headed eventually for the comparative freedoms of San Francisco's African Americans, he is trapped instead by "a woman's treachery," just as the "despicable" white men are trapped off-road by the army detachment on their trail, and Mrs. Arnold is trapped in a remote fort and a remoter marriage. If theirs is to be a continuing story, which Clifford's "episode" quietly suggests, it is a story of uncertain liberties and predatory appetites in the unpicturesque solitudes of the West.

Metaphorically, the bewitching wife, the belittled sergeant, the constant cook, the whimpering boy, and even the off-stage Apaches are all moons of a sort, domestic dependents revolving around the "true-hearted" captain as an imploding sun and a vanishing common good. He is their walking U.S. flag, and the "horrible significance" of his death haunts those who have rebelled. If their center holds, at least on the pages of the *Overland Monthly*, it is thanks to the new frontier wife with binocular vision, the minor character who sees from fort to fort, from barracks to plains, and from black sergeant to white mistress, in whom she sees herself. The frontier spectacle she discovers, as surely as Crary's observer discovers dimension on a pasteboard card, is a Gilded Age image of white display, black service, and parlor complicity in continuing postwar injustice, at least from her distant perspective.

After discovering the moons of Mars in 1877, Asaph Hall thoughtfully observed that in order to get a fix on distant bodies, he had to find a new perspective. "All that was needed was the right way of looking," he would later write, "and that was to get rid of the dazzling light of the planet."[103] If the "dazzling" marketplace success of eastern "quality journals" like the *Atlantic Monthly* is displaced as insistently as Clifford's Captain Arnold, then the "panic" and "terror" that the Civil War engendered recover some of their regional urgency and parallactic promise, especially after emancipation and African American service were imaginatively acknowledged. Long-neglected satellites of another sort, journals like the *Overland Monthly* are always double visioned, always attending to the gravity of eastern norms and their own tangential velocity. They can offer, therefore, a startling integration of national order and local detail, of national opportunity and local expense, especially for growing numbers of readers just discovering grizzly bear claws. Even in postwar San Francisco, however, the stereoscopic shimmer of true national reconstruction, like New Mexico's gilded china and Antietam's Zouave glory, was a distant spectacle, at once beckoning and precarious.

Coda
Depot, Culture, 1876

In May 1876, when the Centennial Exhibition opened in Philadelphia, Julia Ward Howe was already making plans to travel south. On this journey from Boston, she would not accompany her husband, as she had in 1861. The years of the war and its immediate aftermath had brought misfortune to her family. Her son Sammy contracted diphtheria at the age of four and died in 1863. The assassination of Abraham Lincoln in 1865 brought another sudden grief, much like the death in 1867 of John Andrew, wartime governor of Massachusetts and a close family friend. To be sure, these were also the years in which the verses of Howe's "Battle Hymn" were sung more regularly, and she was invited to speak more often in public—at poetry readings, in lecture series, with occasional sermons. The recognition was gladly received, but her husband railed against her travel, her absences, and her pay, even when she vowed to donate profits to the U.S. Sanitary Commission. What Valarie Ziegler sees as a "clash of wills," Elaine Showalter describes as a "battle in that other civil war of emancipation."[1] Theirs was an intermittent feud that ended at last when Samuel Gridley Howe died on January 9, 1876. In his absence, Howe's journey south as the country celebrated the Declaration of Independence would again prove revealing, though in ways she could not have anticipated when the Civil War began.

By 1876 the glory the poet had seen outside Washington in 1861 had faded into the brutalities of the Franco-Prussian War and the 1870 siege of Paris, whose horrors she described in her *Reminiscences* as "a return to barbarism."[2] In her anguished directive to the world's mothers, a rousing message published by the *Woman's Journal* (September 24, 1870), which she helped to found, Howe called on her readers to "arise" and trumpet the message "Disarm, disarm!" As she put it, "Our husbands shall not come to us, reeking with carnage, for caresses and applause. Our sons shall not be taken from us to unlearn all that we have been able to teach them of charity, mercy and patience."[3] She called for a Women's Peace Festival to be held for the first time on June 2, 1872, spoke on behalf of the movement for woman suffrage, and founded the Association of American Women, which she would serve as president for decades to come. When she left for Philadelphia during the fall of 1876, it was to address an international Congress of Women. That October, she would not be visiting the "circling camps" memorialized in a song that many knew by heart.

Instead, she found herself in a city crowded with the travelers drawn by a national celebration that was also a world's fair, one dedicated to progress and organized by the social elites who had made the city's 1864 U.S. Sanitary Fair a financial bonanza. As administrators in 1876, writes Gary B. Nash, the city's upper classes were committed to insuring "symbols of unity for a divided society," with the kind of conciliatory slogans that historian Mitch Kachun has reported: "No North, No South, No East, No West—The Union One and Indivisible."[4] It was a cooperative mission like Howe's own, with a scope as large as the "immense" project of Grand Central Dépôt: Robert Rydell reports five main buildings, seventeen state buildings, nine foreign government buildings, and numerous other installations, as well as "many restaurants, six cigar pavilions, popcorn stands, beer gardens," and 106 gates. From opening day on May 10, those entrances would serve a colossal number of visitors.[5] Before closing on November 10, the grand exposition would welcome nearly ten million sightseers from across the country.[6] "The Centennial hosted a staggering 20% of the American population," writes Jack Noe, "and virtually every literate person amongst the remaining 80% would have been exposed to discussion and descriptions of the fair."[7] Managed by Philadelphia volunteers, the Centennial Exhibition recalls for Nash "the old practice of rollicking local fairs," but with exhibitors spanning the globe and financing that required, according to Matthew Gallman, a $1.5 million loan from Congress and 450 acres of the city's Fairmount Park for more than two hundred buildings.[8]

Construction proceeded even after the exposition's many gates swung open, and in more ways than one. Beyond the continuing work of local builders, the country's anniversary celebrations were subtly designed to obscure accelerating hostilities, particularly in Philadelphia. Just fifteen miles north of the Mason-Dixon Line, as the Sixth Massachusetts had discovered in 1861, the city relied on commercial networks extending deep into the South, together with the regional social connections among many elite families that Nash has noticed. "Philadelphia's ties to the South, both economic and emotional, were so strong," he writes, "that the city remained deeply divided throughout the Civil War."[9] When exposition planning commenced, southern pavilions were thus warmly invited. Yet southern legislatures proved skeptical of the "moneymaking scam," as Noe reveals, and in any case their treasuries remained bare.[10] Only Mississippi and Arkansas built state-supported exhibits. African Americans were still less in evidence at an exposition controlled by a disdainful upper crust. As Philip Foner has declared, "The City of Brotherly Love was the most racist city in the North."[11] Nash likewise sees Philadelphia's postwar racial frictions as palpable and unrelieved; at a time when many black veterans were unemployed, they would not find work at the Centennial Exhibition in construction, only as the help. In Nash's phrase, they were "shoeshine boys, gardeners, waiters, janitors, and an occasional messenger."[12] Just as the facades of Grand Central Dépôt hid unintegrated services, Philadelphia's exposition hid festering injuries that would not soon heal.

By 1876 the author of the republic's "Battle Hymn" was less inclined to notice, but the author of "John Lamar" did. In 1863 Rebecca Harding had married L. Clarke Davis, an outspoken abolitionist, and relocated to Philadelphia. The couple prospered, he as a newspaper editor of increasing stature and she as a contributor to prestigious literary magazines; biographer Sharon Harris has noted that "they would move among the Philadelphia elite."[13] When Centennial festivities began, Davis was well-positioned to provide accounts of the city's auspicious past and tourist bona fides. But the sketches she composed usually included an unpredictable twist. For *Harper's Weekly*, she wrote "A Rainy Day at the Exposition" (November 18, 1876), in which she described the "half-pay" crowds, including a country "squire" and a "small housekeeper" from the city, a "shoe-maker from Kensington" and a "black barber from South Street," a "brilliant young beauty from New York" and a "sharp-nosed New Jersey matron," alongside "pigtail and fez and gold-worked caftan."[14] In "A Glimpse of Philadelphia in July, 1776" (July 1876) for *Lippincott's* some months earlier, she followed a colonial visitor from the South who was "fevered by excitement," but she also paused on his black servant, as well as on a Confederate descendant and the latter-day black congressman who interrupts the Virginian's ardor for the Declaration of Independence.[15] In *Harper's Monthly* as early as the spring, her two-part "Old Philadelphia" (April and May 1876) settled into the commemorative enthusiasms that many readers expected, but only after a lengthy salute to Gustavus Adolphus and the "religious liberty" he had established well before William Penn.[16] In Davis's hands, the anticipated cast always grew.

Her effort to repopulate the Centennial narrative that got into print extended southward, particularly after Radical Reconstruction ebbed. Jean Pfaelzer has aptly summarized the problem Davis consistently encountered: "To justify abandoning the post–Civil War goal of political equality for freed slaves, the North needed to reinvent southern history, indeed, to reinvent the South."[17] Reasserting the plantation romance troubled Davis both after the war and earlier, before its uneasy peace. Her first stories for the *Atlantic Monthly*, particularly "John Lamar" (April 1862), contested the slave master's dubious bonhomie, nowhere more so than in her arresting portrait of Ben and his knife. In *Waiting for the Verdict* (1868), which was serialized in New York's postwar *Galaxy*, the number of her startling portraits proliferated. Her novel introduces, for example, a mulatto doctor in Philadelphia who is passing for white and the doctor's enslaved brother in Virginia, along with the emancipated wife and child who search for him. In Philadelphia's once widely read *Peterson's Magazine*, which rivaled *Godey's Lady's Book*, Davis also published wartime mysteries set in Virginia during the antebellum decades, unusual stories narrated by a well-heeled lawyer whose servant Pine becomes his investigator. Self-taught in the law, the black detective has a knack for discovering evidence that undercuts his master, the epitome of the Old Dominion as blind and deteriorating. "Davis's dramatic choice to use a slaveholding, unreliable, genteel Southern lawyer as her narrator was a notably risky one," Harris observes, "but it becomes her most effective tool for damning the mask of gentility that harbors the horrors of slavery's injustice."[18] Where Howe favored home as it was before "carnage," Davis preferred a remodeled extension, an enlarged cast, and multiple claims on a national future.

The postbellum priorities of Julia Ward Howe and Rebecca Harding Davis exemplify the two most familiar stories about Reconstruction: an obliterating hunger for peace at any cost and, in sharp counterpoint, a resolute grasp of the Civil War's most important social upshot, liberty and justice for African Americans. These two narratives have proved fundamental for students of Reconstruction's literature, which has been only marginally respectable until recently and even now scarcely read. It is therefore curious that the Centennial Exhibition has shared in a similar binary shorthand. Remembered infrequently, the outsized fair has been known generally for two massive structures that visitors encountered early and returned to often: the Main Building and Machinery Hall. Both edifices, located across from the Pennsylvania Railroad depot at the fair's main gates, have been described by Jeffrey Howe as "monstrous expanses," and each had a sense of "unending abundance" with remarkable implications.[19]

According to *Harper's Weekly*, the Main Building was "an enormous structure of iron and glass" that ran a noteworthy 1,876 feet in length and 464 feet across (figure 38). A glimpse of the "magnificent" center aisle reveals why William Dean Howells, who toured the Centennial Exhibition for a week shortly after its opening, praised "that brightness of effect which was so largely owing to

FIGURE 38. Francis H. Schell and Thomas Hogan, *The Centennial—Interior of the Main Building*. Wood engraving from a photograph and sketches. *Harper's Weekly*, July 8, 1876, 552–53. Courtesy of the University of Iowa Libraries.

the handsomeness of the show-cases and pavilions."[20] The newsmagazine commended the exhibits of foreign countries that displayed their tools, household goods, machinery, and fine arts, both public and domestic, in astonishing numbers. The Main Building was, notes James McClelland, "the largest structure of its kind in the world," with eleven miles of walkways to accommodate almost fourteen thousand exhibits from thirty-seven countries.[21] In its purposeful amplitude and global panache, the exposition's Main Building lends credence to the purpose and scope, the intensity and elegance, of Howe's international call for peace. Yet in her distinguished tribute to domestic priorities, which inspired the "charity, mercy and patience" she prized, Howe's universalizing zeal also anticipated Philadelphia's festive assumption that hostilities could be dispelled and that peace was right around the corner—or down the aisle.

Likewise, Davis's recurring case for liberty and justice, one unexpected character at a time, was easier to grasp during 1876 thanks to Machinery Hall's singular achievement. *Harper's Weekly* announced the structure's size as 1,400 feet by 360 feet, somewhat smaller than the Main Building but filled with the sort of "mechanical invention and constructive skill" that culminated in the Corliss engine.[22] On opening day, its twin shafts were fired up by President Grant and Emperor Pedro II of Brazil in a double hiss of steam that fed the hall's assembled machinery (figure 39). The weekly chronicled the dimension and capabil-

FIGURE 39.
Theodore R. Davis,
*Our Centennial—
President Grant and
Dom Pedro Starting
the Corliss Engine.*
Wood engraving.
Harper's Weekly,
May 27, 1876, 421.
Courtesy of the
University of Iowa
Libraries.

ity of every gear and flywheel. More briskly, Howells declared that "the Corliss engine set an example of unwearying application to business, and even while one gazed in fond approval, innumerable spindles began to whirr and shuttles to clack, and a thousand *tête-à-têtes* were broken up as by magic."[23] Metaphorically, the engine's power catches the fateful lightning of transformational social change in new freedoms for those who had been enslaved, an invigorating whirr and clack as the nation was reinvented in the halls of Congress. Jeffrey Howe extols the "unrestrained exuberance" of an exposition that "epitomized the dynamism of the era," which Grant had discovered through hard fighting must lead to both the eradication of slavery and what biographer Brooks Simpson has called "a social and economic revolution."[24] But the urbane whisper of "*tête-à-têtes*," so far from Davis's "half-pay" visitors, raises vexing questions about whose interests such "magic" would ultimately serve. Susanna Gold points out

FIGURE 40. Theodore R. Davis, *The Centennial—Southern Restaurant, the New Jersey Building, the Women's Pavilion*. Wood engraving. *Harper's Weekly*, May 20, 1876, 412. Courtesy of the University of Iowa Libraries.

that Brazil's Dom Pedro II was "the leader of the last great slave nation," which he had ruled for more than thirty years with a well-intentioned policy of gradual emancipation.[25] Who would throw the U.S. levers of power after 1876 remained to be seen.

Because Philadelphia's exposition was also filled with carefully selected regional specimens and fetching state exhibits that served as homes away from home for their citizens, it is worth noticing that both *Harper's Weekly* and William Dean Howells moved beyond the two largest exposition buildings, absorbing as they were. Even before the fair opened, the newsmagazine's special artist ambled through the Grand Plaza to the sprawling enterprise starting to take shape in Fairmount Park. What Theodore Davis drew with increasing detail, Howells eventually toured: the New England Farmer's Home, with vintage furniture from the Pilgrims at Plymouth; Horticultural Hall, with two aging sago palms planted before the Revolution; and Agricultural Hall, with a wealth of specimens that included tall glass canisters packed with the fertile soils of Iowa, proof that the country's chosen roots were sunk deep and continuing to grow. The state buildings were also regional showplaces. Maryland displayed one of the first railroad engines from 1835, while Mississippi built a log cabin out of sixty-eight homegrown woods draped with Spanish moss. The Illinois house offered both an organ and an upright piano, California joined with Nevada to tout mineral resources, and New Jersey covered its house with tiles made from local clay (figure 40). Howells deemed it "the most picturesque building," and Theodore Davis made its tiled tower roof instantly recognizable, tucked as it was between the low Southern Restaurant at the far end of Belmont Avenue and the Women's Pavilion with its flag-topped cupola.[26]

Amid so much local color, devised and funded by the states or developed with their assistance, it is nonetheless these two near neighbors, the Southern Restaurant and the Women's Pavilion, that offer the best opportunity to gauge how "the South" was popularly conceived by 1876 and where African American citizens stood, specifically during the postwar decade that included the *Southern Magazine* and *The Land We Love*, the *Lakeside Monthly* and the *Overland*. James McCabe in his *Illustrated History of the Centennial Exhibition* noted that the restaurant was run by Edward Mercer, an Atlanta hotelier who offered an agreeable "place of rendezvous" for numerous white southerners and their families.[27] His two-story building included four ample dining halls and sixteen private areas, as well as parlors and a reading room. Together, McCabe observed, they could serve up to a thousand guests at once. That was comfortable space for the visitors from southern states whom Theodore Bryant Kingsbury anticipated. In a guidebook designed for their use, the North Carolina newspaper and magazine editor championed the "Restaurant of the South" as "the main rallying point of the two-hundred thousand visitors to the great International Exhibition who will go up from the cities and towns and villages and hamlets and plantations of the land we love."[28] Though Mercer's restaurant would welcome an international clientele, like all of the exposition's dining halls, the astute businessman made a distinctive southern menu both an exotic invitation and an indulgent memory of home.

That canny pitch recalls the postwar success of William Hand Browne's *Southern Magazine*, which gave Baltimore's urban vigor both a Confederate past and an economic future far from the Big House. The magazine was thus positioned at a regional crossroads in a growing metropolis—"the South's largest city in 1860" for Frank Towers, "the financial center for the agrarian west" for Marshall Fishwick, and "a city through which North and South reached each other" for Christopher Phillips.[29] Yet the opportunity to discover both the common interests and the commercial appetites that characterized Atlanta's New South during the 1880s (and the Southern Restaurant a decade earlier) was not the hallmark of Civil War stories in the *Southern Magazine*. Even the "nootral" territory that Mrs. Spriggins claims in her "horspittle" dissolves in a story whose Northern nurse and Southern traveler finally go their separate ways. Instead of embracing the exposition's unifying slogans, the *Southern Mag-*

azine cast border territory as the site of Confederate escape, bayou resistance, and an editorial campaign against "Yankeeisation." Where Browne was outspoken in his defiance, however, those imagined in occupied territory learned to hide Richmond sympathies, southern accents, and Confederate jackets behind well-bred manners and a shrewd self-preservation, which gave postwar Dixie regionalism a distinct political agenda.

That much was apparent when southern hospitality was industriously provided in Mercer's dining rooms by a staff of black waiters, whom Howells dubbed without quibble "lustrous citizens of color."[30] Mercer also arranged for entertainment that would be both alluring and reminiscent, at once foreign and familiar. The only tourist guide actually sold at the exposition advertised an "Old Plantation Darkey Band" that would also "illustrate Southern plantation scenes," while Kingsbury's guidebook for southern visitors praised the "delightful music" of "a genuine, old-time plantation band of negro minstrels from 'way down South.'"[31] Rydell is more skeptical. Noting that the Southern Restaurant was also called simply "The South," he glosses the impression Mercer aimed to make ("newly freed blacks in the South were happy, carefree, and in good hands"), as well as what was suppressed: the "sharecropping, lynching, and political exclusion" thought unsuitable for visitors enjoying their omelets in pork fat. "Feared as insurrectionists and barely tolerated as minstrels," Rydell observes, "blacks were relegated to the shadows of the vision of progress projected at the fair."[32] Where Howells saw "citizens of color" in the Southern Restaurant's attentive staff, Mercer saw antebellum props in an unchanging plantation spectacle.

The *Southern Magazine* was similarly cordial to local white control, which staved off both an imperial North and the threat of amalgamation. But it was Daniel Harvey Hill's *The Land We Love* that proved haunted by unsuppressed Northern violence, even while Charlotte was comparatively thriving. In the lost limbs, lost homes, and lost lives that General Hill's editorials replaced with practical education and Confederate mettle, the monthly's Civil War stories saw the specter of lost white freeholds and a Revolutionary compact undone by Northern destruction and African American liberties. What Patricia Yeager would portray as the ghost of white fears, especially for widows and children, Marianne Hirsch would describe as the lived trauma that others would inherit outside the South, even readers who survived the war with their limbs, their homes, and their lives intact. Still, if trauma's postmemory also incorporated the mettle of a roadside story in perpetual motion, a female Abraham could surreptitiously exchange a failing patriarchy for a housewife's needle and thread. The postwar nation thus remade in Mississippi and Alabama would not secure liberty and justice for all, even metaphorically, but the constraints of coverture would apparently dwindle for autonomous white women on the mend.

How much could be stitched into a renovated version of the nation's origins and prospects was similarly evident in Philadelphia, where the whir and clack of immense halls also gave way to the Women's Pavilion. The building was not anticipated in the fair's original designs because more prominent exhibit space had been assured. When the Women's Centennial Executive Committee was appointed in 1873 to increase sales of the stock subscriptions that helped fund the fair, the great-granddaughter of Benjamin Franklin agreed to serve as committee president in return for a guarantee that the Women's Exhibit would be accommodated in the Main Building. But the efforts Elizabeth Duane Gillespie organized were so successful and the requests from foreign countries encouraged by the women's committee were so numerous that their promised square footage vanished in 1875. Less than a year before the exhibition opened, Gillespie was told that she and her women must construct their own building.

To their credit, they raised the $31,160 required in under four months, an effort that produced what Mary Frances Cordato has called "a self-conscious bid for collective strength and sorority."[33] As Cordato has demonstrated, the subsequent displays tended toward "traditional handicrafts," though the pavilion also included women's household inventions, like a dishwasher and a life-preserving mattress, a self-heating gas iron and a stocking darner.[34] In addition, a six-horsepower steam engine fueled both these inventions and the press that printed the pavilion's paper, the *New Century for Woman*, which also served the international Congress of Women that Julia Ward Howe attended. As the weekly confessed, the quickly constructed building looked to some like "two Saratoga trunks at right angles, crowned by something not unlike a bandbox."[35] But Sylvia Yount calculates that roughly six hundred displays "were intended to illustrate women's progressive influence in many fields," including the "charming sentiment" of the "carved wood-work" that Howells applauded.[36]

In its embrace of a "new century," Chicago was as forward-looking as the Women's Pavilion and as committed to newfound opportunity, so long as Illinois was seen to be the home of both steel webs and upright pianos. Like the two Saratoga trunks and a bandbox, Francis Fisher Browne's *Lakeside Monthly* took to relocation not only in boosting a western metropolis but also in imagining an unsung war in obscure places. The deliberate pause that railroads in Civil War stories repeatedly staged became in western magazines the pause between "a pleasant secluded bend of the creek" where time slows down and the freedmen's schools that hurried a national future. Just as the Women's Pavilion made room for both steam power and handmade goods, the *Lakeside Monthly* in a "go-ahead" city regularly recalled a hinterland war on the crags and sugar fields of unrelieved lives. Yet time and again, the restorative home that western observers feared losing was replaced through trauma by a vigorous future previously unimagined, just as a city decimated by fire would soon scrape the sky. When domestic violence created an underground railroad, the grief that for Dana Luciano recalls the country's origins in 1776 ultimately "refounds the nation" by extending its personal liberties and social justice to the Amelias and Primuses who trade Florida for Massachusetts.[37]

In doing so, they reanimate what home stands for and whose home matters in the *Lakeside Monthly* while also revealing where the Women's Pavilion fell short. Like Gillespie, the project's organizers tended to be from Philadelphia's established families, who favored the parlor values that led back to Revolutionary mothers. There would be little acknowledgment of more recent female "wage-earners," as Cordato has noted.[38] In addition, the hastily organized fund-raising effort almost immediately offended African American women, who were invited to contribute but ordered to limit their efforts to the "colored" community. Segregated as well into a subcommittee, they spoke out through resolutions that were widely reported by the Philadelphia press. In Washington, D.C., the *New National Era* took notice of their "indignity" and of the meeting during which they were told they had "no right to work among white people," a claim that turned the city's patricians into the *New National Era*'s "opponents of justice."[39] As Frederick Douglass's weekly later reported with the measured letter of Dr. Rebecca J. Cole, the subcommittee's black chairwoman, Gillespie's elite group made amends, their apology was accepted, and the Colored Centennial Committee was disbanded.[40] Predictably, its concerns also disappeared when the Women's Pavilion welcomed visitors.

The accounts of an incensed committee member and her more temperate chairwoman thus appeared in the *New National Era* almost in stereo view, differing committee versions of a dispossession that stung. Bret Harte's *Overland Monthly* was similarly geared toward differing points of view in San Francisco, which shared Philadelphia's fraught politics and tourist appeal. Once railroad tracks were laid, both Rincon Hill and Fairmount Park were widely accessible, and so were the narratives that well-thumbed guidebooks offered. But the roles and masks, the stage sets and theatrical space that the *Overland*'s war stories circulated were not acceptable to Dr. Cole's subcommittee in Philadelphia. While a plantation's "Uncle Hampshire" in the San Francisco monthly might play meek to hide his indignation and a Kansas parson's daughter might dream of gold to forget her bed chain, both thereby casting themselves in stereo view, the protest of Philadelphia's Colored Centennial Committee was no more furtive than Harte's euchre brawl. When stereo vision and Miles Orvell's "fraternally twinned images" did not produce the "one apparently solid whole" that Asa Gray expected, the Civil War's imagined aftermath led to anonymous murder and dangerous trails, to national declarations betrayed and local celebrations disrupted.[41] That left Yeager's social fears unresolved, Hirsch's trauma endless, Luciano's grief unavailing, and Orvell's pasteboard resolution as mutilated as Alexander Gardner's battlefield corpses. What was lost behind the scenes would impoverish what met the public eye.

African Americans did not wash their hands of exposition preparations, however, as most southern legislatures did. Although shunned and insulted in Philadelphia, new black citizens across the country refused to be submerged in Centennial sloganeering, which favored white reconciliation while strategically forgetting black victories. Like regional monthlies with unorthodox stories of the Civil War, African American citizens had their own version of what it meant to declare independence, and they were determined to be visible in Fairmount Park. As Philip Foner has observed, "A number of black spokesmen felt that the Centennial offered an opportunity to show the American people the contributions of black Americans to the creation and building of the nation, a subject ignored in nearly all history books then in use in the schools and colleges."[42] How to focus those contributions into one exhibit was the issue when the Arkansas Conference of the African Methodist Episcopal Church offered a plan.

On behalf of "the four millions of American Negroes at the banquet of Nations," Reverend Andrew Chambers proposed a bust of Richard Allen, the first bishop of the first independent black church in the country.[43] Born into slavery in 1760, Allen was sold away from Philadelphia, but he purchased his freedom when he was seventeen and eventually returned to the city. There the AME Church was founded during the late eighteenth century in response to dictatorial white Methodists. Art historian Susanna Gold sums up the first bishop's unusual credentials: "Richard Allen was chosen to represent the collective African American community at the Centennial because his life history was then and remains legendary, his advocacy against racial oppression earning him the reputation as one of the nation's Black Founding Fathers."[44] In his honor, a bust just over three feet high would be made from imported white marble and rendered more elaborate by a Gothic arch, with columns, spires, and figures that would create a pavilion rising to twenty-two feet.[45] Through connections in Cincinnati, the Monument Committee secured the services of sculptor Alfred H. White, and Reverend Chambers in Arkansas began the kind of fundraising campaign that regional periodicals during the 1870s knew all too well.

There the problems began. Fundraising was protracted among those who

FIGURE 41. Alfred H. White, bust of Bishop Richard Allen. 1876. 36.5 inches high. Marble. Photograph. Wilberforce University, on loan to the Richard Allen Museum, Mother Bethel African Methodist Episcopal Church, Philadelphia. Courtesy of Susanna W. Gold.

had so little; as a result, the sculptor went unpaid, and his work progressed fitfully. Meanwhile, the Centennial Commission refused to allow the exhibit to remain permanently in Fairmount Park; instead, the Allen Monument would need to be disassembled within sixty days of the exhibition's closing in November. It was therefore an anxious time as spring slipped into summer and Independence Day passed. With the approach of September 22, the anniversary of the Preliminary Emancipation Proclamation in 1862, the completed bust and its substantial arch were finally loaded onto the cars in Cincinnati, although that train never got much farther than the Pennsylvania border. A broken wheel and a nighttime mishap on a narrow railroad bridge caused several cars to fall into the Chemung River, including the car transporting the monument's arch and, with it, the long-deferred hopes of the AME Church. Against all odds, however, the small bust in its separate packing case was found unharmed and arrived at length in Philadelphia. Instead of lamenting another unjust misfortune, African American supporters were celebrating on November 2, when the marble bust of Bishop Allen was finally installed on a nine-foot granite pedestal just eight days before the Centennial Exhibition closed (figure 41). Like regional periodicals in the wake of the war and then the Panic of 1873, the local tribute so long in coming made its national debut with a clutch of unforeseen stories worth retelling.

Once on display, the bust also became for the fair's black visitors what state exhibits had more often been for white travelers: a restorative gathering place in which fellow citizens could take pride. Mitch Kachun notes that at the unveiling several hundred Africans Americans sang "Joy to the World."[46] Bishop John

M. Brown of Howard University delivered an oration, and "We Are Rising," a poem composed for the occasion by Frances E. W. Harper, was read aloud and printed in the *Christian Recorder*, including these lines:

> Unto God, be *all* the glory,
> That our eyes behold the sight.
> Of a people, peeled and scattered
> Rising into freedom's light.[47]

Such tributes persisted during the limited time that the bust of Bishop Allen was on view. As Gold declares, "Perhaps more significant than the Allen Monument's presence on the fairgrounds, the commemorative speeches, activities, and community assemblies associated with the sculpture afforded the black community the opportunity to unite during this critical re-invention of national identity and claim their place in the social fabric, resisting all mainstream efforts to 'forget.'"[48] Like steadfast contributors in the forums that regional magazines provided, African Americans in Fairmount Park during the waning days of the Centennial Exhibition made sure their voices were heard.

Those days ended too soon, and the partial monument was removed to Ohio's Wilberforce University, where it seemingly disappeared. But the Allen bust has recently resurfaced and returned on loan to Philadelphia and the Richard Allen Museum. In its peripatetic existence, this first public sculpture of an African American subject has provided multiple sites of "rendezvous" that have outstripped the diminished project of the Women's Pavilion, outlived the Southern Restaurant's "Old Plantation Darkey Band," outperformed Machinery Hall's Corliss engine (later sold for scrap), and outclassed the elegant displays in the Centennial Exhibition's Main Building. For the AME Church and its congregations, the Allen Monument enlarged what was worth honoring in the decade that followed the Civil War and, indeed, the century that preceded 1876. "Memories necessarily vary according to the subjective experiences of any specific group," Gold writes, "resulting in any number of alternative narratives and counter-memories."[49] And she concludes, "It is the very dialog and debate between official and specialized community interests that produces the richness of collective memory."[50] Like the monthly magazines issuing from Baltimore and Charlotte, Chicago and San Francisco, the Allen Monument modeled what it meant to be a countermemory and yet, contrary to the fears of W. E. B. Du Bois, visible at last. Miraculously, the bust's lost arch, with its homage to the long swell of African civilization and the more recent history of the AME Church, has also reemerged from the Chemung River, at least on paper (figure 42). Thanks to the keen eye of Metropolitan AME Church member Mar-

FIGURE 42.
Alfred H. White, monument to Bishop Richard Allen. 1876. 22 inches high. Lithograph. Strobridge & Company, Lithographers, Cincinnati, Ohio. Located by Marian Bennett. Courtesy of the Mother Bethel Archives.

ian Bennett, a lithograph of the sculpture's original plan, designed for late fundraising, has been recovered and with it every intricate detail that White once envisioned.[51]

On the November afternoon in 1876 when the simpler marble bust was publicly unveiled, bystanders who arrived at the celebration as tourists could nonetheless become agents of change, as vigorous as Bishop Allen and as mobile as his monument. More broadly, so could those who made their way through the Women's Pavilion, dined at the Southern Restaurant, or strolled the wide avenues of the exposition. Whether more impressed by the official narratives of exposition guidebooks, the countermemories of unexpected exhibits, or their own wayward experiences, the fair's travelers were caught up in filling history's gaps and fissures, just as Civil War stories in regional magazines of the 1860s and

1870s encouraged. Reflecting on what strolling visitors discovered for themselves, Bruno Giberti observes, "This audience did not constitute a passive surface on which the organizers could inscribe their own intentions. It brought its own agenda to the exhibition, which included entertainment as well as education, pleasure, and instruction."[52] Thanks to such travelers, memories of the Centennial Exhibition spread. Some visitors, like Davis, carried their recollections back to Philadelphia homes by foot or streetcar, cab or carriage. Others enjoyed day trips or longer sojourns from nearby cities such as New York, Baltimore, and even Boston for the peaceable Howe and the curious Howells. Those who carried their recollections farthest were most likely to travel on the Pennsylvania Railroad, which advertised "the only direct route from the West, North, and East to the Centennial Exhibition," a "great highway of America" that led to "the very doors of the Exposition."[53] For them, the company built a depot with a pertinent history of its own.

More stately than crowded country platforms and less massive than Vanderbilt's grand terminal in New York, the Centennial Depot afforded easy access to Machinery Hall and the exposition's Main Building while also facing onto palatial lodgings like the Globe, the Transcontinental, and the Grand Exposition Hotels (figure 43). To meet the needs of fairgoers, the station included a general waiting room and a ladies' waiting room, several retiring rooms, a baggage room, a package room, and a ticket office. The building was made of wood and designed to be temporary, provided three tracks for simultaneous arrivals and departures, relied upon seventeen sidetracks for waiting cars, and offered second-floor rooms for railroad officials—Grand Central Dépôt on a smaller scale. Yet its imposing gables and lofty towers, elongated windows and ornamental timbering invoked a deliberate alternative to Second Empire architecture in the revivalist styles of nineteenth-century England. "The fact of the matter is that every architect who has any vitality in him has been captivated by the British buildings," wrote the *New York Times*, and this depot was "worked out in genuine Gothic spirit," especially "the later Tudor styles."[54] The result was a structure that catered to technological progress by recalling a preindustrial past, the inventive plan of a civil engineer turned architect.

The depot built for the Centennial Exhibition was designed by Joseph Wilson, who had served the Pennsylvania Railroad for sixteen years (1860–76) as a designer of bridges, viaducts, and stations. By 1864, as Domenic Vitiello has pointed out, it was Wilson's job "along the northern edge of the Mason-Dixon line" to smooth the transport of Union troops and their matériel.[55] With his brothers John and Henry, also civil engineers like their father before them, he

FIGURE 43. *Panoramic View of Fairmount Park, Taken from the Pennsylvania Railroad.* Wood engraving. *La Ilustración Española y Americana*, May 30, 1876, 352. PRISMA ARCHIVO / Alamy Stock Photo.

founded Wilson Brothers & Co. in January 1876. The firm included several architects and aimed to merge engineering and architecture in assuring "the best professional advice" to individual clients and corporate enterprises, beginning with railway lines.[56] In the "genuine Gothic spirit" of the Centennial Depot, Joseph Wilson favored a conservative British style, which Arts and Crafts designer and social activist William Morris would describe in 1893 as "catching-up the slender thread of tradition" and John Ruskin had championed forty years earlier as fundamentally organic.[57] "In the Gothic vaults and traceries," Ruskin wrote, "there is a stiffness analogous to that of the bones of a limb, or fibres of a tree."[58]

Tudor architecture was somewhat tamer than Ruskin's savage Gothic, its forms harking back nostalgically to the homegrown popularity of William Shakespeare and the Elizabethan Age. Andrew Ballantyne and Andrew Law observe that the "Tudoresque" as a style would continue to be "indigenous, old-fashioned and presented as an image of perfection"—in short, "the very model of Englishness" as "local life."[59] Invoking the Tudor Gothic, Wilson's depot embodied both cosmopolitan import and vernacular tradition, in sharp contrast with New York's Grand Central. Where the Manhattan terminal borrowed from imperial France in its horizontal layering capped by pavilion domes, the Centennial Depot drew upon revivalist England in its vertical thrust, its tall windows and Tudor timbers soaring to pointed gables and towers. The impression of control in New York was thus replaced by the image of aspiration in Philadelphia, mighty ambition acquiescing to local pride.

Self-consciously, Civil War stories in fleeting postwar magazines also held ambition and pride in tension, their multiple regional perspectives bound to the shared upheaval of civil conflict. Like Julia Ward Howe, they generally acknowledged and often hankered for some part of antebellum security; like Rebecca Harding Davis, they also envisioned a borderland future or a replacement home, the Revolution's compact extended or a national "sun" eclipsed. In cities with enough commercial dynamism to support a monthly literary magazine, they surveyed local terrain with inevitable blinders and commemorated both a cause and a new equilibrium that readers could then begin to imagine. From the settings of stories to their plots, from their achronological structure to their differing perspectives, magazines with their own agendas were never transparently representative, but together they traced in short fiction an ambivalent reckoning with fear and terror that never relinquished the country's founding commitment to liberty and justice, later made integral to Francis Bellamy's Pledge of Allegiance in 1892.

How to bring their postwar vision into greater focus, how to pull the levers of Corliss power in a fateful lightning of national moment remained the imaginative task of armchair readers, many of whom were likely among the nearly ten million who passed through Centennial Exhibition turnstiles. Almost all had returned home before the bust of Bishop Allen finally arrived. Against such hefty numbers drawn to other exhibits, what commemorative difference did a small bust and its few hundred witnesses make as they sang? Arguably, not much in 1876; the marble tribute still disappeared from Fairmount Park. But so did many other exhibits, state buildings, and exposition spaces, including the Main Building and Machinery Hall that Joseph Wilson helped design for prompt dismantlement and piecemeal recycling. Unlike so many more auspicious enterprises, however, the Allen bust and his monument's lithograph have returned to Philadelphia, surfacing unexpectedly just when Civil War stories in neglected periodicals have also been rediscovered. As contributions to an ongoing national reconstruction, they may give students of a murky postwar decade much to imagine anew.

NOTES

Introduction: Dépôt Culture

1. Howe told and retold the story of her "battle hymn" and its composition, a tale elaborated by other commentators as well. Most useful for this brief account has been her *Reminiscences*, 269–77, particularly for the enthusiasm of Union soldiers, even in a Richmond prison (276–77). Elaine Showalter underscores how much Howe's words were written to be shared in song. As she puts it, "The words were meant for the ear and not the eye" (Showalter, *Civil Wars*, 167). Significant discussions of the hymn's inception and growing appeal may also be found in Stauffer and Soskis, *Battle Hymn*, 73–105; McWhirter, *Battle Hymns*, 32–58; and Ziegler, *Diva Julia*, 97–100.
2. Howe, "Battle Hymn," 145.
3. Miller, *Raven and the Whale*, 338.
4. "Grand Central Dépôt," 108.
5. Roth, *American Architecture*, 212.
6. "Grand Central Dépôt," 108–9.
7. Fahs, *Imagined Civil War*, 51.
8. Aaron, *Unwritten War*, xvii.
9. Blight, *Race and Reunion*, 4.
10. "President Lincoln's Gettysburg Oration," 469.
11. Ibid.
12. Diffley, *Where My Heart*, xliii.
13. Davis, "John Lamar," 418.
14. Ibid., 415.
15. Pfaelzer, *Parlor Radical*, 92.
16. Sedgwick, *The "Atlantic Monthly*," 109–10; Exman, *House of Harper*, 87–88.
17. Stiles, *First Tycoon*, 19–20. This compact sketch owes much to Stiles's significant research and anecdotal care.
18. Schlichting, *Grand Central Terminal*, 31.
19. Belle and Leighton, *Grand Central*, 36.
20. Mead, "Urban Contingency," 160.
21. Humphreys, "How to Read a Building," 40.
22. Sedgwick, *The "Atlantic Monthly*," 6.
23. Ibid., 77.
24. Stiles, *First Tycoon*, 515–16.
25. Roth, *American Architecture*, 213.
26. Atchison, "Southern Literary Magazines," 60.
27. Bridges, *Lee's Maverick General*, 274.
28. "The Haversack," 427.
29. Hackenberg, "Lakeside Monthly," 199.
30. Kroll, "Civil War Defenses," 8.

31. Schlichting, *Grand Central Terminal*, 32.
32. Condit, *Port of New York*, 92.
33. Belle and Leighton, *Grand Central*, 37.
34. Schlichting, *Grand Central Terminal*, 32.
35. Warner, *Publics and Counterpublics*, 122.
36. Stiles, *First Tycoon*, 515, 518–19.

37. As the *Oxford English Dictionary* further reveals, American writers like Henry Wadsworth Longfellow, James Russell Lowell, and Mark Twain "pronounced" the word in print to rhyme with teapot, a measure of how much play a migrating French coinage could have. See "depot, n." *OED Online*, March 2021, www.oed.com/view/Entry/50387.

38. Young, *Disarming the Nation*, 3.
39. Julia A. Stern, *Mary Chesnut's Civil War Epic*, 5.
40. Jeremy Wells, *Romances*, 2.
41. Fuller, *From Battlefields Rising*, 3.
42. Fahs, *Imagined Civil War*, 4.
43. Okker, *Social Stories*, 109; Frost, *Never One Nation*, xii.
44. Hager, *Word by Word*, 243.
45. Kennedy-Nolle, *Writing Reconstruction*, 19.
46. Ibid., 23.
47. Brook Thomas, *Literature of Reconstruction*, 47.
48. Ibid., 243.
49. "The Boat and the Train," 453.
50. Ibid., 452.

Chapter 1. Potshots

1. As Charles W. Mitchell has remarked, "Many Baltimoreans believed these and other soldiers passing through their city to be the vanguard of a northern assault on the southern states that had seceded from the Union, and for three days following the riot, smoldering anger against the federal government threatened to propel Maryland into the Confederacy" ("'The Whirlwind Now Gathering,'" 203). For varying perspectives on the war's first clash, see Edmund Wilson, *Patriotic Gore*, 395–401; Towers, "'A Vociferous Army'"; and George William Brown, *Baltimore*. More broadly, David Graham ties Baltimore's early upheaval to a late-century cultural effort that reanimated the city's Southern affiliations: "Though it had strong Unionist sentiment, particularly in the business community, Baltimore was also a bastion for Confederate sympathizers and became a central setting for contention between the two sides" ("'She Spurns the Northern Scum,'" 35–36).

2. Quoted in Bright, "In Memoriam," 19.

3. The most valuable sources on Browne are Butts, "*The Southern Review* (Bledsoe's)"; and Bright, "In Memoriam," 3–28.

4. Towers, "Strange Bedfellows." Also of interest are Adam I. P. Smith, *No Party Now*, 49–66; Jonathan Daniel Wells, "Transformation of John Pendleton Kennedy," 292; and Kennedy, *Border States*.

5. See Towers, *Urban South*, 166–82; Bailey, "Pratt Street Riots Reconsidered"; and Brugger, *Maryland: A Middle Temperament*, 274–83.

6. In "Control of the Baltimore Press during the Civil War," Sidney Matthews noted some time ago that the *Daily Republican* was actually suspended midwar for printing "The Southern Cross" (September 10, 1863) with its satire of "The Star-Spangled Banner" in militant stanzas, one of which began "How peaceful and blest was America's soil, / 'Till portrayed by the guile of the Puritan demon" (160).

7. Brugger, *Maryland: A Middle Temperament*, 251. This discussion of Maryland's early commercial development and Baltimore's thriving trade also draws upon Lesher, "A Load of Guano"; Hunter, "Wheat, War"; Arnett, Brugger, and Papenfuse, *Maryland: A New Guide*, 252–61; and Olson, *Baltimore*, 41–101.

8. Silver, "Baltimore Book Trade," 117.

9. Hoyt, "Monday Club"; Sutro, "Wednesday Club."

10. Uhler, "Delphian Club."

11. See Molin, "'Wirt—or Wart?'" Other useful discussions of *The Portico* may be found in Riley, *Magazines of the American South*, 173–76; Ljungquist, "*The Portico*"; and Mott, *History of American Magazines*, 1:293–96.

12. William R. Taylor, *Cavalier and Yankee*, 177–201.

13. "Varieties, Literary and Philosophical," 69.

14. See Brugger, *Maryland: A Middle Temperament*, 196–206. For the status of plantation slavery in Maryland, particularly as tobacco began giving way to other crops such as grains, see *Scraping By*, in which Seth Rockman observes: "The former tobacco plantations of eastern and southern Maryland soon realized the smaller labor requirements of grain agriculture. To be sure, Maryland planters did not abandon slavery wholesale, but their commitment to the institution wavered" (33).

15. This discussion of Baltimore's developing economy draws upon the concept of a "public society" articulated by Browne, *Baltimore in the Nation*, 161–236. In addition, John Stover speaks to the political realignment that railroad routes encouraged and trade guaranteed when he observes: "Not the tobacco from southern plantations, but the flour from the West had made Baltimore prosperous. The B&O hopper cars filled with Cumberland coal did not go south, but rather north to power the plants and factories of New England" (*History*, 101).

16. Browne, *Baltimore in the Nation*, 191.

17. See Lorenz-Meyer, "United in Difference." For related economic concerns, see Mustafa, "'Merchant Culture.'"

18. For the surge in Irish immigration and the Know-Nothing backlash in Baltimore, see Browne, *Baltimore in the Nation*, 191–92, 200–215; and Towers, *Urban South*, 80–98.

19. Grivno, *Gleanings of Freedom*, 197.

20. See Towers, "Job Busting at Baltimore Shipyards," 224–25.

21. The city's black residents had become socially engaged decades before the Civil War. "By the second quarter of the nineteenth century," writes Christopher Phillips, "they had established strong and active social institutions that had transformed a small, disparate, and relatively inert amalgam of transients into a multifaceted community that derived strength from those institutions and exercised power through them" (*Freedom's Port*, 234). For the competition among these several urban groups as their numbers increased, see Olson, *Baltimore*, 117–29.

22. See Brugger, *Maryland: A Middle Temperament*, 310–18, 370–77.

23. Atchison, "Southern Literary Magazines," 28.

24. "Southern Magazine," 768. Just before this "notice" of the journal's momentous change in title, the *New Eclectic*'s editor and publisher, Lawrence Turnbull, revealed in "A Parting Word" that his intent had been "to develop the nascent literature of the South," a goal the new editorial staff shared (766). Five years later in "The Liverpool of America," Edward King would call the *Southern Magazine* "the only monthly periodical of importance in the South" (695).

25. Winston, "Escape from Johnston's Island," 538–39. In the *Southern Magazine*, this narrative was published anonymously; Winston's descendants revealed his authorship when reprinting his story as a booklet in 1915. Charles Rodenbough has since discovered that John Reynolds Winston (1839–88) served in the Forty-Fifth North Carolina Infantry; he was wounded and captured at Gettysburg. Upon his return to Leaksville, North Carolina, he wrote his escape account

and published an unattributed version in the *Greensborough Patriot* (March 10, 1864) before the extended story appeared in the *Southern Magazine*'s postwar pages. See Rodenbough, *Rockingham County*, 76–77.

26. Hoge, "Editorial Notice," 191.

27. For the early financial burden sustained by the magazine's Baltimore publishers, see Margaret J. Preston to Paul Hamilton Hayne, September 13, 1869, in Allan, *Life and Letters*, 250.

28. Turnbull, "New Eclectic Magazine Advertiser," x; Browne to Hayne, March 25, 1872, quoted in Hubbell, *South in American Literature*, 718.

29. Davis, "A Peculiar People," January 10, 1903, 9.

30. George James Atkinson Coulson was the writer behind Alcibiades Jones, a penname that recalled the bold and devious Athenian general whose loyalties shifted during the Peloponnesian War, especially as the number of his enemies grew. Born in Baltimore, Coulson later moved to the Delmarva Peninsula, a proslavery borderland at the intersection of Delaware, Maryland, and Virginia. For further discussion of Coulson's politics and those of fellow Presbyterians in the nineteenth-century South, see Harlow, "Slavery, Race, and Political Ideology," especially 209, 214–15.

31. Baldwin, *Copyright Wars*, 115. For further lucid assessments of copyright debates during the nineteenth century, see 82–125.

32. McGill, *American Literature*, 95. For a discussion of U.S. copyright law just before and after the Civil War, see also McGill, "Role of Government: Copyright." As Claudia Stokes has pointed out, it was only when postwar authors cast themselves as bookworkers, when they "transform[ed] themselves in the public imagination from aristocrats to literary laborers on a par with other manual workers," that the chances for American legislation supporting international copyright markedly improved, ultimately with decisive consequences for an American regional literature. See "Copyrighting American History," 293.

33. Quilibet, "Copyright Struggle," 554.

34. Simms, "International Copyright Law, Part I," 8, 10, 7.

35. "Editor's Table," 117.

36. Ibid., 118.

37. Homestead, *American Women Authors*, 210.

38. In *The Imagined Civil War*, Alice Fahs is usefully specific about differing Northern and Southern investments. "The 1860 census," she writes, "made the disparity dramatically clear: it counted 986 printing offices in New England and the middle states, with only 151 printing establishments in the South. Of these, the 21 presses in Tennessee produced the most work—yet Tennessee, with the only stereotype foundry in the South, fell under Union control early in the war." (21).

39. Parton, "International Copyright," 451.

40. Groves, "Courtesy of the Trade," 146.

41. Browne to Hayne, July 30, 1870, quoted in Hubbell, *South in American Literature*, 718.

42. Browne, "Green Table," December 1874, 647.

43. Ibid.

44. Browne, "Green Table," April 1873, 509; Browne, "Green Table," August 1873, 254.

45. Browne, "Green Table," January 1874, 105.

46. Browne, "Green Table," April 1873, 510.

47. Browne, "Green Table," January 1874, 105.

48. Yeager, "Narrating Space," 5.

49. Marsdale, "Cousin Jack," 713.

50. Yeager, "Narrating Space," 5–6.

51. Ibid., 4.

52. "Midnight Ride from Petersburg," 706; "Trying Journey," 624.
53. Vlach, *Back of the Big House*, 5.
54. Morales-Vázquez, "George Washington," 38.
55. For the varying terms by which the president's house was known, see Seale, *President's House*, 1:23, 364, 366; Gleason, *Sites Unseen*, 84.
56. Seale, "White House," 5. For the similarities to Washington's Mount Vernon, see Dalzell and Dalzell, "Memory, Architecture, and the Future."
57. "Peninsular Sketches," 663; "Revenge of a Goddess," 622.
58. Fitts, "Story of a Mutiny," 224.
59. Ibid.
60. Sheppard, "Sentenced and Shot," 271.
61. Ibid., 274.
62. Ibid., 270.
63. Ibid., 271.
64. Pfaelzer, *Parlor Radical*, 15.
65. "Midnight Ride from Petersburg," 705.
66. Ibid., 703.
67. "A Trying Journey," 624.
68. Marler, *Merchants' Capital*, 4.
69. Schafer, "Part Two," *Louisiana: A History*, 135.
70. See Cutrer, *Theater of a Separate War*, 189–210.
71. Rothman, *Slave Country*, 220.
72. Marler, *Merchants' Capital*, 16.
73. Cutrer, *Theater of a Separate War*, 9.
74. Ibid., 3. For a crisp discussion of the lower Mississippi River as a crucial nineteenth-century locale for growing and exporting cotton, see "Cotton and the U.S. South," in which Sven Beckert describes the Delta as "a kind of Saudi Arabia of the early nineteenth century" (51).
75. Johnson, *Red River Campaign*, 13.
76. For the Confederate cotton trade in Texas, as well as the Union effort to stymie the French, see Cutrer, *Theater of a Separate War*, 272–84; Gentry, "Confederates and Cotton"; and James R. Smith, "Shreveport."
77. For Louisiana's postwar politics and mounting disturbances, see Eric Foner, *Reconstruction*, 262–63, 547–48, 550–52, 554–55; Schafer, "Part Two," *Louisiana: A History*, 212–26; and Marler, *Merchants' Capital*, 171–230, a discussion that includes this observation: "Far from epitomizing the New South, Reconstruction-era New Orleans constituted one of the region's foremost sites of revanchist sentiment and counterrevolutionary resistance" (172).
78. This discussion of a once widely read but now scarcely remembered writer owes much to *Mary Edwards Bryan*, the recent biography by Canter Brown Jr. and Larry Eugene Rivers. In correspondence with the author (July 9, 2017), Brown noted that the stretch of Marsdale's greatest activity coincided with Mary's "relatively fallow period" during the early 1870s, and he added, "She seems to have had trouble placing her material during those years so, perhaps, a pen name made her work seem fresher." Brown also pointed to Mary's appetite for romantic novels during her youth; later, he observed, she would draw pseudonyms from such sources, perhaps including Thomas Peckett Prest's *The Lone Cottage; or, Who's the Stranger?* (1845) and one of that novel's principal characters, Lady Caroline Marsden. The three other lively contributions made to the *Southern Magazine* by "Caroline Marsdale" (or C.M.) were "The Refugees" (September 1873), also set in Louisiana; "Tom" (August 1874), set in Texas; and "My Man Friday" (February 1875), set in Florida.
79. Brown and Rivers, *Mary Edwards Bryan*, 162–63, 182–83. Iredell E. Bryan's Confederate ser-

vice in the Second Louisiana Cavalry, Company B (Natchitoches), has been documented on the Soldiers and Sailors Database for the Civil War, where he is listed erroneously as J. E. Bryan. The presence of the Second Louisiana Cavalry near Opelousas during October and November 1863 and then along the Red River the following spring is detailed in Bergeron, *Guide*, 41–43. For an account of the Second Louisiana Cavalry in action, see "War as I Saw It, Part II," in which Frank L. Richardson notes that at the Battle of Mansfield "men had struggled with each other like wild beasts" (251). Bryan's regiment served in Louisiana throughout the war.

80. Johnston, "Mrs. Mary E. Bryan," 592. Brown and Rivers have identified Johnston as one of Mary's numerous pseudonyms, in this instance taken from Dinah Mulock Craik's *A Life for a Life* (1859). *Mary Edwards Bryan*, xiv.

81. Brown and Rivers, *Mary Edwards Bryan*, 103.

82. Ibid., 104. For further biographical information, see Jonathan Daniel Wells, *Women Writers and Journalists*, 142–51; Susan Sutton Smith, "Mary Edwards Bryan"; Patty, "Bryan, Mary Edwards"; Patty, "Woman Journalist"; and Patty, "Georgia Authoress."

83. Bryan, "Char-Coal Sketches. Lily," 5.

84. "Louisiana," 78. For the significance of Confederate Shreveport, which the Red River Campaign was meant to capture, see Cutrer, *Theater of a Separate War*, 338–59. For the entanglement of the expedition in the cotton trade, see Michael Thomas Smith, "'For Love of Cotton.'"

85. A measured reading of such classical iconography may be taken from "The Divine River," in which Gretchen Meyers writes that "the emergence of Tiberinus onto the Roman stage coincides with the emergence of Rome onto the world stage" (246). Even in postwar Louisiana, the aging water god can be said to embody imperial power both in the distant fields that would reward postbellum Northern capital and on the rivers and bayous where Southern resistance would lurk.

86. See Arthur, "Emblematic Bird of Louisiana."

87. De Forest, "Forced Marches," 712.

88. For detailed accounts of the Red River expedition and the Battle of Mansfield, see Joiner, *Through the Howling Wilderness*, 57–108; Johnson, *Red River Campaign*, 79–169; and Winters, *Civil War in Louisiana*, 317–79.

89. Bonner, "Sketches," 464.

90. Ibid., 466.

91. Lowe, *Greyhound Commander*, 82.

92. Dollar, "Red River Campaign," 413–14.

93. De Forest, "Forced Marches," 708.

94. Johnson, *Red River Campaign*, 119.

95. For the expression widely attributed to the historical congressman from Tennessee, see Ellis, *Life of Colonel David Crockett*, 148.

96. *The Oxford English Dictionary* defines "the mischief" as the devil, a euphemism in regional phrases that spread well beyond the South. An early U.S. usage appeared in an article by Anthony Evergreen for New York's *Salmagundi* in 1807 and another in Maine writer John Neal's *Brother Jonathan: Or, The New Englanders* (1825). See "mischief, n.," *OED Online*, June 2020, www.oed.com/view/Entry/119293.

97. Gay Smith, "Shakespearean Tragedy," 779.

98. "Observations on the 'Caesars,'" 281; Elder, "Servantgalism in Virginia," 632.

99. Conway, "Sacred Flora," 735.

100. Stowe, "First Christmas of New England," 22.

101. Oakes, "Dies Natalis," 3.

102. Vail, "'The Standard of Revolt,'" para. 1.

103. Rangarajan, "*Lalla Rookh*," 80.

104. Vail, "'The Standard of Revolt,'" para. 2.

105. Meagher, "Nineteenth-Century Ireland," 145.

Chapter 2. Old Times There

1. Henkin, *Postal Age*, x.
2. As early as its first volume, the monthly's listed "agents" included Colonel Dudley Evans (Twentieth Virginia Cavalry) in San Francisco and W. L. Springs in Philadelphia. See "Notice to Subscribers," back matter.
3. This succinct sketch is drawn from Welsh, "Lee's Hard Fighter"; Erslev, "'Nearly There'"; Hughes and Johnson, *A Fighter from Way Back*; Bridges, *Lee's Maverick General*; and Wert, "'I Am So Unlike.'"
4. Avery, "Memorial Address," 116.
5. Hill, *Elements of Algebra*, 124. The answer is 100.
6. Bridges, "D. H. Hill's Anti-Yankee Algebra," 220.
7. Kielbowicz, *News in the Mail*, 1.
8. Ibid., 31.
9. Hill, "Editorial," November 1867, 84.
10. John, *Spreading the News*, 4.
11. Adkins, "In a Country Post-Office," 248.
12. Wriston, "Vermont Post Office Locations," 129.
13. Foley, "A Mission Unfulfilled," 616.
14. Kielbowicz, *News in the Mail*, 5. For the establishment of local post offices in more remote states and territories, see, for example, Bergmann, "Delivering a Nation"; Winsberg, "Advance of Florida's Frontier"; Owens, "Overland Mail in Wyoming"; Eigenheer, "Eastward the Frontier"; and Shortridge, "Post Office Frontier in Kansas."
15. "Editor's Easy Chair," 286.
16. Gallagher, *How the Post Office Created America*, 88.
17. Golden, *Posting It*, 105.
18. Hoyo, "Posting Nationalism," 77.
19. Henkin explains why in *The Postal Age* when he observes of the Union, "Throughout the state-banking era (before the Treasury Department began issuing currency in 1863), stamps were the only pieces of paper authorized by the federal government to circulate at a set value throughout the country. During the war, when specie was rare and banknotes depreciated, stamps became useful as money, and stores in cities would give them as change" (37). In "The Postal Service in the Confederacy," Jerry Palazolo makes a similar point about a "severe specie shortage" in the South (10).
20. Gallagher, *How the Post Office Created America*, 100–101.
21. John, *Spreading the News*, 137.
22. Dietz, *Postal Service*, 115.
23. Leonard, *Neither Snow nor Rain*, 17.
24. Reamy and Reamy, *Index*, x.
25. Sternhell, "Communicating War," 197.
26. Thorpe, "New York City Post-Office," 659.
27. Ridgway, *Self-Sufficiency at All Costs*, 50. More broadly, see Anderson, "Money or Nothing."
28. For circulation figures, see Atchison, "*The Land We Love*," 508. Also of interest are Kennedy-Nolle, "Living for Dixie"; and Riley, *Magazines of the American South*, 97–101.
29. William Powell alludes to North Carolina's reputation as Washington Irving's "isolated" folk in *North Carolina through Four Centuries*, 245.
30. Hill, "Education," August 1866, 238.
31. Ibid., 239.
32. Hanchett, *Sorting Out*, 25. This brisk assessment derives from Hanchett's knowledgeable history.

33. Ibid., 42.
34. Ibid., 40.
35. Ready, *Tar Heel State*, 109.
36. "Sketch of Mecklenburg County," 130, 134.
37. Ibid., 144.
38. Greenwood, *Bittersweet Legacy*, 2; Hill "Editorial," July 1867, 269; and Hill, "Editorial," November 1867, 90.
39. Robinson, "Iconography of Postwar Magazine Covers," 56.
40. Bishir, "A Spirit of Improvement," 145.
41. Ibid., 164.
42. Ibid., 131. As Hanchett reveals in *Sorting Out the New South City*, large-scale plantation agriculture depending on an enslaved labor force of fifty or more was nonetheless a rarity near Charlotte before the Civil War, despite the landed authority portrayed on Hill's magazine covers. "In the lowcountry," Hanchett observes, "big plantation owners traded directly with brokers in Charleston or Wilmington and often ignored local towns. Mecklenburg's smaller slaveholders, by contrast, could seldom muster the time, expertise, or economic clout to deal directly with the coast and instead traded their crops to Charlotte storekeepers" (17). Because revenues in this part of North Carolina remained local, Charlotte prospered, just as Governor Morehead had intended.
43. Robinson, "Iconography of Postwar Magazine Covers," 56.
44. *Dred Scott v. Sandford* 60 U.S. at 407.
45. Bardaglio, *Reconstructing the Household*, xi.
46. Zipf, "No Longer under Cover(ture)," 205.
47. Ibid., 210.
48. Hutchison, *Apples and Ashes*, 177.
49. Pollard, *Lost Cause*, 41, 35.
50. Ibid., 743.
51. Ibid., 749.
52. Ibid., 752.
53. Nolan, "Anatomy of the Myth," 12.
54. Maddex, *Reconstruction of Edward A. Pollard*, 3.
55. Hill, "Education," May 1866, 1.
56. Ibid., 3.
57. Pollard, *Lost Cause*, 314.
58. Hill, "Lost Dispatch," 278.
59. Hill, "Editorial," March 1868, 442; Hill, "Editorial," July 1868, 281.
60. Hill, "Editorial," December 1868, 175.
61. Hill, "Editorial," July 1868, 285.
62. Gallagher, "Jubal A. Early," 41.
63. Rubin, "Politics and Petticoats," 180.
64. Hill, "Editorial," August 1868, 369.
65. Hill, "Editorial," September 1868, 444.
66. Hill, "Editorial," August 1866, 303.
67. Hill, "Editorial," November 1868, 87–88.
68. Blight, *Race and Reunion*, 260.
69. McCurry, *Confederate Reckoning*, 13.
70. Hill, "Editorial," November 1867, 87; Hill, "Editorial," December 1867, 171.
71. "To Our Patrons," April 1868, back matter.
72. Hirsch, *Generation of Postmemory*, 5.
73. Keizer, "Gone Astray in the Flesh."
74. McDermott, "Ethics of Postmemory."

75. Edelstein, "'Pretty as Pictures,'" 155.
76. Moody, "Women, Race, Reading, and Feeling," 263.
77. Hirsch, "Presidential Address 2014," 334. In an address entitled "Connective Histories in Vulnerable Times," Hirsch expanded the purview of her term. "Postmemory," she declared, "describes the relationship that later generations *or distant contemporary witnesses* bear to the personal, collective, and cultural trauma of others—to experiences they 'remember' or know only by means of stories, images, and behaviors" (339, emphasis added).
78. Davis, "A Peculiar People," January 17, 1903, 8.
79. Gamerro, "Remembering without memories," 112.
80. Hirsch, "Presidential Address 2014," 335.
81. "Home on Furlough," 36.
82. Porter, "Texas Soldier," 346.
83. Reita, "Elmsville and Its Hospital," 120–27, 225–31.
84. Hill, "Education," May 1866, 2.
85. *Congressional Globe*, 40th Cong., 3rd sess., February 4, 1869, 861.
86. Manheim, "First Campaign of a Fat Volunteer," 4; Davis, "John Lamar," 420.
87. Bagby, "My Uncle Flatback's Plantation," 602; Davis, "John Lamar," 421.
88. "Peninsular Sketches," 669; Davis, "John Lamar," 419, 416.
89. Rose, *Victorian America*, 13.
90. "In an Old Drawer," 161.
91. White, "Life in Civil War," 5–6.
92. See Timothy B. Smith, *Corinth 1862*, xviii; and Hardy, *Civil War Charlotte*, 11.
93. Dossman, *Campaign for Corinth*, 14.
94. Groom, *Shiloh 1862*, 15, 16.
95. Shelby Foote, *Fort Sumter to Perryville*, 351.
96. James Harris, "Short History," 61.
97. Groom, *Shiloh 1862*, 261.
98. Shelby Foote, *Fort Sumter to Perryville*, 330.
99. Judy Atkins Taylor, correspondence with the author, July 28, 2014.
100. Raymond, *Living Female Writers*, 281. Ina Marie Porter would gain a considerable reputation as an author during the war. In 1861 she was attending the South Alabama Female College in Greenville, but she was already publishing poetry and more. Judy Atkins Taylor reports that a "good-bye party," which saw the Greenville Guards off to Richmond in November, sang new words to "Dixie" that Ina Marie had written and her father had printed on his hand press overnight. The United Daughters of the Confederacy later approved her version as the official lyrics of the song, which Confederate veterans' organizations preferred as well ("Ina Marie," 69, 70). Any sketch of the twice-married Porter will owe a good deal to Taylor's acute portrait, much like this one does. As Benjamin Buford Williams has further observed, "Throughout her career the war and its veterans were always the central subjects of her writing" (*Literary History of Alabama*, 128). After the war, the widowed Porter was resourceful in publishing poetry and stories in *The Land We Love*, which paid its contributors.
101. Raymond, *Living Female Writers*, 282.
102. Rogers, *Civil War Corinth*, 7.
103. Cumming, *Kate*, 43.
104. Dossman, *Campaign for Corinth*, 23.
105. Cashin, "Into the Trackless Wilderness," 29, 32.
106. See McCurry, *Confederate Reckoning*, 85–132.
107. Rable, *Civil Wars*, 183.
108. Ibid., 181.
109. McCurry, *Confederate Reckoning*, 88, 89.

110. Ockenden, "Interesting Reminiscences," 10. Also useful is Ockenden, "What I Remember," 12–15.
111. See Walker, "Corinth," 5–22.
112. Cashin, "Into the Trackless Wilderness," 33.
113. Edwards, *Gendered Strife and Confusion*, 7.
114. Rable, *Civil Wars*, 184.
115. Cashin, "Into the Trackless Wilderness," 48.
116. Ockenden, *Confederate Monument*, 8.
117. Janney, *Remembering the Civil War*, 244.
118. Edwards, *Gendered Strife and Confusion*, 8.
119. Ibid., 12.
120. McCurry, *Confederate Reckoning*, 156.
121. Ockenden, *Confederate Monument*, 3.
122. Panhorst, "Devotion, Deception," 166–67.

Chapter 3. Railroaded

1. Gara, *Liberty Line*, 1–18.
2. Blackwell, "Fugitives at the West," 585.
3. Ibid., 589, 585.
4. Ibid., 584.
5. Luciano, *Arranging Grief*, 51, 50.
6. Ibid., 52.
7. Davis, "John Lamar," 420, 421.
8. Ibid., 423.
9. Blackwell, "Fugitives at the West," 588.
10. Ibid., 590, 591.
11. Ibid., 591.
12. Schivelbusch, *Railway Journey*, 35.
13. Sikes, "One of My Scholars," 592.
14. Hastings, "Lois Pearl Berkeley," 552.
15. Ibid., 567.
16. Davis, "Ellen," 33, 26.
17. Gordon, *Passage to Union*, 6.
18. Carlene Stephens has observed that, as early as the 1840s, railroads foresaw the need for standardized time so that freight could be loaded, schedules could be kept, and trains could avoid collisions. Myriad local times slowly gave way to city clocks and then regional norms. "Gradually a network of regional times replaced the patchwork of local times," Stephens writes, "and, as the century progressed, the number of regional times decreased in turn. In 1873 there were over seventy regional railroad times across the United States. In 1883, on the eve of the railroads' introduction of a national standard time, there were about fifty" (*On Time*, 103). Even before the advent of time zones, it seems, railway priorities were transforming local time across the country.
19. Stover, *American Railroads*, 45.
20. Bruns, *Mail on the Move*, 65.
21. "The Fast Mail to Chicago," 818. As the newsmagazine revealed, the first fast mail train left New York's Grand Central Dépôt early on September 16, 1875, and reached Chicago the next morning, just over twenty-four hours later. During the day en route, more than a hundred station deliveries were made before the train arrived at its western terminus, though pauses were getting shorter all the time. Because the Ward mail-bag catcher had been installed relatively recently, the newsmagazine included "Catching Post" (upper left) along with "Catching Mail at Way-Station"

(upper right) in its composite engraving and even spelled out how the mechanism worked: "As soon as a station is reached, the mail-bag for that place is thrown off, and a movable iron crane, acutely angular in shape, is projected from the side of the car to catch the mail-bag that hangs on an arm of a post at the side of the track" (817). Not everyone agreed, however, that shorter pauses meant greater progress. Writing for the *Overland Monthly*, economist Henry George complained in "What the Railroad Will Bring Us" (October 1868) about the small towns killed off to fatten great cities and about a "new era" of "less personal independence among the many and the greater power of the few" (306). His model for such a threat in 1868 was "the tower which men once built almost unto heaven" (306), as if depot "Babel" could stand in for both an older biblical hubris and the railroad's corporate shrug.

22. Stephens, *On Time*, 100.
23. Cronon, *Nature's Metropolis*, 74.
24. "Chicago in 1856," 606, 608.
25. Pierce, *History of Chicago*, 2:5.
26. For the city's wartime neighborhoods, see Karamanski, *Rally 'Round the Flag*, 4–5. For neighborhood population percentages, see Karamanski and McMahon, *Civil War Chicago*, 8–9.
27. Pierce, *History of Chicago*, 2:476.
28. Jentz and Schneirov, *Chicago in the Age of Capital*, 3.
29. Ibid., 13–52.
30. Ibid., 40.
31. Karamanski, *Rally 'Round the Flag*, xiv.
32. Pierce, *History of Chicago*, 2:247–48.
33. Ibid., 2:268–80.
34. Ibid., 2:272.
35. Karamanski, *Rally 'Round the Flag*, 166.
36. William G. Thomas, *Iron Way*, 168.
37. Hicken, *Illinois in the Civil War*, 27.
38. Hackenberg, "Lakeside Monthly," 200. For additional profiles of Browne and his magazines, see Digby-Junger, "Chicago's *Lakeside Monthly*," 15–28, 39–41, 48–61; Flanagan, "Some Midwestern Literary Magazines," 238–40; Mosher, "Chicago's 'Saving Remnant,'" 8–25, 107–73; Binckley, "Life-Story of a Magazine"; Muir, "Browne the Beloved," 492; and Browne, "Francis Fisher Browne," which declares of the *Lakeside Monthly*'s editor that he came from "the purest New England stock" and that "the blood of 'John Brown of Osawatomie' flowed in his veins" (437).
39. Hackenberg, "Lakeside Monthly," 199.
40. Mott, *History of American Magazines*, 3:414.
41. "Editorial—Our Field," 252.
42. Booth, "Suffrage," 85.
43. "Current Notes—the Western Monthly," 437.
44. Ibid., 438.
45. G. Nelson Smith, "East and West," 159–60.
46. Ibid., 162.
47. "New Chicago," 811.
48. Pierce, *History of Chicago*, 1:72.
49. Cronon, *Nature's Metropolis*, 52.
50. For the trumpet blast of "RESURGAM," the issue's final word, see Foster, "New Chicago," 85.
51. "Current Notes," 436; "Editorial—to Western Writers," 58.
52. Mosher, "Chicago's 'Saving Remnant,'" 8.
53. Mott, *History of American Magazines*, 3:414.
54. "William B. Ogden," 2, 3, 4.
55. Ibid., 4, 6.

56. Ibid., 5, 7.
57. Pierce, *History of Chicago*, 1:187.
58. Kellogg, "Self-Made Men," 36.
59. Ibid.
60. "Harriet Beecher Stowe," 196–97, 200.
61. Leslie, "Wife of Garibaldi," 462.
62. Booth, "Suffrage," 86; Hawthorn, "Citizen as a Voter," 208.
63. Hawthorn, "Citizen as a Voter," 208, 207.
64. De Quincey, "New Story of Lee's Surrender," 329, 327.
65. Schivelbusch, *Railway Journey*, 103.
66. Cooley, "Illinois and the Underground Railroad," 88.
67. See Turner, *Underground Railroad in Illinois*, 26, 31, 85, 117–18.
68. For the Thirteenth Amendment, which was drafted in 1861 by Illinois senator Lyman Trumbull, see Eric Foner, *Fiery Trial*, 291–94, 311–17. In Foner's view, "The debates over the Thirteenth Amendment offered a foretaste of the more far-reaching discussion of the meaning of American freedom that would follow the Civil War" (293), not least in the pages of the *Lakeside Monthly*.
69. "Editorial—a Word to the Public," 57.
70. Digby-Junger, "Chicago's *Lakeside Monthly*," 13. Digby-Junger adds, "While the 'pitch' was literature, the first issues were clearly designed for the city's most lucrative magazine market, the upper middle-class commercial and industrial sector" (14), good reason to commence with a portrait of Chicago's "Railway King."
71. See Kevin Phillips, *Cousins' War*, 366–69, for all settlement patterns in Illinois.
72. Bordewich, *Bound for Canaan*, 93.
73. LaRoche, *Free Black Communities*, 56.
74. "William Bross," 324.
75. LaRoche, *Free Black Communities*, 88.
76. Turner, *Underground Railroad in Illinois*, 29. Turner remarks as well on the "instructive geometric shapes" of quilts "hung on a clothesline" (50). Doubts about their hidden messages have arisen, however, among scholar quilters. See Horton, "Truth and the Quilt Researcher's Rage"; and Hood, "An Inconvenient Truth."
77. Turner, *Underground Railroad in Illinois*, 45.
78. Eric Foner, *Gateway to Freedom*, 218.
79. "Anson S. Miller," 194.
80. Ibid., 193.
81. Ibid., 194.
82. Karamanski, *Rally 'Round the Flag*, 181. For extended attention to the significant contributions of John Jones in Illinois, see Bridges, "Antebellum Struggle for Citizenship"; Garb, "Political Education of John James"; Gliozzo, "John Jones"; and Angle, "Illinois Black Laws."
83. Nash, "Jack Dessart," 307.
84. Ibid., 312.
85. Ibid., 311, 315, 316.
86. Ibid., 315, 316.
87. Ibid., 308.
88. Pierce, *History of Chicago*, 2:188–89.
89. Karamanski and McMahon, *Civil War Chicago*, 189.
90. Karamanski, *Rally 'Round the Flag*, 179.
91. Jentz and Schneirov, *Chicago in the Age of Capital*, 122.
92. Ibid., 122–23.
93. Ibid., 21, 15. The anger of the city's laborers was also rising, as Jentz and Schneirov make plain: "They were wage-slaves in the eyes of a producers' republican society that rooted indepen-

dence and liberty in the ownership of productive property. A wage-slave could not be an independent citizen of a producers' republic" (82). For a magazine like the *Lakeside Monthly*, which lionized self-made men and women, stifled workers did not suit the customary script and only occasionally appeared in the stories of a war they rarely escaped.

94. Ibid., 17.
95. Ibid., 79–80.
96. "William Bross," 323.
97. Ibid., 323, 324.
98. Ibid., 326, 325.
99. Ibid., 327.
100. Ibid., 329.
101. Phelps, "Our Adjutant," 374. Phelps graduated Phi Beta Kappa from Schenectady's Union College in 1856 and taught in Alexandria, Louisiana, for three years before enlisting in the Nineteenth U.S. Infantry in 1861 and following his regiment south. After the war he became a lawyer in Joliet, Illinois, while contributing to *The Cosmopolitan* and *The Knickerbocker*, as well as the *Lakeside Monthly*. See Ellis, *Norwich University*, 2:570–71. For his military service, see Hewitt, "Nineteenth Regiment of Infantry."
102. Phelps, "Our Adjutant," 374.
103. Ibid., 380.
104. Ibid., 384, 374, 377, 384.
105. Ibid., 377, 378, 375.
106. Ibid., 386.
107. Ibid., 379–80.
108. Ibid., 380.
109. William G. Thomas, *Iron Way*, 152.
110. Ibid., 160.
111. Phelps, "Our Adjutant," 380.
112. Ibid. For a more stringent view of Bross, see Pierce, *History of Chicago*, 2:169, 281; and Jentz and Schneirov, *Chicago in the Age of Capital*, 94–95.
113. Thomas Graham, *Mr. Flagler's St. Augustine*, 81.
114. Braden, *Architecture of Leisure*, 25. See, too, Poleo, "James Edmundson Ingraham," 93–118.
115. "Three New Hotels," 860.
116. Ibid.
117. Woolson, "Ancient City," 2; Woolson, "South Devil," 176.
118. B., "Death of Mrs. Helen E. Harrington," 2.
119. For Helen E. Griswold's earlier correspondence with Frances Smith in St. Augustine, see Baker, *Websters*, 18, 301n9. For a lengthy sketch of the Reverend Joseph Harrington, whom Griswold married in Chicago on April 6, 1841, see Whiting, *Memoir*, in which the couple's travels during 1844 are noted (33).
120. Griffin, "Life on the Plantations," 180.
121. Vlach, *Back of the Big House*, 187; Wayne, *Sweet Cane*, 10.
122. Wayne, *Sweet Cane*, 98.
123. Mintz, *Sweetness and Power*, 49.
124. Doggett, "Glance at Florida," 223.
125. Ibid., 226.
126. Luciano, *Arranging Grief*, 170.
127. Winsboro and Knetsch, "Florida Slaves," 77.
128. Morrison, *Playing in the Dark*, 17.
129. "Seminole War," 441. For the anxious spurt in the city's population during the mid-1830s, see Dewhurst, *History of Saint Augustine*, 151.

130. Landers, *Atlantic Creoles*, 193. See, too, Klos, "Blacks and the Seminole Removal"; and Porter, "Negroes and the Seminole War."
131. Landers, *Atlantic Creoles*, 179.
132. Rivers, *Slavery in Florida*, 190.

Chapter 4. Emancipation and Grizzly Reckoning

1. "Brady's Photographs," 5. D. Mark Katz writes that, of the seventy photographs made by Brady's operators in Maryland, only eight were large eight-by-ten plates; fully sixty-two were stereo views, including fifty-five taken by Alexander Gardner and another seven by his assistant. See *Witness to an Era*, 45. Robert Taft has noted that wartime operators almost always carried a stereoscopic camera, which was small, easy to use, and likely to produce the popular sales that would underwrite future fieldwork (*Photography and the American Scene*, 234). That was demonstrably the case with the stereo views of Antietam. As Alan Trachtenberg has observed, "Whether translated into wood engravings and lithographs in the daily press and in periodicals or offered for sale as freshly made prints, mainly in stereo-card or carte-de-visite format, the photographs were destined for home consumption . . . with domestic audiences in mind" (*Reading American Photographs*, 88). More than simply a New York event during the weeks that followed the battle, Brady's exhibition was a successful marketing venture.
2. Orvell, *Real Thing*, 78.
3. Berglund, *Making San Francisco American*, 1.
4. Kowalewski, "Romancing the Gold Rush," 208.
5. Sandweiss, *Print the Legend*, 54.
6. Upton, "Plan of San Francisco," 137.
7. Sears, *Landscape Turned Red*, 45.
8. McPherson, *Crossroads of Freedom*, 139.
9. "President Lincoln's Gettysburg Oration," 469.
10. As a self-described "Photographer to the Army of the Potomac," Gardner had been photographing maps and charts for the Secret Service under Allan Pinkerton since early 1862. He had also enjoyed unlimited access to troops in the field and early information about their movements, information that brought him to Antietam before Robert E. Lee's army slipped away during the night of September 18. Particularly useful in documenting Gardner's ties to McClellan's staff and the secret activities of the U.S. Topographical Engineers are Miller, *Photographic History of the Civil War*, 8:14–15, 23; Cobb, "Alexander Gardner"; Katz, *Witness to an Era*, 22–103; Stapp, "'To . . . Arouse the Conscience,'" 23; and, above all, Frassanito, *Antietam*. Earlier accounts that mistakenly place Mathew Brady at Antietam, despite his failing eyesight, should be used with caution.
11. Forbes, "Watching a Battle," 258.
12. For a fuller description of the Ninth New York's extraordinary charge and the brigade's heavy casualties, see Sears, *Landscape Turned Red*, 281–84. For the impact of that charge and its expense, see McPherson, *Crossroads of Freedom*, 125–28.
13. In the description printed alongside his drawing, Forbes failed to mention the late arrival of General A. P. Hill's division, Confederate regiments from Harpers Ferry that appeared just in time to flank the Union advance and force the New Yorkers to fall back. See "Last Bayonet Charge," 45–46. For a brief allusion to the final "repulse" plus Forbes's later recollections of Antietam ("the battle was a dramatic and most magnificent series of pictures"), see Forbes, "Watching a Battle," 258. Further discussion of how special artists functioned at the front may be found in Davis, "How a Battle Is Sketched"; Campbell, *Civil War: A Centennial Exhibition*; Hodgson, *War Illustrators*; Diffley, "'Musquitos, Rattlesnakes, and Perspiration'"; Thompson, *Image of War*; Sneden, *Eye of the Storm*; and Joshua Brown, *Beyond the Lines*, 32–59. For another thoughtful contrast between "image makers" at Antietam, see Lee, "Image of War," 16–43.

14. "Brady's Photographs," 5.
15. Galassi, *Before Photography*, 17.
16. Frassanito, *Antietam*, 131.
17. For revealing discussions of Gardner's practices, see Stapp, "'To ... Arouse the Conscience,'" 27–33; Frassanito, *Gettysburg*, 186–92; and Young, "Verbal Battlefields," 53–54.
18. Snyder, *American Frontiers*, 14.
19. Davis, "'A Terrible Distinctness,'" 152.
20. "Fine Arts. Brady's Incidents," 1.
21. Phelps, "A Sacrifice Consumed," 238, 235, 237, 238, 239.
22. Crary, *Techniques of the Observer*, 120.
23. Nichols, "General's Story," 73.
24. Ibid., 72.
25. Du Bois, "Strivings," 194.
26. Ibid.
27. Holmes, "Professor's Story," 491.
28. "Recent Literature: Higginson's *Oldport Days*," 108; Gray, "Darwin," 231.
29. Holmes, "Doings," 11, 12.
30. Harte, "ETC.," 99.
31. Ibid. For Harte's quick hand with a pencil and his tenure as the *Overland Monthly*'s first editor, see Nissen, *Bret Harte*, 87–112; May, "Bret Harte"; Madeleine B. Stern, "Anton Roman"; Brooks, "Bret Harte in California"; Brooks, "Early Days"; and Bartlett, "Overland Reminiscences."
32. Writing of the president as an American Everyman, Eric Foner describes Lincoln's capacity to listen and change. "He had to take into account the actions of groups with which he had previously had virtually no contact," writes Foner. "Most notable among these groups were the slaves themselves, who seized the opportunity offered by the Civil War to strike for their freedom and who overwhelmingly rejected Lincoln's hope that many of them would agree to emigrate to some other country. Their actions forced the questions of slavery and the future place of blacks in American society onto the wartime agenda" (*Fiery Trial*, xx–xxi). Following 1863, when the Emancipation Proclamation went into effect less than a year after Davis's story was published, the purposes of the war shifted for many.
33. Ethington, *Public City*, 241.
34. Keith Wilson, introduction, 1–2.
35. Bowley, "Dark Night on Picket," 35.
36. Ibid., 35, 32, 33.
37. Ibid., 36.
38. Ibid., 35.
39. Davis, "John Lamar," 417.
40. Ibid., 421.
41. Ethington, *Public City*, 240.
42. Matthews, "Forging," 214.
43. Starr, "Rooted," 6.
44. Matthews, "Forging," 219.
45. Daniels, *Pioneer Urbanites*, 49.
46. Aarim-Heriot, *Chinese Immigrants*, 156.
47. Hittell, *History*, 384.
48. Berglund, *Making San Francisco American*, 10.
49. Hittell, *History*, 361.
50. Watkins, "San Francisco," 21.
51. Brooks, "Restaurant Life," 473.
52. Scharnhorst, *Bret Harte*, 52. For other useful sketches of the *Overland Monthly*, see O'Con-

nor, *Bret Harte*, 96–133; and Mott, *History of American Magazines*, 3:402–9, which includes circulation figures (405).

53. Avery, "ETC.," 281.

54. Roman, "Beginnings," 73.

55. Bartlett, "Overland Reminiscences," 45–46.

56. May, "Bret Harte," 269.

57. Hansen, "Chivalry," 32. For the reach of Gwin's Democrats across wartime California, see Matthews, *Golden State*, 179–202.

58. Hittell, *History*, 349.

59. Ibid., 338. For wartime Union sentiment in northern California and the deep pockets opened for the U.S. Sanitary Commission, see Matthews, *Golden State*, 155–70, 235–46.

60. Scharnhorst, *Bret Harte*, 18.

61. Powers, prefatory, 5. This brisk sketch is drawn from Harwood P. Hinton's engaging introduction.

62. F. Bret Harte to J. W. Bliss, September 30, 1870, Graff 1804, Newberry Library. It is a pleasure to acknowledge the assistance of the Newberry Library's Jill Gage, who located this "lost" correspondence.

63. Hyacinth, "Ruined State," 10, 14.

64. Ibid., 10.

65. Hyacinth, "Some Pine-Knots," 51.

66. Ibid., 49.

67. Ibid., 50.

68. Ibid., 52.

69. Hyacinth, "Solid Days in Texas," 555, 556.

70. Hinton, introduction, xix.

71. Starr, *California*, 13–16, 99.

72. Quoted in Hinton, introduction, xvii.

73. As Linwood Carranco has documented in "Bret Harte in Union," a young Harte moved from setting type to writing editorials for the *Northern Californian*, a weekly paper he was managing as temporary associate editor during the early months of 1860. On February 26, the nearby Wiyot were attacked by whites, who hatcheted sixty Indians, including women and children. Harte wrote of their "indiscriminate massacre" and then left town abruptly (see 107–9). In his biography, Scharnhorst has thus observed of the editor's three years in Union, "In one respect only was Harte's tenure as a printer's devil and editor pro tem of a rural newspaper at all remarkable: he consistently championed the rights of Native Americans in his editorials" (*Bret Harte*, 12). David Wyatt further notes that Harte "deplored the massacre of Indians in Humboldt County and had established himself as a staunch abolitionist" (*Five Fires*, 74). For Harte's activities during the late 1850s more generally, see Murdock, "Bret Harte in Humboldt."

74. Wyatt, *Five Fires*, 86.

75. Ethington, *Public City*, 202.

76. Frost, *Never One Nation*, 140.

77. Indeed, who got noticed in the magazine's short fiction often reveals how the demographic tug of Chinese immigration would position other racial interest groups in cosmopolitan San Francisco when the Civil War was recollected. For long-vulnerable free blacks and the formerly enslaved, the spike in Chinese immigration provided a discernible opportunity. What Helen Jun has termed a "black orientalism" engendered among some in San Francisco a rhetoric privileging domestic citizens such as African Americans at the expense of the "foreign" Chinese. As Jun observes, "The formulaic narration of black military service, Christian morality, and nationalist identification that constructed blacks as American subjects would become a repetitive and frequent articulation with respect to discourses of Chinese exclusion" ("Black Orientalism," 1058–59). While

the Chinese do not appear in the *Overland Monthly*'s war stories, they register as the kind of unseen "presence" that Toni Morrison has made familiar, though here in unusual ways (*Playing in the Dark*, 5).

78. Scharnhorst, *Bret Harte*, 52.
79. Harte, "Plain Language," 287.
80. Ibid., 288; Scharnhorst, *Bret Harte*, 52–57.
81. Harte, "Plain Language," 288.
82. Wyatt, *Five Fires*, 7.
83. Shipley, "Saint Saviour," 347.
84. King, "Cabin," 514, 513.
85. Cooper, "Old Uncle Hampshire," 437.
86. Crary, *Techniques of the Observer*, 129.
87. Bellion, "Vision and Visuality," 22.
88. Genette, *Narrative Discourse Revisited*, 64.
89. McCrackin, "Reminiscences of Bret Harte," 10.
90. Cheryl Foote, "'My Husband Was a Madman,'" in *Women of the New Mexico Frontier*, 74.
91. Clifford, "Marching with a Command," 396.
92. Ibid., 397.
93. James, "Romantic History," 13.
94. For Clifford's account of her escape from New Mexico, see "Toby" and "Flight: A Sequel to 'Toby.'" Both stories were apparently written after her husband was reported dead, and the timing was no accident. As Cheryl Foote observes, "She probably hesitated to publish these stories about her life with Clifford while he was still alive because she feared that he might locate her" ("'My Husband Was a Madman,'" in *Women of the New Mexico Frontier*, 167n41). Foote's portrait of Clifford relies on careful research; her chapter title comes from a line in "Toby" (105). Also useful in tracing Josephine Clifford, who married Jackson McCrackin in 1882, are Egli, "Josephine Clifford McCrackin"; Payne, *Howling Wilderness*, 121–27; and Cummins, *Story of the Files*, 158–59. Less reliable is Vore, "A Famous Western Pioneer."
95. Leonard, *Men of Color to Arms!*, 8.
96. Meier, "Lorenzo Thomas," 267.
97. John David Smith, "Recruitment of Negro Soldiers," 389.
98. Billington, *New Mexico's Buffalo Soldiers*, 204–5.
99. Parker, *Annals of Old Fort Cummings*, 5.
100. Ibid., 12.
101. Ibid., 39, 4.
102. Leonard, *Men of Color to Arms!*, 258n29; Mays, "Battle of Saltville," 205.
103. Quoted in Sheehan, *Planet Mars*, 63.

Coda: Depot, Culture, 1876

1. Ziegler, *Diva Julia*, 3; Showalter, *Civil Wars*, xiv. This return to Howe and her family also draws upon Showalter, *Civil Wars*, 185–205; and Journal 1876, MS Am 2119 (1107), Julia Ward Howe Papers, Houghton Library, Harvard University, Cambridge, Mass.
2. Howe, *Reminiscences*, 328.
3. Howe, "Appeal to Womanhood," 1.
4. Nash, *First City*, 277; Kachun, "Before the Eyes," 307.
5. Rydell, *All the World's a Fair*, 11, 13.
6. Ibid., 10.
7. Noe, "'Everybody Is Centennializing,'" 327.
8. Nash, *First City*, 262; Gallman, *Mastering Wartime*, 336.

9. Nash, *First City*, 231.
10. Noe, "'Everybody Is Centennializing,'" 327.
11. Philip S. Foner, "Black Participation," 288.
12. Nash, *First City*, 279.
13. Harris, *Rebecca Harding Davis*, 75.
14. Davis, "Rainy Day at the Exposition," 930.
15. Davis, "Glimpse of Philadelphia," 30.
16. Davis, "Old Philadelphia," 711.
17. Pfaelzer, *Parlor Radical*, 189.
18. Harris, "Anatomy of Complicity," 297.
19. Howe, "A 'Monstrous Edifice,'" 641.
20. "Our Centennial," 422; Howells, "Sennight of the Centennial," 99.
21. McClelland, "1876 Centennial Craze," 20.
22. "Our Centennial," 422.
23. Howells, "Sennight of the Centennial," 104.
24. Howe, "A 'Monstrous Edifice,'" 638; Simpson, "'The Doom of Slavery,'" 55. See also Sacco, "'I Never Was an Abolitionist'"; and Marszalek, "Writing His Mind."
25. Gold, *Unfinished Exhibition*, 6. For U.S. newspaper response to the emperor's visit, see Roberts, "'All Americans Are Hero-Worshippers.'"
26. Howells, "Sennight of the Centennial," 100.
27. McCabe, *Illustrated History*, 621–22.
28. Kingsbury, *International Exhibition Guide*, 88.
29. Towers, *Urban South*, 8; Fishwick, "*The Portico* and Literary Nationalism," 239; Christopher Phillips, *Freedom's Port*, 4.
30. Howells, "Sennight of the Centennial," 106.
31. *Authorized Visitors' Guide*, 20; Kingsbury, *International Exhibition Guide*, 88.
32. Rydell, *All the World's a Fair*, 29. For the restaurant's bill of fare, see "Exhibition of 1876," 1. It has been hinted that a part of the Southern Restaurant survives to this day in New Jersey as the Red Bank depot station, which still serves in receptive travelers. See Prial, "Buildings from 1876 Centennial," 61.
33. Cordato, "Toward a New Century," 117, 119. This quick sketch of the Women's Pavilion owes much to Cordato's able research.
34. Ibid., 125, 119–24.
35. "Aladdin's Lamp," 2.
36. Yount, "A 'New Century' for Women," 150; Howells, "Sennight of the Centennial," 101. McClelland adds in "1876 Centennial Craze" that many fairgoers were drawn to Emma Allison, who single-handedly ran the steam engine (25). Her clean dispatch, Yount remarks, contrasted sharply with habits in engine rooms run by men (155). See, too, Cordato, "Toward a New Century," 123–24.
37. Luciano, *Arranging Grief*, 51.
38. Cordato, "Toward a New Century," 133.
39. "Color Prejudice," 1. The article reprints an interview arranged by Philadelphia's *Sunday Times* with an African American subcommittee member, someone who mentioned the "dictatorial" tactics of Mrs. Aubrey Smith when she spoke of "remanding" the invited ladies to Africa if they were dissatisfied (1).
40. "Letter from Philadelphia," 1. The "colored" committee's invited leader, who assembled the group of thirty-six, wrote directly to the *New National Era* with "a fuller report" (1).
41. Orvell, *Real Thing*, 78.
42. Philip S. Foner, "Black Participation," 284.
43. Chambers, "Allen Monument a Success!," 1. Reverend Chambers led the Arkansas Confer-

ence, which originated the Centennial Plan. For him, the Allen Monument would become "the Negro's Bunker Hill, Independence Hall, and Liberty Bell" (1).

44. Gold, *Unfinished Exhibition*, 138. This brief overview is indebted to Gold's impressive research on the creation of the monument and its subsequent fate.
45. Ibid., 149.
46. Kachun, "Before the Eyes," 319.
47. "Bishop Allen Monument," 5.
48. Gold, *Unfinished Exhibition*, 11.
49. Ibid., 8.
50. Ibid., 9.
51. For an engrossing account of the lithograph's recovery, see https://www.facebook.com/watch/live/?v=276180560737560&ref=notif&notif_id=1613520165514261&notif_t=live_video_explicit.
52. Giberti, *Designing the Centennial*, 153.
53. "Centennial Dépôt, Pennsylvania Railroad," front matter.
54. "Centennial Traveling," 1. The article was signed by the paper's special correspondent GAR, the penname of J. Garczynski. See Cushing, *Initials and Pseudonyms*, 111.
55. Vitiello, "Engineering the Metropolis," 279.
56. "Circular," 3.
57. Morris, *Gothic Architecture*, 6. The lecture was first delivered in 1889.
58. Ruskin, "Nature of Gothic," 203.
59. Ballantyne and Law, *Tudoresque*, 22, 35, 96.

BIBLIOGRAPHY

Primary Sources
Published before 1877

Adkins, Milton T. "In a Country Post-Office." *Godey's Lady's Book*, September 1876, 247–51.
"Aladdin's Lamp: A Month Ago in the Exposition." *New Century for Woman*, May 13, 1876, 2.
"Alice Bankgrove's Soldier." *Harper's Weekly*, December 13, 1862, 794–95.
"Anson S. Miller." *Lakeside Monthly*, April 1869, frontispiece, 193–97.
Avery, Benjamin P. "ETC.—the New Era in California." *Overland Monthly*, March 1874, 281–83.
B. "Death of Mrs. Helen E. Harrington." *Daily Evening Bulletin*, September 27, 1872, 2.
Bagby, George William. "My Uncle Flatback's Plantation." *Southern Literary Messenger*, October 1863, 590–604.
"Bishop Allen Monument." *Christian Recorder*, November 9, 1876, 5.
Blackwell, Miss S. C. "Fugitives at the West." *Continental Monthly*, May 1862, 582–91.
"The Boat and the Train." *Harper's Weekly*, July 17, 1858, 452–53.
Bonner, Colonel T. R. "Sketches of the Campaign of 1864: Walker's Division—Retreat up Red River—Battle of Mansfield." *The Land We Love*, October 1868, 459–66.
Booth, Sherman M. "Suffrage." *Lakeside Monthly*, February 1869, 81–86.
Bowley, Freeman S. "A Dark Night on Picket." *Overland Monthly*, July 1870, 31–37.
"Brady's Photographs: Pictures of the Dead at Antietam." *New York Times*, October 20, 1862, 5.
Brooks, Noah. "Restaurant Life in San Francisco." *Overland Monthly*, November 1868, 465–73.
Browne, William Hand. "The Green Table." *Southern Magazine*, April 1873, 508–10.
———. "The Green Table." *Southern Magazine*, August 1873, 253–54.
———. "The Green Table." *Southern Magazine*, January 1874, 105–6.
———. "The Green Table." *Southern Magazine*, December 1874, 646–47.
Bryan, Mary E. "Char-Coal Sketches. Lily." *Sunny South*, May 13, 1882, 5.
"Centennial Dépôt, Pennsylvania Railroad." *The Independent*, July 13, 1876, front matter.
"Centennial Traveling." *New York Times*, April 10, 1876, 1.
Chambers, Andrew J. "The Allen Monument a Success!" *Christian Recorder*, September 7, 1876, 1.
"Chicago in 1856." *Putnam's*, June 1856, 606–13.
Clifford, Josephine. "An Episode of 'Fort Desolation.'" *Overland Monthly*, March 1871, 207–14.
———. "Marching with a Command." *Lakeside Monthly*, April and May 1873, 298–306, 389–97.
"Color Prejudice." *New National Era*, May 22, 1873, 1.
Conway, Moncure D. "The Sacred Flora, Part I." *Harper's Monthly*, October 1870, 731–47.
Cooper, Sarah B. "Old Uncle Hampshire." *Overland Monthly*, November 1872, 430–40.
"Current Notes—the Western Monthly and Its Aims." *Lakeside Monthly*, December 1869, 436–38.
Davis, Rebecca Harding. "Ellen." *Atlantic Monthly*, July 1865, 22–34.
———. "A Glimpse of Philadelphia in July, 1776." *Lippincott's*, July 1876, 30.
———. "John Lamar." *Atlantic Monthly*, April 1862, 411–23.
———. "Old Philadelphia." *Harper's Monthly*, April 1876, 711.
———. "A Rainy Day at the Exposition." *Harper's Weekly*, November 18, 1876, 930.

De Forest, John W. "Forced Marches." *Galaxy*, June 1868, 708–18.
De Quincey, Anna. "A New Story of Lee's Surrender." *Lakeside Monthly*, May 1871, 327–30.
Doggett, Kate N. "A Glance at Florida." *Lakeside Monthly*, October 1869, 223–36.
"Editorial—Our Field." *Lakeside Monthly*, April 1869, 252.
"Editorial—a Word to the Public." *Lakeside Monthly*, January 1869, 57.
"Editorial—to Western Writers." *Lakeside Monthly*, January 1869, 57–58.
"Editor's Easy Chair." *Harper's Monthly*, July 1874, 284–86.
"Editor's Table." *Southern Literary Messenger*, February 1863, 117–19.
Elder, Richard B. "Servantgalism in Virginia." *Lippincott's*, June 1871, 630–37.
"The Exhibition of 1876. Notes of the Fair." *New-York Tribune*, May 15, 1876, 1.
"The Fast Mail to Chicago." *Harper's Weekly*, October 9, 1875, 816–18.
"Fine Arts. Brady's Incidents of the War—the Battles of South Mountain and Antietam." *New York Herald*, October 5, 1862, 1.
Fitts, James Franklin. "The Story of a Mutiny." *Galaxy*, August 1870, 224–28.
Forbes, Edwin. "The Last Bayonet Charge of Hawkins's Zouaves at Antietam." *Frank Leslie's Illustrated Newspaper*, October 11, 1862, 40–41, 45–46.
"'Fortune Favors the Brave.'" *Harper's Weekly*, August 16, 1862, 519.
Foster, J. W. "New Chicago." *Lakeside Monthly*, January 1872, 84–89.
George, Henry. "What the Railroad Will Bring Us." *Overland Monthly*, October 1868, 297–306.
"Grand Central Dépôt." *Harper's Weekly*, February 3, 1872, 104–5, 108–9.
Gray, Asa. "Darwin on the Origin of Species." *Atlantic Monthly*, July and August 1860, 109–16, 229–39.
"Harriet Beecher Stowe." *Lakeside Monthly*, September 1869, 196–202.
Harrington, Helen E. "In the Palmy Days of Slaveholding." *Lakeside Monthly*, August 1870, 100–107.
Harte, F. Bret. "ETC." *Overland Monthly*, July 1868, 99–100.
———. "Plain Language from Truthful James." *Overland Monthly*, September 1870, 287–88.
Hastings, Margaret Vane. "Lois Pearl Berkeley." *Continental Monthly*, November 1864, 552–72.
"The Haversack." *The Land We Love*, September 1867, 427.
Hawthorn, Mat. "The Citizen as a Voter." *Lakeside Monthly*, April 1869, 207–8.
Hill, Daniel Harvey. "Editorial." *The Land We Love*, August 1866, 303–4.
———. "Editorial." *The Land We Love*, July 1867, 268–69.
———. "Editorial." *The Land We Love*, November 1867, 84.
———. "Editorial." *The Land We Love*, November 1867, 87–88.
———. "Editorial." *The Land We Love*, November 1867, 88–91.
———. "Editorial." *The Land We Love*, December 1867, 170–74.
———. "Editorial." *The Land We Love*, March 1868, 442–43.
———. "Editorial." *The Land We Love*, July 1868, 281–85.
———. "Editorial." *The Land We Love*, August 1868, 369–70.
———. "Editorial." *The Land We Love*, September 1868, 444–49.
———. "Editorial." *The Land We Love*, November 1868, 87–88.
———. "Editorial." *The Land We Love*, December 1868, 174–75.
———. "Education." *The Land We Love*, May 1866, 1–11; August 1866, 235–39.
———. *Elements of Algebra*. Philadelphia: Lippincott, 1857.
———. "The Lost Dispatch." *The Land We Love*, February 1868, 270–84.
Hoge, Moses Drury. "Editorial Notice." *Richmond Eclectic*, December 1867, 191–92.
Holmes, Oliver Wendell. "Doings of the Sunbeam." *Atlantic Monthly*, July 1863, 1–15.
———. "The Professor's Story." *Atlantic Monthly*, October 1860, 482–92.
"Home on Furlough." *The Land We Love*, November 1866, 26–36.
Howe, Julia Ward. "An Appeal to Womanhood throughout the World." *Woman's Journal*, September 24, 1870, 1.

———. "Battle Hymn of the Republic." *Atlantic Monthly*, February 1862, 145.
Howells, William Dean. "A Sennight of the Centennial." *Atlantic Monthly*, July 1876, 92–107.
Hyacinth, Socrates [Stephen Powers]. "A Ruined State." *Overland Monthly*, July 1869, 9–14.
———. "Solid Days in Texas." *Overland Monthly*, June 1871, 555–61.
———. "Some Pine-Knots." *Overland Monthly*, January 1872, 49–56.
"In an Old Drawer." *The Land We Love*, December 1868, 155–61.
Johnston, Theodora. "Mrs. Mary E. Bryan. A Sketch of Her Life and Writings." *Scott's Monthly Magazine*, August 1869, 590–94.
"Kate's Soldier." *Harper's Weekly*, October 4, 1862, 634–35.
Kellogg, G. M. "Self-Made Men." *Lakeside Monthly*, July 1869, 36–38.
King, Edward. "The Liverpool of America." *Scribner's Monthly*, April 1875, 681–95.
King, Henry. "The Cabin at Pharaoh's Ford." *Overland Monthly*, December 1874, 507–16.
Kingsbury, Theodore Bryant. *The International Exhibition Guide for the Southern States*. Raleigh, N.C.: R. T. Fulghum, 1876.
Leslie, Lawrence. "The Wife of Garibaldi." *Lakeside Monthly*, June 1870, 460–64.
"Letter from Philadelphia." *New National Era*, June 5, 1873, 1.
"Louisiana." *Harper's Weekly*, February 3, 1866, 78.
Manheim, Louise. "The First Campaign of a Fat Volunteer: A Sketch of the John Brown War." *Southern Illustrated News*, January 10, 1863, 4–5.
Marsdale, Caroline. "Cousin Jack." *Southern Magazine*, December 1873, 712–19.
McCabe, James D. *The Illustrated History of the Centennial Exhibition*. Philadelphia: National Publishing Co., 1876.
"A Midnight Ride from Petersburg." *Southern Magazine*, December 1871, 702–8.
Nash, Burdett. "Jack Dessart." *Lakeside Monthly*, October 1871, 307–16.
"New Chicago." *Saturday Review*, December 27, 1873, 811–12.
Nichols, George Ward. "The General's Story." *Harper's Monthly*, June 1867, 60–74.
"Notice to Subscribers." *The Land We Love*, May–October 1866, back matter.
"Observations on the 'Caesars,' of De Quincey." *Southern Literary Messenger*, October 1859, 277–88.
"Our Centennial." *Harper's Weekly*, May 27, 1876, 422.
Parton, James. "International Copyright." *Atlantic Monthly*, October 1867, 430–51.
"Peninsular Sketches." *Southern Literary Messenger*, November/December 1862, 662–72.
Phelps, Egbert. "Our Adjutant." *Lakeside Monthly*, May 1873, 374–86.
Phelps, Elizabeth Stuart. "A Sacrifice Consumed." *Harper's Monthly*, January 1864, 235–40.
Pollard, Edward A. *The Lost Cause; a New Southern History of the War of the Confederates*. New York: E. B. Treat, 1866.
Porter, Ina Marie. "Road-Side Story." *The Land We Love*, August 1866, 255–61.
———. "The Texas Soldier." *The Land We Love*, March 1867, 343–50.
Powers, Stephen [Socrates Hyacinth]. *Afoot and Alone: A Walk from Sea to Sea by the Southern Route*. 1872; repr., Austin: Book Club of Texas, 1995.
"President Lincoln's Gettysburg Oration, November 19, 1863." *Harper's Weekly*, July 24, 1869, 469.
Quilibet, Philip [George E. Pond]. "The Copyright Struggle." *Galaxy*, April 1872, 554–56.
"Ralph Hazlitt, Soldier." *Harper's Weekly*, July 18, 1863, 459.
"Recent Literature: Higginson's *Oldport Days*." *Atlantic Monthly*, January 1874, 108–10.
Reita. "Elmsville and Its Hospital." *The Land We Love*, June and July 1866, 120–27, 225–31.
"The Revenge of a Goddess." *Harper's Weekly*, September 24, 1864, 622–23.
"The Seminole War. Items and Scraps. The Mediation." *Niles' Weekly Register*, February 27, 1836, 441–42.
Sheppard, Richard M. "Sentenced and Shot." *Lakeside Monthly*, November 1870, 270–75.
Shipley, G. T. "Saint Saviour of the Bay." *Overland Monthly*, October 1868, 346–53.
Sikes, William W. "One of My Scholars." *Harper's Monthly*, October 1865, 589–94.

Simms, William Gilmore. "International Copyright Law, Part I." *Southern Literary Messenger*, January 1844, 7–17.
"Sketch of Mecklenburg County." *The Land We Love*, December 1866, 129–45.
Smith, G. Nelson. "East and West." *Lakeside Monthly*, March 1869, 159–62.
"The Southern Magazine, Notice." *New Eclectic*, December 1879, 768.
Stowe, Harriet Beecher. "The First Christmas of New England: Chapter IV. Elder Brewster's Christmas Sermon." *Christian Union*, December 25, 1871, 22.
Thorpe, T. B. "New York City Post-Office." *Harper's Monthly*, October 1871, 645–63.
"The Three New Hotels of St. Augustine." *Harper's Weekly*, November 26, 1887, 860.
"To Our Patrons." *The Land We Love*, April 1868, back matter.
"A Trying Journey." *Southern Magazine*, November 1872, 621–26.
Turnbull, Henry C., Jr. "The New Eclectic Magazine Advertiser." *New Eclectic*, June 1869, x.
Turnbull, Lawrence. "A Parting Word." *New Eclectic*, December 1870, 766–68.
Upton, M. G. "The Plan of San Francisco." *Overland Monthly*, February 1869, 131–37.
"Varieties, Literary and Philosophical." *Monthly Magazine* (London), August 1817, 69.
Watkins, James F. "San Francisco." *Overland Monthly*, January 1870, 9–23.
Whiting, William. *Memoir of Rev. Joseph Harrington*. Boston: Crosby, Nichols and Company, 1854.
"William B. Ogden." *Lakeside Monthly*, January 1869, frontispiece, 1–7.
"William Bross." *Lakeside Monthly*, June 1869, frontispiece, 321–30.
Winston, John. "An Escape from Johnston's Island." *Southern Magazine*, November 1872, 535–44.
Woolson, Constance Fenimore. "The Ancient City." *Harper's Monthly*, December 1874, 1–25.
———. "The South Devil." *Atlantic Monthly*, February 1880, 173–93.

Secondary Sources
Published after 1876

Aarim-Heriot, Najia. *Chinese Immigrants, African Americans, and Racial Anxiety in the United States, 1848–82*. Urbana: University of Illinois Press, 2003.
Aaron, Daniel. *The Unwritten War: American Writers and the Civil War*. 1973; repr., Tuscaloosa: University of Alabama Press, 2003.
Allan, Elizabeth Preston. *The Life and Letters of Margaret Junkin Preston*. Boston: Houghton, Mifflin, 1903.
Anderson, John Nathan. "Money or Nothing: Confederate Postal System Collapse during the Civil War." *American Journalism* 30, no. 1 (Winter 2013): 65–86.
Angle, Paul M. "The Illinois Black Laws." *Chicago History* 8, no. 3 (September 1979): 65–75.
Arnett, Earl, Robert J. Brugger, and Edward C. Papenfuse. *Maryland: A New Guide to the Old Line State*. Baltimore, Md.: Johns Hopkins University Press, 1999.
Arthur, Stanley Clisby. "The Emblematic Bird of Louisiana." *Louisiana Historical Quarterly* 2, no. 3 (July 1919): 248–57.
Atchison, Ray M. "*The Land We Love*: A Southern Post-Bellum Magazine of Agriculture, Literature, and Military History." *North Carolina Historical Review* 37, no. 4 (October 1960): 506–15.
———. "Southern Literary Magazines, 1865–1887." PhD diss., Duke University, 1956.
Authorized Visitors' Guide to the Centennial Exhibition and Philadelphia, 1876. Philadelphia: Lippincott's, 1876.
Avery, Alphonso Calhoun. "Memorial Address: On the Life and Character of Lieut.-General D. H. Hill." *Southern Historical Society Papers* 21 (1893): 110–50.
Bailey, Robert F., III. "The Pratt Street Riots Reconsidered: A Case of Overstated Significance?" *Maryland Historical Magazine* 98, no. 2 (Summer 2003): 152–71.
Baker, Van R., ed. *The Websters: Letters of an American Army Family in Peace and War, 1836–1853*. Kent, Ohio: Kent State University Press, 2000.

Baldwin, Peter. *The Copyright Wars: Three Centuries of Trans-Atlantic Battle*. Princeton, N.J.: Princeton University Press, 2014.
Ballantyne, Andrew, and Andrew Law. *Tudoresque: In Pursuit of the Ideal Home*. London: Reaktion Books, 2011.
Bardaglio, Peter W. *Reconstructing the Household: Families, Sex, and the Law in the Nineteenth-Century South*. Chapel Hill: University of North Carolina Press, 1995.
Bartlett, W. C. "Overland Reminiscences." *Overland Monthly*, July 1898, 41–46.
Beckert, Sven. "Cotton and the U.S. South: A Short History." In *Plantation Kingdom: The American South and Its Global Commodities*, by Richard Follett, Sven Beckert, Peter Coclanis, and Barbara Hahn, 39–60. Baltimore, Md.: Johns Hopkins University Press, 2016.
Belle, John, and Maxinne R. Leighton. *Grand Central: Gateway to a Million Lives*. New York: Norton, 2000.
Bellion, Wendy. "Vision and Visuality." *American Art* 24, no. 3 (Fall 2010): 21–25.
Bergeron, Arthur W., Jr. *Guide to Louisiana Confederate Military Units, 1861–1865*. Baton Rouge: Louisiana State University Press, 1989.
Berglund, Barbara. *Making San Francisco American: Cultural Frontiers in the Urban West, 1846–1906*. Lawrence: University Press of Kansas, 2007.
Bergmann, William H. "Delivering a Nation through the Mail: The Post Office in the Ohio Valley, 1789–1815." *Ohio Valley History* 8, no. 3 (Fall 2008): 1–18.
Billington, Monroe Lee. *New Mexico's Buffalo Soldiers, 1866–1900*. Niwot: University Press of Colorado, 1991.
Binckley, John M. "Life-Story of a Magazine." *The Dial*, June 16, 1913, 489–92.
Bishir, Catherine W. "A Spirit of Improvement: Changes in Building Practice, 1830–1860." In *Architects and Builders in North Carolina: A History of the Practice of Building*, by Catherine W. Bishir, Charlotte V. Brown, Carl R. Lounsbury, and Ernest H. Wood III, 130–92. Chapel Hill: University of North Carolina Press, 1990.
Blight, David W. *Race and Reunion: The Civil War in American Memory*. Cambridge, Mass.: Harvard University Press, 2001.
Bordewich, Fergus M. *Bound for Canaan: The Underground Railroad and the War for the Soul of America*. New York: Amistad-HarperCollins, 2005.
Braden, Susan R. *The Architecture of Leisure: The Florida Resort Hotels of Henry Flagler and Henry Plant*. Gainesville: University Press of Florida, 2002.
Bridges, Hal. "D. H. Hill's Anti-Yankee Algebra." *Journal of Southern History* 22, no. 2 (May 1956): 220–22.
———. *Lee's Maverick General: Daniel Harvey Hill*. 1961; repr., Lincoln: Bison Books, University of Nebraska Press, 1991.
Bridges, Roger D. "Antebellum Struggle for Citizenship." *Journal of the Illinois State Historical Society* 108, no. 3/4 (Fall/Winter 2015): 296–321.
Bright, James Wilson. "In Memoriam, William Hand Browne, 1828–1912." *Johns Hopkins University Circular* 32, no. 252 (February 1913): 1–28.
Brooks, Noah. "Bret Harte in California." *Century Illustrated*, July 1899, 447–51.
———. "Early Days of 'The Overland.'" *Overland Monthly*, July 1898, 3–11.
Brown, Canter, Jr., and Larry Eugene Rivers. *Mary Edwards Bryan: Her Early Life and Works*. Gainesville: University Press of Florida, 2015.
Brown, George William. *Baltimore and the Nineteenth of April, 1861: A Study of the War*. Edited by Kevin Conley Ruffner. 1887; repr., Baltimore, Md.: Johns Hopkins University Press, 2001.
Brown, Joshua. *Beyond the Lines: Pictorial Reporting, Everyday Life, and the Crisis of Gilded Age America*. Berkeley: University of California Press, 2002.
Browne, Gary Lawson. *Baltimore in the Nation, 1789–1861*. Chapel Hill: University of North Carolina Press, 1980.

Browne, Waldo R. "Francis Fisher Browne, 1843–1913." *The Dial*, June 1, 1913, 437–41.

Brugger, Robert J. *Maryland: A Middle Temperament, 1634–1980*. Baltimore, Md.: Johns Hopkins University Press, 1988.

Bruns, James H. *Mail on the Move*. Polo, Ill.: Transportation Trails, 1992.

"Bryan, J. E." Soldiers and Sailors Database for the Civil War. National Park Service. https://www.nps.gov/civilwar/soldiers-and-sailors-database.htm.

Butts, Leonard. "*The Southern Review* (Bledsoe's)." In *American Literary Magazines: The Eighteenth and Nineteenth Centuries*, edited by Edward E. Chielens, 409–13. Westport, Conn.: Greenwood, 1986.

Campbell, William P. *The Civil War: A Centennial Exhibition of Eyewitness Drawings*. Washington, D.C.: National Gallery of Art, 1961.

Carranco, Linwood. "Bret Harte in Union (1857–1860)." *California Historical Society Quarterly* 45, no. 2 (June 1966): 99–112.

Cashin, Joan E. "Into the Trackless Wilderness: The Refugee Experience in the Civil War." In *A Woman's War: Southern Women, Civil War, and the Confederate Legacy*, edited by Edward D. C. Campbell Jr. and Kym S. Rice, 29–53. Charlottesville: University of Virginia Press, 1996.

"Circular." Wilson Brothers & Co. In *Catalogue of Work Executed*, 3. Philadelphia: Lippincott, 1885.

Clifford, Josephine. "Flight: A Sequel to 'Toby.'" In *"Another Juanita" and Other Stories*, 133–67. Buffalo, N.Y.: Charles Wells Moulton, 1893.

———. "Toby." In *"Another Juanita" and Other Stories*, 99–130. Buffalo, N.Y.: Charles Wells Moulton, 1893.

Clifford McCrackin, Josephine. "Reminiscences of Bret Harte and Pioneer Days in the West." *Overland Monthly*, December 1915 and January 1916, 463–68, 7–15.

Cobb, Josephine. "Alexander Gardner." *Image* 7, no. 6 (1958): 124–36.

Condit, Carl W. *The Port of New York: A History of the Rail and Terminal System from the Beginnings to Pennsylvania Station*. Chicago: University of Chicago Press, 1980.

Cooley, Verna. "Illinois and the Underground Railroad to Canada." *Transactions of the Illinois State Historical Society* 23 (1917): 76–98.

Cordato, Mary Frances. "Toward a New Century: Women and the Philadelphia Centennial Exhibition, 1876." *Pennsylvania Magazine of History and Biography* 107, no. 1 (January 1983): 113–35.

Crary, Jonathan. *Techniques of the Observer: On Vision and Modernity in the Nineteenth Century*. Cambridge, Mass.: MIT Press, 1992.

Cronon, William. *Nature's Metropolis: Chicago and the Great West*. New York: Norton, 1992.

Cumming, Kate. *Kate: The Journal of a Confederate Nurse*. Edited by Richard Barksdale Harwell. 1959; repr., Baton Rouge: Louisiana State University Press, 1998.

Cummins (Mighels), Ella Sterling. *The Story of the Files: A Review of Californian Writers and Literature*. San Francisco: Cooperative Printing Co., 1893.

Cushing, William. *Initials and Pseudonyms: A Dictionary of Literary Disguises*. New York: Thomas J. Crowell & Co., 1885.

Cutrer, Thomas W. *Theater of a Separate War: The Civil War West of the Mississippi River, 1861–1865*. Chapel Hill: University of North Carolina Press, 2017.

Dalzell, Robert F., Jr., and Lee Baldwin Dalzell. "Memory, Architecture, and the Future: George Washington, Mount Vernon, and the White House." *White House History* 6 (Fall 1999): 34–45.

Daniels, Douglas Henry. *Pioneer Urbanites: A Social and Cultural History of Black San Francisco*. 1980; repr., Berkeley: University of California Press, 1990.

Davis, Keith F. "'A Terrible Distinctness': Photography of the Civil War Era." In *Photography in Nineteenth-Century America*, edited by Martha A. Sandweiss, 130–79. Fort Worth, Tex.: Amon Carter Museum, 1991.

Davis, Rebecca Harding. "A Peculiar People." *Saturday Evening Post*, January 10, 1903, 9, 20; January 17, 1903, 8–9.
Davis, Theodore R. "How a Battle Is Sketched." *St. Nicholas*, July 1889, 661–68.
Dewhurst, William W. *The History of Saint Augustine, Florida*. New York: Putnam's, 1881.
Dietz, August. *The Postal Service of the Confederate States of America*. Richmond, Va.: Dietz Printing Company, 1929.
Diffley, Kathleen. "'Musquitos, Rattlesnakes, and Perspiration': The Civil War's Special Artist for the *Illustrated London News*." *Books at Iowa* 63 (November 1995): 3–13.
——— . *Where My Heart Is Turning Ever: Civil War Stories and Constitutional Reform, 1861–1876*. 1992; repr., Athens: University of Georgia Press, 2020.
Digby-Junger, Richard. "Chicago's *Lakeside Monthly*: Urban Boosterism in a Literary Magazine." MA thesis, University of Wisconsin–Milwaukee, 1986.
Dollar, Susan E. "The Red River Campaign, Natchitoches Parish, Louisiana: A Case of Equal Opportunity Destruction." *Louisiana History* 43, no. 4 (Autumn 2002): 411–32.
Dossman, Steven Nathaniel. *Campaign for Corinth: Blood in Mississippi*. Abilene, Tex.: McWhiney Foundation Press, 2006.
Du Bois, W. E. B. "Strivings of the Negro People." *Atlantic Monthly*, August 1897, 194–98.
Edelstein, Sari. "'Pretty as Pictures': Family Photography and Southern Postmemory in Porter's *Old Mortality*." *Southern Literary Journal* 40, no. 2 (Spring 2008): 151–65.
Edwards, Laura F. *Gendered Strife and Confusion: The Political Culture of Reconstruction*. Champaign: University of Illinois Press, 1997.
Egli, Ida Rae. "Josephine Clifford McCrackin (1839–1920)." In *No Rooms of Their Own: Women Writers of Early California*, edited by Ida Rae Egli, 111–14. 1992; repr., San Francisco: Heyday Books, 2010.
Eigenheer, Richard A. "Eastward the Frontier: Historic Nevada Post Office Locations, 1860–1910." *Nevada Historical Society Quarterly* 25, no. 4 (December 1982): 315–26.
Ellis, Edward S. *The Life of Colonel David Crockett*. Philadelphia: Porter & Coates, 1884.
Ellis, William Arba, ed. *Norwich University, 1819–1911: Her History, Her Graduates, Her Roll of Honor*. 3 vols. Montpelier, Vt.: Capital City Press, 1911.
Erslev, Brit Kimberly. "'Nearly There': Daniel Harvey Hill, Proponent and Target of the Lost Cause." PhD diss., University of North Carolina at Chapel Hill, 2011.
Ethington, Philip J. *The Public City: The Political Construction of Urban Life in San Francisco, 1850–1900*. 1994; repr., Berkeley: University of California Press, 2001.
Exman, Eugene. *The House of Harper: The Making of a Modern Publisher*. 1967; repr., New York: Harper Perennial, 2010.
Fahs, Alice. *The Imagined Civil War: Popular Literature of the North and South, 1861–1865*. Chapel Hill: University of North Carolina Press, 2001.
Fishwick, Marshall W. "*The Portico* and Literary Nationalism after the War of 1812." *William and Mary Quarterly* 8, no. 2 (April 1951): 238–45.
Flanagan, John T. "Some Midwestern Literary Magazines." *Papers on Language and Literature* 3, no. 3 (Summer 1967): 237–57.
Foley, Michael S. "A Mission Unfulfilled: The Post Office and the Distribution of Information in Rural New England, 1821–1835." *Journal of the Early Republic* 17, no. 4 (Winter 1997): 611–50.
Foner, Eric. *The Fiery Trial: Abraham Lincoln and American Slavery*. New York: Norton, 2011.
——— . *Gateway to Freedom: The Hidden History of the Underground Railroad*. New York: Norton, 2015.
——— . *Reconstruction: America's Unfinished Revolution, 1863–1877*. 1988; repr., New York: Harper Perennial Modern Classics, 2014.
Foner, Philip S. "Black Participation in the Centennial of 1876." *Phylon* 39, no. 4 (1978): 283–96.

Foote, Cheryl J. *Women of the New Mexico Frontier, 1846–1912*. 1990; repr., Albuquerque: University of New Mexico Press, 2005.
Foote, Shelby. *Fort Sumter to Perryville*. Vol. 1 of *The Civil War: A Narrative*. 1958; repr., New York: Vintage Books–Random House, 1986.
Forbes, Edwin. "Watching a Battle." In *Thirty Years After: An Artist's Story of the Great War*, 257–59. New York: Fords, Howard, and Hulbert, 1890.
Frassanito, William A. *Antietam: The Photographic Legacy of America's Bloodiest Day*. New York: Scribner's, 1978.
———. *Gettysburg: A Journey in Time*. New York: Scribner's, 1975.
Frost, Linda. *Never One Nation: Freaks, Savages, and Whiteness in U.S. Popular Culture, 1850–1877*. Minneapolis: University of Minnesota Press, 2005.
Fuller, Randall. *From Battlefields Rising: How the Civil War Transformed American Literature*. New York: Oxford University Press, 2011.
Galassi, Peter. *Before Photography: Painting and the Invention of Photography*. New York: Museum of Modern Art, 1981.
Gallagher, Gary W. "Jubal A. Early, the Lost Cause, and Civil War History: A Persistent Legacy." In *The Myth of the Lost Cause and Civil War History*, edited by Gary W. Gallagher and Alan T. Nolan, 35–59. Bloomington: Indiana University Press, 2000.
Gallagher, Winifred. *How the Post Office Created America: A History*. New York: Penguin, 2016.
Gallman, J. Matthew. *Mastering Wartime: A Social History of Philadelphia during the Civil War*. Philadelphia: University of Pennsylvania Press, 2000.
Gamerro, Carlos. "Remembering without memories." Translated by James Scorer. *Journal of Romance Studies* 13, no. 3 (December 2013): 110–15.
Gara, Larry. *The Liberty Line: The Legend of the Underground Railroad*. 1961; repr., Lexington: University Press of Kentucky, 1996.
Garb, Margaret. "The Political Education of John Jones: Black Politics in a Northern City, 1845–1879." *Journal of the Historical Society* 8, no. 1 (March 2008): 29–60.
Genette, Gérard. *Narrative Discourse Revisited*. Translated by Jane E. Lewin. Ithaca, N.Y.: Cornell University Press, 1990.
Gentry, Judy. "Confederates and Cotton in East Texas." *East Texas Historical Journal* 48, no. 1 (Spring 2010): 20–39.
Giberti, Bruno. *Designing the Centennial: A History of the 1876 International Exhibition in Philadelphia*. Lexington: University Press of Kentucky, 2002.
Gleason, William A. *Sites Unseen: Architecture, Race, and American Literature*. New York: New York University Press, 2011.
Gliozzo, Charles A. "John Jones: A Study of a Black Chicagoan." *Illinois Historical Journal* 80, no. 3 (Autumn 1987): 177–88.
Gold, Susanna W. *The Unfinished Exhibition: Visualizing Myth, Memory, and the Shadow of the Civil War in Centennial America*. New York: Routledge, 2017.
Golden, Catherine J. *Posting It: The Victorian Revolution in Letter Writing*. Gainesville: University Press of Florida, 2009.
Gordon, Sarah H. *Passage to Union: How the Railroads Transformed American Life, 1829–1929*. Chicago: Ivan R. Dee, 1998.
Graham, David K. "'She Spurns the Northern Scum': Maryland's Civil War Loyalty in Mass Culture and Memory." *Maryland Historical Magazine* 109, no. 1 (Spring 2014): 34–50.
Graham, Thomas. *Mr. Flagler's St. Augustine*. Gainesville: University Press of Florida, 2014.
Greenwood, Janette Thomas. *Bittersweet Legacy: The Black and White "Better Classes" in Charlotte, 1850–1910*. Chapel Hill: University of North Carolina Press, 1994.
Griffin, Patricia C. "Life on the Plantations of East Florida: 1763–1848." *Florida Anthropologist* 56, no. 3 (September 2003): 163–81.

Grivno, Max. *Gleanings of Freedom: Free and Slave Labor along the Mason-Dixon Line, 1790–1860*. Urbana: University of Illinois Press, 2011.
Groom, Winston. *Shiloh 1862*. Washington, D.C.: National Geographic Society, 2012.
Groves, Jeffrey D. "Courtesy of the Trade." In *The Industrial Book, 1840–1880*, edited by Scott E. Casper, Jeffrey D. Groves, Stephen W. Nissenbaum, and Michael Winship, 139–48. Vol. 3 of *A History of the Book in America*. Chapel Hill: University of North Carolina Press, 2007.
Hackenberg, Michael. "The *Lakeside Monthly*." In *American Literary Magazines: The Eighteenth and Nineteenth Centuries*, edited by Edward E. Chielens, 199–203. New York: Greenwood Press, 1986.
Hager, Christopher. *Word by Word: Emancipation and the Act of Writing*. Cambridge, Mass.: Harvard University Press, 2013.
Hanchett, Thomas W. *Sorting Out the New South City: Race, Class, and Urban Development in Charlotte, 1875–1975*. Chapel Hill: University of North Carolina Press, 1998.
Hansen, Sandra. "The Chivalry and the Shovelry." *Civil War Times Illustrated* 23, no. 8 (December 1984): 30–33.
Hardy, Michael C. *Civil War Charlotte: Last Capital of the Confederacy*. Charleston: History Press, 2012.
Harlow, Luke E. "Slavery, Race, and Political Ideology in the White Christian South before and after the Civil War." In *Religion and American Politics: From the Colonial Period to the Present*, edited by Mark A. Noll and Luke E. Harlow, 203–24. New York: Oxford University Press, 2007.
Harris, James C. "A Short History of the Corinth Rifles and Their Flag." *Military Collector and Historian* 34, no. 2 (Summer 1982): 61–64.
Harris, Sharon M. "The Anatomy of Complicity: Rebecca Harding Davis, *Peterson's Magazine*, and the Civil War." *Tulsa Studies in Women's Literature* 30, no. 2 (Fall 2011): 291–315.
———. *Rebecca Harding Davis: A Life among Writers*. Morgantown: West Virginia University Press, 2018.
Henkin, David M. *The Postal Age: The Emergence of Modern Communications in Nineteenth-Century America*. Chicago: University of Chicago Press, 2006.
Hewitt, Lieut. C. C. "Nineteenth Regiment of Infantry." In *The Army of the U.S.: Historical Sketches of Staff and Line with Portraits of Generals in Chief*, edited by Theo. F. Rodenbough and William L. Haskin, 657–65. New York: Maynard, Merrill, 1896.
Hicken, Victor. *Illinois in the Civil War*. 1966; repr., Urbana: University of Illinois Press, 1991.
Hinton, Harwood P. Introduction to *Afoot and Alone: A Walk from Sea to Sea by the Southern Route*, by Stephen Powers [Socrates Hyacinth], ix–xxxv. 1872; repr., Austin: Book Club of Texas, 1995.
Hirsch, Marianne. *The Generation of Postmemory: Writing and Visual Culture after the Holocaust*. New York: Columbia University Press, 2012.
———. "Presidential Address 2014: Connective Histories in Vulnerable Times." *PMLA* 129, no. 3 (May 2014): 330–48.
Hittell, John S. *A History of the City of San Francisco and Incidentally of the State of California*. San Francisco: A. L. Bancroft and Company, 1878.
Hodgson, Pat. *The War Illustrators*. New York: Macmillan, 1977.
Homestead, Melissa J. *American Women Authors and Literary Property, 1822–1869*. New York: Cambridge University Press, 2005.
Hood, Yolanda. "An Inconvenient Truth: The Underground Railroad and Quilts in Children's Picturebooks." *Children and Libraries* 11, no. 2 (Summer/Fall 2013): 29–34.
Horton, Laurel. "Truth and the Quilt Researcher's Rage: The Roles of Narrative and Belief in the Quilt Code Debate." *Western Folklore* 76, no. 1 (Winter 2017): 41–68.
Howe, Jeffrey. "A 'Monstrous Edifice': Ambivalence, Appropriation, and the Forging of Cultural Identity at the Centennial Exhibition." *Pennsylvania Magazine of History and Biography* 126, no. 4 (October 2002): 635–50.

Howe, Julia Ward. *Reminiscences, 1819–1899*. Boston: Houghton, Mifflin, 1900.
Hoyo, Henio. "Posting Nationalism: Postage Stamps as Carriers of Nationalist Messages." In *Beyond Imagined Uniqueness: Nationalisms in Contemporary Perspectives*, edited by Joan Burbick and William Glass, 67–92. Newcastle upon Tyne, U.K.: Cambridge Scholars, 2010.
Hoyt, William D., Jr. "The Monday Club." *Maryland Historical Magazine* 49, no. 4 (December 1954): 301–13.
Hubbell, Jay B. *The South in American Literature, 1607–1900*. Durham, N.C.: Duke University Press, 1954.
Hughes, Nathaniel Cheairs, Jr., and Timothy D. Johnson, eds. *A Fighter from Way Back: The Mexican War Diary of Lt. Daniel Harvey Hill, 4th Artillery, USA*. Kent, Ohio: Kent State University Press, 2002.
Humphreys, Barbara. "How to Read a Building: Second Empire Style." *Canadian Heritage* 15, no. 1 (Spring 1989): 40.
Hunter, Brooke. "Wheat, War, and the American Economy during the Age of Revolution." *William and Mary Quarterly* 62, no. 3 (July 2005): 505–26.
Hutchison, Coleman. *Apples and Ashes: Literature, Nationalism, and the Confederate States of America*. Athens: University of Georgia Press, 2012.
James, George Wharton. "The Romantic History of Josephine Clifford McCrackin." In *"The Woman Who Lost Him" and Tales of the Army Frontier*, by Josephine Clifford McCrackin, 1–44. Pasadena, Calif.: George Wharton James, 1913.
Janney, Caroline E. *Remembering the Civil War: Reunion and the Limits of Reconciliation*. Chapel Hill: University of North Carolina Press, 2013.
Jentz, John B., and Richard Schneirov. *Chicago in the Age of Capital: Class, Politics, and Democracy during the Civil War and Reconstruction*. Urbana: University of Illinois Press, 2015.
John, Richard R. *Spreading the News: The American Postal System from Franklin to Morse*. Cambridge, Mass.: Harvard University Press, 1995.
Johnson, Ludwell H. *Red River Campaign: Politics and Cotton in the Civil War*. 1958; repr., Kent, Ohio: Kent State University Press, 1993.
Joiner, Gary D. *Through the Howling Wilderness: The 1864 Red River Campaign and Union Failure in the West*. Knoxville: University of Tennessee Press, 2006.
Jun, Helen H. "Black Orientalism: Nineteenth-Century Narratives of Race and U.S. Citizenship." *American Quarterly* 58, no. 4 (December 2006): 1047–66.
Kachun, Mitch. "Before the Eyes of All Nations: African-American Identity and Historical Memory at the Centennial Exposition of 1876." *Pennsylvania History* 65, no. 3 (Summer 1998): 300–323.
Karamanski, Theodore J. *Rally 'Round the Flag: Chicago and the Civil War*. 1993; repr., Lanham, Md.: Rowman & Littlefield, 2006.
Karamanski, Theodore J., and Eileen M. McMahon, eds. *Civil War Chicago: Eyewitness to History*. Athens: Ohio University Press, 2014.
Katz, D. Mark. *Witness to an Era: The Life and Photographs of Alexander Gardner; The Civil War, Lincoln, and the West*. New York: Viking Penguin, 1991.
Keizer, Arlene R. "Gone Astray in the Flesh: Kara Walker, Black Women Writers, and African American Postmemory." *PMLA* 123, no. 5 (October 2008): 1649–72.
Kennedy, John Pendleton. *The Border States: Their Power and Duty in the Present Disordered Condition of the Country*. Philadelphia: Lippincott, 1861.
Kennedy-Nolle, Sharon D. "Living for Dixie: The Refrain of Postwar Nationalism in Two North Carolina Magazines." *North Carolina Literary Review* 8 (1999): 53–63.
———. *Writing Reconstruction: Race, Gender, and Citizenship in the Postwar South*. Chapel Hill: University of North Carolina Press, 2015.
Kielbowicz, Richard B. *News in the Mail: The Press, Post Office, and Public Information, 1700–1860s*. New York: Greenwood Press, 1989.

Klos, George. "Blacks and the Seminole Removal Debate, 1821–1835." In *The African American Heritage of Florida*, edited by David R. Colburn and Jane L. Landers, 128–56. Gainesville: University Press of Florida, 1995.

Kowalewski, Michael. "Romancing the Gold Rush: The Literature of the California Frontier." In *Rooted in Barbarous Soil: People, Culture, and Community in Gold Rush California*, edited by Kevin Starr and Richard J. Orsi, 204–25. Berkeley: University of California Press, 2000.

Kroll, C. Douglas. "Civil War Defenses of San Francisco Bay." *Journal of America's Military Past* 32, no. 1 (Spring/Summer 2006): 5–20.

Landers, Jane G. *Atlantic Creoles in the Age of Revolutions*. Cambridge, Mass.: Harvard University Press, 2010.

LaRoche, Cheryl Janifer. *Free Black Communities and the Underground Railroad: The Geography of Resistance*. Urbana: University of Illinois Press, 2014.

Lee, Anthony W. "The Image of War." In *On Alexander Gardner's "Photographic Sketch Book" of the Civil War*, edited by Anthony W. Lee, 8–51, 96–100. Berkeley: University of California Press, 2007.

Leonard, Devin. *Neither Snow nor Rain: A History of the United States Postal Service*. New York: Grove Press, 2016.

Leonard, Elizabeth D. *Men of Color to Arms! Black Soldiers, Indian Wars, and the Quest for Equality*. New York: Norton, 2010.

Lesher, Peter. "A Load of Guano: Baltimore and the Fertilizer Trade in the Nineteenth Century." *The Northern Mariner / Le marin du nord* 18, no. 3–4 (July–October 2008): 121–28.

Ljungquist, Kent. "*The Portico*." In *American Literary Magazines: The Eighteenth and Nineteenth Centuries*, edited by Edward E. Chielens, 323–28. New York: Greenwood Press, 1986.

Lorenz-Meyer, Martin. "United in Difference: The German Community in Nativist Baltimore and the Presidential Election of 1860." *Yearbook of German-American Studies* 35 (2000): 1–26.

Lowe, Richard, ed. *Greyhound Commander: Confederate General John G. Walker's "History of the Civil War West of the Mississippi."* Baton Rouge: Louisiana State University Press, 2013.

Luciano, Dana. *Arranging Grief: Sacred Time and the Body in Nineteenth-Century America*. New York: New York University Press, 2007.

Maddex, Jack P., Jr. *The Reconstruction of Edward A. Pollard: A Rebel's Conversion to Postbellum Unionism*. 1974; repr., Chapel Hill: University of North Carolina Press, 2011.

Marler, Scott P. *The Merchants' Capital: New Orleans and the Political Economy of the Nineteenth-Century South*. New York: Cambridge University Press, 2013.

Marszalek, John F. "Writing His Mind." *Civil War Times* 57, no. 4 (August 2018): 24–31.

Matthews, Glenna. "Forging a Cosmopolitan Civic Culture: The Regional Identity of San Francisco and Northern California." In *Many Wests: Place, Culture, and Regional Identity*, edited by David M. Wrobel and Michael C. Steiner, 211–34. Lawrence: University Press of Kansas, 1997.

———. *The Golden State in the Civil War: Thomas Starr King, the Republican Party, and the Birth of Modern California*. New York: Cambridge University Press, 2012.

Matthews, Sidney T. "Control of the Baltimore Press during the Civil War." *Maryland Historical Magazine* 36, no. 2 (June 1941): 150–70.

May, Ernest R. "Bret Harte and the *Overland Monthly*." *American Literature* 22, no. 3 (1950): 260–71.

Mays, Thomas D. "The Battle of Saltville." In *Black Soldiers in Blue: African American Troops in the Civil War Era*, edited by John David Smith, 200–226. Chapel Hill: University of North Carolina Press, 2002.

McClelland, James. "1876 Centennial Craze Sweeps into Philadelphia!" *Pennsylvania Heritage* 32, no. 2 (June 2006): 16–25.

McCurry, Stephanie. *Confederate Reckoning: Power and Politics in the Civil War South*. Cambridge, Mass.: Harvard University Press, 2010.

McDermott, Sinéad. "The Ethics of Postmemory in Bobbie Ann Mason's *In Country*." *Journal of the Midwest Modern Language Association* 39, no. 2 (Fall 2006): 5–21.

McGill, Meredith L. *American Literature and the Culture of Reprinting, 1834–1853*. Philadelphia: University of Pennsylvania Press, 2003.

———. "The Role of Government: Copyright." In *The Industrial Book, 1840–1880*, edited by Scott E. Casper, Jeffrey D. Groves, Stephen W. Nissenbaum, and Michael Winship, 158–78. Vol. 3 of *A History of the Book in America*. Chapel Hill: University of North Carolina Press, 2007.

McPherson, James M. *Crossroads of Freedom: Antietam, The Battle That Changed the Course of the Civil War*. New York: Oxford University Press, 2002.

McWhirter, Christian. *Battle Hymns: The Power and Popularity of Music in the Civil War*. Chapel Hill: University of North Carolina Press, 2012.

Mead, Christopher. "Urban Contingency and the Problem of Representation in Second Empire Paris." *Journal of the Society of Architectural Historians* 54, no. 2 (June 1995): 138–74.

Meagher, Shelley E. "Nineteenth-Century Ireland and the Orient: Tom Moore's *Lalla Rookh*." In *New Voices in Irish Criticism*, edited by Ruth Connolly and Ann Coughlan, 145–53. Dublin: Four Courts Press, 2005.

Meier, Michael T. "Lorenzo Thomas and the Recruitment of Blacks in the Mississippi Valley, 1863–65." In *Black Soldiers in Blue: African American Troops in the Civil War Era*, edited by John David Smith, 249–75. Chapel Hill: University of North Carolina Press, 2002.

Meyers, Gretchen E. "The Divine River: Ancient Roman Identity and the Image of Tiberinus." In *The Nature and Function of Water: Baths, Bathing, and Hygiene from Antiquity through the Renaissance*, edited by Cynthia Kosso and Anne Scott, 233–47. Leiden: Brill, 2009.

Miller, Francis Trevelyan, ed. *The Photographic History of the Civil War*. 10 vols. 1911; repr., New York: Thomas Yoseloff, 1957.

Miller, Perry. *The Raven and the Whale: Poe, Melville, and the New York Literary Scene*. 1956; repr., Baltimore, Md.: Johns Hopkins University Press, 1997.

Mintz, Sidney W. *Sweetness and Power: The Place of Sugar in Modern History*. New York: Viking Penguin, 1985.

Mitchell, Charles W. "'The Whirlwind Now Gathering': Baltimore's Pratt Street Riot and the End of Maryland Secession." *Maryland Historical Magazine* 97, no. 2 (Summer 2002): 203–32.

Molin, Peter. "'Wirt—or Wart?': John Neal's Feud with Baltimore's Literary Elite." *Maryland Historical Magazine* 109, no. 1 (Spring 2014): 6–33.

Moody, Joycelyn K. "Women, Race, Reading, and Feeling: Postmemory in Undergraduate Studies of Slave Narratives." In *Teaching Life Writing Texts*, edited by Miriam Fuchs and Craig Howes, 260–69. MLA Options for Teaching. New York: Modern Language Association of America, 2008.

Morales-Vázquez, Rubil. "George Washington, the President's House, and the Projection of Executive Power." *Washington History* 16, no. 1 (Spring/Summer 2004): 36–53.

Morris, William. *Gothic Architecture: A Lecture for the Arts and Crafts Exhibition Society*. London: Kelmscott Press, 1893.

Morrison, Toni. *Playing in the Dark: Whiteness and the Literary Imagination*. Cambridge, Mass.: Harvard University Press, 1992.

Mosher, Fredric John. "Chicago's 'Saving Remnant': Francis Fisher Browne, William Morton Payne, and the *Dial* (1880–1892)." PhD diss., University of Illinois, 1950.

Mott, Frank Luther. *A History of American Magazines*. 5 vols. Cambridge, Mass.: Belknap Press of Harvard University Press, 1930–68.

Muir, John. "Browne the Beloved." *The Dial*, June 16, 1913, 492.

Murdock, Charles A. "Bret Harte in Humboldt." *Overland Monthly*, September 1902, 301–2.

Mustafa, Sam A. "'Merchant Culture' in Germany and America in the Late-Eighteenth Century." *Yearbook of German-American Studies* 34 (1999): 113–32.

Nash, Gary B. *First City: Philadelphia and the Forging of Historical Memory*. Philadelphia: University of Pennsylvania Press, 2006.
Nissen, Axel. *Bret Harte: Prince and Pauper*. Jackson: University Press of Mississippi, 2000.
Noe, Jack. "'Everybody Is Centennializing': White Southerners and the 1876 Centennial." *American Nineteenth Century History* 17, no. 3 (2016): 325–43.
Nolan, Alan T. "The Anatomy of the Myth." In *The Myth of the Lost Cause and Civil War History*, edited by Gary W. Gallagher and Alan T. Nolan, 11–34. Bloomington: Indiana University Press, 2000.
Oakes, R. A. "Dies Natalis." *The Independent*, December 22, 1887, 3–4.
Ockenden, Ina Marie Porter, ed. *The Confederate Monument on Capitol Hill, Montgomery, Alabama, 1861–1900*. Montgomery, Ala.: Ladies' Memorial Association, 1900.
———. "Interesting Reminiscences of Greenville in the 60's—History and Personal Experiences." *Butler County Historical and Genealogical Society Quarterly* 42, no. 3 (July 2006): 8–11.
———. "What I Remember about Greenville Hospital, 1861–1865." *Butler County Historical and Genealogical Society Quarterly* 42, no. 3 (July 2006): 12–15.
O'Connor, Richard. *Bret Harte: A Biography*. Boston: Little, Brown, 1966.
Okker, Patricia. *Social Stories: The Magazine Novel in Nineteenth-Century America*. Charlottesville: University of Virginia Press, 2003.
Olson, Sherry H. *Baltimore: The Building of an American City*. Baltimore, Md.: Johns Hopkins University Press, 1997.
Orvell, Miles. *The Real Thing: Imitation and Authenticity in American Culture, 1880–1940*. Chapel Hill: University of North Carolina Press, 1989.
Owens, Patricia Ann. "The Overland Mail in Wyoming." *Annals of Wyoming* 61, no. 2 (April 1989): 13–19.
Palazolo, Jerry S. "The Postal Service in the Confederacy." *Memphis Pink Palace Museum Quarterly* 1, no. 1 (Summer 1972): 1–23.
Panhorst, Michael. "Devotion, Deception, and the Ladies Memorial Association, 1865–1898: The Mystery of the Alabama Confederate Monument." *Alabama Review* 65, no. 3 (July 2012): 163–204.
Parker, William Thornton. *Annals of Old Fort Cummings, New Mexico, 1867–8*. Northampton, Mass.: self-published, 1916.
Patty, James S. "Bryan, Mary Edwards." In *Notable American Women, 1607–1950: A Biographical Dictionary*, edited by Edward T. James, Janet Wilson James, and Paul S. Boyer, 1:264–65. Cambridge, Mass.: Harvard University Press, 1971.
———, ed. "A Georgia Authoress Writes Her Editor: Mrs. Mary E. Bryan to W. W. Mann (1860)." *Georgia Historical Quarterly* 41, no. 4 (December 1957): 416–31.
———. "A Woman Journalist in Reconstruction Louisiana." *Louisiana Studies* 3, no. 1 (Spring 1964): 77–104.
Payne, Stephen M. "Josephine Clifford McCrackin." In *A Howling Wilderness: A History of the Summit Road Area of the Santa Cruz Mountains, 1850–1906*, 121–27. Cupertino: California History Center, De Anza College, 1978.
Pfaelzer, Jean. *Parlor Radical: Rebecca Harding Davis and the Origins of American Social Realism*. Pittsburgh, Pa.: University of Pittsburgh Press, 1996.
Phillips, Christopher. *Freedom's Port: The African American Community of Baltimore, 1790–1860*. Urbana: University of Illinois Press, 1997.
Phillips, Kevin. *The Cousins' War: Religion, Politics, and the Triumph of Anglo-America*. New York: Basic Books, 1999.
Pierce, Bessie Louise. *A History of Chicago*. 3 vols. 1937–57; repr., Chicago: University of Chicago Press, 2007.

Poleo, Barbara A. "James Edmundson Ingraham: Florida, Flagler, and St. Augustine." *El Escribano* 40 (2003): 93–118.

Porter, Kenneth Wiggins. "Negroes and the Seminole War, 1835–1842." *Journal of Southern History* 30, no. 4 (November 1964): 427–50.

Powell, William S. *North Carolina through Four Centuries*. Chapel Hill: University of North Carolina Press, 1989.

Prial, Frank J. "Buildings from 1876 Centennial Live On in Spring Lake, N.J." *New York Times*, July 15, 1976, 37, 61.

Rable, George C. *Civil Wars: Women and the Crisis of Southern Nationalism*. Champaign: University of Illinois Press, 1989.

Rangarajan, Padma. "*Lalla Rookh* and the Afterlife of Allegory." *English Language Notes* 54, no. 1 (Spring/Summer 2016): 77–92.

Raymond, Ida M. [Mary T. Tardy]. *The Living Female Writers of the South*. Philadelphia: Claxton, Remsen and Haffelfinger, 1872. 281–82.

Ready, Milton. *The Tar Heel State: A History of North Carolina*. Columbia: University of South Carolina Press, 2005.

Reamy, Martha, and William Reamy. *Index to the Roll of Honor*. Baltimore, Md.: Genealogical Publishing Co., 1995.

Richardson, Frank L. "War as I Saw It, Part II." *Louisiana Historical Quarterly* 6 (April 1923): 239–53.

Ridgway, Richard F. *Self-Sufficiency at All Costs: Confederate Post Office Operations in North Carolina, 1861–1865*. Charlotte, N.C.: Postal History Society, 1988.

Riley, Sam G. *Magazines of the American South*. Westport, Conn.: Greenwood, 1986.

Rivers, Larry Eugene. *Slavery in Florida: Territorial Days to Emancipation*. Gainesville: University Press of Florida, 2000.

Roberts, Phil. "'All Americans Are Hero-Worshippers': American Observations on the First U.S. Visit by a Reigning Monarch, 1876." *Journal of the Gilded Age and Progressive Era* 7, no. 4 (October 2008): 453–77.

Robinson, Lorraine Hale. "The Iconography of Postwar Magazine Covers." *North Carolina Literary Review* 8 (1999): 55–57.

Rockman, Seth. *Scraping By: Wage Labor, Slavery, and Survival in Early Baltimore*. Baltimore, Md.: Johns Hopkins University Press, 2009.

Rodenbough, Charles D. *Rockingham County, NC in the Civil War: Extracted from the Issues of the Rockingham County Historical Society, Inc. Newsletters*. Reidsville, N.C.: Museum and Archives of Rockingham County / Lulu Publishing, 2016.

Rogers, Margaret Greene. *Civil War Corinth, 1861–1865*. Corinth, Miss.: Rankin Printery, 1989.

Roman, Anton. "The Beginnings of the Overland, as Seen by the First Publisher." *Overland Monthly*, July 1898, 72–75.

Rose, Anne C. *Victorian America and the Civil War*. New York: Cambridge University Press, 1994.

Roth, Leland M. *American Architecture: A History*. Boulder, Colo.: Icon-Westview Press, 2003.

Rothman, Adam. *Slave Country: American Expansion and the Origins of the Deep South*. Cambridge, Mass.: Harvard University Press, 2005.

Rubin, Anne Sarah. "Politics and Petticoats in the Same Pod: Florence Fay, Betsey Bittersweet, and the Reconstruction of Southern Womanhood, 1865–1868." In *Battle Scars: Gender and Sexuality in the American Civil War*, edited by Catherine Clinton and Nina Silber, 168–88. New York: Oxford University Press, 2006.

Ruskin, John. "The Nature of Gothic." In *The Stones of Venice, 2: The Sea-Stories*, 151–231. London: Smith, Elder and Co., 1853.

Rydell, Robert W. *All the World's a Fair: Visions of Empire at American International Expositions, 1876–1916*. Chicago: University of Chicago Press, 1984.

Sacco, Nicholas W. "'I Never Was an Abolitionist': Ulysses S. Grant and Slavery, 1854–1863." *Journal of the Civil War Era* 9, no. 3 (September 2019): 410–37.

Sandweiss, Martha A. *Print the Legend: Photography and the American West*. New Haven, Conn.: Yale University Press, 2002.

Schafer, Judith Kelleher. "Part Two." In *Louisiana: A History*, edited by Bennett H. Wall and John C. Rodrigue, 105–232. Oxford: Wiley-Blackwell, 2014.

Scharnhorst, Gary. *Bret Harte: Opening the American Literary West*. 2000; repr., Norman: University of Oklahoma Press, 2016.

Schivelbusch, Wolfgang. *The Railway Journey: The Industrialization of Time and Space in the Nineteenth Century*. 1986; repr., Berkeley: University of California Press, 2014.

Schlichting, Kurt C. *Grand Central Terminal: Railroads, Engineering, and Architecture in New York City*. Baltimore, Md.: Johns Hopkins University Press, 2001.

Seale, William. *The President's House: A History*. Washington, D.C.: White House Historical Association / National Geographic Society, 1986.

———. "The White House: Plans Realized and Unrealized." In *Our Changing White House*, edited by Wendell Garrett, 1–30. Boston: Northeastern University Press, 1995.

Sears, Stephen W. *Landscape Turned Red: The Battle of Antietam*. 1983; repr., New York: Mariner Books / Houghton Mifflin Harcourt, 2003.

Sedgwick, Ellery. *The "Atlantic Monthly," 1857–1909: Yankee Humanism at High Tide and Ebb*. Amherst: University of Massachusetts Press, 1994.

Sheehan, William. *The Planet Mars: A History of Observation and Discovery*. Tucson: University of Arizona Press, 1996.

Shortridge, James R. "The Post Office Frontier in Kansas." *Journal of the West* 13, no. 3 (July 1974): 83–97.

Showalter, Elaine. *The Civil Wars of Julia Ward Howe: A Biography*. New York: Simon and Schuster, 2016.

Silver, Rollo G. "The Baltimore Book Trade, 1800–1825." *Bulletin of the New York Public Library* 57, no. 3 (March 1953): 114–25.

Simpson, Brooks D. "'The Doom of Slavery': Ulysses S. Grant, War Aims, and Emancipation, 1861–1863." *Civil War History* 36, no. 1 (March 1990): 36–56.

Smith, Adam I. P. *No Party Now: Politics in the Civil War North*. New York: Oxford University Press, 2006.

Smith, Gay. "Shakespearean Tragedy in the Nineteenth Century United States: The Case of Julius Caesar." In *The Oxford Handbook of Shakespearean Tragedy*, edited by Michael Neill and David Schalkwyk, 779–94. Oxford: Oxford University Press, 2016.

Smith, James R. "Shreveport, the Heart and Transportation Hub of the Confederate Trans-Mississippi Department." *North Louisiana History* 40, no. 1 (Winter 2009): 3–21.

Smith, John David. "The Recruitment of Negro Soldiers in Kentucky, 1863–65." *Register of the Kentucky Historical Society* 72, no. 4 (October 1974): 364–90.

Smith, Michael Thomas. "'For Love of Cotton': Nathaniel P. Banks, Union Strategy, and the Red River Campaign." *Louisiana History* 51, no. 1 (Winter 2010): 5–26.

Smith, Susan Sutton. "Mary Edwards Bryan." In *American Women Writers: A Critical Reference Guide from Colonial Times to the Present*, edited by Lina Mainiero, 1:262–64. New York: Ungar, 1979.

Smith, Timothy B. *Corinth 1862: Siege, Battle, Occupation*. Lawrence: University Press of Kansas, 2012.

Sneden, Robert Knox. *Eye of the Storm: A Civil War Odyssey*. Edited by Charles F. Bryan Jr. and Nelson D. Lankford. New York: Free Press, 2000.

Snyder, Joel. *American Frontiers: The Photographs of Timothy H. O'Sullivan, 1867–1874*. Millerton, N.Y.: Aperture, 1981.

Stapp, William F. "'To . . . Arouse the Conscience, and Affect the Heart.'" In *An Enduring Interest: The Photographs of Alexander Gardner*, edited by Brooks Johnson, 16–57. Norfolk, Va.: Chrysler Museum, 1991.

Starr, Kevin. *California: A History*. New York: Modern Library / Random House, 2007.

———. "Rooted in Barbarous Soil: An Introduction to Gold Rush Society and Culture." In *Rooted in Barbarous Soil: People, Culture, and Community in Gold Rush California*, edited by Kevin Starr and Richard J. Orsi, 1–24. Berkeley: University of California Press, 2000.

Stauffer, John, and Benjamin Soskis. *The Battle Hymn of the Republic: A Biography of the Song That Marches On*. New York: Oxford University Press, 2013.

Stephens, Carlene E. *On Time: How America Has Learned to Live by the Clock*. Boston: Little, Brown, 2002.

Stern, Julia A. *Mary Chesnut's Civil War Epic*. Chicago: University of Chicago Press, 2010.

Stern, Madeleine B. "Anton Roman: Argonaut of Books." *California Historical Society Quarterly* 28, no. 1 (1949): 1–18.

Sternhell, Yael A. "Communicating War: The Culture of Information in Richmond during the American Civil War." *Past and Present*, no. 202 (February 2009): 175–205.

Stiles, T. J. *The First Tycoon: The Epic Life of Cornelius Vanderbilt*. New York: Knopf, 2009.

Stokes, Claudia. "Copyrighting American History: International Copyright and the Periodization of the Nineteenth Century." *American Literature* 77, no. 2 (June 2005): 291–317.

Stover, John F. *American Railroads*. 1961; repr., Chicago: University of Chicago Press, 1997.

———. *History of the Baltimore and Ohio Railroad*. West Lafayette, Ind.: Purdue University Press, 1987.

Sutro, Ottilie. "The Wednesday Club: A Brief Sketch from Authentic Sources." *Maryland Historical Magazine* 38, no. 1 (March 1943): 60–68.

Taft, Robert. *Photography and the American Scene: A Social History, 1839–1889*. 1938; repr., New York: Dover, 1964.

Taylor, Judy Atkins. "Ina Marie." *Butler County Historical and Genealogical Society* 33, no. 4 (October 1997): 69–83.

Taylor, William R. *Cavalier and Yankee: The Old South and American National Character*. 1957; repr., New York: Oxford University Press, 1993.

Thomas, Brook. *The Literature of Reconstruction: Not in Plain Black and White*. Baltimore, Md.: Johns Hopkins University Press, 2017.

Thomas, William G. *The Iron Way: Railroads, the Civil War, and the Making of Modern America*. New Haven, Conn.: Yale University Press, 2011.

Thompson, William F. *The Image of War: The Pictorial Reporting of the American Civil War*. 1960; repr., Baton Rouge: Louisiana State University Press, 1994.

Towers, Frank. "Job Busting at Baltimore Shipyards: Racial Violence in the Civil War–Era South." *Journal of Southern History* 66, no. 2 (May 2000): 221–56.

———. "Strange Bedfellows: The Union Party and the Federal Government in Civil War Baltimore." *Maryland Historical Magazine* 106, no. 1 (Spring 2011): 7–35.

———. *The Urban South and the Coming of the Civil War*. Charlottesville: University of Virginia Press, 2004.

———. "'A Vociferous Army of Howling Wolves': Baltimore's Civil War Riot of April 19, 1861." *Maryland Historian* 23, no. 2 (December 1992): 1–27.

Trachtenberg, Alan. *Reading American Photographs: Images as History, Mathew Brady to Walker Evans*. New York: Hill and Wang, 1989.

Turner, Glennette Tilley. *The Underground Railroad in Illinois*. Glen Ellyn, Ill.: Newman Educational Publishing, 2001.

Uhler, John Earle. "The Delphian Club: A Contribution to the Literary History of Baltimore in the Early Nineteenth Century." *Maryland Historical Magazine* 20, no. 4 (December 1925): 305–46.

Vail, Jeffrey W. "'The Standard of Revolt': Revolution and National Independence in Moore's *Lalla Rookh*." *Romanticism on the Net* 40 (November 2005), https://www.erudit.org/en/journals/ron/2005-n40-ron1039/012459ar/.

Vitiello, Domenic. "Engineering the Metropolis: William Sellers, Joseph M. Wilson, and Industrial Philadelphia." *Pennsylvania Magazine of History and Biography* 126, no. 2 (April 2002): 273–303.

Vlach, John Michael. *Back of the Big House: The Architecture of Plantation Slavery*. Chapel Hill: University of North Carolina Press, 1993.

Vore, Elizabeth. "A Famous Western Pioneer." *Overland Monthly*, August 1911, 167–70.

Walker, Cam. "Corinth: The Story of a Contraband Camp." *Civil War History* 20, no. 1 (March 1974): 5–22.

Warner, Michael. *Publics and Counterpublics*. Brooklyn, N.Y.: Zone Books, 2002.

Wayne, Lucy B. *Sweet Cane: The Architecture of the Sugar Works of East Florida*. Tuscaloosa: University of Alabama Press, 2010.

Wells, Jeremy. *Romances of the White Man's Burden: Race, Empire, and the Plantation in American Literature, 1880–1936*. Nashville, Tenn.: Vanderbilt University Press, 2011.

Wells, Jonathan Daniel. "The Transformation of John Pendleton Kennedy: Maryland, the Republican Party, and the Civil War." *Maryland Historical Magazine* 95, no. 3 (Fall 2000): 290–307.

———. *Women Writers and Journalists in the Nineteenth-Century South*. New York: Cambridge University Press, 2011.

Welsh, William E. "Lee's Hard Fighter." *Military Heritage* 16, no. 6 (May 2015): 24–31.

Wert, Jeffry. "'I Am So Unlike Other Folks': The Soldier Who Could Not Be Understood." *Civil War Times Illustrated* 28, no. 2 (April 1989): 14–21.

White, Kristy Armstrong. "Life in Civil War Tishomingo County, Mississippi." MA thesis, Mississippi State University, 1998.

Williams, Benjamin Buford. *A Literary History of Alabama: The Nineteenth Century*. Rutherford, N.J.: Fairleigh Dickinson University Press, 1979.

Wilson, Edmund. *Patriotic Gore: Studies in the Literature of the American Civil War*. 1962; repr., New York: Norton, 1994.

Wilson, Keith. Introduction to *Honor in Command: Lt. Freeman S. Bowley's Civil War Service in the 30th United States Colored Infantry*, edited by Keith Wilson, 1–41. Gainesville: University Press of Florida, 2006.

Winsberg, Morton D. "The Advance of Florida's Frontier as Determined from Post Office Openings." *Florida Historical Quarterly* 72, no. 2 (October 1993): 189–99.

Winsboro, Irvin D. S., and Joe Knetsch. "Florida Slaves, the 'Saltwater Railroad' to the Bahamas, and Anglo-American Diplomacy." *Journal of Southern History* 79, no. 1 (February 2013): 51–78.

Winters, John D. *The Civil War in Louisiana*. 1963; repr., Baton Rouge: Louisiana State University Press, 1991.

Wriston, John C., Jr. "Vermont Post Office Locations." *Vermont History News* 37, no. 6 (November/December 1986): 129–31.

Wyatt, David. *Five Fires: Race, Catastrophe, and the Shaping of California*. 1997; repr., New York: Oxford University Press, 1998.

Yeager, Patricia. "Narrating Space." In *The Geography of Identity*, edited by Patricia Yeager, 1–38. Ann Arbor: University of Michigan Press, 1996.

Young, Elizabeth. *Disarming the Nation: Women's Writing and the American Civil War*. Chicago: University of Chicago Press, 1999.

———. "Verbal Battlefields." In *On Alexander Gardner's "Photographic Sketch Book" of the Civil War*, edited by Anthony W. Lee, 52–94, 100–106. Berkeley: University of California Press, 2007.

Yount, Sylvia. "A 'New Century' for Women: Philadelphia's Centennial Exhibition and Domestic Reform." In *Philadelphia's Cultural Landscape: The Sartain Family Legacy*, edited by Katharine Martinez and Page Talbott, 149–60. Philadelphia: Temple University Press, 2000.

Ziegler, Valarie H. *Diva Julia: The Public Romance and Private Agony of Julia Ward Howe*. New York: Trinity Press International, 2003.

Zipf, Karin. "No Longer under Cover(ture): Marriage, Divorce, and Gender in the 1868 Constitutional Convention." In *North Carolinians in the Era of the Civil War and Reconstruction*, edited by Paul D. Escott, 193–219. Chapel Hill: University of North Carolina Press, 2008.

INDEX

Afoot and Alone, by Stephen Powers (1872), 164–67
African Americans: at Centennial Exhibition, 195, 197–201; and citizenship, 76–77, 78–79, 160–61, 195–96; and free blacks in Baltimore, 27; freedpeople, portrayal in newsmagazines, 97, 99, 166; and self-emancipation, 104–7, 142–43 (*see also* Seminoles and Black Seminoles); women, racial segregation of, 197
African Methodist Episcopal (AME) Church, 198, 200–201
"Alcibiades Jones": "Mrs. Spriggins, the Neutral" (*Southern Magazine,* February 1871), 30–31
"Alice Bankgrove's Soldier" (*Harper's Weekly,* December 13, 1862), 69
Allen, Richard, 198
Allen Monument, 198–201, 204
Allison, Emma, 222n36
American Revolution, 64, 71–73, 77–79, 105–6
Andrew, John, 187
Antietam, Battle of, 149–58
architecture, 202–4. *See also* Grand Central Dépôt (New York)
Association of American Women, 188
Atlantic Monthly: circulation and subscription, 6; countermovement against, 9; counter-narrative to, 12; elitism and prestige of, 8, 159–60
Avery, Benjamin P., 163

Bagby, George William: "My Uncle Flatback's Plantation" (*Southern Literary Messenger,* October 1863), 82–83
Baltimore, Md.: border status of, 35–36; demography of, 9, 22, 26–27, 61; economy of, 9, 25, 26; literary culture of, 9, 25–26; occupation of during Civil War, 24; as refuge for former Confederates, 22; and War of 1812, 25
Baltimore and Ohio Railroad, 25, 26
Banks, Nathaniel, 42–43
Barnard, George M., 154
Bartlett, William C., 163
Bellamy, Francis, 204
Bennett, Marian, 200–201
Black Laws of Illinois and a Few Reasons Why They Should Be Repealed, The, by John Jones (1864), 121–22
"black orientalism," 220n77
Blackwell, S. C.: "Fugitives at the West" (*Continental Monthly,* May 1862), 105–7
Booth, Sherman: "Suffrage" (*Lakeside Monthly,* February 1869), 113
borderlands and violence, 29–30. See also *Lakeside Monthly; Overland Monthly*
Bowley, Freeman Sparks, 160–61, 169
Brady, Mathew, 146–47, 150–57
Brilliant and Decisive Bayonet Charge of Hawkins's Zouaves, by Edwin Forbes, 151
Bross, William, 121, 125–26
Brown, John, 120, 122
Brown, John M., 199–200
Browne, Francis Fisher, 33, 113. See also *Lakeside Monthly*
Browne, William Hand, 23–24, 29, 33–35. See also *Southern Magazine*
Bryan, Iredell, 52
Bryan, Mary Edwards, 52–53
Buckholt, Isaac C., 11
Butler, Benjamin, 24, 41

Calhoun, John C., 75
Camp Bayard, 182
casualty lists, 68–69
Centennial celebrations, 37

243

Centennial Depot, 202–4
Centennial Exhibition: and African Americans, 195, 197–98; Machinery Hall, 191–93; Main Building, 190–91; and reconciliation, 188–89; Southern Restaurant, 194–95; state buildings, 193–94; travelers to, 187, 201–2; Women's Pavilion, 194, 196
Chambers, Andrew, 198
Charlotte, N.C.: and American Revolution, memory of, 71; demography and population of, 10, 71, 94; economy of, 10, 70–71, 94; and the New South, 63, 70
Chicago, Ill.: and abolitionism, 10, 112, 119–20, 122–23; and capital, 114; demography of, 10, 111–12, 124; geography and layout of, 110–11, 114, 124; and laborers, 104; railroads of, 10, 111, 112
Chicago fire (1871), 104, 111, 124
Chickamauga, Battle of, 123
Chinese Exclusion Act, 162
Christmas, literary allusions to, 59–60
"Citizen as Voter, The," by Mat. Hawthorn (*Lakeside Monthly*, April 1869), 117–18
Clay, Henry, 75
Clifford, James, 181–82
Clifford, Josephine, 181–83; "Marching with a Command" (*Lakeside Monthly*, April and May 1873), 181. *See also* "An Episode of 'Fort Desolation,'" by Josephine Clifford (*Overland Monthly*, March 1871)
Cole, Rebecca J., 197
Confederate Congress, 32
Confederate States of America: postal system of, 68–69
Congress of Women, 188, 196
Cooper, Sarah B.: "Old Uncle Hampshire" (*Overland Monthly*, November 1872), 169
copyright law, international, 31–32
Corinth, Miss., 94–96
Corliss engine, 191–92
cotton, 53–55
counterpublics: definition of, 13
"Cousin Jack," by Caroline Marsdale (*Southern Magazine*, December 1873), 44–50; and military campaigns, 53–55; and Reconstruction Louisiana, 51–52; reversals in, 58–61; setting of, 55–57
Cumming, Kate, 95–96

"A Dark Night on Picket," by Freeman S. Bowley (*Overland Monthly*, July 1870), 160–61
Darwin, Charles, 159
Davis, Alexander Jackson, 73
Davis, Jefferson, 71, 73; image on stamps, 68
Davis, L. Clarke, 189
Davis, Rebecca Harding, 40, 80, 189–90; "Ellen" (*Atlantic Monthly*, July 1865), 107–8; "A Glimpse of Philadelphia in July, 1776" (*Lippincott's*, July 1876), 189; "John Lamar" (*Atlantic Monthly*, April 1862), 5, 29–31, 82–83, 84, 106–7, 160–61, 190; "Old Philadelphia" (*Harper's Monthly*, April and May 1876), 189; "A Rainy Day at the Exposition" (*Harper's Weekly*, November 18, 1876), 189; *Waiting for the Verdict* (1868), 190
Davis, Theodore R., 193–94
De Forest, John William, 53–55
Delphian Club, 25–26
depot culture, 15
"depot," pronunciation of, 206n37
De Quincey, Anna: "A New Story of Lee's Surrender" (*Lakeside Monthly*, May 1871), 118–19
Doggett, Kate: "A Glance at Florida" (*Lakeside Monthly*, October 1869), 141–42
"Doings of the Sunbeam," by Oliver Wendell Holmes (*Atlantic Monthly*, July 1863), 159
double consciousness, 158
Douglas, Stephen A., 10, 112
Douglass, Frederick, 197
Du Bois, W. E. B.: "Strivings of the Negro People" (*Atlantic Monthly*, August 1897), 158

"East and West," by G. Nelson Smith (*Lakeside Monthly*, March 1869), 114
Elements of Algebra, by Daniel Harvey Hill, 64–65
"Elmsville and Its Hospital" (*The Land We Love*, June and July 1866), 81
Emancipation Proclamation: and black enlistment, 182; and meaning of war, change of, 149, 219n32; preliminary proclamation, 97, 148
"Episode of 'Fort Desolation, An,'" by

Josephine Clifford (*Overland Monthly*, March 1871), 171–79; and African Americans, role of, 184–85; narrator of, 185–86; setting of, 180–81, 183; and spectacle, 183–84

"Escape from Johnston's Island, An," by John Winston (*Southern Magazine*, November 1872), 28–29

Executive Mansion, 36

Eytinge, Solomon, 167–69

Federal authority, strength of, 36–38, 102, 146

Fifteenth Amendment, 78, 81–82, 113

Flagler, Henry, 139

Forbes, Edwin, 150–53

Fort Craig, 182

Fort Cummings, 182–83

"'Fortune Favors the Brave'" (*Harper's Weekly*, August 16, 1862), 69

Fourteenth Amendment, 78

frame narratives, use of, 60, 93–94, 97, 118–19, 158

France, invasion of Mexico, 43

Franco-Prussian War, 187

Frank Leslie's Illustrated Newspaper, 151, 152

Franklin, Benjamin: image of on stamps, 67–68

"Fugitives at the West," by S. C. Blackwell (*Continental Monthly*, May 1862), 105–7

Fugitive Slave Law (1850), 120, 121

Gardner, Alexander, 147, 150–57

Gathered Together for Burial: After the Battle of Antietam, by Alexander Gardner, 155–56

"General's Story, The" by George Ward Nichols (*Harper's Monthly*, June 1867), 158

Gettysburg, Battle of: photographs of, staged, 153

Gibson, James, 150

Gillespie, Elizabeth Duane, 196

"Glimpse of Philadelphia in July, 1776," by Rebecca Harding Davis (*Lippincott's*, July 1876), 189

Grand Central Dépôt (New York), 2–3, 7–8, 9, 11–12, 13–14, 203–4

Grant, Ulysses S., 191–93

Gray, Asa, 159

Griswold, Helen E. (Harrington), 140. *See also* "In the Palmy Days of Slaveholding," by Helen E. Harrington (*Lakeside Monthly*, August 1870)

Gwin, William, 163

Hall, Asaph, 146, 186

Harper, Frances E. W.: "We Are Rising," 200

Harrington, Helen E., 140. *See also* "In the Palmy Days of Slaveholding," by Helen E. Harrington (*Lakeside Monthly*, August 1870)

Harrington, Joseph, 140

Harte, Bret, 159, 163, 164, 167; "Plain Language from Truthful James" (*Overland Monthly*, September 1870), 167–69. *See also Overland Monthly*

Hastings, Margaret Vane: "Lois Pearl Berkeley" (*Continental Monthly*, November 1864), 107

Hatfield, R. G., 11

hauntings, 35–36

Hawthorn, Mat.: "The Citizen as Voter" (*Lakeside Monthly*, April 1869), 117–18

Higginson, Thomas Wentworth, 159

Hill, Daniel Harvey, 62, 64–65, 76–78. *See also The Land We Love*

Hittell, John S., 162

Hoban, James, 36

Hoge, Moses Drury, 29

Holmes, Oliver Wendell, 159

"home," 35–38, 41, 123–24, 126–27, 196–97

"Home on Furlough" (*The Land We Love*, November 1866), 81

Hotel Ponce de Leon, 139

household and domesticity, 99, 100–101

Howe, Julia Ward, 1, 187–90

Howe, Sammy, 187

Howe, Samuel Gridley, 187

Howells, William Dean, 190–94

Hull, Joseph, 167–69

Hyacinth, Socrates (pseudonym for Stephen Powers), 164

Illinois, 120–23. *See also* Chicago, Ill.

Illinois and Michigan Canal, 111

illness and disease, 96

"In an Old Drawer" (*The Land We Love*, December 1869), 84

International Copyright Association, 32

"In the Palmy Days of Slaveholding," by Helen E. Harrington (*Lakeside Monthly*, August 1870), 129–37; and labor, 141, 144–45; narrator of, 140–41
"Italian" villas, 72–74
itinerancy of white Southerners, 96–98

"Jack Dessart," by Burdett Nash (*Lakeside Monthly*, October 1871), 123
Jackson, Andrew: image of on stamps, 67–68
Jackson, T. J. "Stonewall," 75
Jefferson, Thomas: image of on stamps, 68
"John Lamar," by Davis, Rebecca Harding (*Atlantic Monthly*, April 1862), 5, 29–31, 82–83, 84, 106–7, 160–61, 190
Jones, John, 121–23
Jones, Mary Jane, 122
Julius Caesar, 58–59

"Kate's Soldier" (*Harper's Weekly*, October 4, 1862), 69
Kellogg, G. M.: "Self-Made Men" (*Lakeside Monthly*, July 1869), 116–17
Kennedy, John Pendleton, 25–26
Kentucky, 182
Key, Francis Scott, 25
King, Edward, 207n24
Kingsbury, Theodore Bryant, 194–95

labor, 104, 117–19, 124–28
Ladies' Memorial Association (LMA), 98, 101
Ladies' Society for the Burial of Deceased Alabama Soldiers, 98
Lakeside Monthly: and African Americans excluded from self-promotion, 121–23; antislavery principles of, 10, 113, 121, 141–42; broken and replaced, theme of Civil War stories, 103; founding of, 33; and gender, 116–18; on home, meaning of, 196–97; on labor and manufacturing, 124–28; and self-promotion, 114, 115–17, 121–23, 125–26; subscription and circulation of, 113, 120; as Western voice, 33, 113–16. *See also* "In the Palmy Days of Slaveholding," by Helen E. Harrington (*Lakeside Monthly*, August 1870)
Lalla Rookh, by Thomas Moore, 60
The Land We Love: and agrarianism, romantization of, 71–75; and black equality, opposition to, 73; overview of, 10; and Pollard, attacks on, 77–78; and Revolutionary era, memory of, 64, 71–73, 76, 78–79; and Southern independence, cultivation of, 70, 75; and trauma and replacement, theme of, 63–64, 80–84, 195–96. *See also* "Road-Side Story," by Ina M. Porter (*The Land We Love*, August 1866)
Lawton, Charles, 141
Lawton, Joseph, 141
Leslie, Lawrence: "The Wife of Garibaldi" (*Lakeside Monthly*, June 1870), 117
Lincoln, Abraham, 112, 121, 164; assassination of, 187. *See also* Emancipation Proclamation
Lost Cause: emergence of, 76–79; and postmemory, 79–84; white women's role in, 101
Lost Cause, The, by Edward A. Pollard (1866), 76–78
Louisiana: as borderland, 41–43; Federal occupation of, 23, 41; as literary setting, 37–41; and wartime campaigns, 53–55. *See also* sugar production
Lovejoy, Elijah, 119
Lyell, Charles, 159

Manheim, Louise: "The First Campaign of a Fat Volunteer" (*Southern Illustrated News*, January 10 and January 17, 1863), 82–83
Mansfield, Battle of, 53–55
marriage/households, 75
Marsdale, Caroline, 52–53. *See also* "Cousin Jack," by Caroline Marsdale (*Southern Magazine*, December 1873)
Maryland, 22–23, 26, 27. *See also* Baltimore, Md.
masculinity, 116
Mason-Dixon Line, 22
McCabe, James, 194
McCrackin, Jackson, 221n94
Mercer, Edward, 195–96
"A Midnight Ride from Petersburg" (*Southern Magazine*, December 1971), 40
Miller, Anson S., 121
Missouri Compromise, 22
Moore, Thomas: *Lalla Rookh*, 60
Morehead, John Lindsay, 73–74

Morehead, John Motley, 73–74
Morris, William, 203
"Mrs. Spriggins, the Neutral," by "Alcibiades Jones" (*Southern Magazine,* February 1871), 30–31
"The Mutiny" (*New National Era,* August 11, 1870), 38–39
"My Uncle Flatback's Plantation," by George William Bagby (*Southern Literary Messenger,* October 1863), 82–83

Nash, Burdett: "Jack Dessart" (*Lakeside Monthly,* October 1871), 123
Nast, Thomas, 6
Native Americans, 138, 166–67, 180, 182–83. *See also* Seminoles and Black Seminoles
Neal, John, 25
New Century for Woman, 196
New National Era, 197
"New Story of Lee's Surrender, A" by Anna De Quincey (*Lakeside Monthly,* May 1871), 118–19
Nichols, George Ward: "The General's Story" (*Harper's Monthly,* June 1867), 158

observer, 158, 164, 169–70, 185–86
Ogden, William B., 116
"Old Philadelphia," by Rebecca Harding Davis (*Harper's Monthly,* April and May 1876), 189
"Our Adjutant," by Egbert Phelps (*Lakeside Monthly,* May 1873), 126–28
Overland Monthly: financing of, 162; founding of, 33, 159; and minor characters, role of, 169–70, 185–86; perspectives in, differing, 197–98; politics of, 167–69; railroad, role of, 159; readership of, 11, 162–63; themes of, 160, 164; as unillustrated, 154. *See also* "An Episode of 'Fort Desolation,'" by Josephine Clifford (*Overland Monthly,* March 1871)

parallax: explanation of, 146
Parton, James, 32
patriarchal guarantees, breakdown of, 96–98
Pedro II, emperor of Brazil, 191–93
"Peninsular Sketches" (*Southern Literary Messenger,* November–December 1862, July 1863), 36, 82–83

Pennsylvania Railroad, 190, 202
periodicals: circulation and readership of, 15, 65, 102, 151–52; illustrations in, 72–75, 154–57; locations of, 19; scholarship on, 16–17
Phelps, Egbert: "Our Adjutant" (*Lakeside Monthly,* May 1873), 126–28
Phelps, Elizabeth Stuart: "A Sacrifice Consumed" (*Harper's Monthly,* January 1864), 157
Philadelphia, 22, 188–89. *See also* Centennial Exhibition
Phillips, Wendell, 121
photography, 146–47, 150–57. *See also* stereoscope
Pinkerton, Allan, 218n10
"Plain Language from Truthful James," by Bret Harte (*Overland Monthly,* September 1870), 167–69
plantation as literary setting, 36–38, 55–57
Pledge of Allegiance, 204
Pollard, Edward A.: *The Lost Cause* (1866), 76–78
Porter, Ina M., 95, 98, 101, 213n100; "Interesting Reminiscences of Greenville in the 60's," 97; "Road-Side Story" (*The Land We Love,* August 1866), 85–92; "Road-Side Story" (*The Land We Love,* August 1866), setting of, 93–97
Portico, The, 25–26
Postal Law of 1863, 110
Postal Service: and casualty lists, 68–69; as federal and local enterprise, 65–66; and railroads, 108–11; reorganization of, postwar, 63; stamps, introduction of, 66–68
postmemory, 79–84, 195–96
Post Office Act (1794), 65
Powers, Stephen, 164–67
"Professor's Story, The," by Oliver Wendell Holmes (*Atlantic Monthly,* December 1859), 159
Putnam, George Palmer, 32

Radical Reconstruction, 189
raids and scavenging, 96
railroads: in Chicago, 111, 112; and circulation of periodicals, 65, 102; in fiction, 93–94, 99, 102, 104, 107, 123–24; in Florida,

railroads (*continued*)
139–40; and markets, 70–71, 74, 108; and military, 102, 127; and postal service, 108–11; standardization, versus local control, 108; transportation cars, 119; women's use of, 97–98
"Rainy Day at the Exposition, A" by Rebecca Harding Davis (*Harper's Weekly*, November 18, 1876), 189
"Ralph Hazlitt, Soldier" (*Harper's Weekly*, July 18, 1863), 69
Reagan, John Henniger, 68
Reconstruction: and African Americans, liberty and justice for, 189–91; and constitutional amendments, 78–79, 81–82, 113, 120; and Radical Reconstruction, 189; as reconciliation, 188–89, 190–91; and Revolutionary era, link to, 64
Reconstruction Acts, 76, 78–79
Red Bank depot station (Red Bank, N.J.), 222n32
Resolution in Relation to International Copyright (1861), 32
Richard Allen Museum, 200
Richmond Eclectic. See *Southern Magazine*
"Road-Side Story," by Ina M. Porter (*The Land We Love*, August 1866), 85–92; setting of, 93–97
Robert (African American man in Raleigh), 166
Roman, Anton, 162–63
royalties, 33
"Ruined State, A" by Stephen Powers (*Overland Monthly*, July 1869), 165
Ruskin, John, 203

"Sacrifice Consumed, A" by Elizabeth Stuart Phelps (*Harper's Monthly*, January 1864), 157
San Francisco, Calif.: and Confederacy, 10–11; demography and social order of, 148–49, 160–63, 167–69; gold rush, 161
Scenes on the Battlefield of Antietam, by Mathew Brady, 155
self-emancipation, 104–7, 142–43. See also Seminoles and Black Seminoles
"Self-Made Men," by G. M. Kellogg (*Lakeside Monthly*, July 1869), 116–17
Seminoles and Black Seminoles, 138, 141, 144

Seminole Wars, 143–44
"Sentenced and Shot" (*Lakeside Monthly*, November 1870), 39
Sherman, William Tecumseh, 62, 113, 127
Shiloh, Battle of, 94–95
silver, 163
Simms, William Gilmore, 32
"Sketch of Mecklenburg County" (*The Land We Love*, December 1866), 71–73
slave insurrections, 161
slavery, in literature: erasure of, 30; slave quarters, focus on, 37; and violence, 142, 143; weight of on protagonists, 36. See also "In the Palmy Days of Slaveholding," by Helen E. Harrington (*Lakeside Monthly*, August 1870)
Smith, Aubrey, 222n39
Smith, Frances, 140
Smith, G. Nelson: "East and West" (*Lakeside Monthly*, March 1869), 114
Snook, John Butler, 7
Southern Historical Society, 29, 34
Southern Illustrated News, 24
Southern Literary Messenger, 32, 59
Southern Magazine: founding of, 23; on infrastructure, need for, 34–35; mission of, 33–35; pro-Confederacy content, 9–10, 28–29, 194–95; and resistance, theme of, 29–31, 34; second chance, stories of, 23–24; setting of stories, 35–43; and sites of containment, 30–31; subscription and circulation of, 29. See also "Cousin Jack," by Caroline Marsdale (*Southern Magazine*, December 1873)
special artists, 150–53
specie shortage, 67
stamps, 66–68
Stanford, Leland, 164
stereoscope, 146–50, 153–59; in literature, figuratively, 167, 169–70, 180–81, 185
"Story of a Mutiny, The" (*Galaxy*, August 1870), 38–39
Stowe, Harriet Beecher, 117; "The First Christmas of New England" (*Christian Union*, December 25, 1871), 59–60; *Uncle Tom's Cabin*, 105–6
suffrage: for African Americans, 117–18; for women, 188. See also Fifteenth Amendment

"Suffrage," by Sherman Booth (*Lakeside Monthly*, February 1869), 113
sugar production, 138, 141–42; destruction of, 143–44

Tallahassee Railroad, 139–40
Taney, Roger B., 75
Taylor, Richard, 55
Texas, 43
"Texas Soldier, The" (*The Land We Love*, March 1867), 81
textile mills, 43
Thirteenth Amendment, 78–79, 120
Tribes of California, by Stephen Powers (1877), 166–67
"Trying Journey, A" (*Southern Magazine*, November 1872), 40–41
Turnbull, Lawrence, 207n24

Underground Railroad, 104–7, 119–20, 121, 122, 138, 142–43
United States Colored Troops (USCT), 126, 160–61, 180, 182–84, 188–89
Upton, M. G.: "The Plan of San Francisco" (*Overland Monthly*, February 1869), 149
U.S. Sanitary Commission, 1, 164, 187
U.S. Sanitary Fair, 188

Vanderbilt, Cornelius, 6–7. *See also* Grand Central Dépôt (New York)

Waiting for the Verdict, by Rebecca Harding Davis (1868), 190

Walker, John, 55
Ward mail-bag catcher, 110
Warner, Willard, 81–82
War of 1812, 25
Washington, George, 36, 74; image of on stamps, 67–68
Watkins, James F., 162
Waud, Alfred, 154
"We Are Rising," by Frances E. W. Harper, 200
Webster, Daniel, 75
Western Monthly. See *Lakeside Monthly*
Western Theater, 112–13, 123
White, Alfred H., 198
Wilson, Henry, 202
Wilson, John, 202
Wilson, Joseph, 202–4
Wilson Brothers & Co., 202–3
Winston, John: "An Escape from Johnston's Island" (*Southern Magazine*), 28–29
Woempner, Georg Heinrich Ernst, 181
Woempner, Josephine (Clifford), 181–83; "Marching with a Command" (*Lakeside Monthly*, April and May 1873), 181. *See also* "An Episode of 'Fort Desolation,'" by Josephine Clifford (*Overland Monthly*, March 1871)
"Woman Order," 41
Woman's Journal, 187–88
Women's Centennial Executive Committee, 196
Woolson, Constance Fenimore, 140

www.ingramcontent.com/pod-product-compliance
Lightning Source LLC
Chambersburg PA
CBHW010719300426
44115CB00020B/2961